The Demand for Energy in the Soviet Union

David Wilson

CROOM HELM
London & Canberra

ROWMAN & ALLANHELD
Publishers

© 1983 David Wilson
Croom Helm Ltd, Provident House, Burrell Row,
Beckenham, Kent BR3 1AT
Croom Helm Australia, PO Box 391,
Manuka, ACT 2603, Australia

British Library Cataloguing in Publication Data

Wilson, David
    The demand for energy in the Soviet Union.
    1. Energy consumption − Soviet Union
    2. Energy industries − Soviet Union
    I. Title
    333.79'12'0947   HD9502.R9
    ISBN 0-7099-2704-5

First published in the United States of America
in 1983 by Rowman & Allanheld, Publishers
(a division of Littlefield, Adams & Co.)
81 Adams Drive, Totowa, New Jersey 07512

Library of Congress Cataloging in Publication Data

Wilson, David, 1947-
    The demand for energy in the Soviet Union.

    Bibliography: p.
    Includes index.
    1. Energy consumption − Soviet Union. 2. Soviet Union −
Industries − Energy consumption. 3. Energy industries −
Soviet Union. 4. Power resources − Soviet Union.
I. Title
HD9502.S652W54   1983   333.79'12'0947   83-16141
ISBN 0-86598-157-4

Typeset by Mayhew Typesetting, Bristol
Printed and bound in Great Britain by
Biddles Ltd, Guildford and King's Lynn

CONTENTS

MAPS

1 FORECASTING FUEL SUPPLY AND DEMAND

Not so very long ago, it was the conventional wisdom among Western pundits that the USSR had an energy crisis. Its reserves of oil were said to be running out, and because its oil-finding and producing technology was so primitive (with a technological level 40 years behind that of the USA) there was no way that it could find the necessary amount of new oil sufficiently quickly to prevent a downturn in production. According to a CIA report of April 1977, this would take place during the early 1980s at the latest when Soviet oil production would peak at a maximum 600 mn tons before suffering a precipitous decline to between 400 and 450 mn tons in 1985. The Russians would not only be forced to leave their Eastern European allies to fend for themselves, but would also be importing large quantities of oil on their own account.

This would leave them at the mercy of the world oil market, and in order to avoid such a fate, they would have to acquire (by fair means or foul) access to oilfields beyond their borders. It was widely thought that they had their eyes on Iran, and consequently the Iranian revolution, which took place within 18 months of the publication of the CIA report, was initially seen by many in the West as the first stage of the oil-grab with some newspapers even regaling their readers with the names of the KGB men alleged to be behind the Islamic revival.

According to one point of view, the purpose of the CIA report was to terrify the governments of the Middle Eastern oil-producing countries with the spectre of a Soviet drive on the Gulf. This could only be averted by stronger links between the Gulf states and the USA, with the Americans providing military protection in return for Arab support for the Camp David Agreement. In this respect, the CIA was highly successful. Although some Gulf rulers remained dubious, the implications of its report were largely accepted by others. The Saudi oil minister, Sheikh Yamani, was even sufficiently confident to claim that all observers expected Soviet oil production to decline, with the only disagreement between them centring on whether Eastern Europe alone, or Eastern Europe *and* the Soviet Union, would be eventually pleading for OPEC oil.

The success of the CIA report as a political exercise was inversely proportional to its success as an economic forecasting exercise. Oil production has not declined, nor has it peaked, although it is growing more slowly than before; this is due to factors quite different to those discussed by the CIA. The report's findings were never accepted by informed students of the Soviet fuel industry, particularly in Western Europe, and few were surprised when the CIA, after increasingly desperate attempts to justify its predictions, ditched the report in late 1980 and set about writing a new one.

This should have been the end of the matter. However, it is surprising to note that the latest report is little different from that of 1977 — it has some slightly bigger numbers in it, and doomsday has been postponed, with oil production now expected to decline more slowly to 500–550 mn tons in 1985 and 400 mn in 1990. It is likely that this latest effort will prove no more accurate than the last, and if oil output in 1983 gets anywhere near the annual plan target of 619 mn tons, then the CIA should find themselves having to write a third report.

The CIA's misconceptions about the technological standard of the USSR's oil-producing equipment and about its oilfield management techniques have been described elsewhere. Suffice it to say here that the Soviet petroleum engineering industry is far more advanced than most Western observers had believed possible, and even those analysts who make an honest attempt to be objective in their assessment of Soviet achievements have been surprised by the quality and capabilities of some of the new machines which have emerged during the last few years. In some fields, such as automatic welding machines for large diameter pipelines, laminar pipe and drilling rigs designed for super-deep holes, the Russians are several years ahead of the Americans, and in others (such as seismic surveying equipment, pipelayers, electric submersible pumps, marine rigs, etc.) they have made up a considerable lag in a very short time.

This programme of technological advance, generally referred to as a process of intensification of the economy, has been a key element of policy since the late 1960s, but has only really begun to gather pace since 1975. It is a programme embracing all industrial sectors, not just petroleum engineering, and has therefore had an important consequence for the other side of the energy equation, the demand for fuel. The development of larger and more fuel-efficient power station sets, cement kilns, iron-reduction and steel-making furnaces, and the growth of those sectors not requiring fossil fuels, such as atomic and hydro power generation and electric railways, has lead to a marked reduction in fuel demand as well as greater opportunities for fuel substitution, especially gas for oil. There is abundant evidence that poor plant management and organisation has meant that the full potential of these technological advances has not been realised, but there has nevertheless been a useful decline in the average fuel rates of power station boilers, iron and steel plants, etc. due largely to technical improvements in plant and equipment.

In short, most Western analysts have failed to comprehend the scope and depth of Soviet technological advances during the last decade. Indeed, some American observers even believe that the Russians are unable to innovate, with the lack of a profit motive and the power of an entrenched bureaucracy combining to prevent new ideas developed in research institutes from ever reaching the serial production stage. The belief that the USSR depends on the West, mainly the USA, for its 'high technology' goes virtually unquestioned in some quarters; this is why the US government was misled into believing that its sanctions on equipment for the Siberian gas pipeline could prevent the pipeline from being built, or at least delayed for two or more years. Yet within weeks of the imposition of the sanctions, the prototypes of alternative equipment designed and built entirely by the Russians had appeared and factories were tooling up for their mass production. Western specialists who have examined the GPA-25 compressor and the TG-502 pipelayer have confirmed that they are as good as the embargoed American models, and in some respects are better. When it is realised that these are not isolated examples, and that highly efficient new models of machines with very low fuel rates are being installed by most sectors of industry, then Soviet success in reducing their fuel consumption per unit of output can be better appreciated.

Some economists, Soviet as well as Western, contend that the influence of new technology has been exaggerated, and that it has been the change in the fuel mix (i.e. from coal to oil and gas, with gas now gaining at the expense of oil — see Tables 1.1 and 1.2) which has been the primary cause of declining fuel rates. They argue that when the efficiency of fuel consumption is analysed from the standpoint of heat usefully utilised, i.e. the net rather than the gross consumption of fuel, then the level of efficiency has risen very slowly. They estimate that the ratio of net to gross consumption of fuel per unit of output has risen only from 35% in 1960 to 40% in 1980 and is not likely to exceed 42% in the future. The Russians claim that it has already reached 43% (they say it amounts to only 30% in the countries of the EEC) and that it should rise to 60% in 1990. If these figures are correct, then this may confirm the belief that Soviet industry is undergoing a wide-ranging technological renewal, which is now beginning to result in better fuel

Table 1.1: Production of Fuel by Type (mn tsf*)

	1960	1970	1975	1978	1979	1980	1985 Plan
Coal	373.1	432.7	471.8	487.0	486.2	484.4	524.0
Oil	211.4	502.4	701.9	817.3	837.4	862.6	900.9
Gas	54.4	233.5	342.9	441.1	481.8	515.7	746.5
Peat	20.4	17.7	18.5	9.2	13.6	7.3 ⎫	
Shale	4.8	8.8	10.8	11.6	11.8	11.9 ⎬	50.0
Firewood	28.7	26.6	25.4	24.1	24.2	23.8 ⎭	
Total	692.8	1,221.7	1,571.3	1,790.3	1,855.0	1,905.7	2,221.4

Note: * tons of standard fuel.

Table 1.2: Production of Fuel by Type, as a Share of the Total (%)

	1960	1970	1975	1978	1979	1980	1985 Plan
Coal	53.9	35.4	30.0	27.2	26.2	25.4	23.6
Oil	30.5	41.1	44.7	45.7	45.2	45.3	40.6
Gas	7.9	19.1	21.8	24.6	26.0	27.1	33.6
Peat	2.9	1.5	1.2	0.5	0.7	0.4 ⎫	
Shale	0.7	0.7	0.7	0.6	0.6	0.6 ⎬	2.2
Firewood	4.1	2.2	1.6	1.4	1.3	1.2 ⎭	
Total	100	100	100	100	100	100	100

efficiency. If they are wrong, and the ratio of net to gross fuel consumption is not improving, then any further decline in the fuel rate must stem entirely from changes in the fuel mix. With the share of coal set to fall only slightly, and gas likely to replace fuel oil which is nearly as efficient, then it is apparent that the Russians can expect to obtain no more than a marginal improvement in their fuel rates during the next decade.

This would have serious implications for Soviet economic development. The atomic energy programme is in serious trouble, and any growth in industrial output must therefore depend largely on a similar growth in primary fuel production. This has amounted to less than 3% a year since 1979, and with little prospect of this rate rising significantly, it is clear that future economic growth must depend heavily on fuel-saving.

This book will examine the nature of fuel consumption by the main fuel-using sectors — the household and municipal sector, electricity and thermal energy generation, iron and steel, construction materials, petrochemicals and oil-refining, transport, agriculture and foreign trade

— with particular reference to the factors affecting the fuel rate and the scope for its reduction. Estimates of likely fuel consumption in 1985, 1990 and 2000 are provided. These are based on anticipated fuel rates and likely volumes of output by the individual sectors in those years, which in turn are derived from my own model of the future development of the Soviet economy.

Economic forecasting has been likened to most marriages — a triumph of hope over experience. Ostensibly, it should be easier to forecast the development of centrally-planned economies, with five-year plans giving an indication of the broad strategies chosen by their governments, and bearing in mind that these policies are seldom radically altered within a five-year-plan period. It might even be true to say that once a policy has been agreed upon, and the multitude of organisations with a responsibility and/or interest in seeing the policy fulfilled have formulated their own place in the scheme of things, then the nature of the system is such that it is almost impossible for the policy to be subsequently changed. It is inconceivable, for example, that the nuclear power programme of the USSR could be scrapped now that it has so many vested interests promoting it at practically every level of society. Radical changes in the structure of agriculture with (for example) a strengthening of the vertical links between the farm, the transport enterprise, the wholesale organisation, the food processing plant and the shop are proving difficult to carry out in spite of the fact that everybody claims to agree on the need for them.

Major changes in policy generally take place during the transition from one five-year plan to the next. However, the complexity of the debate sometimes means that important changes cannot be foreseen, even by planners. The administrative structure of Soviet society is not *always* quite as rigid as has been suggested above. In particular spheres at particular times it can be quite fluid, with the power of some regional or sectoral interest groups growing while that of others wanes. The aims of a very powerful interest group may even be challenged by a mighty alliance of other weaker groups, able to exert considerable influence where it really counts, on the decision-making committees in the Party and government apparatus. The fuel industry has had its share of situations where quite unexpected decisions have been taken, sometimes relatively late during the plan formulation process, the most recent example being the all-out drive for Siberian gas at the expense of oil.

During the formulation of the Eleventh Five Year Plan, several variants of the fuel production strategy for the period 1980 to 1990 were considered. As late as the summer of 1980, it was thought that the Glavtyumenneftegaz organisation, responsible for the production of oil in Tyumen oblast in Western Siberia (which accounted for just over half of the USSR's oil in 1980), would be asked to continue raising its output by the 30 mn tons a year typical of the 1970s. This would imply a plan target of 450–460 mn tons for 1985, and would entail a vast amount of extremely costly capital construction work, not only on drilling wells, building connector pipelines between the well-heads and installing oil treatment plants, water injection systems, repair workshops, etc. at up to 40 new deposits, but also on building housing, amenities, roads, power lines, etc. in the swamps of Western Siberia. This would have to be undertaken, not by the Ministry of Oil, but by the Ministry of Oil and Gas Construction, the Ministry of Industrial Construction and a host of other ministries which are normally tightly-stretched in meeting their plan targets without venturing out to more distant locations in the Siberian swamps.

It was believed that the Ministry of Oil's political power was great enough to enable it to prevail over its smaller and weaker brethren. However, the finally agreed guidelines for the Eleventh Five Year Plan revealed that an entirely different variant had been adopted. Instead of rising by 150 mn tons during 1981 to 1985, the output of oil by Tyumen oblast has been projected to grow by only 82 mn tons to 385 mn tons in 1985. The Ministry of Gas has consequently been called upon to raise the production of gas in the northern part of Tyumen oblast from 156 bn* cu m in 1980 to 357 bn in 1985. While this is an ambitious programme for the Ministry of Gas, whose prestige (and power) has been growing rapidly recently and is likely to grow further in the future, the capital construction work required for raising annual gas output by 201 bn cu m is much less than that necessary for increasing oil output by 150 mn tons a year. This is because practically all the envisaged growth in gas production will come from just one deposit, Urengoi, and the construction ministries apparently feel more confident in their ability to carry out the necessary work.

This is just one example of where the balance of power within a particular sector has changed dramatically — the switch from coal to oil in the 1950s is another. The decision to move into Western Siberia rather than concentrate on searching for new oil and gas in the European part of the USSR is an example of where the regional power balance has changed within the relevant ministries. These abrupt

* bn = one thousand million throughout.

changes of policy are not common, but when they take place, they can wrench the entire Soviet economy onto a new path of development. The new emphasis on gas at the expense of oil, for example, has necessitated a massive programme of converting oil-fired boilers to burn natural gas while oil refineries are being upgraded so that oil can be more deeply refined allowing a rapidly growing output of light and middle products from a slowly growing throughput of crude.

These major, often unforeseeable, changes in policy make the long-term forecasting of the Soviet economy a hazardous business, dependent on a correct understanding of the relative importance of different interest groups, and the extent to which their power is changing. Another problem is that the Russians themselves frequently over-estimate their ability to overcome obstacles to plan fulfilment. Five-year and annual plans are often too ambitious, both for the economy as a whole and for most industrial sectors, and the performance of industry is indirectly influenced by that of agriculture. The reasons for plan underfulfilment would require an entire book to discuss them adequately, and a few thoughts on the subject should suffice here.

'Waste' and 'inefficiency' are probably the two most common words used by Western observers when describing the Soviet economy. Soviet economists are tempted to employ the same description when thinking of dole queues and empty factories characteristic of Western economies. In fact, different definitions are being used; waste and inefficiency in the Soviet Union is indicated by the low productivity of labour and capital rather than unemployed workers and unused production capacity. Many Soviet factories tend to work to notional capacity with little ability to raise the level of output in response to a sudden surge in demand, and when bottlenecks arise through a shortage of components or materials, it is often a long time before they can be resolved. It can, therefore, be said that the Soviet economy is in a state of permanent crisis; nowhere is this crisis more evident than in the atomic energy sector, where new generating sets are delayed for up to four years while the atomic engineering factories work flat out in attempting to meet an insatiable demand for their products. Bottlenecks in a few key sectors can hold down the growth rate of the entire economy.

The late commissioning of new plant is another important reason for plan underfulfilment. The increasing size and complexity of new factories has created new problems for planners, and it is difficult to formulate critical path analysis schedules for plants which may consist of different sections, all of which are interrelated. Some new Soviet plants are amongst the largest in the world, and there is little practical experience of completion times which can be used as a yardstick. The problem is compounded by the Russian predilection for building very large plants in green-field locations where a whole range of infrastructural and auxiliary items have to be built, and planners have failed notoriously to calculate the time and effort required to provide these. The poor infrastructure has been the greatest single problem encountered by the oil and gas workers in Western Siberia, for example. The large size of new plants has recently been criticised by a number of economists, who have pointed out that the increasing returns to scale available from large factories are often outweighed by the costs incurred due to lengthy construction periods. These costs are tending to rise as the pace of technological change quickens — in some cases a new factory employing a particular production process has become technologically obsolete before it has been completed. There is an argument that it is better to build a large number of small, highly specialised plants, which can be built quickly and brought on stream one after the other rather than large integrated plants which take years to build tying up vast amounts of capital, and do not begin to pay for themselves until they are completed.

Labour shortages are a frequent occurrence in Soviet factories, in spite of the fact that the USSR has one of the fastest growing populations, and workforces, among European countries. Part of the problem is that, during the 1970s, nearly 28% of the population increase has taken place in the relatively unindustrialised republics of Central Asia among people, who, for the most part, live in rural locations and are not inclined either to move to Central Asian cities or to other parts of the country where more labour is needed. But the crux of the problem is low mobility of labour. Workers are not made redundant when new labour-saving machines are installed, and there is no 'unemployment mechanism' for directing labour from factories suffering from overemployment to those short of workers. On the contrary, standardised wage rates mean that factories have to compete for scarce labour by providing non-wage services such as their own housing, food shops, entertainment facilities, etc. Workers are positively discouraged from changing jobs, even when they are no longer required. It is a frequent experience for long-established factories in city centres to be overstaffed while newer factories in the suburbs or beyond city boundaries to suffer from labour shortages. Yet it is these new factories where the potential labour and capital productivities are highest, and on which the fulfilment of sectoral production plans depends.

An additional reason for the poor performance of the Soviet economy since 1978 has been the succession of poor harvests. In order to maintain *per caput* meat consumption at over 55 kg a year, the Soviet government has been importing sufficient grain to keep the size of animal herds at more or less constant levels. Heavy expenditure on grain imports has lead to a sharp cutback in new contracts for the purchase of Western machinery and equipment, and while the value of such imports amounts to less than 1% of the Soviet gross social product (GSP), they are of considerable importance in particular industrial sectors. A large proportion of new plant installed by the petrochemical sector, for example, has been imported from France, West Germany, Italy, the USA and Japan, with a small number of plants also equipped and built by UK firms. In early 1979, the number of foreign-assisted petrochemical facilities under construction reached a record 112 but by the end of 1982 this number had fallen to 55 and is due to fall further. This will hold back the growth of what ought to be a rapidly expanding sector for a country at the USSR's stage of development, and will impede the performance of the economy as a whole.

Forecasting the likely development of the Soviet economy is, therefore, much more difficult then it would appear at first consideration. Most Western attempts to foresee the extent of fulfilment of even five-year plans have foundered, and consequently it does not seem to be either possible or useful to try and predict what may be happening as much as 20 years ahead. This does not mean, however, that forecasting does not have any value. On the contrary, it is possible to draw up a series of quantified constraints on economic growth and make a number of strict assumptions about such variables as the growth of the workforce, the development of urbanisation, the importance of trade and the speed of technology transfer, the capacity for technological innovation and a very large number of other determinants of growth rates, thereby building a model of development which permits a minimum acceptable growth rate without violating any of the given constraints. In other words, such a model is not predictive; I am not going to place any bets on the USSR producing, for example, 137 mn tons of cement in the year 2000 (see Chapter 5 on the construction materials industry). All the model predicts is that if the economy is to grow at a rate sufficient to permit steadily rising living standards for the population and to allow enough resources to sustain the military potential of a superpower, then it is going to need to be producing at least 137 mn ton of cement in 2000.

The model, therefore, quantifies the minimum levels of output required for the main industrial sectors in 1985, 1990 and 2000 and is both realistic and feasible. Some dynamic leadership by the new Party leader with the weeding out of inefficient administrators and plant directors, a string of several years of uncommonly good weather with equally good harvests, the renewal of *détente* with a recognition by Western bankers that the Soviet Union (with a *per caput* debt of a mere $63 in 1981) is one of the best customers for Western loans plus a recognition by Western firms, and governments that the division of labour between the resource-rich USSR and the technologically-developed Western Europe is highly profitable to both sides and many other possible factors, could enable the USSR to grow much more rapidly than the minimum rates projected by the model. If, on the other hand, the model's forecasts are not achieved, then the Soviet leaders will have to choose between guns and butter to an extent not previously experienced with the real risk that either living standards may begin to decline or the country may begin to lag behind in the arms race, or both. Any of these eventualities would be potentially explosive.

How much fuel will be required to sustain these minimum growth rates, and is the Soviet Union capable of producing this fuel from its own resources? This is a question which has been exercising the minds of Western analysts, particularly since 1977 when the CIA issued its report on Soviet oil as well as a report on gas which also assumed the worst possible scenario. Various attempts have been made to forecast overall fuel consumption by the USSR by considering observed historical changes in the ratio of fuel consumption to gross social product or industrial production, or any other variable that comes to hand, and with the aid of some highly tendentious assumptions, project forward into the future. The problem with this approach is that it fails to account for changes in the importance of individual sectors in the economy as a whole; it does not take into account the possible growth of non-fossil-fuel sources of energy (nuclear, hydro and renewable power, synfuels, etc.); and it does not consider the different potentials for fuel-saving of different sectors. In other words, it assumes that there should be a smooth, fairly predictable relationship between fuel consumption and gross social product at fixed prices, when there manifestly is not.

Realistic forecasts of aggregate demand for fuel can only be made by analysing the levels of fuel consumption by individual major fuel-using sectors. This has hardly been attempted in the West before, primarily because of deficiencies in source material. These stem from three main causes. First, many Soviet authors either work for a specific ministry or are employed by research institutes sponsored by particular ministries. Consequently, they concentrate their efforts on their own industries rather than the economy as a whole. This means that an analysis of national fuel consumption requires an exhaustive survey of books and magazines published by a wide range of organisations. Secondly, most of these books and magazines deal with the problems and prospects of the industry in its entirety, and the amount of discussion devoted to fuel consumption depends largely on the importance of fuel and energy in the industry's total costs. The fuel rate is, therefore, an important aspect of research into the electricity, iron and steel and cement industries, while books on textiles and food processing are unlikely even to give it a mention. Therefore, assumptions have to be made about the fuel rates of these less-fuel-intensive sectors. Thirdly, official analyses of fuel consumption by type are helpful only when gas is considered − there are practically no data on the volumes and rates of coal consumption, and the production and consumption of oil products as well as refinery capacities, throughputs, costs, etc. are a state secret. The petrochemical industry is another sector shrouded in a veil of secrecy, although occasionally some useful data burst through in the most unlikely places. The coal and oil product requirements of the various industries have to be estimated with the help of hints, allusions and vague indications from a host of different sources, and these estimates are obviously open to distortions from a variety of causes.

It is, therefore, with some trepidation that one embarks on the task of forecasting fuel consumption by the USSR during the next two decades, especially when some highly respectable Western sovietologists have arrived at the conclusion that this sort of exercise leaves its author on a hiding to nothing. However, it is my contention that as much can be learned when a forecast, drawn up in good faith from a purely objective standpoint, turns out to be wrong as when it proves correct. If the forecast is wrong, then it is possible that an important (but not necessarily announced) policy shift has taken place, and the extent by which the forecast is wrong may give an indication of the extent of the policy change and of the realignment of interest groups which has brought it about. Much of the fragmentary evidence which has been collated about the oil versus gas debate during the formulation of the Eleventh Five Year Plan fits neatly into a framework created when my own forecasts of oil and gas production by Western Siberia in 1985 overestimated oil and underestimated gas. It is now much easier to marshal such evidence into a theory of how (and on whose initiative) the current Eleventh plan guidelines for fuel production were drawn up.

In short, economic forecasting can provide a valuable tool of analysis by enabling comparisons to be made between (for example) the official plan for 1990 drawn up in 1985, the eventual outcome in 1990, and the forecast for 1990 made on the basis of existing evidence in 1982. There are very few other ways of calculating what may be going on in the Kremlin's corridors of power between 1982 and 1985.

This book will have surprisingly little to say on the subject of regional aspects of fuel supply and demand. It has been an economic law, sustained with almost religious fervour, since the First Five Year Plan, that manufacturing must take place at the source of fuel and raw materials so as to minimise transport costs. This law has been unquestioned to the extent that a coherent theory of industrial location has never been elaborated for the world's largest centrally-planned economy.

In fact it made a great deal of sense to locate new industry near the source of fuel when the principal fuel was coal which (being bulky in relation to its heat rate and hence value) was expensive to transport, when the railway system was greatly overloaded and thus heavily congested, and when Stalin was frantically trying to diversify the economy eastwards in case of war with the West. It makes little sense today, when natural gas is planned to account for 73% of the total increase in fuel production during 1981 to 1985, when all this additional gas is expected to come from one of the more inaccessible places on earth where the siting of new gas-using industry would be most impractical, and when Siberian gas can be piped to practically anywhere in the Sovet Union at small cost compared with that of railing coal. For the first time in 50 years, it is now being suggested that it pays to locate new industry in the western part of the country at the market for its products, and much of the earlier enthusiasm for the *Drang nach Osten* has disappeared.

Pressure on capital investment resources has lead to a new policy of increasing production by expanding existing plants rather than building new ones. This basically means a heavier concentration of industrial capacity in the European part of the USSR. While there is a continuing interest in the creation of Territorial Production Complexes in the Asiatic USSR, with a number of technologically-linked energy-intensive plants located in close proximity to a major source of energy like a hydroelectric power station or a coalfield, the immensity of the problems connected with building an infrastructure and attracting sufficient workers of the right kind as well as the transport costs of bringing in consumer goods, food, production materials, etc. and shipping out finished products has led planners to envisage TPCs only for those sectors such as non-ferrous metal smelting, paper and cellulose which cannot be reasonably sited in Europe. Otherwise, practically all new factories are to be located in Europe, and the guidelines of the Eleventh Five Year Plan even largely dropped the ritual references of previous plans to increasing the share of industry in the eastern part of the country. It has finally been recognised that the Soviet Union's economic problems are big enough without trying to industrialise Siberia.

Apart from a number of combined heat-and-power plants (CHPPs) and peak-load gas turbine stations, new power stations in the European USSR will be non-fossil-fuel. These will be nuclear stations for covering base loads, and hydro and pumped storage stations for peak loads. Nuclear power stations can be built almost anywhere, with an adequate supply of water being the only real requirement. Giant new stations like Smolensk, which should have a capacity of 7,000 MW when completed, will force out many existing coal- or oil-fired stations, and also assist the increasing electrification of the economy with electricity replacing the direct combustion of fuel in many processes. The location of new atomic stations has been calculated with a number of variables in mind, one of which is the need to close down the coal- or oil-fired stations operating on fuel brought over long distances by rail. Thus, as the construction of new atomic sets builds up to eight per year of 1,000 MW each with the completion of the Atommash reactor manufacturing plant, the limits of distribution of coal and fuel oil will contract. Already, very little Donbass coal is shipped beyond the frontiers of the Ukraine, and the delivery of Kuzbass coal to the western republics should decline when the Ignalina atomic station in Lithuania is commissioned; imports of Kuzbass coal by Leningrad virtually disappeared with the build-up of the Leningrad atomic station to 4,000 MW.

The other key factor in covering new energy demand by the European USSR is natural gas. The cost of building a pipeline from Western Siberia to the Centre region is immense, amounting to 4–6 bn roubles. It requires up to 3 mn tons of steel pipe of 1,420 mm diameter, most of it imported from the West with a heavy drain on foreign currency reserves, and perhaps 20,000 skilled workers employed for almost a year on building the line. Yet the large amount of fuel that can be delivered (33 bn cu m, equivalent to 46 mn tons of high quality coal, a year) means that the pipeline will pay for itself in less than three years. Moreover, the capital construction cost of a pipeline is partly

Table 1.3: The Share of Fuel and Energy in Total Costs by Sector (%)

	1970	1975	1979	1980
Electricity and thermal energy	55.7	52.0	50.2	49.6
Cement	37.2	35.1	33.4	33.4
Iron and steel	14.9	13.5	13.2	13.1
Cellulose and paper	14.2	12.4	11.8	12.0
Glass	13.3	11.4	11.0	10.8
Chemicals and petrochemicals	10.9	10.2	9.6	9.4
Forestry	5.2	5.3	6.6	6.6
Fuel industry	6.9	6.5	6.4	6.3
Timber processing	3.7	4.0	4.2	4.2
Engineering and metalworking	3.6	3.2	3.1	3.0
Food processing	1.9	1.8	2.0	2.0
Textiles	1.2	1.2	1.2	1.2
Clothing	0.3	0.3	0.3	0.3
All industry	6.4	6.0	5.9	5.9

offset by the running costs, which are comparatively low compared with those of rail transport, and the fact that conversion from coal or fuel oil to gas helps to relieve congestion on the railways. The delivered cost of natural gas is very low compared with those of other fuels, and consequently the share of fuel and energy in the total costs of most sectors has been declining to the point where fuel costs are hardly significant in many cases as gas has replaced coal.

Even if all new industry were to be located along the western border of the USSR at the greatest possible distance from the Siberian gasfields, this would have comparatively little effect on industrial costs. It has already been mentioned that the siting of a substantial amount of new manufacturing capacity in Western Siberia is impractical. At the very least, Tyumen gas has to be piped westwards to the Urals region (over a distance of 1,100 km) and the difference in delivered costs of gas in the Urals and the westernmost parts of the USSR is not very great. These days, industrial location is determined more by the availability of a labour force and the proximity of the market than by the distance from the Tyumen gasfields.

Therefore the regional nature of the fuel mix is of little importance so long as the gas keeps flowing. The North West, Centre, Baltic, Belorussia and South West (i.e. western Ukraine) regions are supplied by the Siyanie Severa pipeline system which runs from Tyumen oblast across the northern Urals and down through the Komi republic, passing to the north of Moscow and south of Leningrad, to Minsk before finishing at Uzhgorod on the Czech border. The Urals, Volga, Volga Vyatka

Table 1.4: Prospective Delivered Costs of Tyumen or Central Asian Gas (roubles per tsf)

Baltic and Belorussia	43–45
Western Ukraine	43–45
Caucasus	43–45
North West	41–43
North Caucasus	41–43
Eastern Ukraine	40–43
Centre	40–42
Volga	37–39
Urals	35–37
Kazakhstan	31–33
Central Asia	28–31
Far East	27–29
Western Siberia	25–28
Eastern Siberia	23–25

and Central regions are served by a system of pipelines running from Tyumen oblast through Perm, Kazan and Gorki to Moscow, and the Urengoi-Chelyabinsk-Petrovsk pipelines serve the Urals, Volga and Central Chernozem regions. The Urengoi-Novopskov system passes through the Urals, Volga and Central Chernozem regions before ending in the Donets-Dnepr region (eastern Ukraine) where it provides gas to supplement that from the Ukrainian deposits which have stabilised at 50-55 bn cu m a year. This system also extends into the North Caucasus and Caucasus regions where Caspian Sea gas cannot cover demand by the Caucasian republics, and it joins a dense network of pipelines in the Ukraine, conveying gas to much of the republic including the Southern region and Moldavia.

So Siberian gas is supplied in growing quantities to every region in the European USSR, and most areas are equally well-served with oil products since the start-up of the Mazheikiai (Lithuania) and Lisichansk (Donets-Dnepr) oil refineries. The tendency for the importance of coal to decline in many sectors as it is replaced by gas is likely to continue for the rest of the century, and its use will be limited to firing large base-load power stations, especially in the east of the country. All the anticipated increase in coal production of nearly 300 mn tons a year between now and 2000 will come from Kazakhstan, Siberia and the Far East, and it is most unlikely that, in spite of heavy investment programmes, the European coalfields will do better than maintain current levels of output. Consequently, the impact of increased coal production in the eastern USSR will be felt in the western USSR through the transmission of electricity in power lines of 1,150 and 1,800 kV AC and 1,500 and 2,200 kV DC, running westwards for thousands of kilometres from large mineside power stations. The first of these (from Ekibastuz to the Urals and Central Chernozem regions) should be commissioned before 1985, and they should be commonplace by 1990 as the Kansk-Achinsk coal and power complex comes to life. Like natural gas pipelines and atomic power stations, these super-high-tension power lines can be built almost anywhere, and their capacity is so great that it makes little difference to the delivered cost of power whether they are 2,000 or 4,000 km long.

Although it is broadly true to say that the regional aspects of fuel supply and demand have little, and declining, significance, there are still several problem areas. One is the supply of oil products to Central Asia, which has a rapidly growing population with the USSR's fourth largest city (Tashkent), the fastest growing industry of any region of the USSR, and a great military importance, bordering on Iran and Afghanistan. While a small oil refinery at Fergana works inefficiently and spasmodically on local Uzbek oil, nearly all oil products are brought by rail from Krasnovodsk on the eastern shore of the Caspian Sea or Pavlodar in northern Kazakhstan. Moving oil products over distances of more than 2,000 km on Central Asia's overburdened railways is expensive and unreliable, and accordingly it was decided during the early 1970s to build two new refineries at Chardzhou (Turkmen republic) and Chimkent (southern Kazakhstan) to be supplied by a pipeline bringing Siberian crude via Omsk and Pavlodar. The final section from Pavlodar to Chimkent was completed in November 1982, and the Chimkent refinery should begin operating in 1983. Branches of the pipeline will be built to the Fergana refinery and to Chardzhou, where the refinery will start up in 1984. By 1985, the region should be self-sufficient in oil products.

Paradoxically, there are no plans at the present time to bring natural gas to the large cities of Siberia. At the moment, Novokuznetsk, Tomsk and Kemerovo are supplied with 16 bn cu m a year of dried casinghead gas from Samotlor and a small amount of bottled gas from the Volga region. But large cities like Novosibirsk (1.34 mn people), Omsk (1.04 mn), Krasnoyarsk (0.82 mn), Irkutsk (0.57 mn) and Vladivostok (0.57 mn) are not yet supplied with mains gas, largely because of the abundance of local coal. Although the coal is cheap to produce, it is expensive, inefficient and pollutive to use. The construction of the first eastwards-running gas pipeline from the Tyumen gasfields must be a matter of some priority during the next plan period.

But on the whole, the regional distribution of fuel must be regarded as being reasonably adequate, and it is distortions in sectoral provision that are most significant, particularly in the household and municipal sector.

2 THE HOUSEHOLD AND MUNICIPAL SECTOR

Since the last war, profound changes in the nature of Soviet society have transformed the life of the average citizen. In 1940, he was more than likely to have lived in one of the tens of thousands of tiny villages that dotted the landscape from Leningrad to beyond the Urals; some 131 mn people, 67% of the total population, were officially described as rural inhabitants at the beginning of that year. A large part of their daily lives was devoted to the task of simply maintaining a precarious existence, with several hours a day taken up by the basic tasks of providing heat and light and cooking food under generally primitive conditions.

As the economy has grown, the lure of the large cities has drawn people from the countryside, to the extent that the rural population has been declining both relatively and absolutely. This trend has accelerated since the mid 1960s — between 1951 and 1966 the number of rural inhabitants remained stable at 108.5 mn, but has since declined at an annual average of over 700,000 to 97.7 mn in 1981. The urban population, on the other hand, has been growing at an average 3.2 mn a year since 1951, reaching 168.9 mn or 63% of the total population, by the beginning of 1981. Much of this rural-urban migration has been destined for the larger towns. In 1959, the 48 towns which by 1981 had more than half a million people, had 33.2 mn inhabitants or 15.9% of the total population. By 1981 they had 54.2 mn people, or 20.3% of the total, and this trend is likely to continue so long as the large towns remain much more attractive than the small or medium-sized towns.

Even today, when electricity reaches the remotest village, life in these big cities is very different to that of the countryside. Light and heat are obtainable with the flick of a switch or turn of a knob, with space-heating accomplished by central heating from large combined heat-and-power plants (CHPPs), regional or municipal boilers, or smaller boilers serving an individual block of flats. It is apparent that, so long as the urbanisation process continues, it will pay to build more (and larger) centralised sources of heat supply, and that these will account for the provision of heat to an increasing share of the total population. At the other end of the settlement scale, it is anticipated that many of the tiny villages, with populations frequently amounting to less than

100, will disappear, as their inhabitants migrate, according to the aspirations of Soviet planners, into the so-called 'perspective villages' with populations of 2,000-4,000 or (more likely) to the larger towns. It is conceivable that, some time in the distant future, an insignificant number of people will be living in settlements of less than 2,000 inhabitants, and the supply of centrally-produced heat to practically the entire population will become possible.

For the time being, however, this is simply a planner's dream. Even in some of the largest cities, many people have to provide their own heat from stoves or boilers using the most inefficient types of fuel. It has been estimated, for example, that firewood is used by 30% of all dwellings in Riga, a large and relatively sophisticated city, capital of Latvia, the republic with perhaps the highest overall living standards in the Soviet Union. It goes without saying that in the countryside, the programme of supplying centrally produced heat has hardly begun, and for most villages it is not even feasible. Even if it were possible to lay the necessary length of hot water pipes, the operation of a boiler designed to serve up to 200 people would not require appreciably less fuel (in terms of heat content) than is now burned in the individual stoves belonging to the same people.

Household and Municipal Consumption of Fuel

The fuel requirements of households and public buildings for heating and cooking purposes are still dominated by coal and other lower-rank fuels. While the extensive programme of gas supply is making a large dent in the share of these relatively inefficient fuels, especially in the Ukraine, where mains and bottled gas accounts for over 35% of fuel consumption by the household and municipal sector, their continuing importance means that the social cost of burning them remains unacceptably high. Social costs include the time spent on the acquisition of fuel, especially the large volume of 'self-produced fuel by the population', the unreliability of supply at times when industry is running short (for example coal in the Ukraine during the winter of 1981/2, or gas in Azerbaidzhan after the Iranian revolution) and the pollution stemming from the burning of low-rank fuels. It is estimated that more than 130 hours are spent by each household annually in collecting and igniting fuel, and in this respect the USSR today compares with many Western countries prior to the First World War.

During 1965 to 1975, the total consumption of fuel by the household

Table 2.1: Fuel Consumption by Households and Public Buildings, Excluding Fuel Burned by Centralised Sources of Heat (mn tsf)

	1965	1970	1975	Share of Total % 1965	Share of Total % 1975
Coal and brickettes	68.3	82.9	90.0	44.0	45.0
Peat and brickettes	3.4	4.0	8.9	2.2	4.5
Wood (state supplied)	12.0	11.9	12.0	7.8	6.0
Mains gas	17.8	29.9	42.6	10.8	21.3
Bottled gas	1.1	3.1	5.2	0.7	2.6
Heating oil	4.9	2.6	13.0	3.2	6.5
Coke	1.0	–	–	0.7	–
Others	0.9	4.6	3.3	0.6	1.6
Self produced fuel by the population	46.6	44.0	25.0	30.0	12.5
Total	156.0	183.0	200.0		

and municipal sector rose from 212 mn tsf to 276 mn tsf, with the share burned in individual stoves and boilers declining only marginally from 73.7% to 72.5%. This means that while the consumption of fuel by stoves and boilers rose by 28% over the decade, that by centralised sources of heat serving the household sector rose only slightly faster, by 35.7%.

By 1980, the situation did not seem to have improved very much over 1975, with one source indicating that 'about two-thirds' of all energy for space-heating and hot water came from small boilers, burning an average 0.220 tons of standard fuel (tsf) per G-cal (Gigacalorie) compared with the 0.173 tsf required by CHPPs and district heating centres. This indicates that, if anything, the share of fuel destined for the household economy burned in individual stoves and small boilers actually rose above the 72.5% of 1975. It is estimated that if 50% of these small boilers were scrapped in favour of centralised sources of heat supply, then annual savings of 25–26 mn tsf would accrue.

Consumption of fuel for the heating of dwellings amounted to 275 mn tsf in 1980, at a rate of 1.033 tsf per person; this excludes the burning of gas and other fuels for cooking food, but probably includes the consumption of fuel for heating some industrial buildings such as small workshops, etc.

Given the heavy capital investment constraint on significantly accelerating the programme for building CHPPs and district heating centres designed specifically to serve the household sector, and the fact that their construction is uneconomical for population centres with less than 10,000 inhabitants, it makes sense to try and reduce the economic and social costs of the fuel mix (see Table 2.1) by replacing lower-rank fuels by natural gas or heating oil. This is particularly true of the eastern regions of the USSR where lower-rank fuels account for well over 90% of total household consumption, and where the burning of particularly pollutive fuels can have a traumatic effect on the environment. In the Far East, for example, there has been an increasing tendency for households to burn coal from the South Yakutsk basin now that the steam coal section of the Neryungri open-cast mine has reached its project capacity of 4 mn tons a year. This coal is extremely pollutive because it cannot be fully burned in small stoves or boilers; it gives off smoke which deposits a greasy dust that cannot be washed away. Only in larger boilers, like those of the Neryungri district heating centre commissioned in 1982, is full combustion possible, and pollution kept to a minimum. It is evidently preferable to reserve Yakutsk coal for large boilers and make bottled gas available to households.

(a) Coal Consumption by Households and Public Buildings

In 1980, about 120 mn natural tons of coal were burned by households, compared with 114 mn in 1975, 105 mn in 1970 and 86 mn tons in 1965. It is suggested by some sources that these figures include coal consumption by a number of small industrial plants. Coal consumption has risen by an average 2.3% a year between 1965 and 1980, and is probably approaching its peak. Most of the coal is supplied to municipal authorities for use in small boilers which come under their jurisdiction, or directly to individual consumers (principally miners and other inhabitants of the coalfield towns and villages) by the mines in an undressed state. Only a comparatively small, but rising, volume is supplied to the population through retail outlets.

The sale of coal by co-operative and state retail centres to the population has grown at an average annual rate of 3.8% between 1965 and 1980 to 30.2 mn tons. Sales have grown most strikingly in the cities by 11.8% a year, from 4.6 mn tons in 1965 to 24.6 mn tons in 1980 as the use of firewood for open hearths, stoves and boilers declines. Sales to rural inhabitants, on the other hand, have declined since 1970 for reasons that are not immediately obvious. It may be that those rural areas where coal, rather than firewood, was the predominant fuel for cooking and space-heating (i.e. the Ukraine and some parts of European Russia) have received mains or bottled gas before the other major rural regions where firewood has traditionally been the principal domestic fuel.

Table 2.2: Sales of Coal by Co-operative and State Organisations to the Population (mn tons)

| | Sales of Coal (mn tons) | | | Consumption per Inhabitant (kg) | | |
	Total	Urban	Rural	USSR	Urban	Rural
1965	17.4	4.6	12.8	76	38	117
1970	24.4	9.3	15.1	101	68	143
1975	27.6	17.4	10.2	108	115	101
1978	29.2	23.0	6.2	112	143	62
1979	29.8	23.8	6.0	113	145	61
1980	30.2	24.6	5.6	113	146	57

Table 2.3: Household Consumption of Coal (inc. Coke and Patent Fuel), 1980

	Household Consumption (mn tons)	Share of Total Consumption (%)	Household Consumption (kg/person)
USSR	120	17.2	450
UK	11.7	9.4	209
West Germany	8.8	4.0	149
France	4.8	9.9	89
Japan	5.4	5.9	46
USA	5.8	0.9	25
Italy	0.3	1.7	10

The USSR is the only major industrial country where the use of coal by households has increased in recent years. Consumption by West German, French and Japanese homes is declining quite steeply, and in some countries like Italy, its use by households is insignificant.

Where gas is not available, it is economical to use fuel oil for firing domestic boilers rather than coal, with savings estimated at 4.5 to 7 roubles/tsf. These consist of 2 to 3.5 R/tsf from the higher boiler efficiency and 2.5 to 3.5 R/tsf from lower capital investment costs. Gas is better than fuel oil, with savings of a further 6 to 10 R/tsf possible (2.5 to 4 R/tsf from higher boiler efficiency and 3.5 to 6 R/tsf from lower capital costs).

(b) Peat

The burning of peat by households, mainly in brickette form, rose significantly during 1965 to 1975 from 9.1 mn tons to 26 mn tons before declining to an estimated 5 mn tons in 1980.

Table 2.4: Consumption of Peat (mn tons)

	Total	By the Household Sector	Share of Household Sector (%)
1965	45.7	9.1	19.9
1970	57.4	13	22.6
1975	53.8	26	48.3
1980	21.6	5	23.1

The production of peat (and hence its consumption) is very irregular, depending on climatic conditions in the main producing areas — the western Ukraine, Belorussia and the Central and North Western regions of the RSFSR. The only other important consumer of peat is the electricity sector, with a number of power stations burning peat in specially designed boilers. Their requirements must take precedence over households, especially at times of coal shortages, and this explains the dramatic fall in household consumption in 1980.

Peat is a more efficient fuel than some types of coal. When burned in a domestic furnace, the efficiency rate of peat amounts to 0.758, and peat brickette to 0.817 compared with 0.678 for brown coal. The use of peat is particularly effective in the western Ukraine, where it competes with Lvov-Volynsk coal with an efficiency rate of only 0.596, and costs less per unit of heat than high-quality hard coal railed in from the Donbass as long as it is burned within a radius of 150 km from its place of extraction. It is estimated that in the western Ukraine alone, a further 2.1–2.4 mn tons of peat could be burned by households above the level typical of a normal year, thereby forcing out lower-rank coal and firewood. Less than half the capacity of peat-bricketting plants was utilised during 1976 to 1980 in the Ukraine, so an expansion of peat utilisation would be relatively inexpensive.

While peat accounted for 3.5% of Ukrainian household fuel consumption in 1975, its share in the Volyn and Rovno oblasts reached 17%, and it was also significant in the Zhitomir and Lvov oblasts.

(c) Firewood

The provision of firewood by the state to industry and households has declined only marginally during the post-war period, from a peak of 33.5 mn tsf in 1965 to 26.6 mn in 1970, and then at an average annual rate of 1.1% to 23.8 mn tsf in 1980. Approximately half of this is supplied to the population for burning in open hearths or stoves, and its use is widespread throughout most of the USSR with the exception of Kazakhstan, Central Asia and the Caucasian republics.

In addition, large volumes of firewood are collected by the population, but these have been declining rapidly since 1965, and should not
exceed 15 mn tsf at the present time. The programme of supplying
bottled gas to rural localities is likely to have a bigger impact on the
consumption of firewood than that of any other fuel, and it is possible
that by the end of the century, the widespread use of firewood will
have practically disappeared.

(d) Lighting Kerosene

The arrival of electricity at even the remotest village has resulted in a
sharp decline in the sale of lighting kerosene to the population by state
organisations and co-operatives. In 1965, 2.27 mn tons, worth 177 mn
roubles, of kerosene were made available, but the 1965–80 period has
seen sales decline at an annual rate of 9.9%, including 11.8% a year
during 1975 and 1980, to only 554,000 tons in 1980. The decline has
been particularly noticeable in urban localities – these tend to be
remote settlements in Central Asia, Siberia or the Far East which have
not yet been connected to an electricity grid, and where local sources
of electric power are subject to frequent breakdowns.

**Table 2.5: Sales of Lighting Kerosene by State Organisations and
Co-operatives to the Population ('000 tons)**

	1965	1970	1975	1980
Volume – total	2,270	1,686	966	554
urban	785	485	237	123
rural	1,485	1,201	729	431
Value – total (mn roubles)	177	131	84	51

(e) Gas

Natural gas is becoming an increasingly important fuel for cooking in
Soviet homes. At the beginning of 1982, some 57.1 mn homes received
either mains or bottled gas, but the rate at which new dwellings are
drawn into the gas supply system is declining. In 1975, a peak of 3.6
mn dwellings were connected up, but in 1981 only 1.9 mn new
consumers (1.3 mn urban and 0.6 mn rural) received gas. The gas
supply programme has been running behind schedule for a number of
years now; according to the Tenth Five Year Plan, 18.8 mn new homes
should have been supplied with gas during the period 1976 to 1980,

Table 2.6: Extent of Gas Provision to Dwellings in the USSR

| | Number of Gas-served Dwellings (million) | | | | | Gas-served Homes per Thousand People | | | |
	1960	1970	1975	1979	1980	1970	1975	1979	1980
USSR	3.2	23.5	41.6	53.3	55.2	95.9	163.4	203	207
Baltic Republics	0.1	1.0	1.5	1.9	1.9	139.5	212.4	257	254
Belorussia	0.0	0.8	1.6	2.2	2.3	89.0	168.5	230	237
Moldavia	0.1	0.4	0.6	0.9	1.0	97.3	164.9	228	250
Ukraine	0.7	4.9	8.9	11.3	11.7	102.8	181.6	227	233
Russia	2.0	11.7	21.4	27.5	28.6	89.3	159.8	200	206
Kazakhstan	0.0	1.5	2.4	2.9	3.0	112.1	164.8	197	199
Caucasus	0.2	1.4	2.2	2.7	2.7	114.7	164.4	192	188
Central Asia	0.1	1.8	3.0	3.9	4.0	87.2	127.2	153	150
USSR – urban		18.7	28.9	35.6	37.0				
– rural		4.7	12.8	17.7	18.2				

bringing the total to 60.5 mn at the end of 1980, including 38 mn in urban and 22 mn in rural localities. In fact only 13.6 mn new customers were supplied, with 80% of the shortfall taking place in rural locations.

The failure to meet the plan target is mainly due to the fact that in many large cities, where the provision of gas is a comparatively simple process, nearly all dwellings are now supplied with mains gas. In Moscow and Leningrad, for example, over 95% of dwellings receive mains or bottled gas. Consequently, the gas supply campaign is now having to be extended to smaller towns and villages where it is impracticable to lay gas mains. These localities must be provided with liquified gas and it is the slow construction of gas liquifaction and bottling plants which is holding up the process.

About 72% of all Soviet homes receive gas, including 75% in the cities and 68% in the countryside. The people of the European non-Russian republics are more likely to be supplied with gas than those of other regions of the country. The Central Asians are least provided for because the high proportion of them living in small villages makes distribution more difficult. Firewood and local coal are more likely to be used for cooking and heating purposes than gas.

Most cities and a large proportion of the urban-type settlements are now supplied with gas. In 1960, 492 towns and 184 settlements were supplied, and by 1970 these figures had risen to 1,720 and 1,866. By 1975, 105.1 mn people living in 1,921 towns and 2,558 settlements were receiving gas, and while the Tenth Five Year Plan expected that 136 mn urban and 79 mn rural inhabitants would be receiving gas by 1980, i.e. 81.4% and 80.6% of the total respectively, the plan was significantly underfulfilled. By the end of 1980, over 2,000 towns and 2,900 settlements were supplied with gas.

The number of villages receiving gas has grown from six in 1960 to 38,070 in 1970 and 143,500 in 1980. At the beginning of 1981, 96% of all towns and 75% of all settlements were getting gas. By 1980, the extent of gas provision was reaching the limit in some areas. In the Turkmen republic, all towns and settlements and 90% of the villages belonged to the gas distribution network, and 98% of the population received mains or bottled gas. In Moldavia, 90% of the population were supplied, and the programme is to be completed by 1985. In Siberia, on the other hand, it will be the turn of the century before the gas supply programme nears completion, although the Sibgazifikatsiya organisation, responsible for installing gas cookers in Siberian towns and villages, is stepping up its operations during the Eleventh Five Year Plan period.

Table 2.7: Number of Households Burning Gas, by Type of Delivery ('000)

	From Gas Mains	In Bottles	Total
1977	19,882	28,344	48,226
1978	20,974	29,950	50,924
1979	21,994	31,264	53,258
1980	23,042	32,186	55,228

In 1980, 58% of Soviet gas-users received their supplies in bottled form rather than through gas mains. Of the 18.7 mn gas-served dwellings in urban areas in 1970, 11 mn were connected to the gas mains and 7.7 mn used bottled gas. The respective figures for 1975 were 17.1 and 11.7 mn and by 1980 more than 20 mn households in over 4,000 locations received mains gas. The continuing importance of bottled gas, even in urban locations, lies in the cost of installing gas mains. This rises considerably, by 70% per unit of consumed gas, when gas mains are installed in a small town of less than 50,000 inhabitants compared with large cities of up to half a million people.

In oblast centres, normally large towns with multi-storey buildings, 85-90% of flats are connected to the mains, and a further 5-10% use bottled gas. Natural gas has been used widely since 1965 when the construction of urban pipeline networks started. In large cities of between 100,000 and 500,000 people, 80-85% of all dwellings use mains gas and 5-10% use bottled gas. In small towns, 40-50% of

Table 2.8: Cost of Construction of Urban Gas Mains

Population of the City ('000)	Consumption of Gas (mn cu m/yr)	Gas Main Construction Cost* (roubles/thousand cu m per year)
Up to 50	34	9.2
50–100	142	7.9
100–250	366	6.4
250–500	853	5.4

Note: * including a 12.5% charge for capital.

households receive mains gas and 20–30% bottled gas; here, the extent of the gas mains network grows only slowly, mainly in new housing areas, and hardly at all in the countryside, where mains gas is virtually unknown. In 1970, 4.3 mn rural dwellings were served with bottled gas and 0.4 mn with mains gas. In 1975, the respective figures were 11.9 and 0.9 mn.

The extent to which the supply of bottled gas can be increased depends on improvements in transport facilities between the gas plants and consumers. Most bottled gas is delivered to regional distribution centres (RDCs) by rail in special propane cisterns able to carry 46 cu m of gas at a pressure of 20 kg/sq cm. The main constraint on the faster growth of bottled gas output is the shortage of rail cisterns, even though new, larger models with a capacity of 84 cu m have been introduced. The importance of building more cisterns can be appreciated from the fact that each 84 cu m cistern is able to distribute fuel with the same heat content as 330 cu m of firewood.

For RDCs located less than 300 km from the gas plant, the transport of bottled gas by road in specialised autocisterns becomes economical, but the use of pipelines is not feasible as yet because no RDC takes sufficient gas to cover pipeline construction costs. Only where an RDC operates in close proximity to another major consumer like a petrochemical plant will the building of a pipeline prove worthwhile.

From the RDC, gas is distributed to consumers in canisters holding either 5.27 or 50 litres. Households in remote regions of Siberia are served by riverboats delivering 3,000-6,000 canisters, each holding 27 litres, and occasionally helicopters are used. In recent years, an increasing amount of gas is being sold in brickette form as a jelly-like substance in a plastic wrapping. A 30-gram brickette is sufficient to heat 1 cu m of water.

Greater emphasis will be placed on bringing gas to rural consumers during the rest of this century, while in the largest cities, the trend now

Table 2.9: Number of Dwellings Using Gas and Electricity for Cooking in Moscow

	Total No. of Dwellings	Gas	Using: Electricity	Others
1966	1,398,000	1,328,000	70,000	
1976	2,279,000	2,142,000	123,000	16,000
1977	2,346,000	2,140,000	192,000	14,000
1978	2,415,000	2,137,000	266,000	12,000
1979	2,479,000	2,132,000	337,000	10,000
1980	2,542,000	2,123,000	409,000	10,000

seems to be moving away from gas in favour of electricity. As long ago as 1960, more than 90% of the living area of Moscow was served with gas mains, the total length of which reached nearly 2,000 km. By 1979, the distribution network had grown to 2,716 km and carried 17.36 bn cu m of gas, of which 1.48 bn was destined for houses and public buildings. The growth in the supply of gas, which now accounts for over 70% of Moscow's fuel requirements, has enabled deliveries of solid fuels to the capital to be reduced. In 1955, residential and municipal customers purchased 1.2 mn tons of coal and 590,000 cu m of firewood, but in 1976 these figures had fallen to 150,000 tons and 8,000 cu m. However, an interesting development has been the rapid growth in the number of homes using electric rather than gas stoves. In 1980, these accounted for 16.1% of the total number of dwellings compared with 5.4% in 1976.

It would appear that, in Moscow at least, most newly-built dwellings are expected to use electricity rather than gas for cooking purposes, and a small number of gas-users are converting to electricity. No more than 10,000 homes out of 2½ mn now use coal or firewood for cooking.

The degree of provision of gas to Leningrad has also reached a very high level, but may be starting to decline. In 1970, the city had 1,076,000 families consisting of 3,987,000 people, and gas was provided to 825,000 homes. By 1976, 1,092,000 homes (95% of the total) were supplied.

The Baku conurbation, with 1.6 mn people and 760,000 gas stoves, is another major area where practically all the inhabitants receive natural gas. Consequently, they suffered severe hardship in 1980 when deliveries of gas from Iran were cut off, but the extension of the Urengoi-Novopskov gas pipeline through Aksai and Mozdok to Kazi

Table 2.10: Provision of Gas to Leningrad City

	1950	1960	1970	1975	1976
Length of gas mains network (km)	322	1,102	1,861	2,120	2,155
Volume of mains and bottled gas (bn cu m)	0.25	1.78	5.20	5.74	6.17
Volume of gas used by the population (mn cu m)			438	461	463
Number of dwellings served with gas ('000)	125	340	825	1,055	1,092

Table 2.11: Consumption of Gas for Residential and Municipal Purposes

	1965	1970	1975	1980
Mains gas (bn cu m)				
dwellings	4.5	7.4	11.5	16.0
urban	4.4	7.1	10.9	14.8
rural	0.1	0.3	0.6	1.2
public buildings	10.8	17.9	21.7	36.0
urban	10.8	17.5	20.7	n.a.
rural	0.0	0.4	1.0	n.a.
total*	15.3	25.3	33.2	52.0
Bottled gas (mn tons)				
dwellings	0.65	1.65	3.00	4.1
public buildings	0.07	0.21	0.30	0.4
total	0.72	1.86	3.30	4.5

Note: * after 1975, the definition of public buildings was changed, possibly to include small workshops, etc.

Magomed should have relieved the situation, with Siberian gas now reaching Baku.

The volume of gas used by the household and domestic sector of the USSR has risen rapidly, particularly since 1965.

It is interesting to note that whereas most Western countries are devoting an increasing share of their natural gas resources to cooking and space-heating in homes, the comparable share of Soviet gas resources has been continuously declining. Most of the increase in bottled gas production, on the other hand is directed towards residential and municipal consumers.

In spite of the fact that nearly three-quarters of Soviet households receive gas, the volume involved is very small by Western standards, because the gas is used only for cooking, and hardly ever for space-heating. In 1980, *per caput* household consumption of mains gas

Table 2.12: Share of Mains and Bottled Gas Used by Households

	Mains Gas (bn cu m)			Bottled Gas (mn tonnes)		
	Production	Household Consumption	Share	Production	Household Consumption	Share
1970	198	7.4	3.7	4.91	1.86	37.9
1975	289	11.5	4.0	6.95	3.30	47.5
1976	321	12.1	3.8	7.30	3.56	48.8
1977	346	12.9	3.7	7.66	3.80	49.6
1978	372	13.7	3.7	7.94	4.05	51.0
1979	407	14.6	3.6	8.34	4.25	51.0
1980	435	16.0	3.7	8.52	4.52	53.1

amounted to only 0.50 mn kcals a year compared with 8.98 in the Netherlands and 5.92 in the USA. Only in countries like Spain, where the gas industry has not really become established, is *per caput* consumption lower than in the USSR (Table 2.13).

The future rate of provision of gas to dwellings and public buildings is difficult to predict. The Eleventh Five Year Plan foresees continued growth in supply, basically to new mikrorayons (urban neighbourhoods), of natural gas delivered to flats and to heating boilers. This will facilitate the transfer from solid fuel to gas. In small and medium-sized towns connected to gas pipelines, it is necessary to accelerate the construction of gas distribution networks, especially those serving buildings of more than four storeys. This will release liquified gas for single houses and rural areas. For towns where mains gas is not yet delivered, the decisions to connect them up to the country's trunk pipeline system must be taken after analysing the effectiveness of using gas in both industrial and domestic sectors. It is not likely, for example, that the major cities of Western and Eastern Siberia will receive gas for many years because of the availability of very cheap local coal. For these regions, and rural areas in the European part of the Soviet Union, greater use of bottled gas is planned.

Multi-storey flats, especially in new mikrorayons, are highly effective and top-priority customers of natural gas. It has been estimated that the supply of gas to the 31.4 mn new flats connected up between 1966 and 1975 has resulted in savings to the population of 786 mn roubles. However, the existing price system does not encourage a more rapid construction of urban distribution pipelines. At the present time, the price of gas sold to residential customers does not permit the recoupment of costs (i.e. it is subsidised), and in particular does not include the costs of the construction and operation of a low-pressure

Table 2.13: Household Consumption of Gas* by Selected Countries, 1980

	Household Consumption (tcals)	Share of Total Supply (%)	Consumption *per caput* (mn kcals)	Rate of Growth 1975–80 (% yr)
USSR	133,443	3.7	0.50	6.9
Netherlands	126,857	37.5	8.98	5.4
USA	1,320,877	25.2	5.92	0.7
UK	212,662	47.4	3.81	7.4
West Germany	137,629	29.2	2.31	17.2
Italy	94,398	37.5	1.65	7.4
France	63,111	26.4	1.17	9.1
Japan	62,170	18.3	0.53	6.0
Spain	3,729	17.2	0.10	5.1

Note: * The data for all Western countries includes gas used by the agricultural sector for production purposes, such as heating buildings for animals, and cannot be distinguished from gas consumption by households.

distribution network with regulation points. Domestic heating boilers pay a wholesale price of 11 to 15 roubles per thousand cu m for gas. This is lower than the prices at which the gorgazy (city gas sales organisations) sell gas to industrial enterprises, although heating boilers create seasonal irregularities in the consumption of gas, which leads to higher costs, i.e. on the construction of underground storage reservoirs. This encourages the gorgazy to supply industrial enterprises at the expense of residential customers, and 'privilege prices' of gas to the residential sector, therefore, lead to delays in the supply of gas to it.

Raising the price level could result in an acceleration of gas supply to the population. At the moment, urban dwellings are equipped for food preparation with gas stoves using mains gas (40%) or liquified gas (25%), electric stoves (5%) and coal-burning stoves (30%). The users of mains gas spend an average of 2 roubles a year. Raising the price of gas, even by 100%, will have only a small effect on household expenditures, but it may encourage its more economical use. Users of bottled gas spend on average 8 to 10 roubles a year, the same as electric stove owners.

The provision of gas on a large scale has contributed to a fall in the share of fuel costs in a family's total expenditure. In 1960, the family of an individual worker spent 0.6% of its income on fuel; by 1965 it had fallen to 0.4%, by 1970 to 0.3% and since 1973 it has been only 0.2%. The cost of fuel as a proportion of total expenditure for the family of a collective farmer is eight times higher than that for an industrial worker, or 1.6% of its income in 1977. This is partly because the collective farmer earns less, but also because fuel tends to be more expensive in rural areas, reflecting not only higher transport costs, but also a higher share of coal and firewood in total fuel utilisation.

Future Consumption of Gas by Households. Estimates suggest that by the end of the century, 89% of all Soviet dwellings will be supplied with mains or bottled gas. This share would be higher were it not for the recent trend towards a very rapid growth in the number of electric stoves in those regions in the west of the country where the distance from the major gas fields makes the delivered price of gas rather high compared with that of electricity from large atomic power stations. While the consumption of bottled gas will grow much more rapidly than that of mains gas during the period up to the early 1990s, it will stabilise at about 6.7 mn tons a year (a rise of 48% over 1980) as small towns and settlements previously dependent on bottled gas are connected to the mains system. At the moment, towns like Kirov (396,000 people), and Gomel (405,000) are still being connected up, but by the end of the century, all towns of more than 20,000 people will be plugged into the nation's trunk network. There should be a surge in the consumption of mains gas towards the end of the 1980s as major trunk lines are (for the first time) laid eastwards from Tyumen oblast, and large towns such as Novosibirsk, Irkutsk, Khabarovsk, Vladivostok and those of the Kuzbass conurbation receive mains gas.

Table 2.14: Estimated Future Consumption of Gas by Households

Year	No. of Dwellings Served with Gas (mn)	Consumption of Mains Gas (bn cu m)	Consumption of Bottled Gas (mn tons)
1979	53.3	14.6	4.25
1980	55.2	16.0	4.52
1985	60.8	18.0	5.4
1990	66.0	20.0	6.2
2000	74.5	22.6	6.7

(f) Thermal Energy

All new housing estates in Soviet cities are provided with networks for the distribution of steam and hot water produced by municipal boilers in district heating centres or by combined heat-and-power plants. Not only are central heating requirements covered in this way, but in some cases hot water is also piped to dwellings and recycled through purification systems back to the boiler for heating and subsequent redistribution.

Table 2.15: Consumption of Centrally Produced Heat

| | Consumption, mn G-cals | | | Consumption *per caput* G-cals/yr | |
	Total	Household and Municipal	Share of Total	Total	Household and Municipal
1965	853	114	13.4	3.67	0.49
1970	1,296	212	16.4	5.34	0.87
1975	1,738	335	19.3	6.86	1.32
1980	2,260	500	21.7	8.69	1.89
1981	2,315	530	22.3	8.92	1.98
1982 Plan	2,365				

In 1970, it was estimated that centralised sources of thermal energy accounted for 25% of the household and municipal sector's heat and hot water needs, with the remaining 75% covered by boilers serving individual houses, blocks of flats, etc., or by individual stoves and open hearths. In 1965, the centralised sources of heat (i.e. heat-and-power plants, district heating centres and large household boilers with productivities of 20 G-cals and more a day) produced 853 mn G-cals of heat, of which 114 mn (13.4%) went to the household and municipal sectors. The consumption of centrally produced heat by homes and public buildings has since grown at an average annual rate of 10.0% to 530 mn G-cals in 1981 (Table 2.15).

Consumption of heat by the household and municipal sector from all sources grew by 25% over the period 1970 to 1975 from 830 to 1,040 mn G-cals, or from 3.40 G-cals per person to 4.07 G-cals. The share of this energy coming from centralised sources rose from 25.5% to 34.1%. During the period 1976 to 1980, output of heat from all sources rose from 2,500 mn G-cals to 3,150 mn, or by 26%, and the volume going to the household and domestic sector rose from 1,040 mn G-cals in 1975 to 1,300 mn in 1980. This means that heat production from small, non-centralised boilers, rose from 762 to 870 mn G-cals (by 14.2%) while that despatched to homes and public buildings rose from 705 to 800 mn G-cals. In 1980, the share of household and municipcal heat coming from centralised sources amounted to 40.8% compared with 34.1% in 1975.

When the provision of heat to the household and municipal sector of *urban* locations alone (i.e. cities and urban-type settlements) is considered, the situation is somewhat better, with centralised sources providing 31.4% in 1970, 40.4% in 1975 and 52% in 1980.

It is natural that, with their heavy capital investment costs, thermal

Table 2.16: Structure of Thermal Energy Consumption by the Household and Municipal Sector in Urban Locations (%)

	1970	1975	1980
Combined heat and power plants	24.6	28.3	31.0
District heating centres	6.8	12.1	21.0
Total centralised sources	31.4	40.4	52.0
Local boilers	28.0	27.5	22.9
Individual stoves	40.2	31.7	25.0
Electric boilers	0.4	0.4	0.1
Total local sources	68.6	59.6	48.0

energy systems should be more prevalent in the cities, and in 1975, some 660 mn G-cal were consumed in towns and urban-type settlements (4.21 G-cals per person) and 380 mn in rural localities (3.84 per person). It is apparent that, as with the distribution of gas, the gap between urban and rural living standards is being rapidly narrowed. However, the larger the city, the more economical the laying of a thermal energy system, and the larger the share of consumption that may be covered by heat-and-power plants. Thus Mosenergo covered 67% of Moscow's residential and municipal requirements in 1975, as well as a great part of the demand from the Ryazan, Stupino and Orokhovo-Zuevo regions. For the country as a whole, the comparable figure was 28%, and this was expected to rise to 31% by 1980. In 1970, heat-and-power plants accounted for 24.6% of residential and muncipal consumption nationally, but for more than 30% in over 200 towns including Kiev (60%), Leningrad (58%) and Moscow (47%). In some new towns created on the basis of a large industrial complex, such as Nizhnekamsk or Naberezhnye Chelny, the share reached 100%.

Demand in Moscow by residential and municipal consumers has grown from 1,018 G-cal an hour in 1950 to 3,920 in 1960, 12,400 in 1970 and 14,500 in 1973. A demand of 33,000 G-cals an hour is foreseen in the long-term, of which 24,000 will be covered by heat-and-power plants. Although their development is much more advanced in Moscow than in most other cities, even here much more needs to be done. The centralised supply of thermal energy is partly covered by peak-supply boilers, some of which have become base-suppliers and operate for an unduly large number of hours. This is because the construction of heat-and-power plants is lagging behind – the Yuzhnyi station was supposed to have begun serving the Biryulev, Yasenev and Teplyi Stan mikrorayons in 1975, and its six units of 250 MW each should have been completed and producing 11 bn kWh of electricity a year by 1980. However, the first unit started up only in July 1981.

An idea of the cost to the nation that this sort of delay entails can be gathered from the fact that while heat-and-power plants required only 178.4 kg of standard fuel per G-cal in 1965, municipal boilers needed 195.4 and small residential boilers 220 kg.

In other cities, the failure to make full use of the potential offered by heat-and-power plants stems from opposite reasons. In order to obtain the greatest possible savings of fuel, it is necessary to join up consumers to the stations as rapidly as possible by laying the thermal energy pipelines in good time. This, on the whole, has been accomplished, and the problem has been delays in the construction of industrial enterprises, which has lead to the heat-and-power plants working mainly on an uneconomical condensing cycle, primarily producing electricity at rates of fuel usage higher than those of condensing power stations.

Because centralised sources of heat generally operate on premium fuels, great emphasis is laid by Soviet planners on trying to raise their levels of efficiency. Of the 120 mn tsf burned in 1980 by heat-and-power plants and district heating stations for the provision of heat to the household and municipal sector (consisting of 100 mn tsf for housing and 20 mn for public buildings) it is said that up to 25% of this was wasted. There are three principal points at which the wastage occurs: fuel is burned inefficiently in the boilers (1.9 bn cu m of gas was wasted in this way in 1980); there is a shortage of equipment able to regulate the flow of heat to buildings depending on the ambient temperature; and Soviet citizens are notoriously wasteful in their use of hot water.

It is a common complaint of the Soviet press that, during warm weather, radiators in flats continue to blaze and the residents have to leave their windows wide open. This phenomenon is most common in spring and autumn when outside temperatures fluctuate considerably and the suppliers of heat are unable to react sufficiently quickly. They operate according to a 'classic graph' relating the temperature at which heat is circulated round a housing estate to that of the atmosphere — as atmospheric temperatures rise, that of the heat is steadily reduced. But the classic graph only extends as far as 2.5° above zero, at which point the temperature of the hot water despatched by the supplier has been reduced to 70°, and for atmospheric temperatures of 3° or higher, it will remain at 70°. This is because, as well as heating rooms, the heat supply must also heat up cold water (through a heat exchanger) to an officially prescribed minimum of 60° for the hot water supply of kitchens and bathrooms. Consequently, millions of tons of fuel are wasted annually in heating flats to an unnecessarily high temperature.

The installation of automatic equipment at central heat points (CHPs) is expected to resolve this problem eventually. Each heat-and-power plant or district heating station has a number of CHPs (the thermal energy equivalents of electricity substations), each serving five to ten blocks of flats. In Moscow, 100 CHPs have been automated, saving an estimated 500,000 roubles' worth of fuel annually. They are now able to monitor the ambient temperature, and their electronically operated regulators can despatch precisely as much heat as is needed for heating rooms and for maintaining the hot water supply at the required 60°. It is planned to regulate the heat supply in this way throughout the USSR eventually, but a shortage of necessary equipment is holding up the process. In the meantime, 60% of all suppliers of thermal energy in the RSFSR, and 50% throughout the USSR, are not even fitted with devices for measuring the volume of heat they produce.

While hot water consumption in most Western countries amounts to 60-80 litres a day per person, the average Soviet citizen manages to use 100-120 litres. Fuel consumption for the supply of hot water now amounts to 70% of that needed for space-heating, and it is readily conceded by planners that the artificially low price of hot water (16 kopecks per person per month) does not encourage people to conserve it, and that exhortations have only a limited effect. But there is not likely to be any radical change in Soviet policy, which has endured since the Revolution, to provide such a basic necessity of life practically free of charge.

It has been estimated that the regulation of hot water consumption by the population could achieve savings of 12-14 mn tsf a year. A consumption norm based on the number of people in the family could be set for each household; a measuring device would record the actual rate of consumption, and a raised tarriff could be charged for consumption above the norm. This would preserve the policy of cheap necessities while discouraging profligacy.

In 1980, homes, public buildings and industrial plants required 390 mn tsf for space-heating, the provision of hot water and the cooking of food, including 170 mn for the firing of centralised sources of heat. According to Gosstroi and Gosgrazhdanstroi (*Izvestia*, 15 November 1981), 50-60 mn tsf a year could be saved if all the decrees passed by the Council of Ministers had been fulfilled. As it was, savings of only

Table 2.17: Forecast Production of Heat (mn G-cals)

	1980	1985	1990	2000
Total production	3,130	3,550	4,000	4,930
for household and municipal sector	1,300	1,450	1,600	1,900
By centralised sources	2,260	2,670	3,100	4,000
for household and municipal sector	500	620	740	1,000
By local boilers	870	880	900	930
for household and municipal sector	800	830	860	900

2.6 mn tsf were achieved in 1980.

It would appear that while the amount of heat going into a flat is determined by the local suppliers, or while the price of fuel supplied to the population is kept very low, there is little incentive for individuals to employ fuel-saving techniques widely used in the West, such as double-glazing or insulation. And while planners are continually urging the population to install double-glazing, there is an acute shortage of materials. In 1980, the demand for penopolyurethane was estimated at 1,260 tons, but only 100 tons were made available, and there was a similar shortage of triple-layer wall materials.

But, whatever the success or otherwise of such conservation measures, the production of heat by heat-and-power plants and boilers (centralised and local) will continue to rise fairly rapidly, basically at the expense of lower-rank fuels burned in hearths and stoves. While Soviet planners would like to see the disappearance of small local boilers because of their high fuel rates, this is not likely to happen before well into the next century. This is because the policy of encouraging the rural population into large villages for which centralised boilers can be built is not succeeding as rapidly as hoped, and the improvement of rural living standards will lead to the installation of many more small boilers serving individual houses and burning bottled gas. These boilers will, at least, cut the huge amount of time spent on collecting and burning lower-rank fuels in the countryside during a period when farms in some areas will be experiencing acute labour shortages, and the question of how the country-dweller spends his time becomes more topical.

(g) Electricity in the Home

A comparatively small share of Soviet electricity production is consumed in the home. Only 78 bn kWh (6.0% of total output) was used in this way in 1980, and the importance of household use is not

Table 2.18: Household Consumption of Electricity by Selected Countries, 1980

	Household Consumption (bn kWh)	Share of Total Output (%)	*Per caput* household Consumption (kWh)
USSR	78.0	6.0	295
USA	717.4	28.9	3,220
UK	86.1	30.2	1,544
West Germany	85.6	23.2	1,440
France	72.9	28.2	1,356
Japan	121.5	21.0	1,040
Italy	38.1	20.5	668
Spain	18.2	16.4	486
Portugal	3.3	21.5	333
Turkey	5.4	23.2	119

growing; in 1970 5.9% (43 bn kWh out of 740 bn) was used for this purpose.

In complete contrast, household use accounts for 15-30% of total electricity production in the West, ranging from 16.4% in Spain to 30.2% in the UK. There is an extraordinary difference in the *per caput* consumption of electricity between the USSR and some Western countries. While the average Soviet citizen uses 295 kWh a year, his American counterpart, for example, uses 3,220. Moreover, household consumption of electricity in most Western countries is growing more rapidly than in the USSR.

However, it should be borne in mind that the data for Western countries in Table 2.18 probably includes electricity used on farms or in shops which would be defined as 'agricultural' or 'municipal' consumption in the USSR.

The differences in *per caput* consumption between the USSR and advanced Western countries (and between Western countries with similar levels of development) is largely explained by the extent to which electricity is used for space-heating and cooking. In most Western countries, electricity is practically the only alternative to gas for cooking, and the use of fuels other than gas and electricity for space-heating is declining. Consequently, the use of electricity depends to some extent on the availability and price of gas. In the USSR, on the other hand, space-heating in cities is often accomplished by boilers which range from very large municipal boilers or heat-and-power plants, which can heat a whole city suburb, to small boilers serving a house or block of flats. In Moscow, for example, 99.6% of housing was provided with

Table 2.19: Ownership of Domestic Electrical Goods (number per 100 families)

	1965	1970	1975	1980	1985 Plan
Radios	59	72	79	85	89
Televisions	24	51	74	85	90
Refrigerators	11	32	61	86	95
Washing machines	21	52	65	70	78
Electric vacuum cleaners	7	12	18	29	38

Table 2.20: Ownership of Consumer Durables in Urban and Rural Locations

	1970		1975		1980	
	Urban	Rural	Urban	Rural	Urban	Rural
Radios	78	55	86	68	90	75
Televisions	61	32	83	59	91	73
Refrigerators	43	13	77	34	99	61
Washing machines	64	26	77	45	78	58
Vacuum cleaners	16	3	24	7	37	13

central heating from these sources in 1980. In rural areas, as well as the older parts of cities, firewood or coal burned in stoves is used for heating. Electric fires are few and far between, and electric underfloor heating is non-existent. For cooking, the Russians use piped or bottled gas in the cities and bottled gas, coal or firewood in the countryside.

The growing sophistication of the economy has permitted much of the drudgery of human existence to be removed by the use of labour-saving devices such as washing machines, vacuum cleaners and refrigerators. It has also enabled life to become more varied and interesting, with most Soviet families now owning a television, radio, record player, etc.

The incidence of ownership of electricity-using consumer durables is greater in the cities than in the countryside, even though electricity is now universally available in rural areas. This is a reflection of the higher living standards in towns, and the more immediate availability of these goods, although it can be seen that the rural-urban gap is narrowing rapidly (Table 2.20).

The production of these goods has stabilised during the last few years, with the emphasis now on producing bigger and better products. The output of televisions, for example, has grown at an average annual rate of only 1.2% since 1970 to 7.53 mn sets in 1980. But while the production of black and white sets has declined from 6.6 to 5.3 mn in

Table 2.21: Production of Domestic Electrical Goods

	1965	1970	1975	1980	1981
Televisions – black & white	3.7	6.6	6.4	5.3	5.5
– colour	–	0.1	0.6	2.3	2.7
Radios	5.2	7.8	8.4	8.5	8.7
Tape recorders	0.5	1.2	2.5	3.0	
Refrigerators	1.7	4.1	5.6	5.9	5.9
Washing machines	3.4	5.2	3.3	3.8	3.9
Electric vacuum cleaners	0.8	1.5	2.9	3.2	

1980, the annual output of colour sets has grown from 46,000 in 1970 to 2.3 mn in 1980. During the latter half of the 1970s, the production of domestic refigerators has stabilised at 5.8 to 6 mn a year. That of washing machines has remained at 3.5 to 3.8 mn, although this compares with 5.2 mn in 1970 and reflects a tendency towards the production of more sophisticated machines with spin dryers. The annual output of electric vacuum cleaners exceeded 3 mn for the first time in 1979, and is likely to grow considerably during the next decade because of the high level of demand for them.

As more households purchase these electric consumer durables, and new, more powerful models are developed, their consumption of electricity will rise beyond the 41.5 bn kWh used for this purpose in 1980. This trend will be particularly noticeable in the countryside, where in 1980 98.2 mn people used only 9.2 bn kWh (94 kWh per person) while 166.2 mn urban dwellers used 32.3 bn kWh (194 kWh per person).

Increased electricity consumption in the home is inevitable if people are to be freed from time-consuming and onerous domestic chores. It is estimated, for example, that the washing of clothes accounts for 20% of the time spent on housework, and that this can be saved with the acquisition of an automatic washing machine.

But time-saving appliances need more electricity, and a major cause for concern to planners is that some new models have unnecessarily high rates of power consumption. The 12-programme 'Vyatka-avtomat' washing machine, for example, is a fully automatic washer which operates with the preheating of the washing solution – an unnecessary refinement given the supply of centrally-produced hot water to many urban dwellings – and this requires a power rating of 2.2 kW compared with 0.5 to 0.65 kW for conventional models. Fortunately, its high price of 500 roubles and problems with installation (it requires a power supply from heavy-duty wiring which is found in only 10% of dwellings) means that few are sold, but other modern models of washing machines are designed to wash clothes more thoroughly than is necessary, thereby wasting considerable amounts of power. It is said that an old-fashioned vibration type machine, dating from 1959, does the job just as well with a power rating of only 40 watts.

Soviet refrigerators are another good example of power-guzzling appliances; they use 36-40% more electricity than comparable foreign models, and the 'Oka-6' made in Murom even uses 50% more, at a rate of 22 kWh/day in summer, due to the low quality of its insulation materials.

While Soviet televisions have traditionally been more power intensive than foreign models, this is changing with the production of new models such as the 'Foton Ts-202', made by the Simferapol Television Plant, which is said to use 50-60% less power than other comparable televisions. When they are sold nationwide, it is estimated that their use will yield savings of 36 mn kWh a year.

It can be tentatively estimated that by the year 2000, 79 bn kWh will be needed for powering household consumer durables. This assumes that the Soviet population will have grown to 305 mn, and that practically every family will have a radio, television, refrigerator, washing machine and electric vacuum cleaner. It also assumes that the ownership of other, more sophisticated durables will have become widespread; already by 1980, a million families (1.1% of the population) had electric air conditioners, and the ownership of record-players, tape recorders, hair dryers and freezers was growing rapidly. Of the anticipated increase of 37.5 bn kWh over 1980, 17% can be attributed to the population increase, 61% to the greater incidence of ownership of consumer durables and 22% to the increase in their unit rates of power consumption due to their greater capacity, etc. The gap between urban and rural inhabitants in the ownership of consumer durables will have practically disappeared, with all Soviet inhabitants requiring an average 259 kWh a year for their use.

The fact that practically all dwellings now receive electricity in the USSR is not reflected in data on electricity consumption for domestic lighting. Some 24.8 bn kWh were used for this purpose in 1980, consisting of 17.4 bn in the cities (105 kWh per person) and 7.4 bn in the countryside (75 kWh per person). Some of the 30 kWh difference can be attributed to the fact that a substantial share of rural inhabitants live in the southern regions (Central Asia, Kazakhstan, the Caucasus, etc.) where the hours of daylight tend to be more regular, and also to the fact that rural inhabitants tend to organise their waking moments more in accordance with daylight hours than is the case in the cities. Nevertheless, the fact still remains that, all other things being equal, they use less electricity for lighting than urban dwellers. It can be estimated that by the end of the century, the consumption of electricity for domestic lighting will have risen to 35 bn kWh a year.

The amount of electricity spent on lighting can be greatly reduced if luminescent lights were used more widely (a luminescent lamp of 32 watts gives as much light as an incandescent light of 100 watts and lasts five to seven times longer) yet they account for only 7% of total production. On the contrary, more and more chandeliers carrying five, six or even seven light bulbs are being produced, giving off far more light than is necessary, although a Moscow factory is now manufacturing chandeliers with variable light selection. If this example were to be followed by other manufacturers, then up to 0.4 bn kWh a year could be saved.

Consumer durables and lighting account for the overwhelming share of electricity consumed by households, because its use for cooking, heating and hot water is not very common in the USSR. In 1980, only 6.6 bn kWh (5.3 in towns and 1.3 bn kWh in the countryside) were used for cooking, and by the end of 1980 only 5 mn families out of 90 mn had electric stoves. Yet even here, significant savings are possible because 3.5 mn of these cookers have stamped-plate rings with an efficiency rating of only 56%. This compares with 72% for tubular heating elements, but these are found on only 650,000 cookers, and they are not being produced in sufficient quantity. Heat regulators can save large amounts of electricity, but they are being produced at the wholly inadequate rate of only 200,000 a year.

In 1980, only 5.1 bn kWh of electricity (3 in urban dwellings and 2.1 bn kWh in the countryside) were used for heating and hot water.

In all, domestic consumption of electricity had grown to 78 bn kWh in 1980, or 295 kWh per person. The level of consumption was higher in towns, where 58 bn kWh (349 kWh per person) were used, than in the countryside where the total of 20 bn kWh provided a *per caput* consumption of only 204 kWh.

The acquisition of more consumer durables has led to a steady rise in the *per caput* consumption of electricity, from 217 kWh per urban inhabitant in 1970 to 276 in 1975 and 349 in 1980. It is anticipated that it will grow to 450 before levelling out shortly before the end of the century, and by this time the gap between urban and rural consumers will have been virtually closed. It is estimated that household electricity requirements will grow to a total 135 bn kWh in 2000, i.e.

at an average rate of 2.8% a year over the period 1980 to 2000.

For urban inhabitants, the *per caput* growth rate will average only 1.3% a year over the 20-year period, compared with 4.9% during 1970 to 1975 and 4.8% during 1976 to 1980. It can be surmised that the *per caput* growth rate will fall to 3% a year during 1981 to 1985, 1.5% during 1986 to 1990, and 0.3% a year during 1990 to 2000. People living in rural areas will continue to increase their consumption of electricity at high rates until well into the 1990s; for the 20-year period as a whole, it will grow at an average 4.0% a year including 7% during 1981 to 1985 (although the Eleventh Five Year Plan calls, rather implausibly, for an average annual growth rate of 13–15%), 4% during 1986 to 1990, and 2.5% a year during the last decade of the century.

(h) Electricity Consumption by the Municipal Sector

In 1980, the expenditure of electricity for municipal purposes amounted to 104.2 bn kWh after practically doubling during the 1970s. Growth was somewhat faster during the first half of the decade (8.1% per year) than the second (5.6%).

Table 2.22: Expenditure of Electricity for Municipal Purposes

	Total Consumption (bn kWh)			Consumption per Person (kWh)		
	1970	1975	1980	1970	1975	1980
Total	53.7	79.4	104.2	222	313	394
Urban	50.7	74.4	97.0	373	490	584
Rural	3.0	5.0	7.2	28	49	73

Almost half the municipal power needs are spent on electric motors for pumping water and sewage, etc. Some 50.9 bn kWh (47.9 bn in the cities and 3 bn in the countryside) were used for this purpose in 1980. The lighting of public buildings took 33 bn kWh, and street lighting 5.5 bn kWh. This is a rather miserable amount compared with that spent in other countries; the provision of street lighting is very poor in Soviet cities, especially in streets which are not major thoroughfares, and it is practically non-existent in the countryside. About 11.3 bn kWh were used for cooking food in restaurants, municipal canteens, hospitals and educational institutions, where the large volume of food being prepared makes the use of electric cookers economical compared with homes, where gas cookers and stoves dominate. A further 3.5 bn kWh were used for heating and hot water in public buildings.

Table 2.23: Municipal Consumption of Electricity by Purpose, 1980

	Total Consumption (bn kWh)			Consumption per person (kWh)		
	Total	Urban	Rural	USSR	Urban	Rural
Electric Motors	50.9	47.9	3.0	192	288	31
Lighting public buildings	33.0	30.0	3.0	125	181	31
Street lighting	5.5	5.2	0.3	21	31	3
Food preparation	11.3	10.7	0.6	43	64	6
Heating and hot water	3.5	3.2	0.3	13	19	3
Total	104.2	97.0	7.2	394	584	73

Table 2.24: Consumption of Electricity for 'Commercial and Public Service' Purposes, 1980

	Consumption (bn kWh)	*Per caput* consumption (kWh)	Share of Total (%)
USSR	104.2	394	8.1
USA	558.7	2,507	22.5
West Germany	58.2	979	15.8
UK	53.8	965	18.9
France	28.2	524	10.9
Japan	53.0	454	9.2
Italy	20.3	356	10.9
Spain	9.6	255	8.7
Portugal	2.3	225	14.8
Turkey	1.4	49	6.0

When compared with most Western countries, it can be seen from Table 2.24 that the amount of electricity which the USSR allots to its municipal economy is very small both in *per caput* terms, and as a share of total output of power.

According to official forecasts, municipal consumption of electricity in the USSR will grow at an annual average rate of 4.6% to 131 bn kWh in 1985, including 117 bn in the cities and 14 bn kWh in the countryside. It is thought that it will rise further to 160 bn kWh in 1990 (135 bn kWh in the cities and 25 bn in rural areas) and 215 bn kWh in 2000 (170 urban, 45 rural). This will provide 705 kWh per person, with 745 kWh/person in the cities and 590 in the countryside.

3 DEMAND FOR FUEL BY THE ELECTRICITY AND THERMAL ENERGY INDUSTRY

In 1981, the USSR produced 1,325 bn kWh of electricity. Since 1965, output has grown at a rate slightly faster than that of other advanced industrial countries, but *per caput* consumption of power is still very much lower than in most Western countries. By 1980, the USSR was still producing little more than half as much as the USA.

Table 3.1: Output of Electricity by the USSR and USA (bn kWh)

| | Output of Electricity | | Growth Rate of Output | | USSR as a |
	USSR	USA	USSR	USA	% of USA
1960	292	842			34.7
1970	741	1,640	9.8	6.9	45.2
1975	1,038	2,003	7.0	4.1	51.8
1978	1,202	2,286	5.0	4.5	52.6
1979	1,238	2,319	3.0	1.4	53.4
1980	1,295	2,356	4.6	1.6	55.0
1981	1,325	2,368	2.3	0.5	56.0

The growth rate of output has been falling in recent years, and is planned to fall still further during the Eleventh Five Year Plan period to 3.7% per year compared with 4.5% per year over 1976 to 1980. On this basis it is reasonable to expect that the USSR will not catch up with the USA in output of electricity before well into the twenty-first century. If the 1985 target of 1,555 bn kWh is fulfilled, and the growth rate of 1981 to 1985 is maintained, then electricity production by the USSR will reach 1,865 bn kWh in 1990 and 2,700 bn at the end of the century.

The Soviet Union has recently experienced a marked change in the relationship between the growth rate of its electricity supply industry and those of the other major national economic indicators. The period 1961 to 1965 was characterised by a huge expansion of staple energy intensive industries such as ferrous and non-ferrous metallurgy, basic chemicals, etc. and the annual growth rate of power production (11.6%) exceeded that of industrial output as a whole (8.6%) and that of produced national income (6.5%). Since 1965, the emphasis has switched to the less electricity-intensive industries, and the

Table 3.2: Output of Electricity and Gross Social Product

	GSP at current prices (bn roubles)		Output of electricity (kW/rouble of GSP)	
	Total	Industrial	Total	Industrial
1960	304	189	0.96	1.54
1965	420	266	1.20	1.90
1970	644	409	1.15	1.81
1975	863	558	1.20	1.86
1978	996	638	1.21	1.88
1979	1,032	657	1.20	1.88
1980	1,072	680	1.21	1.90

Table 3.3: Regional Output of Electricity (bn kWh)

	1960	1970	1975	1980	1985 Plan
RSFSR	196.2	469.2	639.1	804.4	942.5*
North West	17.0	34.4	52.3 ⎫	209.0 ⎫	
Centre	30.7	81.5	114.6 ⎭		
Volga Vyatka	8.3	14.9	14.9	16.6	
Central Chernozem	5.0	8.6	15.0	33.0 ⎬	640*
North Caucasus	9.6	29.8	39.1	49.2	
Volga	32.5	80.6	101.9	121.9	
Urals	49.1	87.1	112.1	141.9 ⎭	
Western Siberia	22.5	44.2	70.1	78.9 ⎫	
Eastern Siberia	16.2	74.0	97.2	123.4 ⎬	310*
Far East	5.3	14.1	21.9	30.5 ⎭	
Baltic	4.7	21.6	28.6	35.3	46.5
Ukraine	53.9	137.6	195.2	236	278.9
Moldavia	0.7	7.6	13.7	15.6	16.7
Belorussia	3.6	15.1	26.7	34.1	34.6
Caucasus	13.0	27.1	35.5	43.2	53.6
Central Asia	8.9	26.9	47.2	63.4	84.4
Kazakhstan	10.5	34.7	52.5	61.5	97.9
Total	291.5	739.8	1,038.5	1,293.5	1,555

Note: * These figures are presented as given by Soviet plan documents — no explanation is offered for their failure to add up.

production of electricity is now growing about as fast as industry as a whole. During 1976 to 1980, industrial production grew by 24.3% while the output of electricity rose by 24.7%. Since 1965, there has been a very close correlation between the production of electricity and the Gross Social Product.

The regional development of generating capacity has been uneven, with a wide variation in the levels of production of electricity per inhabitant between the regions. Table 3.3 shows the growth of output of electricity by region, and Table 3.4 indicates the variation in *per caput* production of electricity between the regions.

Table 3.4: *Per Caput* **Production of Electricity by Region**

| | Production (kWh/person) | | | | USSR = 100) | | | |
	1960	1970	1975	1980	1960	1970	1975	1980
RSFSR	1,650	3,606	4,760	5,818	118	118	116	119
North West	1,565	2,830	4,189	n.a.	112	92	102	n.a.
Centre	1,194	2,947	4,089	n.a.	85	96	99	n.a.
Volga Vyatka	1,006	1,785	1,796	1,986	72	58	44	41
Central Chernozem	644	1,075	1,902	4,184	46	35	46	85
North Caucasus	827	2,087	2,645	3,124	59	68	64	64
Volga	2,034	4,387	5,434	6,242	145	143	132	127
Urals	3,463	5,736	7,385	9,041	247	187	179	185
Western Siberia	2,000	3,650	5,742	5,966	143	119	139	122
Eastern Siberia	2,503	9,916	12,702	14,801	179	323	308	302
Far East	1,096	2,439	3,551	4,341	78	80	86	89
Baltic	711	2,850	3,680	4,756	51	93	90	97
Ukraine	1,287	2,920	4,047	4,724	92	95	98	96
Moldavia	243	2,129	3,681	3,931	17	69	89	80
Belorussia	447	1,677	2,901	3,548	32	55	70	72
Caucasus	1,368	2,204	2,747	3,037	98	72	67	62
Central Asia	644	1,359	2,187	2,431	46	44	53	50
Kazakhstan	1,147	2,667	3,833	4,146	82	87	93	85
USSR	1,400	3,065	4,100	4,896	100	100	100	100

Apart from nuclear and hydro stations, electricity is produced by base-load condensing power stations, known in the USSR as 'state regional power stations' (SRPSs) combined heat-and-power plants (CHPPs) and small diesel-powered mobile plants used on construction sites or in remote areas. In 1980, these stations produced 1,055 bn kWh from a total of 1,295 bn.

Thermal energy is produced by CHPPs, SRPSs and large public utility boilers serving residential and/or industrial customers. These are known by the Russians as 'centralised' sources of supply. Local sources include small boilers serving individual dwellings, blocks of flats or specific factories.

Thermal Power Stations

Thermal power stations accounted for 75.4% of generating capacity and 81.5% of electricity output in 1980, but these figures will fall in the future as an increasing share of the USSR's electricity needs is generated from nuclear and hydro stations which, during the 1981 to 1985 period, are expected to account for 77% of the planned increase in electricity output. The aggregate capacity of thermal power stations

Table 3.5: Output of Electricity by Type of Station (bn kWh)

	Total	Conventional Thermal	Atomic	Hydro
1960	292	241	–	51
1970	641	517	–	124
1975	1,038	892	20	126
1978	1,202	988	44	170
1979	1,239	1,012	55	172
1980	1,295	1,038	73	184
1981	1,330	1,063	86	181
1982 Plan	1,365	1,063	107	195
1985 Plan	1,555	1,105	220	230

Table 3.6: Capacity and Output of Thermal Power Stations in the USSR

	Capacity in MW (year end)	Output in bn kWh
1960	51,900	241
1970	133,200	613
1975	170,800	885
1978	188,800	988
1979	192,800	1,012
1980	198,500	1,038

amounted to 198,500 MW at the end of 1980, after growing by 5.1% a year during 1971 to 1975 and 3.0% during 1976 to 1980.

The total capacity of thermal power stations is planned to grow very slowly during the current plan period, from 198,500 MW at the end of 1980 to perhaps 225,000 MW at the end of 1985. Although 34,000 MW of new thermal capacity is to be installed, this will be accompanied by the scrapping of a large number of small, fuel-inefficient and technologically obsolete sets at the country's older power stations.

The Eleventh Five Year Plan expects thermal power stations to produce 1,105 bn kWh in 1985, compared with 1,038 bn in 1980 – this implies an average annual increase of only 1.3%. The production of thermal energy by power stations is planned to grow somewhat faster, by 2.8% a year from 1,090 mn G-cals in 1980 to 1,250 mn in 1985, by which time thermal power stations (basically CHPPs) should be accounting for 35.2% of the total national output of thermal energy compared with 34.8% in 1980.

In 1980, the total capacity of thermal power stations of 198,500 MW was made up as follows:

Map 3.1: **Thermal Power Stations, European USSR**

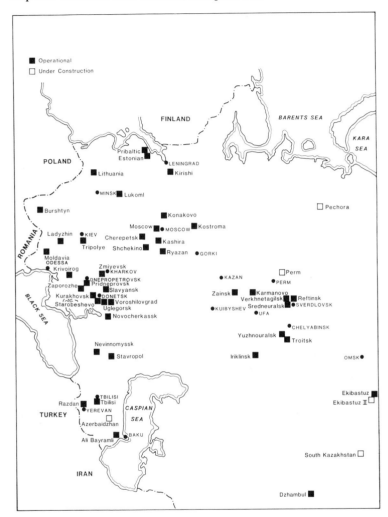

Condensing power stations	117,200 MW
Combined heat-and-power plants	76,000
Diesel and mobile power stations	5,300
Total	198,500 MW

Some 170,650 MW of thermal capacity in 1980 was owned by the Ministry of Power (Minenergo) with the remaining 27,850 MW (mostly CHPPs) belonging to factories owned by other ministries.

At the end of 1970, the USSR had 35 power stations, including 30 thermal and five hydro stations, with a capacity of 1,000 MW and more each. During 1970, these stations produced 38.9% of the USSR's electricity. By the beginning of 1981, the number of 1,000 MW+ stations had more than doubled to 76, including 57 thermal, 14 hydro and five atomic stations. They had a total capacity of 155,500 MW, 58.3% of the national total, and Table 3.7 shows their distribution by region of the USSR.

Table 3.7: Location of Power Stations with Capacity of 1,000 MW+ by Region, 1980 ('000 MW)

	Thermal	Hydro	Atomic	Total
North West	2,070	–	5,320	7,390
Centre	16,500	–	–	16,500
Volga Vyatka	–	–	–	–
Central Chernozem	–	–	4,455	4,455
North Caucasus	5,930	1,000	–	6,930
Volga	4,200	8,270	–	12,470
Urals	11,925	–	–	11,925
Western Siberia	6,410	–	–	6,410
Eastern Siberia	4,550	18,180	–	22,730
Far East	–	1,290	–	1,290
RSFSR	51,585	28,740	9,775	90,100
Baltic	4,835	–	–	4,835
Ukraine	29,100	1,486	3,000	33,586
Moldavia	2,520	–	–	2,520
Belorussia	2,400	–	–	2,400
Caucasus	3,480	1,640	–	5,120
Central Asia	7,390	3,900	–	11,290
Kazakhstan	5,630	–	–	5,630
USSR	106,940	35,766	12,775	155,481

Boilers

In 1980, the sector produced 3,130 mn G-cals of thermal energy, of which 2,260 mn G-cals came from 'centralised' sources (including 1,090 mn G-cals from CHPPs) and 870 mn G-cals from 'local' sources. The share of centralised sources in the total output of heat is planned to grow, as local sources are inefficient in fuel usage and usually pollutive, often being fired by lower-rank fuels. Within the 'centralised sources' category, it has been policy to extend the share of heat-and-power plants, but the share of municipal and industrial boilers may begin to grow in the future. It could be cheaper to cover base-load electricity requirements from very large nuclear stations and produce heat from boilers rather than to combine the two processes in situations where demand for both power and heat can only be met by running the CHPP at less than optimality.

During the decade 1970 to 1980, the production of thermal energy from all sources grew at an annual rate of 5.1%, while output from centralised sources rose by 5.7% a year, and that from local sources by 3.7%. The fact that output by local sources has continued to grow is a reflection of the failure to meet plan targets for the installation of large municipal boilers and new sets at heat-and-power plants.

In 1985, it is expected that the total output of thermal energy will grow to 3,550 mn G-cals, at an average annual rate of 2.4% over 1980. Output from centralised sources is planned to grow by 3.0% a year to 2,670 mn G-cals, while that from local sources will grow by 0.7% a year to 880 mn G-cals.

Consumption of Fuel by the Electricity and Thermal Energy Sector

In 1980, the generation of electricity and thermal energy accounted for 43% of the 1,677 mn tsf consumed by the USSR; this compares with 41% in 1970 and 32.6% in 1960. The country's power stations also increased their share of national fuel consumption to 32.2% from 31.2% in 1970 and 23.3% in 1960, while the share of centralised boilers rose to 10.9% from 9.8% in 1970 and 9.3% in 1960.

The USSR has made considerable strides since the Second World War in reducing the amount of fuel it requires to produce a unit of electricity. In 1945, 627 grams of standard fuel (gsf) were needed for the generation of 1 kWh of electricity, but in 1980 only 52% as much fuel was needed. The generation of 1 G-cal of thermal energy required

Table 3.8: Consumption of Fuel for the Generation of Electric and Thermal Energy (mn tsf)

	A	B	C	D	E	F
1960	678	221	158	113	45	63
1970	1,117	458	348	225	123	110
1975	1,412	614	460	301	159	154
1978	1,593	677	515	327	187	162
1979	1,621	705	528	334	194	177
1980	1,677	722	540	340	200	182

Notes:
A. Total consumption of fuel by the USSR.
B. Total Consumption of Fuel for the production of electricity and thermal energy from power stations and large municipal and industrial boilers.
C. Consumption of fuel for production of electricity and thermal energy by power stations only.
D. Consumption of fuel for production of electricity by power stations.
E. Consumption of fuel for production of thermal energy by power stations.
F. Consumption of fuel for production of thermal energy by large municipal and industrial boilers.

Table 3.9: Consumption of Fuel per Unit of Electricity and Thermal Energy

	Production of Electricity (gsf/kWh)	Production of Thermal Energy (kgsf/G-cal)
1945	627	204.6
1960	468	181.2
1965	415	178.4
1970	367	175.7
1975	340	173.6
1978	331	173.1
1979	330	173.0
1980	328	173.0
1981	327	173.0

204.6 kgsf in 1945, but only 173.0 (84.6% as much) in 1980.

Within the USSR, there is a wide variation in the consumption of fuel per kWh between different regions. This stems from a number of factors, such as the size and technical sophistication of generating sets (which means that regions dominated by a few large modern stations should have a better fuel rate than rural areas with a great many small, inefficient stations), the share of heat-and-power plants in the total generating capacity of the region (CHPPs can charge some of their fuel intake to their output of thermal energy, thereby leaving a very low fuel rate for the production of electricity — they burned only 267 gsf/kWh in 1978 compared with 358 gsf for condensing stations) and the share of oil and gas in the fuel mix (these fuels have high heat rates and therefore less fuel is required).

The Ukraine has consistently experienced a higher fuel rate than the USSR as a whole, and the gap has been growing. In 1965, the USSR burned 414 gsf/kWh compared with 422 for the Ukraine, and the respective figures for 1979 were 330 and 347.7. This is because most Ukrainian stations burn local coal and some, such as Zuevka-1 which dates back to the First Five Year Plan of 1928–32, are very old and should have been scrapped long ago.

In 1970, the energy systems with the highest fuel rates were Yakutenergo (610 gsf/kWh) and Magadanenergo (574 gsf/kWh), both in the Far East. They have the disadvantage that they are remote from extensive grids dominated by large highly-efficient stations. They cover large areas, and in the past it has proved cheaper to provide each small settlement with its own small, highly fuel-intensive station than to build large stations and spend large capital investment sums on transmission lines. This may be changing, because the increasing cost of delivering fuel to remote local stations has made power transmission over a wide area more economical and the commissioning of the 900 MW Kolyma hydro station should allow many of Magadanenergo's most inefficient thermal stations to be closed.

In other areas, the fuel rate is vey much better than for the USSR as a whole. The Mosenergo directorate, for example, serves Moscow and administers several base-load stations and 25 CHPPs – not surprisingly its fuel rate is only 188 gsf/kWh. Other directorates which are able to use a large part of their generating capacity for the production of thermal energy, such as Barnaulenergo (75%), Kustanaienergo (60%) and Bashkirenergo (46%) also have very low fuel rates. The Soviet republic with the best fuel rate is Belorussia, which has one large condensing station at Lukoml and a large number of efficient gas-burning CHPPs. During the 1976 to 1980 period, its average fuel rate was reduced from 314.8 gsf/kWh to 300.9, thereby saving 1.4 mn tsf, and after declining further to 298 in 1981 a target of 296 gsf/kWh was set for 1982. This is only 90.8% of the average for the USSR as a whole.

The contribution of joint electricity and heat production to lowering the fuel rate will be discussed later; suffice it to say now that at some of the Mosenergo CHPPs, where all the generating capacity is used for the production of power and heat, the fuel rate for power production has been reduced to below 150 gsf/kWh, while the USSR's most efficient condensing station in 1980 was the 2,400 MW Iriklinsk in Orenburg oblast, which produced 16.6 bn kWh for 318 gsf/kWh.

Soviet power engineers believe tht the fuel rate can be reduced even further than the 327 gsf/kWh achieved by the nation in 1981, and the Eleventh Five Year Plan has set a target of 320 gsf/kWh for 1985.

Since the Second World War, the share of coal in the total consumption of fuel by power stations has fallen from 70.9% in 1960 to 37.9% in 1980. The Tenth Five Year Plan expected coal to account for 42.5% in 1980, primarily due to increased coal production from the Ekibastuz and Kansk-Achinsk fields, but this target was not met because of problems with coal production which amounted to only 716 mn tons in 1980 compared with the planned 805 mn tons. Accordingly, only 417.6 mn tons were burned by the sector as a whole instead of the planned 468 mn tons, with a subsequent higher consumption of oil and gas than was anticipated by the plan.

In 1980, 343.4 mn natural tons of coal (47.9% of natural output), 150 mn natural tons of fuel oil (73.2%) and 110 bn cu m of gas (25.3%) were burned in power stations. According to the Eleventh Five Year Plan, there is to be a radical change over 1981 to 1985, with the share of coal rising from 37.9% to 39.6%, oil declining from 35.2% to 25.9% and gas rising from 24.2% to 31.5%. This implies a rise in coal consumption from 343.4 mn tons to 388.7 mn (50.2% of planned total output compared with 47.9% in 1980), a fall in fuel oil requirements from 150 mn tons to 120 mn and a rise in the consumption of gas from 110 to 155 bn cu m (24.6% of planned output compared with 25.3% in 1980).

In 1980, power stations belonging to Minenergo burned 299.3 mn tons of coal, an increase of just 5.1% over the 284.7 mn tons consumed in 1975. Consumption of Ekibastuz coal rose by 41.5% from 44.1 to 62.4 mn tons, Kansk-Achinsk coal by 20.7% from 19.3 to 23.3 mn tons, and Kuznetsk coal by 44.9% from 27.4 to 39.7 mn tons. Consumption of Donetsk coal declined from 64.8 to 59.7 mn tons after peaking at 71.6 mn in 1976, and the burning of Moscow coal fell from 29 to 21.8 mn tons, Chelyabinsk coal from 12.3 to 10.1 mn tons, Kizel coal from 2.8 to 2.1 mn tons, Lvov-Volynsk coal from 9.8 to 7.3 mn tons, and in some cases the decline in supplies by European coalfields forced power stations to turn to other suppliers. The Cherepetsk station, for example, started using Karaganda coal railed thousands of kilometres from Kazakhstan instead of local Moscow coal.

Of the 110 bn cu m of gas burned in 1980, 88.3 bn were used by general purpose power stations owned by Minenergo, and 21.7 bn by stations (basically heat-and-power plants) owned by other ministries for

Table 3.10: Structure of Fuel Consumption by Power Stations* (per cent)

	1960	1970	1975	1980	1985 Plan
Coal	70.9	46.1	41.3	37.9	39.6
Gas	12.3	26.0	25.7	24.2	31.5
Fuel oil	7.5	22.5	28.8	35.2	25.9
Peat	7.0	3.1	2.0 ⎤		
Shale	1.0	1.7	1.7 ⎬	2.8	2.9
Others (mostly wood)	1.3	0.6	0.5 ⎦		

Volume of Fuel Consumed by Power Stations (mn tons of standard fuel)

	1960	1970	1975	1980	1985 Plan
Coal	112.0	160.4	190.0	204.7	231.7
Gas	19.4	90.5	118.2	130.7	184.3
Fuel oil	11.9	78.3	132.5	190.0	151.5
Peat	11.1	10.8	9.2 ⎤		
Shale	1.6	5.9	7.8 ⎬	15.0	17.0
Others	2.1	2.1	2.3 ⎦		
Total	158.0	348.0	460.0	540.0	584.5

Note: * All power stations, i.e. those owned by Minenergo and all other ministries.

providing factories with electricity, heat and steam. Since 1970, when general purpose stations used 48.8 bn cu m and factory stations 20.3 bn, the importance of factory-owned stations has declined in relative terms with their share of gas consumption by power stations falling from 29.4% to 19.9%.

In the Ukraine, fuel consumption by power stations consists mainly of Donbass coal, with small amounts of coal being imported from the Kuzbass, Karaganda and Pechora coalfields. During the period 1975 to 1980, coal consumption by Ukrainian power stations fell from 41 to 33.9 mn tons of standard fuel, with coal being replaced by fuel oil and, to a lesser extent, gas. Consequently, the volume of fuel oil burned in Minenergo's Ukrainian stations doubled during the period, from 10.6 to 21 mn tons.

The structure of fuel consumption by centralised boilers is dominated by natural gas, which accounted for 56% in 1978. Fuel oil accounted for 23%, coal 19% and other fuels (principally firewood in some remote areas of Siberia) 2%. It is unlikely that any major change had taken place by 1980, in which year centralised boilers burned 182 mn tsf, comprised of an estimated 102 mn tsf of natural gas, 42 mn tsf of oil, 34.5 mn tsf of coal and 3.5 mn tsf of other fuels. Natural gas consumption amounted to 85.8 bn cu m (19.7% of total production), and 33.1 mn tons of fuel oil (16.1%) and 46.1 mn tons of coal (practically all of it hard coal) or 6.4% of total output in that year, were burned. In the Ukraine, 52% of all fuel burned by boilers was natural gas, 25.5% fuel oil and 22.5% coal and peat in 1975.

An important reason for the much better fuel rates of centralised boilers compared with those of small local boilers is the 79% share of their total fuel consumption claimed by oil and gas. By contrast, oil and gas accounted for only 13% of local boilers' requirements, with coal (46%) and other fuels (41%) providing the rest. Of the 191 mn tsf burned in small factory and household boilers in 1980, natural gas accounted for 23 mn tsf (i.e. 19.5 bn cu m, or 4.5% of total output of gas), fuel oil 1.9 mn tsf (some sources say that 16 mn tsf of 'liquid fuels' were used by these boilers), coal 87.9 mn tsf (117 mn tons, 16.4% of coal production) and other fuels 78.5 mn tsf. This last category seems rather high, and must include bottled gas, some other types of heating oil, coal brickettes, peat, firewood and fuel collected by the population.

In the European part of the USSR, the principal source of coal for power stations up to 1960 was the Donbass, with only a small amount of Kuznets coal being used. The development of open-cast mining in the Kuzbass and the increase in mining depths and growing complexity of geological conditions in the Donbass has led to a big increase in the volume of Kuznets coal being carried over the Urals. Although the Donbass will remain the principal source of coal for the European USSR, many power stations, particularly in the Volga, Centre and North West regions were forced during the 1960s to turn to alternative sources of coal, including the Kuzbass. The production of coal in the Donbass has fallen to less than 200 mn tons a year compared with its peak of 225 mn tons in 1976 and, although the Eleventh Five Year Plan expects it to begin growing again, to 212 mn tons in 1985, much of the increased output will be coking coal.

A priority now is to eliminate the use of Donbass coal in the power stations of the North West, Centre, Volga and Belorussian regions in favour of other fuels, principally gas. It was planned to restrict Donbass steam coal to power stations of the Southern Energy System (i.e. Ukraine and Moldavia) by 1975 with the exception of small stations in the Lower Volga area and the Central Chernozem region.

In recent years, the production of low-heat high-cost brown coal from the Moscow coal basin has declined from a peak of 45 mn tons/yr in the late 1950s to little more than 20 mn tons/year today. The ageing power stations which burned it have either been scrapped or converted to gas, and the new large-capacity mines like Berezovskaya, which will allow the field to maintain output at above 25 mn tons/year until into the 1990s are designed to serve new, technologically advanced stations.

The significance of Ekibastuz coal is growing very rapidly. Its importance is particularly apparent in the Urals where, until 1960, power stations worked primarily on local coals (Sverdlovsk, Chelyabinsk, Kizel, etc.) plus a small amount of Karaganda and Kuznets coal, peat, coking gas and blast furnace gas. However, as the Urals has been experiencing a decline in coal output from a peak of 59 mn tons in 1960 to 32 mn tons in 1980, the share of other fuels has been growing rapidly. The completion of the Urengoi-Chelyabinsk gas pipeline system has permitted a big rise in the share of gas, largely at the expense of fuel oil from local refineries, while increased deliveries of Ekibastuz coal have compensated for the decline in local coal production. It can be envisaged that Urals stations will, in the long-term, run almost solely on Tyumen gas and Ekibastuz coal, which is almost as economically effective in the Urals as Tyumen gas. The two largest Urals customers for Ekibastuz coal are the Reftinsk (3,800 MW) and Troitsk (2,500 MW) power stations.

Delays in the construction of the system of minehead power stations at Ekibastuz mean that deliveries of the coal to the Urals have grown particularly rapidly, from 22.2 mn tons in 1975 to 33.3 mn in 1980, when the Urals used 53.4% of all Ekibastuz coal burned in power stations. This volume could have been greater but for congestion on the railways, which delayed deliveries and forced dual-fired stations to burn more gas and less coal.

During 1981 to 1985, coal consumption by Minenergo stations is planned to rise by 36 mn tons to 335 mn, and the Ekibastuz coalfield will supply 55% of the increase, i.e. 20 mn tons. Supplies from the Kansk-Achinsk field will grow by 10 mn tons, and an extra 5 mn tons will be obtained from the Kuzbass.

Siberian thermal power stations work almost entirely on coal, with small amounts of gas burned by minor stations like the heat-and-power plants at Yakutsk, Norilsk and Okha (Sakhalin island). This position is not likely to change in the long-term, considering the heavy demand for oil and gas in the European USSR and the extremely low cost of open-cast coal-mining of Siberian coals in the Kuzbass, Kansk-Achinsk and Far Eastern fields, which makes the use of oil and gas inexpedient. However, in some cases the use of fuel oil is justified, where it is burned (for example) in boilers which are used to cover peak demand for thermal energy for less than 1,000 hours a year. For such a low level of utilisation, the savings in capital investment obtained by building oil-burning boilers instead of coal-burning types, exceed the difference in costs of the two fuels. Coal-burning boilers are still needed to provide base-loads of thermal energy.

In the Ukraine, Donbass coal remains the principal fuel for thermal power stations. The level of consumption is likely to be maintained in the future, in spite of a declining output of steam coal by the Donbass, because deliveries out of the Ukraine will be reduced. Waste from coal-dressing plants is likely to be extensively used, and the only large new thermal station planned for the Ukraine, the Zuevka-2 station (2,400 MW planned capacity) will be fired in this way. New heat-and-power plants will burn local gas, the consumption of which will rise in the Ukraine as the flow of gas to the Central region from Western Siberia is increased and that from the Ukraine correspondingly reduced. However, most of the increase in base-load generating capacity during the foreseeable future will be provided by atomic stations. The Ukraine has one station operating at Chernobyl with a capacity of 3,000 MW, and six more under construction. They should have an aggregate capacity of 30,000 MW by the end of the century.

Locally produced oil-shale is burned by two of the three large thermal stations in the Baltic republics, and Belorussia's largest station at Lukoml (2,400 MW) uses coal.

In Kazakhstan, all the base-load stations burn local Karaganda or Ekibastuz coal, and most Central Asian stations use gas. The largest oil-burning station, the Syr Darya (3,200 MW), ran into difficulties in obtaining regular deliveries of fuel oil which had to be railed in over distances of more than 1,600 km from Krasnovodsk refinery on the Caspian Sea. At one point, only half of its generating capacity was operational, and a decision was taken to convert it to gas, delivered through a 420-km pipeline from the Shurtan deposit in the Karshi Steppe. The Angren power station in Uzbekistan burns coal from the nearby coalfield, as will the Angren-2 station now under construction, but all other major base-load stations such as Mary (1,260 MW), Navoi (1,250 MW) and Tashkent (1,200 MW) work on gas.

The rapid development of the natural gas industry has had a profound effect on the power sector. Gas, unlike coal or oil, flows directly from the point of production to the point of consumption. Gas usage is subject to seasonal variations because of the large share used for the generation of heat for dwellings and public buildings in winter, and it is necessary to increase industrial consumption during the summer if the degree of utilisation of pipelines and gas processing equipment is to be improved. The creation of underground gas reservoirs in worked-out gas deposits or salt domes, into which surplus gas is pumped in summer to be drawn on when demand rises in winter, provides a partial solution, but the Soviets have also favoured converting oil- or coal-burning power stations so that they can also burn gas during the summer. The creation of these so-called 'buffer consumers' has been particularly apparent in the European part of the USSR and the Urals.

The consumption of fuel per G-cal of thermal energy has fallen slowly since the Second World War, mainly because there is little scope for further reduction. The efficiency of power station boilers varies between 85% and 95% depending on the type of boiler and fuel used, and any further reduction in the fuel rate must stem from raising this level of efficiency. The Tenth Five Year Plan expected the fuel rate to decline from 173.6 kgsf/G-cal in 1975 to 172 in 1980, but in fact it only fell to 173, and the 172 kgsf/G-cal target has been put back to 1985. It is likely that the scope for any further reduction is almost exhausted.

The fuel rate for the production of thermal energy by power stations is much lower than for industrial boilers, where it varied between 190 and 210 kgsf/G-cal in 1980. Municipal boilers required 180–200 kgsf/G-cal in 1980.

Factors Influencing the Fuel Rate of the Sector
(a) The Centralisation of Thermal Energy Production

Particularly large savings can be made by the centralisation of thermal energy production, not only in the sphere of fuel consumption (where the fuel rate can be improved by up to 100% compared with the production of heat on localised boilers), but also through lower capital investment and fuel transportation costs, smaller numbers of servicing personnel, etc.

The centralisation of thermal energy supply is accomplished by the construction of heat-and-power plants and large industrial and municipal boilers with productivities of more than 20 G-cals a day. These cover practically the entire demand for heat and steam by industrial enterprises and 40% of demand for household and municipal purposes. The share of centralised production in the total output of thermal energy seems to have stabilised at 72–73%; complete centralisation cannot be achieved because of the need to supply rural localities with heat from small boilers characterised by low densities of thermal loading and great irregularity of output. However, it is estimated that the

Table 3.11: Sources of Thermal Energy

	1970 mn G-cals	1970 Share	1975 mn G-cals	1975 Share	1980 mn G-cals	1980 Share
Centralised sources	1,296	67.9	1,738	72.4	2,260	72.2
CHPPs	699	36.7	915	38.1	1,170	37.3
General purpose	507	26.6	680	28.3	900	28.7
Factory-owned	192	10.1	235	9.8	270	8.6
Large boilers	547	28.7	740	30.8	960	30.7
Heat exchangers	50	2.5	83	3.5	130	4.2
Local sources	610	32.1	662	27.6	870	27.8
Total	1,906	100	2,400	100	3,130	100

extent of centralisation can be raised to 80–85%, mainly by scrapping small boilers in the cities. At the moment, CHPPs and large municipal boilers in district heating stations serve only half their potential household and municipal customers. The rest are served by 250,000 small boilers burning 50 mn tsf a year and needing 3.5 million workers to operate them. Slightly more than half of all thermal energy from centralised sources is produced by CHPPs.

So far as saving fuel is concerned, the most efficient methods of producing thermal energy are by heat exchangers and combined heat-and-power plants. Heat exchangers transform secondary energy resources, like heat from a non-ferrous metal smelter or cement kiln, into steam and hot water, thereby saving fuel and lowering the production costs of the sectors to which they are attached. They also enable capital investment to be saved by the fuel industries whose products have been saved. Consequently, thermal energy from heat exchangers tends to be much cheaper than that from boilers and even from CHPPs.

The most efficient heat exchangers are the KU series. The cost of installing them can be recouped in 10 months to 2½ years depending on the capacity of the installation.

Heat exchangers are now providing a significant share of national thermal energy needs. In 1977 they supplied 5.9% of the Ukraine's requirements, saving 3 mn tsf. But even if the most optimistic plans for the installation of heat exchangers were fulfilled, these plants would not satisfy more than a small share of the demand for thermal energy. The basis of the Soviet government's policy in this sphere has been the CHPP, to which the Directives of the 24th Congress (1971) referred when they said '. . . to foresee the rational concentration and centralisation of production of steam and hot water for technological and heating needs, and the gradual disappearance of small boilers'.

Table 3.12: Characteristics of KU Heat Exchangers

Model	Productivity (G-cals/hour)	Annual Fuel Savings ('000 tons)	Construction Cost ('000 R)	Cost Recoupment Period (months)
KU-16	1.8	1.2	30	30
KU-40	5	4	40	12
KU-60	14	10	110	13
KU-80	20	17	135	10
KU-100	25	20	160	10
KU-125	30	25	200	10

The importance of this policy has not diminished since 1971, but its justification has become more complex. On the one hand, it is necessary (according to Borisov and Shitsman of Mosenergo, writing in *Elektricheskaya Stantsiya*, 1976, no. 4, p. 5) to strive to 'accelerate the development of CHPPs, to maintain and even increase their share in the total capacity of thermal power stations'. On the other hand, atomic power stations and large thermal stations are being built to improve the fuel balance, and this has lead to 'slightly higher capital investments in the energy sector' resulting in a 'tendency towards a limitation on the construction of CHPPs in favour of municipal and industrial boilers'. Borisov and Shitsman are saying that the large new power stations can satisfy demand for electricity, and it could be cheaper to meet the demand for thermal energy by means of boilers.

The total capacity of Soviet CHPPs was expected by the Ninth Five Year Plan to rise from 47,000 MW in 1970 to 65,000 MW by the end of 1975, but only reached 59,800 MW, an increase of 12,800 MW. During 1976 to 1980, construction proceeded more rapidly, with total capacity rising to 76,000 MW at the end of 1980, or by 16,200 MW over 1975. The share of CHPPs in the total generating capacity of thermal power stations fell from 38.15% in 1970 to 36.91% in 1975, but then rose to 37.75% in 1980.

The physical limit on the capacity of a CHPP is the demand for thermal energy by its customers. The efficiency of the plant stems from its combined production of two commodities, but this efficiency is lost without a correct balance between the output of electricity and thermal energy. The fuel rate for the production of electricity by the condensing cycle of a CHPP turbine is always higher than by a condensing power station. However, the more thermal energy it produces, the greater the share of fuel consumption that can be attributed to the generation of thermal energy rather than electricity, and the lower the fuel rate for electricity production. The size of the CHPP is there-fore limited by its customers' maximum demand for thermal energy and this, in turn, is limited by the length of the thermal energy net-work; the longer the steam or hot water pipeline, the greater the consumption of fuel. For a steam network carrying 350 tons of steam per hour, the lengthening of the network by 1 km raises the fuel consumption by 3,500 tsf a year. For a hot water network carry-ing 350 G-cals of heat per hour, its extension by 1 km raises fuel consumption by 550 tsf/year.

The maximum radius of a steam network is thought to be 3 km, and 15 km for a hot water network. For an average living space of 12 sq m per person, a 250 MW CHPP set produces enough heat for houses and buildings serving about 250,000 people. To ensure reliability, at least three or four sets are used together, and a 750 MW CHPP is sufficient for a city of 500,000 people. At the present time, the optimal size of CHPP's is 600–750 MW for factories and 1,000–1,250 MW for residen-tial areas.

In 1970, CHPPs produced 232 bn kWh of electricity, or 37.8% of the total output by thermal stations. Their average productivity was 4,936 kWh/kW, which amounted to 86.7% of the average productivity of all thermal stations. In 1980, they produced 388 bn kWh, or 37.4% of total output with an average productivity of 5,109 kWh/kW, 89.9% of the average productivity of all thermal stations. More than 800 Soviet cities were served by CHPPs in 1980.

Savings of fuel resulting from the combined production of electricity and thermal energy are considerable. In 1970, 29 mn tsf were saved compared with the production of electricity by condensing stations and of thermal energy by municipal and industrial boilers. Of this amount, 23 mn tsf was saved due to the co-generation of electricity and thermal energy, and 6 mn due to the lower fuel rates resulting from the scrapping of small boilers. If the thermal energy had been produced by small, local boilers, an additional 55 mn tsf would have been required. In 1975, 35 mn tsf were saved, and by 1980, annual savings were amounting to more than 40 mn tsf a year.

The fuel rate for the production of electricity has been falling more rapidly for CHPPs than for condensing stations, this being due to the inreasing size of newly installed sets and to the rising share of electricity produced on the thermal energy cycle, which grew from 54% in 1970 to 64.0% in 1980. Meanwhile, the fuel rate for thermal energy produc-tion by CHPPs is declining slightly while that claimed by large boilers is growing. This may be because as district heating centres replace

Table 3.13: CHPP Fuel Rates

	For the Production of Electricity (gsf/kWh)		Thermal Energy (kgsf/G-cal)	
	CHPPs	Condensing Stations	CHPPs	Large Boilers
1970	324	388	175.7	184.3
1975	279	365	173.6	187.1
1980	272	356	173.0	189.6

small boilers heating blocks of flats, the average rate of capacity utilisation for the municipal boiler sector is being dragged down, leading to a small rise in the average fuel rate. In other words, boiler usage is assuming a more seasonal character, with a higher significance of peak loading.

This adverse tendency is to be counteracted in two ways. First, some extremely large boilers are planned for the 1981 to 1985 period. They will burn natural gas, and while designed to fulfil a base-load function will be very flexible in their operation, allowing peak loads to be covered without raising average fuel rates. Secondly, some condensing power stations are to be converted to enable them to produce hot water for households, and this will help to relieve municipal boilers of the task of covering household peak loads. One of the first stations to be converted in this way is the Pridneprovsk station (2,400 MW) at Dnepropetrovsk. After all its eight sets have been converted (the first was completed in 1982), it should be able to serve nearly all the homes in Dnepropetrovsk, a Ukrainian city of 1.1 mn people, and permit the closure of 1,000 small and medium boilers burning fuel oil and natural gas. The fuel savings from this one station alone will approach 4,000 tsf/yr.

(b) The Trend Towards Larger Power Stations and Large Generating Sets

Large fuel savings can be achieved by the phasing out of small, obsolete and highly inefficient sets and the simultaneous construction of large base-load stations consisting of sets with capacities of 300 MW and more.

At the end of 1970, there were seven thermal stations with a capacity of 2,000 MW or more, six of which were located in the Ukraine. By the end of 1975, the number of 2,000 MW+ thermal stations had risen to 18, and by the end of 1980 to 23, including six of 3,000 MW and more. The largest thermal station is Reftinsk in the

Urals, with a capacity of 3,800 MW, but five stations with projected capacities of 4,000 MW each are being built at Ekibastuz, a 4,800 MW station is under construction at Perm, and a complex of up to ten stations of 6,400 MW each will be created on the Kansk-Achinsk coalfield.

The largest heat-and-power plant is Moscow No. 25 (1,350 MW) and there are currently six with capacities of 1,000 MW and more – four in Moscow and two in Eastern Siberia at Irkutsk and Krasnoyarsk. More of 1,000-1,500 MW will be built in Moscow, Leningrad, Kiev and Kharov, with atomic CHPPs being built in Minsk and Odessa.

The aggregate capacity of thermal stations (excluding heat-and-power plants and gas turbine peak-load stations) of less than 1,000 MW each is likely to decline in the future from 26,690 MW at the end of 1980.

The construction of very large stations has been made possible by the mastering of the construction (and operation) of large sets. Although the first models of 500 MW and 800 MW were installed in 1966 at Nazarovo and 1967 at Slavyansk respectively, the basic unit until recently has been that of 300 MW, of which the Soviet Union had 143 operating at the end of 1980. Sets of 500 MW are now being manufactured on a serial basis; so far, nine have been installed and perhaps 50-60 more will be built before the end of the century, including a further 35 at the Ekibastuz complex. Very few sets of 800 MW have been built, but their successful operation at Ryazan has paved the way for their serial production and subsequent installation at Perm and the Kansk-Achinsk complex. The world's first set of 1,200 MW was commissioned at Kostroma in December 1980, and although it has been rumoured that more are to be manufactured for a new station at Surgut in Western Siberia, this will not take place before 1986.

While sets of less than 300 MW are still being installed – the first Surgut station is continuing to grow on the basis of 210 MW and 180 MW sets, for example – their importance in the total capacity of thermal stations (excluding heat-and-power plants, where the size of sets varies between 50 and 250 MW) is declining.

The size of the power station, usually a reflection of the size of the sets employed, has a striking influence on the fuel rate. In 1970, this amounted to 388 gsf/kWh for all Minenergo condensing stations, but 23 of the 28 stations of 1,000 MW and more each had fuel rates lower than the national average, and the five stations with fuel rates higher than 388 gsf/kWh used low-rank fuel (for example Pribaltic, burning oil shale, and Shchekino, using Moscow coal) or were very old, like Slavyansk, dating from 1954.

Table 3.14: Number of Generating Sets of Different Capacities

	300 MW	500 MW	800 MW	1,200 MW
1970	69	1	1	–
1975	132	2	4	–
1980	143	9	9	–
1981	145	11	10	1
1985 Plan	152	18	16	1

The influence of station size on the level of fuel consumption is recognised by the planners. The consumption of Donbass coal, for example, by a projected Saratov station falls from 360 gsf/kWh to 348 as the size of the station is increased from 1,200 MW to 4,800 MW and 800 MW sets are employed instead of 200 MW models. If natural gas is used, the fuel rate falls from 327 to 320 gsf/kWh.

One reason for this is that large condensing stations generally cover the base-loading for the area in which they are situated, and can therefore benefit from a constant usage regime. This enables a high degree of automation to be usefully employed. But the main reason for the low fuel rate by large stations is that their large-capacity sets have high steam parameters of 130 ats (atmospheres) and more, which raise the productivity of the fuel input. In 1973, Soviet generating sets with steam pressures of 45 ats and below burned an average 401 gsf/kWh while those of 130 ats and above used only 336 gsf/kWh.

Over the period 1970 to 1974, the increase in the share of large, high-pressure sets in total generating capacity accounted for 62% of the fall in the average fuel rate. Improvements in the operation of existing equipment due to increased mechanisation, greater experience in handling new sets by the operating personnel and a higher degree of exploitation, etc. contributed 34.6% with the remaining 3.6% attributable to a number of factors including a small rise in the share of electricity produced on the thermal energy cycle of CHPPs from 19.4% in 1970 to 20.1% in 1974. Most of the fuel savings from improvements in the operation of existing equipment resulted from the running-in of 300 MW sets, which reduced their average fuel rates by 31 gsf/kWh between 1970 and 1974 compared with 0.1 by 200 MW sets, 11.1 by 150 MW sets and 3.2 gsf/kWh by low pressure sets. But the importance of fuel savings from the 300 MW sets is declining as experience in their use is diffused throughout the industry.

By 1980, the average fuel rate of the country's 143 operating 300 MW sets had been reduced to 334.8 gsf/kWh compared with 362.3 by

69 sets in 1970. Sets of 200–210 MW needed an average 358.1 gsf/kWh compared with 364 in 1970 and sets of 150–160 MW burned 366.8 gsf/kWh. The 500 MW sets averaged 342.3 gsf/kWh — a rather high figure because they are mostly burning poor-quality Ekibastuz coal or Kansk-Achinsk coal, and there have been numerous technical problems including the fouling of water pipes with accumulations of ash — and the 800 MW sets achieved an average of 327.3 gsf/kWh.

The scope for further falls in fuel consumption as a result of the increasing size of sets is declining. As long ago as 1974, sets with pressures of 130–240 ats produced 424 bn kWh, or 52% of the total output from Soviet thermal stations. Consequently, while a fall of 26 gsf/kWh in the fuel rate was achieved over 1971 to 1975, the comparable figure for 1976 to 1980 was 12, and over 1981 to 1985 it is likely to fall to less than 8 gsf/kWh.

(c) Type of Fuel

During the period 1960 to 1980, there has been a massive change from coal to oil and gas by Soviet power stations, with the share of hydrocarbons in their total fuel consumption rising from 19.8% to 59.4%. The consumption of fuel oil has grown particularly strongly, at an average annual rate of 14.8%.

An important reason for this is the declining quality of coal, especially that of the Donbass steam coal used by most coal-burning stations in the European USSR. The ash content is increasing, as is the moisture content, and the calorific value of coal burned in Soviet power stations is only 5,500 kcals/kg compared with 6,650 in the USA.

A station of 2,400 MW size with eight 300 MW sets will consume, during one hour of work, some 870 tons of Kuznets coal, 1,400 tons of Kansk-Achinsk coal, 2,000 tons of peat, 2,230 tons of Moscow brown coal or 2,470 tons of shale. Up to 150 tons of ash will have to be removed. The costs of transportation (i.e. within the station), storage and preparation of fuel and removal of the ash can provide a significant share of the cost of power production. The advantages of oil- and gas-burning stations can be immediately recognised in this context. Moreover, their own power requirements are far smaller than those of coal-burning stations due to the absence of coal-grinding and loading equipment.

It is not surprising then, that the consumption of fuel in terms of tsf/kWh of released electricity is less for oil- and gas-burning stations than for the coal-burning variety. A study of the fuel rates of 34 condensing stations shows a remarkable difference between the fuel rate of shale-burning stations at one extreme, and that of stations burning oil at the other.

Shale	445 gsf/kWh,	2 stations in the sample
Coal and gas	386	4
Coal	381	13
Coal, oil and gas	374	2
Oil and gas	367	6
Coal and oil	365	2
Gas	351	3
Oil	345	2

These figures are distorted by local considerations, such as the quality of the fuel and the proportion of different fuels in the fuel mix employed by multi-fuel stations, by the extent to which gas is used as a basic fuel and as a buffer fuel in summer, and by the age and technical characteristics of the generating sets. Thus, very modern coal-fired stations such as Lukoml and Moldavia can have better fuel rates than oil-burning stations such as Karmanovo.

Economists working on projects for new power stations tend to consider gas to be the most efficient fuel. In the project calculations for a 1,200 MW station at Saratov, the consumption of fuels of different types per 1 kWh of electricity are:

Donets Coal	360 gsf/kWh
Kuznets coal	351
Oil	332
Natural gas	327

However, the further use of gas has to be seen in the context of its importance in other spheres. In the North West economic region, for example, the savings from the use of gas as a basic fuel in condensing stations amount to 1.0–1.3 roubles/tsf, assuming an identical price of coal and gas charged to the consumer. When used in households and by heating furnaces, the savings rise to 12 R/tsf, and 15 R/tsf when gas serves as a raw material for the chemical industry. The gas industry's research institute, VNIIgaz, has proposed that gas should only be used in the last resort for boilers and power stations.

In fact, the prices of coal and gas are not identical — the cost of burning gas is much lower than that for coal because gas costs less to produce and less to utilise. Consequently, it is being used to replace oil wherever possible and coal in particularly pollutive cases, and its share of fuel consumption by power stations is expected to grow from 24.2% to 31.5% over 1981 to 1985. This should contribute to the continuing fall in the average fuel rate for Soviet power stations.

On factor influencing the choice of fuel is the greater cost of construction of coal-burning stations. According to project data for new power stations in Siberia and Central Asia, coal-burning stations of 1,200 or 2,400 MW capacity cost 14-15% more to build than gas-burning stations of similar size, although for 4,800 MW stations the margin is only 8-9%.

The differences are even greater when running costs are taken into account. Whole processes can be cut out when oil or gas are used, and the running cost of an oil- or gas-fired station is very small compared with that of a station burning coal. The cost of production of electricity, including a capital charge calculated at an annual rate of 12% of the capital cost of the station, of projected stations using different fuels is shown in Table 3.15.

Table 3.15: Cost of Electricity Production at Projected Thermal Power Stations (kop/kWh)

Location and Size of Station* (MW)		Donets Coal	Kuznets Coal	Tyumen Gas	Central Asian Gas
Centre	2,400	1.02	0.97	0.59	0.78
	4,800	0.98	0.94	0.55	0.76
Volga Vyatka	2,400	1.04	0.94	0.59	0.71
	4,800	1.00	0.90	0.55	0.69
Central Chernozem	2,400	0.76	1.08	0.60	0.68
	4,800	0.73	1.05	0.58	0.66

Note: * assumes that the stations produce for 7,000 hours a year.

In the Urals, the choice of fuel also has a considerable influence on the production cost of electricity, although not as great as in the Centre region because the Urals region is closer to major sources of fuel. Electricity can be produced at a 2400 MW station at the following costs.

Kuznets coal	0.89 kop/kWh
Ekibastuz coal	0.78
Central Asian gas	0.77
Tyumen gas	0.65
Orenburg gas	0.60

Table 3.16: Cost of Electricity Produced by a Projected 2,400 MW Station at Volgograd

Fuel	Cost of Capital Construction (rouble/kWh)	Fuel Rate (gsf/kWh)	Electricity Production Cost (kop/kWh)
Donets coal	126	348	0.99
Kuznets coal	126	348	1.00
Orenburg gas	117	320	0.55
Central Asian gas	117	320	0.77
Tyumen gas	117	320	0.71

Prospective power stations in the Volga region will use the same fuels as those of the Urals, except that Donets coal will be considered and Ekibastuz coal excluded.

It is apparent that Minenergo planners would prefer to use natural gas on all their projected thermal stations. Its use leads to much lower electricity production costs, and although its share in total fuel consumption by power stations has risen slowly (compared to that of fuel oil) in the past because of the heavy demand for gas by other industries where it can be used more profitably, it is planned to grow rapidly over 1981 to 1985 to 31.5%, entirely at the expense of fuel oil. This will take place, not through the construction of new stations — most new thermal power stations other than heat-and-power plants are to be coal-burning — but by the conversion of existing oil-fired stations to gas. At dual-fired stations burning oil in winter and gas in summer, the number of months in which the station burns gas is to be raised from five to seven; this should allow a 300 MW set to save about 100,000 tons of fuel oil a year.

Eventually, all CHPPs will run on gas except for those located in Siberia and the Far East where local coal will remain the only availaable fuel. The increased use of gas stems from the importance given by the Soviet government to measures designed to reduce air pollution. This is particularly relevant to CHPPs which, because of their role as suppliers of thermal energy and the physical limitations on the distance over which thermal energy can be delivered, need to be built near the centres of cities. Moreover, their small size does not enable them to draw on the economies of scale which enable coal-burning condensing stations to produce electricity at economical costs.

Some idea of planners fuel preferences can be gained from a survey of new thermal condensing stations currently under construction, and new ones being extended. They include:

* Zuevka-II, Donets-Dnepr region, projected capacity 2,400 MW, burning waste from coal-dressing plants.
* Kharanor, Eastern Siberia, 1,260 MW, local Kharanor brown coal.
* Novo-Angren, Central Asia, 2,400 MW, local brown coal.
* Gusino-ozersk, Eastern Siberia, expansion by 1,260 MW, local brown coal.
* Primorskii, Far East, six more sets totalling 660 MW to be built, local brown coal.
* Perm, Urals region, 4,800 MW, will burn Kuzbass and Ekibastuz coal, and Tyumen gas.
* Ekibastuz I, Kazakhstan. Currently 3,000 MW and planned to reach 4,000 MW. Will be part of a mineside complex of five stations of 4,000 MW each being built on a flowline basis. Uses Ekibastuz brown coal from the 50 mn tons/year Bogatyr pit. The complex may include the 'South Kazakhstan' station (sometimes known as the 'Balkhash') with a planned capacity of 4,000 MW.
* Berezovo I, Eastern Siberia. Will have a capacity of 6,400 MW when completed in the early 1990s, and will be served by the Berezovo open-cast mine, Kansk-Achinsk coalfield, with a planned capacity of 60 mn tons of brown coal a year.
* Neryungri, Far East, 630 MW, but could be doubled, local Neryungri hard coal.
* Pechora, North West, two more sets totalling 420 MW, Komi gas.
* Surgut I, Western Siberia, two more sets totalling 360 MW, Western Siberia casinghead gas.
* Surgut II, planned capacity 4,000 MW, Western Siberian gas.
* Urengoi, Western Siberia, 4,000 MW, Western Siberian gas.
* Azerbaidzhan, two more sets totalling 600 MW, Caspian gas.
* Talimardzhan, Central Asia, 3,200 MW, Uzbek gas.

The last major oil-burning set was that of 1,200 MW installed at Kostroma in December 1980. For the plan to reduce oil consumption from 35.2% of power station requirements in 1980 to 25.9% in 1985 to be met, no new oil-burning sets must be installed and 20,000–25,000 MW of existing capacity must be scrapped or converted. The Eleventh Five Year Plan expects only 6,000–7,000 MW of old sets to be scrapped, and it can be assumed that many of the candidates for dismantling will be very old coal-burning stations in the Ukraine (for example the 300 MW Zuevka-I) and the Centre region. This implies that a very big conversion programme is under way, probably involving the conversion of oil-fired sets to a dual-fuel regime, burning fuel oil in winter and gas in summer.

Current Fuel Strategy

In the future, the largest energy complexes will be created on the basis of huge resources of very cheap fuel, notably the brown coal deposits of Ekibastuz and Kansk-Achinsk. Plans for Ekibastuz seem to change periodically, involving different variants of four or five stations with individual capacities of 4,000 or 5,000 MW, but five stations of 4,000 MW each seems most likely. Until recently, power from Ekibastuz-I station, currently 3,000 MW, has been used locally in Pavlodar, Karaganda and Ekibastuz itself. A 500 kV line is under construction to Omsk, but in the future the principal customers for Ekibastuz power will be located in the Urals and the Central Chernozem regions. Super-high-tension lines of 1,150 kV AC (to the Urals) and 1,500 kV DC (to Tambov) are being built with the former reaching Kokchetav by the end of 1982.

If the capacity of the complex grows to 20,000 MW, and assuming it operates at 6,000 hours a year, then its annual output will amount to 120 bn kWh, and it will require about 120 mn tons a year of Ekibastuz coal. At the moment, it is using 18 mn tons a year, with the remaining 54 mn tons of the coalfield's annual output of 72 mn tons going to other consumers, including 20 other power stations in Kazakhstan, the Urals and Western Siberia. The largest of these are Troitsk in the Urals (2,500 MW) and Yermakovo in Kazakhstan (2,400 MW). Of the long-term target of 170 mn tons, coal deliveries beyond the complex will fall slightly to 50 mn tons. By this time, the new Turgai coalfield in Kazakhstan will be operating, and it has been suggested that the annual output of coal at Turgai may be brought to a level sufficient to sustain a power complex of 12,000 MW burning 70 mn tons of coal a year.

While the Soviets are now convinced, after many years of tests and debate, that power lines of up to 1,500 kV are technically feasible and economically justifiable, they are still unsure about the prospects for lines of greater capacity. While lines of 1,800 kV have been tested at Leningrad, and designs of 2,200 kV lines have been drawn up, there are no plans at the moment for their construction. Yet the future of the Kansk-Achinsk mineside power scheme, which currently envisages the building of up to ten stations of 6,400 MW each, depends on the ability to transmit a large share of this power westward to the Central region. This entails a distance of 3,350 km, although a line to the Urals (2,100 km to Chelyabinsk) seems more feasible.

Difficulties with burning Kansk-Achinsk coal have arisen, and the 500 MW sets of the Nazarovo thermal power station are said to be operating at only 400 MW because of ash accumulation in the boilers. Although specially designed by the Podolsk Boiler Plant to burn low-grade high-ash coal, the boilers are highly metal intensive and extremely expensive to build and maintain, and it is arguable whether power generated from Kansk-Achinsk coal is really as cheap as might be expected from the price of the coal.

Construction of the complex has fallen a long way behind schedule, paradoxically because of a shortage of power among other things. A 500 kV transmission line has now been erected from the Sayano-Shushenskoe hydro station to the coalfield (it reached Itatsk substation in 1981) and is being extended to the Kuzbass. The initial plans expected several sets of the first station in the complex, Berezovo-I, to begin generating before 1980, but as construction work began as late as 1975, these plans were never really feasible, and the first set is now supposed to begin operating in 1984. Like all the sets planned for the complex, it will be of 800 MW, and will be similar to the latest sets installed at Ryazan thermal station which burns Moscow coal. When its eight sets have been completed the station will burn 13 mn tsf a year, or 26 mn tons of Kansk-Achinsk coal, amounting to half of the annual output of the open-cast mine under construction nearby. The whole complex should consume 260 mn tons a year, and with the Kansk-Achinsk field expected to yield 350 mn tons/year eventually, it appears that there are plans to ship some of the coal out of the region. Its tendency for spontaneous combustion means that transportation in its crude form is difficult and dangerous, and it is likely that towards the end of this century, a number of bricketting plants will be built in the region. Coal liquifaction is a long-term aim, and experimental plants are under construction, but progress is painfully slow. Another way of utilising the surplus coal is to mix it with water, forming a slurry which can be piped westwards; however, no firm plans have been announced.

Another long-term option for supplying the Urals and central Russia with cheap electricity is the construction of a series of large power stations fired with casinghead gas from the Middle Ob oilfields of Tyumen oblast. The existing Surgut power station has a capacity of 2,910 MW, which will be extended to 3,090 MW by the end of 1984 and a second Surgut station with six sets of 800 MW each has been under construction since 1980. It has been stated, perhaps optimistically, that 5,300 MW of new capacity will be installed in Tyumen oblast during the 1981 to 1985 plan period. Four sets of Surgut-II will be commissioned, including one in 1984 and three in 1985, and Tobolsk heat-and-power plant will be completed. Construction of a 4,000 MW station designed to work on natural gas has begun at Tikhii, near the old settlement of Urengoi, and the building of Nizhnevartovsk heat-and-power plant and Tyumen CHPP-II will begin. During the 1986 to 1990 plan period, a third station at Surgut with a capacity of 7,200 MW, and consisting of six sets of 1,200 MW each, will be built.

As with the Kansk-Achinsk and Ekibastuz power complexes, long-term plans for that of Tyumen oblast are rather vague. One of the most recent statements has confirmed earlier reports that its capacity will reach 20,000 MW by the end of the century, with electricity consumption by Tyumen oblast doubling to 40 bn kWh a year. This suggests that up to 80 bn kWh a year will be available for delivery to the Urals, with three or four more 500 kV transmission lines following the existing 500 kV Refta-Tyumen-Demyansk-Surgut line, along which the power flow will be reversed.

Minister of Power Neporozhnyi has said that the eventual capacity of the Surgut complex alone (presumably excluding the station being built at Tikhii) will reach 30,000 MW some time during the next century, and it can be estimated that its annual consumption of gas will exceed 50 bn cu m. It is hard to believe that all this will be casinghead gas, unless some oil deposits with very high gas factors remain to be exploited, and/or Middle Ob reserves of oil are very much higher than even the most optimistic Western estimates. At the present time, the Tyumen oilfields yield 17.5 bn cu m of gas a year, of which 4.5 bn are used by the Surgut-I station, and 13 bn are despatched by pipeline to the Kuzbass. My research suggests that a maximum of 30 bn cu m/year of casinghead gas can be produced.

Apart from these three power complexes, very few new thermal stations are to be built. Almost all of them will be related to the exploitation of local deposits of coal and gas, which will render their power cheaper than that generated by nuclear or hydro stations and transmitted over long distances to the consumer.

Future Consumption of Fuel

Any forecast of the future consumption of fuel by the electricity and thermal energy sector must depend on a number of assumptions concerning:

(1) Future levels of demand for, and production of, electricity and thermal energy.

(2) The share of hydro and atomic power in total electricity output.
(3) Fuel rates, which in turn depend on assumptions concerning:
    (a) The share of electricity produced on CHPPs.
    (b) The rate of modernisation of equipment.
    (c) The nature of the fuel mix in the electricity and thermal energy sector.

Future Levels of Production of Electricity

The Eleventh Five Year Plan has called for the production of electricity to grow at an annual rate of 3.7% between 1981 and 1985, and towards the end of 1982 it was beginning to look as if even this modest programme would not be met. The problem is principally that of building new atomic stations, with all the attendant infrastructural problems, now that the policy of a heavy commitment to atomic power has become finally accepted in the USSR. Almost 57% of the increase in electricity generation will come from atomic stations consisting of sets of 1,000 MW or 1,500 MW each, and a failure to commission just three or four of these sets can effectively wreck the five-year plan for power production. In 1981, the Russians failed to commission three sets of 1,000 MW planned for that year at the Smolensk, Kursk and South Ukraine stations; towards the end of 1982 they still had not become operational, and the sets initially planned for 1982 were nowhere near completion.

Even more ominous for Soviet planners is the fact that construction of the Atommash plant at Volgodonsk, which will eventually produce ten reactors of 1,000 MW each a year on a flowline basis, and on which the nuclear programme is highly dependent, is falling further and further behind schedule. And on top of all this, acute problems in the coal industry mean that many coal-fired power stations, especially in the Ukraine, are operating at well below capacity.

On present performance, the Russians will be hard pressed to produce more than 1,475 bn kWh in 1985 compared with the plan target of 1,555 bn, giving an annual average growth rate of only 2.6%.

This must be seen as something of a disaster for the Soviet economy, because not only must the electricity sector meet a growing demand for its products, it must also replace the direct combustion of gas and oil products in cases where the use of electricity is cheaper and more efficient. In the medium-term perspective (i.e. up to 1990), 35% of the entire increase in electricity production is intended to replace the

Table 3.17: Share of the Increase in Electricity Output to be Devoted to the Substitution of Oil and Gas (%)

	Replacing:		
	Oil	Gas	Total
Medium-term perspective (to 1990)	15	20	35
Power processes	4	8	12
Stationary	–	8	8
Mobile	4	–	4
High-temperature processes	1.5	11.5	13
Medium- and low-temperature processes	9.5	0.5	10
Long-term perspective	17	21	38
Power processes	5.5	8.5	14
Stationary	–	8.5	8.5
Mobile	5.5	–	5.5
High-temperature processes	1	11	12
Medium- and low-temperature processes	10.5	1.5	12

direct use of gas (20%) and oil products (15%).

Given that the rapid growth of atomic power is planned to save huge volumes of gas and oil, it must be expected that the Russians will make great efforts to overcome their problems in this sphere, and it can be assumed that during the Twelfth and subsequent plan periods nuclear sets will be installed according to schedule. With large new stations building up to rated capacity, a growth rate of 3.5% a year, somewhat better than that of 1981 to 1985, is a reasonable assumption. By this time, the process of demolishing obsolete thermal plant will be accelerating, to the extent that by 2000 the commissioning of sets at the Ekibastuz, Kansk-Achinsk and Tyumen complexes will barely cover the scrapping rate of old sets in the European part of the USSR, and the total capacity of thermal stations may even be declining in absolute terms. Table 3.18 gives a tentative view of how the Soviet electricity sector might evolve during the period to 2000. While a 3.5% a year growth rate is the more likely outcome, variants of 3% and 4% have been included for the production projections. The forecasts for capacity assume a growth rate of 3.5% a year, and are subdivided into thermal, atomic and hydro capacity on the basis of current plans for the construction of new stations.

At the present time, construction work is taking place on extensions to existing stations, or on completely new stations, with an aggregate capacity of 137,714 MW. This does not include generating capacity at stations which are planned, but for which no construction work has yet taken place; it includes, for example, only two of the five stations

Table 3.18: Forecasts for Output of Electricity and Capacity of the Sector, 1980–2000

	Output, Assuming growth of:			Capacity (MW)			
	3%	3.5%	4%	Thermal	Atomic	Hydro	Total
1980		1,295[1]		198,500	15,900[3]	52,310	266,710
1985		1,475[2]		215,700	30,300	64,000	310,000
1990	1,710	1,750	1,790	226,000	60,000	74,000	360,000
1995	1,980	2,080	2,180	238,000	100,000	82,000	420,000
2000	2,300	2,470	2,660	240,000	160,000	90,000	490,000

Notes:
1. Actual.
2. My estimate, not the official plan target.
3. Official Soviet data does not include the Siberian facility.

Table 3.19: Distribution of Current Construction Work at Power Stations (MW)

	Thermal	Atomic	Hydro	Total
Western zone	12,580	65,440	10,354	88,374
Eastern zone*	30,500	–	18,840	49,340
Total	43,080	65,440	29,194	137,714

Note: * Siberia, Far East, Central Asia and Kazakhstan.

planned for the Ekibastuz complex, and only one at Kansk-Achinsk. Nor does the figure take into account a large volume of work taking place at new heat-and-power plants, about which little information is available. The spatial distribution of this construction work is shown in Table 3.19.

Bearing in mind that capacity utilisation at hydro stations is normally 60–65% that of thermal and atomic stations, it can be estimated from Table 3.18 that by the end of the century, nuclear power will be accounting for 35% of total output (Soviet estimates say 40%) while the share of thermal stations will have fallen to 53% and will continue to fall rapidly. It is even conceivable that the output of electricity from thermal stations will be declining in absolute terms.

To what extent is the assumption that the USSR will have 160,000 MW of atomic capacity by the end of the century realistic? There are now 13 stations operating with a total capacity of 16,500 MW at Leningrad (4,000 MW), Chernobyl (3,000 MW), Novovoronezh (2,455 MW), Kursk (2,000 MW), Kola peninsular (1,320 MW) Beloyarsk (900 MW), Armenia (880 MW), Rovno (880 MW), Shevchenko (350 MW),

Map 3.2: Nuclear Stations, European USSR

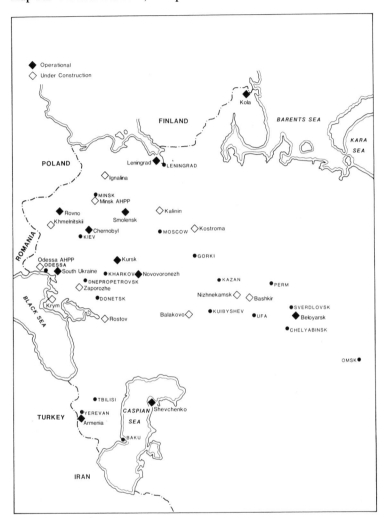

Dimitrovgrad (62 MW), Bilibino (48 MW) and Obninsk (5 MW). There is also the 600 MW station which the Russians refer to as 'the Siberian facility' or as 'Troitskii', which some Western observers have assumed means the town of the same name in Orenburg oblast. Its exact location is a secret, implying that it produces material for weapons.

The 65,440 MW of atomic capacity listed in Table 3.19 consists of:

South Ukraine (Ukraine)	4,000 MW
Chernobyl (Ukraine)	3,000 (extension)
Zaporozhe (Ukraine)	4,000
Rovno (Ukraine)	4,000 (extension)
Krym (Ukraine)	4,000
Khmelnitskii (Ukraine)	4,000
Odessa ACHPP (Ukraine)	1,000
Kola (North West)	440 (extension)
Smolensk (Centre)	4,000
Kalinin (Centre)	4,000
Kostroma (Centre)	6,000
Balakovo (Volga)	4,000
Nizhnekamsk (Volga)	4,000
Bashkir (Volga)	6,000
Rostov (North Caucasus)	4,000
Kursk (Central Chernozem)	2,000 (extension)
Ignalina (Baltic)	6,000
Minsk ACHPP (Belorussia)	1,000

These are firm projects, and in addition a number of other possible projects have been mooted. One of these, for a station at Krasnodar, has recently been confirmed, although no other information is available. Plans for an extension of the Armenia station, and for new stations in Azerbaidzhan and the Urals are still being considered.

It can be assumed that the rate of building 8,000–10,000 MW a year by 1990 will continue into the next century. The grounds for such confidence are that the manufacture of reactors is being undertaken by special-purpose shops at plants like Izhora of Leningrad and Ural-khimmash of Sverdlovsk, and eventually by Atommash, and the creation of this entirely new engineering sector is extremely expensive. It must produce a large number of reactors to prove economically justifiable, and for this reason alone the prospects of a sudden curtailment of the Soviet nuclear power programme are most remote. There is certainly no possibility that it will be halted by cost considerations; although the capital construction cost of building an atomic station is 50-100% higher than that for a comparable fossil-fired station, the cheapness of the fuel means that the production costs of atomic power is 40-50% less than that of power from a conventional coal-fired station. Costs may fall even further as larger reactors are employed. Power from a 1,000 MW reactor costs only 0.6 kop/kWh to produce compared with 0.95 kop/kWh from a 210 MW reactor, and the use of 1,500 MW reactors, now being installed at Ignalina, should bring the cost down to 0.5-0.55 kop/kWh. Stations with capacities of 10,000 MW made up of five fast breeder reactors of 2,000 MW each are now being designed, and it is thought that electricity from such a station may cost no more than 0.4 kop/kWh at current prices.

Forecasts for hydro station construction can be made with much less confidence. Once the decision has been taken to build a new station, and a particular point has been reached during the lengthy and expensive process of dam construction, it is unlikely that the station will not be completed. However long-term plans have no firm basis at all — there is no engineering sector uniquely devoted to the manufacture of equipment for hydro stations (like the reactor manufacturing sector for atomic stations) where expensive machinery must be depreciated by the continued output of specifically hydro equipment. Hydro turbines, for example, are made by plants like the 'Kirov' turbine plant at Kharkov, which can readily turn its hand to turbines for atomic, hydro or thermal stations as required.

Another factor complicating forecasts for hydro stations is that the largest of them will be located on remote rivers in Eastern Siberia and the Far East, and using the potential of rivers like the Nizhnyaya Tunguska is limited by the 'state of the art' in building 1,800 and 2,200 kV transmission lines. A design has been drawn up for a 20,000 MW hydro station at Turukhansk, and it is technically feasible to have it operating by the mid-1990s, but it would be foolish to try and make any assumption. In any case, the new hydro capacity under construction is quite sufficient, together with new thermal and atomic stations, to cover Soviet power needs until well into the next century. This capacity consists of:

Sayano-Shushenskoe (Eastern Siberia)	2,560 MW (extension)
Boguchany (Eastern Siberia)	4,000
Kureisk (Eastern Siberia)	500
Moksk (Eastern Siberia)	2,000

Mainsk (Eastern Siberia)	400
Kolyma (Far East)	720 (extension)
Bureya (Far East)	2,000
Rogun (Central Asia)	3,600
Baipazinsk (Central Asia)	600
Kurpsai (Central Asia)	200 (extension)
Tashkumyr (Central Asia)	450
Miatli (Central Asia)	220
Andizhan (Central Asia)	140
Tyuya Muyun (Central Asia)	100 (extension)
Nizhnekamsk (Volga)	624 (extension)
Cheboksary (Volga Vyatka)	1,092 (extension)
Dnestrovsk (Ukraine)	468 (extension)
Konstantinovsk pumped storage (Ukraine)	380
Tashlyk (Ukraine)	1,800
Khudoni (Caucasus)	740
Shamkhor (Caucasus)	760
Zhinvali (Caucasus)	140
Spandaryan (Caucasus)	76
Zaramag (North Caucasus)	374
Irganai (North Caucasus)	800
Shulba (Kazakhstan)	1,350
Daugavpils (Baltic)	300
Kaisyadorys pumped storage (Baltic)	1,600
Zagorsk pumped storage (Centre)	1,200

Stations for which designs have been drawn up, and on which construction may begin during the next decade, include:

Nizhnyaya Tunguska (Eastern Siberia) (preparations for construction begun)	12,000 MW
Sredneyeniseisk (Eastern Siberia) (planning begun)	7,000 MW
Turukhansk (Eastern Siberia) (feasibility report drawn up)	20,000 MW
Pskem cascade (Central Asia)	1,000 MW
Kambaratin (Central Asia)	2,000 MW

It has been estimated that the potential total capacity of hydro stations is 450,000 MW, of which 240,000 MW were technically feasible and 125,000 MW economically justifiable in 1974. The technical and

Map 3.3: Hydro Stations, European USSR

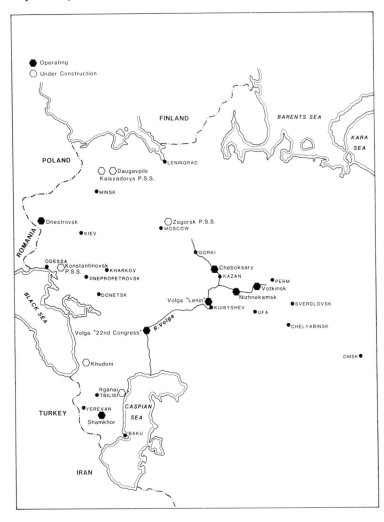

Map 3.4: Thermal and Hydro Stations, Operating or Under Construction, Siberia and Central Asia

economic limits should have widened since 1974, especially with the development of new types of 'diagonal' turbines able to operate on rivers flowing down gentle gradients, and on which it is impossible to build up a large head of water. This could give grounds for believing that my forecast of 90,000 MW for the end of the century is on the low side. Projections drawn up by Gosplan in 1970 for a long-term plan to 1990 foresaw a total hydro capacity of 100,000–130,000 MW in that year, with as much as 40% of the increase (i.e. 28,000–40,000 MW) located in the western zone. However, this scenario was created before the final decision to all out for nuclear power was taken, and in fact less than 10,500 MW of new hydro capacity is under construction in the western zone. It is now too late to begin work on any more stations and have them operational before 1990, and apart from some pumped storage stations planned for Leningrad, the Dnepr and the Dnestr, no other large hydro stations are foreseen at the present time.

The greatest constraint on utilisation of the hydro potential is the slow progress in designing super-high-tension lines of 1,800–2,200 kV able to transmit the power westwards. A technological breakthrough in this sphere could alter radically the forecast of Table 3.18, and the construction of the very large stations listed above would almost certainly be undertaken. The feasibility study for the Nizhnyaya Tunguska station, for example, estimated an electricity production cost less than 10% the national average at the present time (0.1 kop/kWh compared with 1.55) with the huge construction cost recouped in five years.

Some Soviet planners have even raised the possibility that technological breakthroughs in long-distance transmission through the use of liquid gas insulation, cryogenic cable transmission, etc. could render the atomic power programme redundant. But they also recognise that once the Atommash reactor plant has been completed, a certain number of atomic stations must be built for the cost of building the plant to be recouped. This does not preclude the eventual construction of hydro stations like Nizhnyaya Tunguska, particularly if the relocation of industry to the eastern zone can be effected to any significant extent. It is likely that the next 50 years will see both policy variants — European atomic stations and large Siberian hydro stations — being pursued to cover base-loads in their respective regions, with long-distance transmission lines built, if this is technically and economically feasible, from Siberia to Europe to cover peak loads in the western zone of the USSR.

The Fuel Rate

According to my forecasts, thermal power stations will be producing 1,300 bn kWh a year by the end of the century, and their output will grow at an average annual rate of 1.13%, declining from 1.26% during 1981 to 1985 to only 0.63% over the last five years of the century.

Table 3.20: Forecast Output of Electricity and Thermal Energy, and Consumption of Fuel, by Thermal Power Stations

| | Output | | Fuel Rates | | Fuel Consumption | | |
	Electri-city (bn kWh)	Thermal Energy (mn G-cals)	Electri-city (gsf/kWh)	Thermal Energy (kgsf/ G-cal)	Electri-city	Thermal Energy (mn tsf)	Total
1980	1,038	1,170	328	173.0	340	202	542
1985	1,105	1,340	320	172.7	354	231	585
1990	1,180	1,540	313	172.4	369	265	634
2000	1,300	1,970	300	172.0	390	339	729

It is reasonable to assume that the share of electricity produced on thermal energy cycles of CHPPs will rise slightly from the present 20% of Minenergo output to 25% by 1990. The basis of this assumption is the official expectation that the share of CHPP electricity output derived from their thermal energy cycles will grow from about 54% at the present time to 70–75% in the long-term. The share of CHPPs in total thermal generating capacity belonging to Minenergo is likely to stabilise at the current level of 38%. On this basis, the total capacity of CHPPs should rise from 76,000 MW in 1980 to 82,000 in 1985, and 91,000 MW by the end of the century.

Some CHPPs are now producing electricity for as little as 160 gsf/ kWh. Such a rate is unlikely to be achieved universally, due to the different demands for thermal energy facing different stations. But the increasing degree of concentration of CHPP sets in large stations and technological improvements may well bring the average fuel rate for CHPPs to 200 gsf/kWh by the end of the century.

For condensing stations, the fuel rate should fall further as old coal-fired sets are replaced by new gas-burning ones. This tendency could be partly offset by the greater use of low-rank coal from the Ekibastuz and Kansk-Achinsk fields, although Ekibastuz coal is projected to give fuel rates of 334 gsf/kWh on the 500 MW sets being used by the Eki-bastuz power complex. It must be assumed that highly efficient units of 300 MW, 500 MW and 800 MW will dominate the condensing stations of the end of the century, and an average fuel rate of 335 gsf/kWh does not seem unreasonable.

Another factor helping to bring down the fuel rate of condensing stations will be the widespread conversion of sets to a heat-and-power regime, similar to that taking place at Dnepropetrovsk. The very low fuel rates claimed by MHD (Magnetohydrodynamic) sets will be starting to have an impact by 2000, by which time the 500 MW station at Ryazan (now under construction), and several other larger stations, will be operating.

If 25% of all electricity is produced on CHPPs with an average fuel rate of 200 gsf/kWh, and the remaining 75% on condensing stations and small gas turbine stations with an average rate of 335 gsf/kWh, then the average rate for all thermal stations will be about 300 gsf/kWh. Consequently, the generation of 1,300 bn kWh of electricity at the end of the century will require 390 mn tsf, or 50 mn more than in 1980. If there is no decline in the fuel rate from the 328 gsf/kWh of 1980, then 426 mn tsf will be needed; it can therefore be argued that improving technology in the electricity production sector will effect fuel savings of 36 mn tsf a year by 2000 compared with 1980. During the Eleventh Five Year Plan period, savings of 12 mn tsf must be effected, primarily by reducing the fuel rate for the production of electricity.

With the production of thermal energy by power stations expected to grow by 2.6% a year from 1,170 mn G-cals in 1980 to 1,970 mn in 2000, and the fuel rate likely to decline only marginally, it can be estimated that the consumption of fuel for this purpose will rise to 339 mn tsf a year by 2000, giving a total fuel requirement by power stations of 729 mn tsf. The growth in output of thermal energy implies a rise in the productivity of CHPPs from 15,400 mn G-cals per MW of capacity in 1980 to 21,650 mn in 2000. In fact the improvement will not be quite as dramatic as this, because a significant share of the additional output of thermal energy will come, not from CHPPs, but from converted sets at condensing stations.

Large municipal and industrial boilers could well improve their share of overall thermal energy output in the future, with production rising slightly faster than that from CHPPs at perhaps 3% a year. These boilers are already extremely efficient, and technical improvements and the replacement of obsolete equipment should not permit the fuel rate to fall beyond 180 kgsf/G-cal by the end of the century.

It should be noted that the production of thermal energy by large boilers (Table 3.21) added to that by power stations (Table 3.20)

Table 3.21: Forecast Fuel Consumption by Municipal and Industrial Boilers

	Production of Thermal Energy (mn G-cals)	Fuel Rate (kgsf/G-cal)	Fuel Consumption (mn tsf)
1980	960	189	182
1985	1,150	184	212
1990	1,330	182.5	243
2000	1,700	180	306

Table 3.22: Forecast Fuel Consumption by Localised Boilers

	Production of Thermal Energy (mn G-cals)	Fuel Rate (kgsf/G-cal)	Fuel Consumption (mn tsf)
1980	870	220	191
1985	880	215	189
1990	900	210	189
2000	930	200	186

comes to slightly less than the forecast output by all centralised sources (Table 1.17). This is because a small, but increasing amount of heat will be obtained from heat exchangers.

By the end of the century, the production of thermal energy from localised boilers is likely to have stabilised at about 930 mn G-cals, mainly in remote regions of Siberia and the Far East, and in rural areas throughout the USSR, where these boilers will have replaced household stoves burning firewood and other low-rank fuels.

Although the average fuel rate for large centralised boilers will fall by only 4.8% over the 20 years 1980–2000, it is expected to fall by over 9% for localised boilers. This is because many of these boilers are extremely inefficient due to their poor design, with fuel rates of up to 350 ksgf/G-cal. The Soviet engineering industry has already turned its attention to the manufacture of much more efficient boilers designed to burn mains or bottled gas, and it can be anticipated that these will be installed in increasing numbers in the 'prospective villages' in the countryside, where they will provide heat and hot water to cottages in place of individual stoves. Meanwhile, the most inefficient localised boilers serving blocks of flats in the towns will be scrapped as the network of CHPPs and municipal boilers is extended. In Leningrad alone, 800 small boilers were scrapped during 1976 to 1980, providing a fuel saving of 50,000 tsf/ year.

These forecasts therefore foresee the production of thermal energy rising from 3,130 mn G-cals in 1980 to 3,550 mn in 1985, 4,000 mn in 1990 and 4,930 mn in 2000, at an average annual rate of 2.3% over the 20-year period.

The consumption of fuel by the entire electricity and thermal energy generating sector should grow from 915 mn tsf in 1980 to 986 mn in 1985, 1,066 mn in 1990 and 1,221 mn tsf in 2000. Considering the plans for new thermal power stations, and taking into account some (unofficial) Soviet long-term projections of fuel consumption by centralised and localised boilers, it is possible to calculate that by the end of the century, the share of gas in overall fuel consumption should have risen to over 40% compared with 28% in 1980. The share of fuel oil will have declined from 25.6% to under 10% while that of coal will have risen from 35.8% to 41.4%.

Table 3.23: Forecast Fuel Consumption by the Electricity and Thermal Energy Sector by Type of Fuel (mn tsf)

	1980	1985	1990	2000
Power stations − total	542	585	634	730
coal	205	232	264	380
gas	131	169[2]	200	260
fuel oil	190	167[2]	150	90
others	15	17	20	−
Centralised boilers − total	182	212	243	306
coal	35	40	50	80
gas	102	122	133	160
fuel oil	42	50	60	66
others	3	−	−	−
Local boilers − total	191	189	189	186
coal	88	76	69	46
gas	23	35	45	70
fuel oil	16	18	20	20
others[1]	64	60	55	50
Total	915	986	1,066	1,222
coal	328	348	383	506
gas	257	326	378	490
fuel oil	248	235	230	176
others[1]	82	77	75	50

Notes:
1. Includes secondary energy from factories via heat exchangers, coke and oil products other than fuel oil as well as peat, firewood, etc.
2. The official plan targets of 190 mn tsf of gas and 151.5 mn tsf fuel oil imply the successful achievement of an ambitious conversion programme.

4 THE IRON AND STEEL INDUSTRY

After power and transport, the iron and steel industry is the next largest consumer of fuel. It is of particular significance to planners trying to divide a limited volume of capital investment between competing fuel production sectors like oil, gas and coal, because its principal fuel requirement is of coking coal, for which the Russians have the greatest difficulty in meeting demand.

There are five distinct sectors of the iron and steel industry: iron ore mining and concentration; coke production; iron-smelting; steel production; and steel-rolling.

Being one of the staple industries of any industrially developed society, ferrous metallurgy grew very rapidly after the Second World War, but the production of steel in the Soviet Union has now reached a plateau of about 150 mn tons a year with the emphasis now on extending the range of finished products and improving their quality. The USSR is the world's largest producer of all the products listed in Table 4.1. In 1980, it produced 147.9 mn tons of steel compared with 103.8 mn by the USA, the second largest producer.

Table 4.1: Output of Sectors of the Ferrous Metallurgy Industry (mn tons)

	Iron Ore	Coke	Pig-iron	Steel	Rolled Steel	Pipes
1960	105.9	56.2	46.8	65.3	43.7	5.8
1970	197.3	75.4	85.9	115.9	80.6	12.4
1975	235.0	83.5	103.0	141.3	98.7	16.0
1978	246.4	89.3	110.7	151.5	105.4	17.6
1979	241.7	87.8	109.0	149.1	103.2	18.2
1980	244.7	86.0	107.3	147.9	102.9	18.2
1981	242.5	86.1	108.0	148.5	103.0	18.3

The Soviet iron and steel industry is concentrated in a small number of large plants. In 1973, six plants accounted for 43.6% of the total output of iron, with 19 plants, each producing more than 2 mn tons, accounting for 92.6%. In the steel sector, 26 plants with an output of more than 1 mn tons each yielded 90.6% of total output. The world's largest metallurgical plant is the Magnitogorsk Combine in the Urals;

Map 4.1: Iron and Steel Plants, European USSR

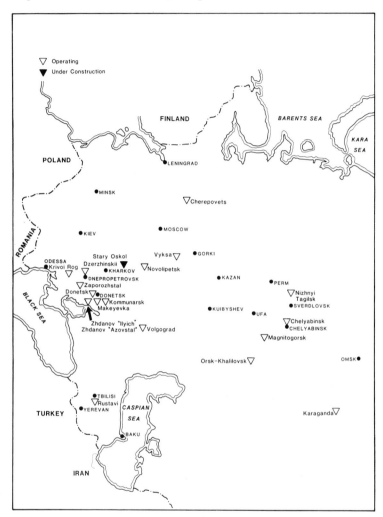

by 1985 it is planned to produce 14 mn tons of iron, 17 mn tons of steel and 15 mn tons of rolled steel annually.

The major determinants of the location of the industry are the location and size of deposits of iron ore and coking coal and the presence of a skilled labour force. The eastern Ukraine and the Urals have been the principal centres of the industry, but in recent years it has become more widely diffused, with iron and steel combines being built in the North West, Central Chernozem, Western Siberia and Kazakhstan regions, and small steel plants in Belorussia, Latvia, Uzbekistan, Azerbaidzhan, the North Caucasus and the Far East.

Table 4.2: Regional Output of Iron and Steel (mn tons)

	1960	1970	1975	1980
Pig iron – total	46.8	85.9	103.0	107.3
RSFSR	21.6	42.0	52.2	
Ukraine	24.2	41.4	46.4	
Kazakhstan	0.3	1.8	3.6	
Georgia	0.7	0.8	0.8	
Steel – total	65.3	115.9	141.3	147.9
RSFSR	36.6	63.9	79.9	
Ukraine	26.2	46.6	53.1	
Kazakhstan	0.3	2.2	4.9	
Caucasus	1.7	2.1	2.3	
Others	0.5	1.1	1.2	

The most significant development during the last 20 years is that the Ukraine has lost its place as the largest producer of iron to the RSFSR. This is because the output of Donbass coking coal has grown more slowly than that of the Kuzbass. The fuel base appears to be the most important factor in location policy; one expert says 'the volume of fuel consumption in metallurgical plants amounts to 0.9-1.0 tsf per ton of rolled steel, therefore the fuel base is as important as that of iron ore'. In fact, when all types of fuel and energy are taken into consideration, this figure is very much higher, amounting to 1.3 tons in the Ukraine in 1970. It is therefore iron ore, rather than fuel, which is having to be transported over increasingly long distances, from the Kursk Magnetic Anomaly, for example, to the Urals. In 1980, 34 mn tons of coke, and 191.8 mn tons of ferrous metals, including iron ore, were transported by rail.

Fuel Consumption by the Iron and Steel Industry

The Soviet iron and steel industry consumed 155.3 mn tsf in 1972 and 175 mn in 1977; during these five years consumption grew at an average annual rate of 2.5%, but since 1977 it is unlikely to have risen at all, and has probably fallen, in connection with the failure of the industry to expand and with the increasing use of secondary energy resources and more fuel-efficient production methods. These figures represent fuel in its secondary, i.e. processed form, and include by-products of coking, such as 'koksik', coke fines and coking gas, blast furnace gas, coal-dressing plant wastes and slurry.

Of the five principal sectors of the industry, iron-making is the most important in terms of fuel consumption, using 68.8 mn tsf in 1972 and an estimated 77.5 mn tsf in 1977. In 1972, 59.5 mn tsf were used in the blast furnaces including 51.4 mn of coke and 7.9 mn tsf of natural gas, and a further 9.3 mn tsf was required for heating the blast – this included 8.7 mn tsf of blast furnace gas. The steel-making sector required 12.6 mn tsf, including 7.05 mn of natural gas and 4.13 mn of oil. The steel-rolling sector consumed 15.6 mn tsf; natural gas and coking gas were the principal fuels.

Some 10.6 mn tsf were used in the ore-dressing process, 9.3 mn in the coke batteries and 24.4 mn tsf for energy needs, i.e. by the CHPPs and industrial boilers owned by the Ministry of Ferrous Metallurgy. Other sectors (production of fireproofing and lime, transport, etc.) used 14 mn tsf in 1972.

In 1972, iron-smelting used 44.3% of all fuel consumed by the industry, including fuel used for heating the blast. Energy needs took 15.7%, steel-rolling 10.0% and steel-making 8.3%.

The most important fuel, in terms of volume, is coke, with 53.4 mn tsf (34.4% of the total) being consumed in 1972 and about 60 mn tsf (34.3%) in 1977. This amounts to more than 80% of the total output of coke by the USSR, with the non-ferrous metal industry being the only other major consumer. Together with its by-products, coke accounts for virtually half the fuel inputs to the iron and steel industry.

Natural gas is the other major fuel; consumption rose from 27.8 bn cu m in 1970 to 33 bn in 1975 and 39.3 bn in 1980. In 1973, natural gas accounted for 12% of fuel used by the blast furnace sector, 40% of fuel consumed in steel-rolling and 63% of that needed for steel-making.

Significant volumes of coking gas and blast furnace gas are acquired from the coking and iron-smelting processes. In 1973, they accounted for practically all the fuel needed to transform coal into coke, and

Table 4.3: Fuel Consumption by the Iron and Steel Industry in 1972 (by Sector) and 1977 (mn tons of standard fuel)

	Ore-dressing	Coke Production	Iron-smelting	Steel-making	Steel-rolling	Energy Needs	Others	Total 1972	1977
Hard coal	2.8	—	—	0.1	—	3.1	2.4	8.4	9.3
Oil	0.2	—	0.2	4.1	0.8	1.2	1.2	7.8	10.0
Coke	0.4	—	51.4	—	0.1	—	1.5	53.4	67.7
Koksik	0.1	—	—	—	1.1	—	0.2	1.4	
Coke fines	5.1	—	—	—	—	—	0.3	5.4	
Natural gas	1.3	0.1	8.2	7.0	6.2	7.6	5.0	35.4	42.3
Coking gas	0.5	5.5	0.2	1.2	4.1	3.3	2.1	16.9	17.5
Blast furnace gas	0.2	3.7	8.8	0.1	3.3	7.2	0.6	23.8	25.1
Dressing plant waste and slurry	—	—	—	—	—	1.7	—	1.7	2.1
Others	—	—	—	0.2	—	0.2	0.7	1.1	1.0
Total	10.6	9.3	68.8	12.7	15.6	24.3	14.0	155.3	175.0

Table 4.4: Consumption of Gas During 1970 to 1980 (bn cu m)*

	Natural Gas			Coke Oven Gas			Blast Furnace Gas		
	Total	Iron and Steel	Share	Total	Iron and Steel	Share	Total	Iron and Steel	Share
1970	196.0	27.8	14.0%	14.9	13.3	89.1%	20.6	18.9	92.1%
1977	346.0	35.7	10.3	16.8	14.8	88.1	22.4	21.2	94.5
1978	372.2	36.6	9.8	16.8	14.9	88.6	22.6	21.5	95.1
1979	406.6	38.4	9.4	16.5	14.7	89.0	22.4	21.2	94.8
1980	435.2	39.3	9.0	16.6	14.9	89.7	22.2	20.9	94.3

Note: * Coking gas and blast furnace gas are converted to the same calorific value as natural gas.

The Iron and Steel Industry 101

provided 47% of the fuel needed for steel-rolling and 43% of that required for the CHPPs and energy boilers.

At the Cherepovets plant, coking gas and blast furnace gas have pressures of up to 3.5 ats and can be used to drive turbines. The plant has turbines of 8 MW and 12 MW capacity working on gas in two blast furnaces, and the same process has been employed at another two blast furnaces at Krivoi Rog. The use of each of these turbines saves an estimated 10,000 tsf a year, but so far only 18 turbines have been produced, of which five have been sold to Japan. During the current plan period, their serial production is to begin.

Table 4.4 shows how the consumption of different types of gas has grown over the period 1970 to 1980. The total consumption of gas has grown from 60.0 bn cu m in 1970 to 75.1 bn in 1980 at an average annual rate of 2.3%. During the three years 1977-80, the rate declined to only 1.1% a year in connection with the levelling out of steel production.

(a) Iron Ore Mining and Concentration

As the quality of crude ore has deteriorated, with the best deposits becoming exhausted and more marginal deposits being worked at the major fields of Krivoi Rog, Kachkanar and Rudnyi, the iron input to Soviet blast furnaces has come to be dominated by concentrate and pellets, with crude ore now accounting for less than 2%.

In 1972, the concentration sector consumed 10.6 mn tsf of fuel, more than half of which was by-products of the coking sector. By 1980, the usage of natural gas had risen from 1.3 mn tsf to 3.1 mn (including 0.75 mn for concentration and 2.35 mn for pelletisation) while that of coking gas remained at 0.5 mn tsf and the consumption of blast furnace gas declined slightly to 0.17 mn tsf. Ore-processing is power-intensive, using considerable quantities of electricity. The comparatively small amount of fuel used is consumed in the process of the reduction roasting of ores. But, as a proportion of the total cost of production of concentrate and pellets, the cost of fuel is not very significant − 1.61% of the cost of concentrate from Krivbass Mining Enrichment Combine, and 5.25% of the cost of pellets from the Central MEC. The average fuel rate for concentrate production amounts to 66 kgsf of solid fuel per ton of concentrate plus 18.6 cu m of gas for conversion, and for pelletisation 57.6 cu m of natural gas are required.

(b) The Coking Sector

Coking coal is regarded as a deficit fuel in the USSR, in that demand for it places a severe strain on existing supplies. However the USSR is the world's largest producer of coking coal with an output in 1975 of 181 mn tons; data for all aspects of coke and coking coal production since 1975 have not been published. Proven reserves of coking coal exceeded 24,500 mn tons in 1971, and these are sufficient to sustain current rates of output for perhaps 135 years. Probable reserves are very much greater.

The coking coal production sector is based on six coalfields, and is dominated by the Donbass which accounts for 45% of national output and claims 24.3% of reserves. The biggest reserves of coking coal are found in the Kuzbass (40.3%) with the Pechora field (5.8%), Karaganda (5.4%) and South Yakutsk containing significant volumes. About 70% of all coking coal is despatched to the iron and steel industry, and coke is produced in seven economic regions of the USSR.

North West. Coke production takes place at the Cherepovets kombinat using local coal from the Pechora basin mixed with imported Kuznets coal. Pechora coking coal is relatively expensive, costing 12 R/ton to produce. The coke has a low sulphur (0.90%) and fairly high ash (10.30%) content, and suffers from the extremely variable nature of Pechora coal, which often contains a heavy concentration of fines and a variable ash content. The Cherepovets coke shop is modern with a high degree of mechanisation, including dry-quenching facilities which raise the quality of the coke. However, the high cost and variable quality of the coal means that the coke is expensive at 30-32 R/t.

Central Chernozem. Coke is produced at the Novolipetsk kombinat, which is very modern with the mechanisation and automation of production processes, including the dry-quenching of coke. The plant uses a blend of Pechora, Donbass and Kuzbass coke. The sulphur content has been reduced to 1.1% as a result of the greater use of low-sulphur Pechora coal. In 1973, 9.7 mn tons of coke was produced in the Central Chernozem and North West regions.

Caucasus. The Caucasus region has one metallurgical plant with a coking shop at Rustavi, Georgia, which requires about one million tons of coal a year. It was hoped to phase out the imports of Donbass coal by raising the output of Georgian coal to 3.6 mn tons a year, including 3.25 mn tons of coking coal, by 1975, but in fact output has stabilised at 1.8 mn tons. The quality of Rustavi coke is low, with high contents of ash (15.2%) and sulphur (1.45%).

Urals. The Urals is a region with comparatively small reserves of coking coal, although it is a major iron- and steel-producing centre. Urals coke is produced from a mixture of Kuzbass and Karaganda coals together with small amounts of Pechora and local Kizel coal. Coke production takes place in the coking shops of a number of metallurgical plants and in the Gubakha chemical plant, which uses local Kizel coking coal mixed with Kuznets coal. The Magnitogorsk coking shop uses a mixture of 67% Kuznets and 33% Karaganda coal. Urals coke is of poor quality in terms of strength and ash content (12.2%) due to the high ash content of Karaganda coal, but it should improve as new coking coal deposits in the Kuzbass come on stream. Some coke batteries, such as the latest to be commissioned at Magnitogorsk in 1982 with a capacity of one million tons of coke a year, produce high quality coke at a comparatively low cost. In 1973, 18.7 mn tons of coke was produced in the Urals region.

Ukraine. In 1970, 50% of Soviet coke was produced in the Ukraine, using local Donbass coking coal which is the most expensive in the country, costing 12-14 R/ton to produce. Ukrainian coke is of indifferent quality and is likely to get worse because, as the share of gas-coal and other coals with poor coking qualities grows, the quality of the coking coal blend will worsen. Although it has a low ash content of only 9.51%, the coke is extremely sulphurous (1.75% sulphur content), and its quality fluctuates considerably, both between plants and over a period of time in the same plant. This is partly due to the poor technical level of some plants, but also to the irregular quality of coking coal. The Donetsk, Makeyevka and Kommunarsk plants are notorious for the production of poor-quality coke. As with the coking shops of the Urals, those of the Ukraine were built at different periods and consequently have diverse technical characteristics; while many plants have advanced systems of mechanisation and automation of production, others are stocked with obsolete and dilapidated equipment. The cost of Donbass coke at the newest plants varies between 34.1 R/ton when produced in a large (41.6 cu m) chamber at a plant with eight batteries, and 41.5 R/ton in a small (30.0 cu m) chamber at a plant with four batteries.

Western Siberia. The West Siberian coke plant at Novokuznetsk, and the new Altai coking plant, the first two of a planned four batteries of which have begun operating with capacities of one million tons a year each, use local Kuzbass coal. The Altai plant is the first in the USSR designed to transform poor-quality coals into coke in a continuous process developed in the Soviet Union and first tested in an experimental coke shop at Kharkov coke and chemical plant. In 1973, only 10.1 mn tons of coke were produced in Western Siberia, but as Kuzbass coking coal is the cheapest in the country, costing 7.2 R/ton to produce, it may pay to expand the coking plants and transport coke to the rest of the country. At the present time, Kuzbass coke is very cheap (21-23 R/ton) with a fairly low ash content of 10.9% and a very low sulphur content of 0.45%.

Kazakhstan. In Kazakhstan, coke is produced at the coke shop of the Karaganda kombinat using local coal which costs 9.2 R/ton to produce. Karaganda coal has a high ash content, and so, therefore, has the coke at 12.4%, with consequently a low strength. The quality of both coal and coke worsened during the 1970s, with the coke plant rejecting some coal deliveries because of their excessive ash content. During the 1981 to 1985 plan period, a new 1 mn ton/year battery is to be built, specially designed to produce high-quality coke from Karaganda coal.

Table 4.5: Output of Coke (6% Moisture Content) (mn tons)

	1960	1970	1975
Output – USSR	56.2	75.4	83.5
RSFSR	25.4	34.4	39.1
Ukraine	30.1	37.5	40.4
Kazakhstan	–	2.8	3.3
Georgia	0.7	0.7	0.7
Imports	–	0.7	0.9
Exports	2.6	4.0	4.2
Available for consumption	53.6	72.1	80.2

The national output of coke has apparently stabilised at 80 to 90 mn tons a year – no official data is available for the years after 1975 – and because of frequent shortages, inferior alternatives often have to be used in order to keep the blast furnaces operating.

The future development of the coking coal industry is likely to see the phasing out of the two smallest producing basins, Kizel and Georgia. Georgian coal will become prohibitively expensive in spite of recent modernisation work, and the decline in the quality of Kizel coal will lead to its being used exclusively as steam coal. It will be replaced as a source of coke by increased deliveries to the Urals of Kuznets coal.

The western part of the country will be supplied from the Donbass and Pechora basins until the beginning of the next century when coke production begins to decline as the direct reduction process grows in importance. The main problem is the continuing decline in coke quality because the construction of new mines has been taking place in areas of poorer quality coking coal. Output of coking coal by the Pechora mines has been growing, and it is used primarily for the Cherepovets and Novolipetsk metallurgical plants, and the chemical plants at Moscow and Kaliningrad.

It is more economical to use Kuzbass coal for the coking plants of the central regions than either Donbass or Pechora coal. The high quality of Kuzbass coal, its low sulphur content and low cost of extraction and dressing more than compensate for the cost of transport to consumers over the distance of 3,700 km. During the last decade, western regions have been importing 45-50 mn tons of Kuzbass coal each year, and this volume is likely to rise in the future, conceivably to as much as 100 mn tons/year by 1990.

The future of the Karaganda basin is not very bright. The extraction costs are higher than those of the Kuzbass, and the principal customers of Karaganda coking coal will be the local metallurgical plant and, to a lesser degree, the Urals plants.

The South Yakutsk field is now being developed. When completed, the open-cast Neryungri mine will produce 9 mn tons a year of coking coal and 4 mn tons of steam coal. So far, the two steam coal stages of the mine have been commissioned, and sufficient overburden has been removed for the coking coal section to start up in 1983. Initially, the coking coal will be exported to Japan under a long-term agreement signed in 1974, but eventually a full-cycle metallurgical plant will be built in the Far East using iron ore from the Taldanskii iron ore field, located close to the Neryungri mine.

As a direct result of the shortage of coking coal, methods of direct reduction of iron ore have been elaborated. The Stary Oskol plant in the Kursk Magnetic Anomaly is under construction with the aid of West German technology, and its first stage should start up in 1985. The first facility of the combine, a plant for producing 2.43 mn tons of oxidised iron ore pellets, came on stream in November 1982.

In 1972, the Soviet iron and steel industry used 9.3 mn tsf for the production of coke in the coking shops of metallurgical combines and coking plants belonging to the Ministry of Ferrous Metallurgy. This consisted almost entirely of by-products of the coking process (i.e. coking gas), or of other internal processes of the industry such as blast furnace gas. Some 110,000 tsf of natural gas and an insignificant quantity of hard coal were used. There has been little change since 1972, with fuel consumption falling to 9.22 mn tsf, consisting of 5.71 mn tsf of coking gas (up from 5.5 mn in 1972), 3.37 mn tsf of blast furnace gas (down from 3.7 mn) and 0.14 mn tsf of natural gas compared with 0.11 mn.

It can be anticipated that total fuel consumption may fall further in the future as more of the highly fuel-efficient 1 mn ton/year batteries come on stream and smaller ancient batteries are scrapped. During the two years 1981-2, four such batteries were commissioned, at Zaporozhe (replacing a group of obsolete batteries), with a second now under construction, Magnitogorsk and the Altai coking plant at Zarinsk in Western Siberia, where two batteries are now operating. The planned group of four at Altai, to be completed by 1985, will cost 275 mn roubles and will use natural gas; the coking gas will be used for firing a CHPP serving the plant, and for a nitrogenous fertiliser plant to be built alongside the coke batteries. In addition, a new battery of 0.2 mn tons/year has been installed at the Kirov Coke and Chemical Plant of Donetsk, bringing its total capacity to 0.4 mn tons/year, and two of the four batteries of Chelyabinsk Metallurgical Plant have been renewed. The remaining two will be renewed by 1985, enabling the plant to raise its annual output of coke by 270,000 tons in 1985 compared with 1980. The Eleventh Five Year Plan has called for the programme of coke battery construction and renewal to be accelerated over the Tenth plan period, when 18 battieres were commissioned in the USSR.

(c) Iron-smelting

In 1972, iron-smelting required 68.8 mn tsf, or 44.3% of total fuel consumption by the iron and steel industry. By 1977, requirements had risen to 77.5 mn tsf before growing more slowly to 79.8 mn tsf in 1980.

In 1980, fuel accounted for 46% of the total cost of blast furnace production in the USSR compared with 43% in 1970. This varies within wide limits depending on the region in which the blast furnaces are located, with fuel being more expensive, and therefore more important, in the western part of the country.

The amount of fuel required to smelt a ton of iron fell steadily until 1970, since when it has stabilised at about 0.65 tsf per ton. In 1980, 70.0 mn tsf (excluding fuel used for heating the blast) were required to produce 107.3 mn tons of iron, giving a rate of 652 kgsf/ton. This compared with 646 kgsf/ton in 1970 and 753 in 1961, and suggests

Table 4.6: Consumption of Fuel by the Iron-smelting Sector, 1972 and 1977 (mn tsf)

| | Heating the Blast | | Blast Furnace | | Total | |
	1972	1977	1972	1977	1972	1977
Oil	–	–	0.2	0.2	0.2	0.2
Coke	–	–	51.4	57.0	51.4	57.0
Natural gas	0.3	0.4	7.9	12.8	8.2	13.2
Coking gas	0.2	0.3	–	–	0.2	0.3
Blast Furnace Gas	8.7	9.1	–	–	8.7	9.1
Total	9.3	9.8	59.5	70.0	68.8	79.8

Table 4.7: Consumption of Coke by Soviet Blast Furnaces

	Volume (mn tons)	Rate of Consumption (kg per ton of iron)
1960	33.3	711
1970	49.4	575
1975	56.3	547
1978	59.0	533
1979	58.3	535
1980	57.1	532
1981	57.3	531

that the potential for further declines in fuel consumption is becoming exhausted.

In 1980, coke accounted for 81% of the total fuel consumption of Soviet blast furnaces, showing a significant decline over 1970. However, the rate of consumption of coke per ton of iron has been falling steadily, from 935 kg in 1950 to 711 in 1960, 575 in 1970 and 532 in 1980.

In 1980, 57.1 mn tons of dry coke were required, a decline of 1.9 mn tons over the peak year of 1978, although the rate of 532 kg/ton was much higher than the planned 509 kg/ton; this meant that the supply of an additional 2.47 mn tons of coke proved necessary. Soviet sources normally quote the coke consumption rate in terms of dry skipped coke, i.e. coke which has had the fines removed from it before it enters the furnace. These fines amount to about 27 kg per ton of coke, or 2.90 mn tons in 1980, and although they serve as a useful fuel for iron ore concentration, it is Soviet policy to try and reduce their creation during the movement of coke from the coke ovens to the blast furnace.

It has been suggested that the coke usage rate can ultimately fall as

Table 4.8: Consumption of Coke Per Ton of Iron in Kg, Selected Countries

	1970	1975	1980
USA	658	612	596
UK	625	609	588
USSR	575	547	532
France	626	532	520
West Germany	559	498	515
Japan	478	444	423

low as 350–400 kg/ton, and in some Japanese plants it has already fallen to 350. Japan boasts by far the world's best coke usage rate; it was lower in the early 1960s than the level attained by the Soviet Union today. The West German and French iron-smelting sectors are also highly efficient, but the USSR scores better than the USA and the UK.

Consumption of coke for iron-smelting in the USSR varies widely region by region and plant by plant. The regional variations are largely a reflection of the characteristics of plants in those regions. For instance, the Caucasus and Volga regions have one plant each, both of which are comparatively small and inefficient, and consequently the coke usage rate for these regions is very high. The North West and Central Chernozem regions each have one plant, respectively Cherepovets and Novolipetsk, which are very modern and highly efficient, and this is reflected in their very low usage rates.

The major influences on the coke consumption rate are: the size of the blast furnace; the temperature of blasting; the quality of the iron ore; the method of work of the blast furnace; and the quality of coke.

Size of the Blast Furnace. Considerable savings of coke can be made by increasing the size of blast furnaces. In 1970, consumption of coke varied between 818 kg/ton by furnaces of less than 600 cu m, and 517 for those of 1,700–2,000 cu m, with a national average of 575 kg/ton. By 1980, the average size of Soviet furnaces had grown from 1,199 cu m in 1973 to 1,363 cu m, and a furnace of 5,000 cu m had been installed at Krivoi Rog. The consumption of coke and natural gas per ton of iron by the 5,000 cu m furnace was only 91.7% and 85.2% respectively of the consumption level typical of a 1,033 cu m furnace in 1976, and the cost of iron was 94.6%. Labour productivity was 87% greater.

However it is misleading to believe that reductions in the coke consumption rate are brought about solely as a result of the increased size of the furnaces. When larger furnaces are employed (a) the temperature at which iron is smelted can be raised, (b) it becomes more economical to lay pipes bringing natural gas to the furnaces and to install plants for the provision of oxygen, (c) larger batches of ore and coke can be delivered to the furnaces, enabling a greater degree of stability in their quality to be maintained and (d) other factors tending to reduce the level of coke requirements can be introduced. When the influence of all these factors is excluded, there is a very small decline in the coke usage rate as the size of the furnace is increased.

The Temperature of Blasting. Raising the temperature of the blast leads to a lowering of coke consumption because it introduces to the furnace an additional quantity of thermal energy in the hotter blast, thereby raising its productivity. The predominant fuel used for heating the blast is blast-furnace gas, although small amounts of natural gas and coking gas are used. Raising the temperature of blasting has proved particularly effective in those plants where natural gas is blown into the furnace.

In 1980, the average blast temperature in Soviet furnaces was approaching 1,100°C compared with 1,040° in 1971. At the present time, however, the projected blast temperature has not been achieved in many furnaces, and this leads to a large over-expenditure of coke. It has been found that for every rise of 100° in the temperature, the savings of coke amount to 15.9 kg per ton of iron.

The Quality of the Iron Input. As well as providing heat, coke acts as a deoxidising agent on the iron ore. If the content of pure iron in the ore can be raised, then less coke is required to smelt each ton of converted iron.

Crude iron ore is now practically absent from the iron part of the blast furnace burden. In 1981, 1,822 kg of ore was smelted for each ton of pig-iron, including 502 kg of pellets, of which 54.1 mn tons were produced. The share of pellets has been growing (in 1975, 27.2 mn tons were produced, or 264 kg per ton of converted iron) and is set to rise further at the expense of sinter and the tiny amount of crude ore still delivered to furnaces. However some experts have argued that the use of pellets, while raising the productivity of blast furnaces, also raises the volume of coke required for smelting a ton of iron.

A number of experiments have been carried out to determine the extent of the reduction in the coke rate for an increased pure iron content in the burden. At Krivoi Rog, the usual sinter with an iron content of 51.5% was replaced by sinter with a 59.5% content, and the coke rate was reduced from 585 to 507 kg per ton.

Method of Work of the Blast Furnace. The coefficient of blast furnace volume use, measured in terms of cubic metres of furnace volume required for the smelting of one ton of iron, is greatly influenced by the extent to which reduction reagents such as natural gas, oil and coal dust are blown into the furnace, and the degree of enrichment of the blast with oxygen.

While in 1960, 0.741 cu m of furnace space was required for the smelting of a ton of iron, in 1970 and 1980 the comparable figures were 0.597 and 0.571. In Soviet blast furnaces, the most important additional reduction agent is natural gas, and the combined use of natural gas and oxygen has become standard practice in most furnaces. The presence of natural gas has a positive influence on the blasting process by providing an increase in the quantity of the deoxidisers acting on a unit of oxide. This lowers the consumption of coke. However, an increase in the amount of natural gas blown into the furnace considerably increases the volume of hearth gases and thereby lowers the temperature in the furnace hearth.

Therefore the optimal volume of natural gas is between 80 and 110 cu m per ton of iron. But when combined with oxygen, the optimal consumption of natural gas can considerably exceed this level, reaching 280 cu m according to some sources because oxygen and natural gas have opposite influences on the blast temperature and furnace pressure.

When a mixture of gas and oxygen is used, the saving of coke amounts to only 0.8-0.9 kg per cubic metre of gas, compared with 1.25-1.4 when gas is used by itself. But a very much larger volume of gas can be employed, bringing about a very big reduction in the consumption of coke. The effect of the use of oxygen can be seen from the results of experiments at the 'Dzerzhinskii' Plant in the Ukraine. When natural gas alone was blown into the blast furnace, the coke rate was reduced by 13.4%, but when it was enriched with oxygen, the coke saving rose to 19.7%. According to the Gipromez Institute a mixture of oxygen and natural gas, accounting for an optimal 35% of the blast blown into the furnace, permits a reduction in the consumption of coke to only 400 kg per ton of iron.

The USSR was the first country in the world to use natural gas for iron-smelting, at the Petrov plant in 1957. A combination of gas and oxygen was first used in 1958 at the 'Dzerzhinskii' and Zaporozhstal

Table 4.9: Consumption of Natural Gas and Oxygen for Iron Smelting

	1960	1970	1975	1980	1981
No. of blast furnaces	122	132	136	138	138
using natural gas	46	103	108	115	115
Total iron production (mn tons)	46.8	85.9	103.0	107.3	107.8
using natural gas	19.3	73.8	86.0	98.3	99.9
using oxygen	1.8	48.2	77.5	88.9	91.7
Consumption of natural gas (bn cu m)	1.76	5.9	8.1	10.8	

plants. Table 4.9 shows how the use of natural gas and oxygen has grown.

In 1960, 90.9 cu m of gas were used for each ton of iron produced using gas. By 1970, this figure had fallen to 80 due to shortfalls in the production of gas, but in 1980 109.9 cu m were used. The use of natural gas is far more common in the Ukraine that in other regions, due to the proximity of a large gasfield centred on Shebelinka. Consumption has been rising at the Urals plants, especially since the completion of the Urengoi-Chelyabinsk pipelines, and gas was delivered to the two Western Siberian plants at Novokuznetsk in 1980 when the pipeline was bringing dry casinghead gas from Nizhnevartovsk was completed.

The use of natural gas is far more extensive in the USSR than in other countries, and in view of the scarcity and cost of production of coke in the USSR, the iron and steel industry provides one of the most effective uses for natural gas. Its value has been estimated at 58 roubles per thousand cubic metres when used in blast furnaces.

It has been demonstrated that the blowing of one cubic metre of gas into the furnace leads to a lowering of the consumption of coke by between 0.7 and 2.0 kg per ton of iron. In 1980, about 8 mn tons of coke were saved as a result of the employment of gas.

The blowing of natural gas and oxygen into the blast furnace proves most effective in plants which are technologically advanced. In other plants, the blowing of liquid or solid fuels can result in a substantial lowering of the expenditure of coke. Oil was first used at Magnitogorsk in 1958. Although the expenditure of coke was reduced by 12-15 kg/ton for an oil usage of 4-5 kg/ton, the method did not become popular. In 1964, 25 small blast furnaces, in which 4.6% of all smelting took place, were using oil, but by 1970, these had dwindled to only five, in which 1.2 mn tons of iron (1.4% of the total) were smelted using 27,000 tons of oil. Since then, there has been a renewal of interest in the potential of oil, particularly during the fuel oil glut of the late 1970s, and in 1978 a record 560,000 tons were blown into blast furnaces. The use of oil is more widespread in other countries, especially Japan.

The first experiments using coal dust as a reduction agent were carried out at 'Dzerzhinsk' in 1948, but the process has not become widespread due to the complexity of the equipment delivering coal dust to the hearth of the furnace. Some experts say that the use of coal dust or fuel oil can be more effective than the blowing of gas. In recent years, the inclusion of natural gas in the blast has accounted for only 17.5 kg/ton of the 46 kg/ton decline in the coke rate, or 38% of the total. It has been argued that coal dust could make a more substantial cut in coke use if it is applied correctly.

Quality of the Coke. The quality of the coke, i.e. its strength, the size of its lumps, and its content of ash, fines and sulphur, has a considerable influence on the level of consumption of coke.

There is a relationship between the size of coke, its strength and its content of fines. If the lumps of coke are too large, their strength is reduced and they crush more easily, thereby producing fines. Losses of coke due to pulverisation can amount to as much as 12% of the total quantity of coke despatched to the furnace.

Although the ash content of Soviet coke has been considered unduly high in the past, recent experiments have shown that it has a comparatively small effect on the level of coke consumption. One experiment has shown that by lowering the ash content of coke from 10% to 8%, the consumption of coke per ton of iron would fall from 536 to 520 kg, but that the cost of coke per ton of iron would rise from 24.25 to 25.95 roubles.

A high level of sulphur in the coke leads to a greater requirement of flux, thereby raising the output of slag. This worsens the conditions of smelting, and raises the level of coke consumption. Experiments have shown that a change of 0.1% in the sulphur content of coke brings about a corresponding change in coke consumption of 0.3-0.5%.

Conclusions. Soviet experts have established the following norms for the reduction of coke consumption by different means.

	Saving of Coke (%)
Raising the content of pure iron in the blend by 1%.	1.5
The exclusion of small fractions of coke and agglomerate from the blend, by each 1% of fractions.	0.5
Raising the temperature of blasting by 100°C.	2.0–3.0
Raising the consumption of natural gas by each cubic metre per ton of iron.	0.8–1.0
Raising the pressure of the furnace gas by each 0.1 ats.	0.4–0.5

Although the Soviet Union's first large reduction plant is now under construction at Stary Oskol, Kursk oblast, this method of de-oxidisation of iron will not account for a significant share of output of pig-iron before 1990.

The smelting of iron in electro-furnaces is another method of reduction which has attracted attention in recent years. Much less fuel is required than by blast furnaces, and the basic fuel is either coke nuts or anthracite, depending on the method used. However, electro-furnaces would not be suitable in the main iron-producing areas of the USSR, which are short of electricity.

(d) Steel-making

During the period 1970 to 1980, the consumption of fuel and energy per ton of steel rose from 144 to 146 kg after falling to 138 in 1975. The total consumption of fuel by the steel-making sector is comparatively small — in 1980 it amounted to 13.0 mn tsf for the production of 89.1 mn tons of steel by the open-hearth method (compared with 12.7 mn tsf in 1972), consisting of 7.8 mn tsf of natural gas (7.0), 2.2 mn tsf of oil (4.1) and 3.0 mn tsf of coking gas and blast furnace gas (1.6).

Between 1960 and 1970, there was a substantial fall in the fuel rate from 175.5 kgsf/ton to 144, mainly because of the increasing use of natural gas instead of inferior fuels. Since 1970, the fuel rate has risen because few new open-hearth furnaces are being built now that the emphasis has switched to oxygen-converter furnaces, and consequently the extent of obsolescence among the remaining open-hearth furnaces is growing. In the Ukraine, however, the fuel rate is still continuing to fall, albeit slowly, from 166 kgsf in 1960 to 134 in 1970 and 132 in 1980.

There is a considerable variation in the fuel rates of different plants, from 62 to 280 kgsf/ton. This is because the plants were built at different times and employ technological processes of different periods. The metallurgical combines, i.e. plants with a full metallurgical cycle, tend to be more modern, and their large size permits them to make profitable use of the newest conversion processes. Fuel rates like 87 kgsf/ton for Zaporozhstal and 91 for Krivoi Rog are typical of the most modern plants, while the small steel-making plants in Eastern Siberia and the Far East have rates of 248-251 kgsf/ton.

The principal factors influencing fuel rates for steel-making are the size of the furnace; the productivity of the furnace; the extent of the use of natural gas; and the nature of the method of steel conversion.

Furnace Size. As with blast furnaces, it would be incorrect to think that the size of the furnace alone has a major influence on the level of fuel consumption, although the fuel rate falls dramatically the larger the furnace. In 1973, the average furnace with a floor area of less than 20 sq m required 316 kgsf per ton of steel, while a furnace of area more than 90 sq m needed only 120.

Furnace Productivity. When considering Soviet open-hearth furnaces from the point of view of fuel consumption, it is possible to divide them into three basic groups.

The first group consists of modern open-hearth shops equipped with furnaces of 200-900 tons capacity, working on high-calorie fuel in conjunction with oxygen. The fuel rate amounts to 80-160 kgsf/ton. The second group has open-hearth shops equipped with furnaces of 130-200 tons capacity using partially oxygen and, to a greater degree, compressed air, and the fuel rate varies between 160 and 210 kgsf/ton. The third group consists of small furnaces of 45-130 capacity, largely operating without the use of oxygen or compressed air, and fuel consumption generally exceeds 210 kgsf/ton.

During 1960 to 1970, the fuel rate fell as a result of furnaces in the third group being phased out, and the characteristics of steel production in the furnaces of the other two groups being improved. Because of the increasing share of plants of the first group in total smelting capacity, the productivity of open-hearth furnaces has grown rapidly in recent years. While in 1960, the average daily output of steel per square metre of furnace floor in Soviet open-hearth furnaces amounted to only 7.69 tons, by 1970 it had risen to 9.15, and by 1980 to 9.30 tons. The Ukraine has traditionally claimed a higher furnace productivity due to the importance of modern plants such as Zaporozhstal (14.10 tons) and Krivoi Rog (14.00 tons).

The Use of Natural Gas. The use of natural gas in open-hearth furnaces instead of a mixture of coking and blast-furnace gases gives a number of technical and economic advantages, principally that the high heat rate of natural gas allows it to be delivered to the furnace without being preheated in regenerators. Consequently, the construction of the furnace can be simplified.

According to calculations made by Gipromez, transferring the heating of an open-hearth furnace producing 500 tons of steel per shift to natural gas lowers the fuel consumption per ton of steel by 2-3 kgsf. Some plants have achieved much greater savings; when a large open-hearth furnace at Zaporozhstal was converted to natural gas, its productivity rose by 7.5-8.2%, and its fuel rate was reduced by 7-9% to only 91.9 kgsf/ton.

Table 4.10: Consumption of Natural Gas and Oxygen for Steel-making

	Production of Steel (mn tons)			Consumption in bn cu m of:	
	Total Output of Steel	Using Natural Gas	Using Oxygen	Natural Gas	Oxygen
1965	91.0	47.6	43.8	4.76	1.48
1970	115.9	64.8	71.4	5.49	2.15
1975	141.3	77.3	98.4	6.00	n.a.
1980	147.9	85.0	106.7	6.58	n.a.

In 1975, natural gas was employed at 285 open-hearth furnaces from an operating total of 360, and 82.2% of all open-hearth steel was produced in them. Of the furnaces employing gas, 67% used a mixture of gas and fuel oil, with the fuel oil fulfilling a carburisation function.

The use of fuel oil for steel-making declined during the 1970s with the elaboration of new methods of heating open-hearth furnaces by gas with self-carburisation properties, i.e. enriched with carbonaceous fractions obtained from the thermic decomposition of natural gas liquids. Table 4.11 compares the performance of furnaces fired with fuel oil, a gas-oil mixture and gas with self-carburisation additives. For the largest furnaces, savings of between 12.9 and 15.4 roubles per ton of standard fuel can be obtained by converting furnaces from fuel oil to gas.

Table 4.11: Fuel Rates of Open-hearth Furnaces by Type of Fuel

	Fuel Oil	Gas/Fuel Oil	Natural Gas
Furnace productivity	1	1.10	1.15
Fuel rate	1	0.95	0.80
Fuel rate in kgsf/ton by furnace capacity:			
50–70 tons	266	252	213
200 tons	242	230	194
400–500 tons	128	122	102
600–900 tons	105	102	84

Changes in the Nature of Steel Conversion. Considerable savings of primary fuel can be achieved by the use of oxygen-converter furnaces because their fuel requirements amount to only 5–10 kgsf/ton compared with 146 for open-hearth furnaces. However, the large amounts of electricity needed by oxygen-converters means that their overall fuel/energy requirements can be 200 kgsf/ton higher.

The advantage of oxygen-converters is that a large share of their energy requirements can be covered by secondary thermal energy produced by other sectors of the plant. Thus, in 1970, each ton of oxygen-converter steel required 1,150 kgsf of fuel (including that needed for iron-smelting and other processes), and secondary energy resources provided 440 kgsf (38%) of this. It is generally believed that fuel savings of 27% overall can be made if the oxygen-converter rather than the open-hearth conversion method is used.

There are other advantages stemming from the production of steel by the oxygen-converter method, in terms of lower costs. This is the main reason why the share of oxygen-converter steel is rising, although the USSR is still lagging behind many other nations in this respect.

Table 4.12: Output of Steel by Process (mn tons)

	1960	%	1970	%	1975	%	1980	%
Total	65.3	100	115.9	100	141.3	100	147.9	100
Open-hearth	55.1	84.4	84.1	72.6	91.5	64.8	89.1	60.2
Bessemer	1.9	2.9	1.2	1.0	1.1	0.8	0.8	0.5
Electro-steel	5.8	8.9	10.7	9.2	14.0	9.9	15.9	10.8
Oxygen-converter	2.5	3.8	19.9	17.2	34.8	24.6	42.2	28.5

Of the increase in steel output between 1970 and 1980, steel produced by the oxygen-converter process accounted for 69.7%, and electro-steel for 16.3% compared with only 14% for open-hearth steel. Consequently, the total consumption of primary fuel by the steel-making sector is likely to fall as the oxygen-converter and electro-steel processes become comparatively more important.

(e) The Steel-rolling Sector

There has been a comparatively small fall in the fuel rate of the steel-rolling sector, from 154 kgsf/ton in 1960 and 137.8 in 1970 to about 135 at the present time, because of the increase in the variety of finished products and the share of fuel-intensive thermally processed steels. For pipes, the fall has been even smaller, from 147 kgsf/ton in 1960 to 134.6 in 1970 and about 132 at present.

The principal types of fuel are natural gas, coking gas and blast furnace gas, with the proportion of natural gas increasing as the techno-logical level of the plant is raised. In 1980, steel-rolling plants used 6.66 mn tsf of natural gas, 4.45 mn tsf of coking gas and 3.14 mn tsf of blast furnace gas plus a small amount of (0.6–0.7 mn tsf) of fuel oil. Pipe-rolling plants used 2.61 mn tsf of natural gas and an insignificant amount of coking gas. In all, about 18 mn tsf of fuel was used by the sector, of which about 14.2 mn was used directly for steel-rolling and pipe manufacture.

In 1972, the sector used 14.75 mn tsf of fuel, including 12.73 mn for steel-rolling, 1.71 mn for pipes and 0.31 mn for the production of ferrous alloys. Over the period 1972 to 1980, total fuel consumption rose at an average annual rate of 2.5%, while that of natural gas in-creased from 6.23 mn tsf at 5.1% a year, and coking gas from 4.1 mn tsf at 1.0%.

Natural gas was burned in 199 of the USSR's 389 steel-rolling plants in 1975, but these tended to be the largest and most technologically advanced, accounting for the overwhelming share of rolled steel products. The fuel usage rate varies considerably from plant to plant, depending on the type of finished product and the technical level of the plant. The highest rates are found at plants concentrating on plate-rolling, for which the consumption of fuel is higher than for section-rolling. The lowest rates are experienced at those plants which have succeeded in utilising the largest share of their secondary energy resources, in particular the plants (representing 58% of the total in 1975) equipped with heat-exchangers. It has been shown that where the heat from waste gases can be captured, and used for preheating the furnace to 400°, 18% of fuel requirements can be saved, and 27% when a preheating of 600° is achieved.

In 1975 the fuel rate varied among plants from 65 to 230 kgsf/ton, and among products from 41 kgsf/ton for blooming in '900' mills to 61-94 kgsf/ton for section-rolling and 102 for sheet-rolling to over 300 kgsf/ton for some products.

The continuous casting of steel can provide useful fuel savings. The Russians claim to be the initiators of the process, but in 1980 only 12% of steel production was continuously cast while in Japan, which bought the licence for the process from the Soviet Union, the share reached 50%. It is believed that 1 mn tons of fuel a year could be saved by raising the share of continuous casting from 12% to 40%.

(f) The Energy Sector

Fuel requirements for the production of electricity and thermal energy by heat-and-power plants and industrial boilers belonging to the Ministry of Ferrous Metallurgy came to 24.3 mn tsf in 1972, or 15-16% of the industry's total fuel needs. About 75% of this fuel was gas of various types. By 1980, the usage of natural gas had declined to 7.1 mn tsf from 7.8 mn in 1972 while that of coking gas had risen from 3.3 to 3.4 mn, and the consumption of blast furnace gas had jumped from 7.2 to 9.0 mn tsf.

Practically all this energy is produced by 'centralised' sources, which have been considered in Chapter 3.

All the large iron and steel combines have a CHPP which provides all their electricity and most of their thermal energy, with the rest supplied by heat-exchangers. The smaller plants, especially the oxygen-converter and electro-steel plants and steel-rolling mills, produce their thermal energy on industrial boilers and receive electricity from the national grid. So while fuel consumption by the energy sector of the iron and steel industry has been growing very slowly in recent years, the amount of electricity drawn from the grid has grown rapidly, from 29.2 bn kWh (10% of total national output) in 1960 to 70.7 bn (9.5%) in 1970 and 120.4 bn kWh (9.3%) in 1980. Electricity usage rose at an average rate of 9.2% over 1960 to 1970, and by 5.5% a year over 1970 to 1980. The electricity-intensity of the iron and steel industry rose from 447 kWh per ton of crude steel in 1960 to 610 in 1970 and 814 kWh in 1980.

In 1973, the fuel rate for the generation of electricity on the ferrous metallurgy industry's 3,060 MW of CHPP's was 411.6 gsf/kWh, with the output of thermal energy requiring 179.1 kgsf/G-cal, and these rates are unlikely to have changed substantially since that year. These fuel rates are very high by Soviet standards, partly because the CHPPs are generally very old, operating with low pressures, and partly because their output of thermal energy is very low (48.3 mn G-cals in 1973). Iron and steel plants are finding it increasingly profitable to produce their heat on large boilers and obtain their power supplies from general-purpose base-load power stations.

Consumption of thermal energy rose from 55 mn G-cals in 1965 to 71 mn in 1970 and 85 mn in 1975. Iron and steel is by far the most successful sector in utilising waste heat, the volume of which rose from 13.3 mn G-cals in 1965 to 20.9 mn in 1970 and nearly 32 mn in 1975. In 1972, utilised waste heat accounted for 28% of the sector's output of thermal energy, 32% of its consumption and 42.4% of consumption by the plants at which the thermal energy was saved. At some plants, practically all the consumed thermal energy consisted of utilised waste heat; the Kommunarsk plant in the Ukraine, for example, captured 860,000 G-cals which covered 82% of its thermal energy requirements of 1.05 mn G-cals. In 1978, Zaporozhstal covered 90% of its needs, and Kramatorsk 80%. But the most successful Soviet plant in this respect is Cherepovets; in 1978 it produced 1.16 mn G-cals from heat exchangers, 0.68 mn from evaporative cooling systems and 1.00 mn from plants for the dry-quenching of coke. The dry-quenching method was first used at the Cherepovets plant, and a quenching plant can produce 25 tons/hour of steam, saving 10,000 tsf a year. During 1981 to 1985, four more of these plants are to be built.

However, Cherepovets is rather exceptional, and only 35% of the waste heat potential is realised by the iron and steel sector as a whole.

Future Fuel Consumption

The Tenth Five Year Plan called for the production of steel to grow from 141.3 to 168.5 mn tons over 1975 to 1980. In fact it reached only 147.9 mn tons after declining from a peak of 151.5 mn tons in 1978. The Eleventh Plan has called for the production of 168 mn tons of steel in 1985, and 117 mn tons of rolled steel, compared with 102.9 mn in 1980. However, the indications are that even these modest targets will not be reached, and an output of 160 mn tons of steel seems more likely – this implies an annual growth rate of 1.6%. The current and planned capital construction programme suggests that growth rates of no more than 1% a year are likely beyond 1985, yielding 168 mn tons in 1990 and 186 mn tons in 2000.

The rate of growth of pig-iron production is likely to be slightly lower than that of steel, in view of the increasing contribution made by scrap to the iron inputs of the steel-making plants. This will become more apparent during the late 1980s, when the share of steel produced in oxygen-converters will approach half the total steel output. During the 1970s, the input of scrap to oxygen-converters rose from 208 to 257 tons per 1,000 tons of produced steel (and to 262 tons in 1981) with a corresponding decrease in the required tonnage of pig-iron, and it is possible to surmise that the annual rate of growth of pig-iron output will fall from 1.6% over 1981 to 1985 to 0.5% during the last decade of the century.

It may be expected that the relationship between the production of steel and rolled steel products will continue to remain stable, implying the production of 130 mn tons of products per year at the end of the century.

Table 4.13: Forecast Production of Pig-iron, Steel and Rolled Steel Products (mn tons)

	Pig-iron	Crude Steel	Rolled Steel Products
1980	107.3	147.9	102.9
1985	116.2	160	111.4
1990	122	168	117
2000	128	186	130

According to the Eleventh Five Year Plan, the iron and steel sector must save 8 mn tsf over 1981 to 1985, principally by replacing open-hearth steel-smelting by the oxygen-converter method, by a more careful preparation of the blast-furnace burden, and the faster development of continuous casting.

As a result of measures designed to reduce the consumption of coke, it can be expected that the coke rate per ton of smelted iron will continue to fall. The intention to replace the small delapidated pre-war blast furnaces of the Urals and Ukraine with new furnaces of capacities 3,200 and 5,000 cu m, the piping of Tyumen and Orenburg gas in growing quantities to these furnaces where it will be used in conjunction with increased volumes of oxygen, and the improvement of the iron part of the burden through the increased use of pellets, as well as other technological measures, should allow the average coke rate of the

Table 4.14: Consumption of Coke by the Iron-smelting Sector

	Output of Pig-iron (mn tons)	Coke Rate (kg/ton*)	Consumption of Dry Coke (mn tons)
1980	107.3	532	57.1
1985	116.2	510	59.3
1990	122	489	56.7
2000	128	450	51.8

Note: * blast furnace iron only.

USSR to fall by the end of the century to 450 kg/ton, although this is still much higher than the rate currently enjoyed by Japan of about 420 kg/ton. Table 4.14 assumes that the coke rate will fall uniformly at 0.08% a year from the 532 kg of dry coke recorded in 1980, and that direct reduction smelting will be accounting for 5% of pig-iron output in 1990 and 10% in 2000.

As Table 4.14 suggests, coke consumption will probably continue to grow until 1985, when it will peak and then start to fall quite rapidly. It has been assumed that the annual decline in the coke rate will be uniform over the 20-year period; in fact it may be slower during the 1980s and faster in the 1990s as the growth of direct reduction enables the rate of scrapping of the oldest and most coke-inefficient blast furnaces to be speeded up.

The forecast of an average coke rate of 450 kg/ton in 2000 is based on the fact that this rate has already been achieved by some of the Soviet Union's most efficient plants, such as Cherepovets, and it neces-sarily implies that the technical conditions currently existing at Chere-povets will apply for the USSR as a whole. This suggests that the average consumption of natural gas per ton of smelted iron for the whole country will be 100 cu m compared with 84 in 1977 when 84.3% of pig-iron was smelted with the use of natural gas. This share will rise gradually until 1990, when most of the small furnaces will have been replaced by large, modern furnaces adapted to the use of gas. The consumption of gas by blast furnaces could rise from 10.8 bn cu m in 1980 to 11 bn in 1985, 11.2 bn in 1990 and 11.5 bn in 2000.

It has been suggested that fuel oil or coal dust could be more efficient than natural gas as fuel additives, and it is claimed that during the decade when the coke rate fell from 586 to 540 kg per ton, only 17.5 of the 46 kg decline could be attributed to the use of gas, and this figure may well have been higher if fuel oil had been used. However, the new domestic prices set for oil products in January 1982 make it

Table 4.15: Forecast Consumption of Fuel by the Iron-smelting Sector (mn tsf)

	For Iron-smelting			For Heating the Blast		Total
	Coke*	Natural Gas	Others	Natural Gas	Others	
1980	56.4	12.8	0.6	1.0	10.0	80.8
1985	58.6	13.0	0.3	5.0	6.9	83.8
1990	56.0	13.3	–	8.0	3.8	81.1
2000	51.1	13.6	–	11.8	–	76.5

Note: * at 6% moisture content.

extremely unlikely that the use of fuel oil in blast furnaces will rise above the 0.5 mn tons in 1980, and will probably decline when the Karaganda Metallurgical Plant, which accounts for well over half the 0.5 mn tons, is connected to the natural gas distribution network. It is reasonable to assume that the use of fuel oil will be phased out by 1990.

As the size of Soviet blast furnaces increases, leading to an increase in the average temperature of blasting, it may be that the fuel requirements for heating the blast will also increase. These consist mainly of blast furnace gas, but as the smelting of iron becomes more technologically advanced, the output of blast furnace gas will fall, and in any case should be used to replace the more valuable natural gas currently being squandered on meeting energy needs. Natural gas should be used to heat the blast, and the higher heat rate of natural gas compared with blast furnace gas may well offset the increase in the volume of fuel needed to heat the blast. It therefore seems reasonable to presume that fuel needs for heating the blast will change in direct relationship to the change in output of blast furnace iron, from 11 mn tsf in 1980 to 11.9 mn in 1985, and then stabilise at 11.8 mn tsf a year until the end of the century.

Consumption of fuel for steel-making has grown very slowly in recent years as a result of the rapid development of oxygen conversion, the increased use of natural gas (which now accounts for 60% of the fuel used by the sector) and other technical developments. Yet there are still considerable savings to be made because some plants get very much better results than the national average of 146 kg per ton. Over 1976 to 1979, open-hearth production at Cherepovets, for example, required only 90.5 kgsf/ton, although the small decline over the 1971 to 1975 period when the fuel rate averaged 91.9 kgsf/ton suggests that

Table 4.16: Forecast Fuel Consumption for Steel Conversion (mn tsf)

	Total Steel Output (mn tons)	Open-hearth Steel Output (mn tons)	Fuel Rate (kgsf/ton)	Fuel Consumption (mn tsf)
1980	147.9	89.1	146	13.0
1985	160	79	129	10.2
1990	168	68	114	7.8
2000	186	46	90	4.1

the physical limit is being approached. Some of the smaller plants burn up to 280 kgsf to make a ton of steel. In keeping with the assumptions made for the iron-smelting sector, it seems reasonable to take Cherepovets as a model for the country as a whole in 2000, and assume that fuel consumption for steel conversion in open-hearth furnaces will fall to 90 kgsf/ton, i.e. at an average annual rate of 2.5% over 1980 to 2000. Towards the end of the 1980s, natural gas will have completely replaced the small amounts of expensive oil and inefficient coking gas used in 1980. Natural gas has the important advantage that its consistent quality enables a regular rhythm of work to be achieved, thereby reducing costs and raising the quality of the steel.

It must be assumed that the shares of oxygen-conversion and electro-steel production will rise, and Soviet sources suggest that they will account for 75% of total Soviet steel output by the end of the century. Primary fuel consumption by oxygen-converter and electro-steel furnaces is practically negligible − 0.6 mn tsf for 58 mn tons of steel in 1980 − and this should amount to about 1.1 mn tsf in 2000.

Consumption of fuel by the steel-rolling and pipe manufacturing sector is not very great, amounting to only 10% of all fuel consumed by the industry. However, it has been rising at a faster rate than that of any other sector, and its importance is likely to increase.

A major problem in forecasting fuel consumption by this sector is that technological advances in equipment tend to result in a wider assortment of products and an improvement in their quality, rather than a reduction in fuel consumption. In 1971, the Magnitogorsk combine was acknowledged to possess the most modern steel-rolling mill in the USSR, but its fuel rates frequently exceeded those of the USSR as a whole. Thus, while the average Soviet blooming mill used 41 kgsf/ton, the No. 3 blooming mill at Magnitogorsk needed 47.

However, it is believed that considerable reductions in fuel consumption are possible. These will stem from measures designed to reduce the idling time and speed up the rate at which the steel passes

Table 4.17: Forecast Fuel Consumption for Steel-rolling and Pipe Manufacture

	Total Fuel Consumption	Natural Gas	Others
1980	18.0	9.3	8.7
1985	19.0	15	4
1990	20.0	20	–
2000	22.0	22	–

Table 4.18: Forecast Fuel Consumption for Coke Production

	Production of Coke (6% moisture content) (mn tons)	Fuel Needs for Coking (mn tsf)	Coking Coal Requirements (mn tons)
1980	88	9.9	121
1985	93	10.4	128
1990	93	10.4	128
2000	95	10.6	131

through the mills. It is reasonable to assume that these measures will no more than outweigh the tendency for the fuel rate to rise because of the greater share of plates in the product mix, and that overall fuel consumption will increase at the same rate as the output of rolled products, i.e. by 1.2% a year. As with steel-making, natural gas (already the most important fuel) will become dominant because of its consistently good thermal qualities.

For coke production, 112 kgsf/ton of coke were required in 1980. The coking process in Soviet metallurgical plants is comparatively efficient, and further improvements achieved by modernisation may be offset by the declining quality of coking coal, at least until 1990 when new coking coal mines being created at the Kuzbass on the basis of high-quality coking coal deposits come on stream. It is a fair assumption that the 1980 fuel rate will pertain until the end of the century, giving a fuel requirement of 10.6 mn tsf in 2000.

In the past, some 80% of produced coke has been used by metallurgical plants, with the rest going to other industries requiring coke, such as engineering and metalworking, non-ferrous metallurgy and chemicals, and small amounts have been used by factories which normally burn anthracite but have been unable to obtain it. But while the consumption of coke by these other sectors will continue to rise beyond the end of the century by perhaps 2% a year, demand by the ferrous metallurgy industry will begin to decline after 1985, resulting in a very slow increase in coke requirements after that year, to 95 mn tons in 2000. Consequently, the demand for coal by the coking sector will also grow very slowly, from 128 mn tons in 1985 to 131 mn in 2000; this assumes that the coal/coke conversion ratio will remain at the current 1.375 to 1.

Very little has been said on the subject of the energy-producing sector of the metallurgical industry. This is because practically all the fuel consumed by this sector (25.1 mn tsf in 1980) was used by in-house heat-and-power plants and industrial boilers which have already been considered in Chapter 2. In the future, strenuous efforts will be made to replace oil and natural gas by blast furnace gas and coking gas at the combines with full metallurgical cycles, although individual steel conversion plants and rolling mills must obviously use primary fuel.

The demand for electricity and thermal energy will grow rapidly because of the increasing importance of oxygen-converter and electro-steel plants, the direct reduction of iron and new steel treatment processes. This will enable larger and more efficient boilers and CHPPs to be installed, eventually leading to a considerable fall in the fuel rate for the sector.

It can be assumed that the output of iron ore, and hence concentrates, will grow at a rate similar to that of pig-iron. If the 1980 fuel rate of 50 kgsf/ton of ore for ore mining and dressing is maintained, then the sector will need 13.3 mn tsf in 1985, 13.9 mn in 1990 and 14.6 mn in 2000 compared with 12.2 mn tsf in 1980.

For the iron and steel industry as a whole, a reasonable forecast of fuel requirements suggests that these will rise from 175 mn tsf in 1980

Table 4.19: Forecast Consumption of Fuel by the Iron and Steel Industry (mn tsf)

	1980	1985	1990	2000
Ore mining and dressing	12.2	13.3	13.9	14.6
Coke production	9.9	10.4	10.4	10.6
Iron-smelting	80.8	83.8	81.1	76.5
Steel-making	13.0	10.2	7.8	4.1
Steel-rolling and pipe manufacture	18.0	19.0	20.0	22.0
Energy needs	25.1	26.0	26.2	25.1
Others	16.0	17.3	18.2	20.1
Total	175.0	180.0	177.6	173.0

to about 180 mn in 1985, but will then stabilise at this level before falling slightly to 173 mn tsf at the end of the century.

The expenditure of fuel by type will depend partly on the volume of blast furnace gas and coking gas produced by the industry. In 1970, the smelting of 85.9 mn tons of iron produced 24.4 mn tsf of blast furnace gas at an average rate of 284 kgsf/ton, and in 1980 the respective figures were 107.3 mn tons, 26.3 mn tsf and 245 kgsf/ton. As the blast furnace process becomes more technologically advanced, the output of gas per ton of iron will continue to fall. If it does so at the same rate as during the period 1970 to 1980, i.e. by 1.5% a year, then the gas factor will amount to 227 kgsf/ton in 1985, 211 in 1990 and 181 kgsf/ton in 2000. Therefore the total volume of production of blast furnace gas will be 26.4 mn tsf in 1985, 25.7 mn in 1990 and 23.2 mn in 2000.

A similar forecast can be made for the output of coking gas, although a complication is that coking gas contains valuable inputs for the chemical industry, and the iron and steel industry has traditionally used only 90% of the available gas. In 1970, 75.4 mn tons of coke were produced, yielding 17.7 mn tsf of coking gas, at an average rate of 234 kgsf/ton, and in 1980 the respective figures rose to 88 mn tons, 19.7 mn tsf and 224 kgsf/ton. However, it seems unlikely that the gas factor will fall much further, and it can be estimated that the production of coking gas will grow to 21 mn tsf in 1985 and that it will stabilise at this level until the end of the century. However, some of this gas will be used by sectors other than iron and steel, such as nitrogenous fertilisers at the new plant under construction at the Altai coking plant.

It can be surmised that the share of natural gas in total fuel consumption by the iron and steel industry will rise from 26.6% in 1980 to 38.3% in 2000, mainly at the expense of oil and coal.

Table 4.20: Forecast Demand for Fuel by Type (mn tsf)

	1980	1985	1990	2000
Coke (including fines and koksik)	66.1	68.8	66.6	62.5
Blast furnace gas	26.3	26.4	25.7	23.2
Coking gas	17.7	18.8	19.0	19.0
Natural gas	46.6	54.0	60.3	66.3
Oil	10.3	7.0	4.0	2.0
Coal	8.0	5.0	2.0	–
Total	175.0	180.0	177.6	173.0

5 THE CONSTRUCTION MATERIALS INDUSTRY

Every year, some 350–400 new large factories are put into operation as well as thousands of smaller ones, and existing plants are reconstructed and extended. In addition, two million new dwellings are built as well as schools, hospitals, shops, administrative buildings, etc. for new towns or new suburbs of existing towns.

During the immediate post-war years, the policy was to build as many factories and houses as possible with the limited available materials. Consequently, dwellings were small and badly built, although their average size has been gradually increasing from 42.3 sq m of 'useful' floor space in 1960 to 52.5 in 1980.

Table 5.1: Construction of Dwellings in the USSR

	Number of Dwellings ('000)	Floor Area (mn sq m)	Average Size of Dwelling (sq m)
1960	2,591	109.6	42.3
1970	2,266	106.0	46.8
1975	2,228	109.9	49.3
1980	2,050	107.7	52.5

This massive construction programme has necessitated the development of a large cement industry, and as long ago as 1964 the USSR become the world's largest producer of cement. The output of bricks, on the other hand, has never been significant by world standards, and has been declining by 2.5% a year from the peak of 47.2 bn in 1975; this is because nearly all construction work by state organisations depends on the use of precast sections for the erection of blocks of flats and other buildings. Bricks are used basically for the construction of homes by individuals using state credit or by collective farms. Since 1960, the share of dwellings built by state organisations has steadily grown; from 51% of the floor area of newly built homes to 72% in 1970 and over 80% by 1980.

It can be confidently predicted that the continuing housing shortage in Soviet cities will mean that the housing construction rate will be maintained at over two million units a year. The future volume of non-residential construction work is more difficult to predict. On the one

Table 5.2: Output of Cement (mn tons)

	1960	1970	1975	1980	1985 Plan
USSR total	45.5	95.2	122.1	125.0	140–142
RSFSR	29.5	57.7	73.1		
Ukraine	8.1	17.3	22.5		
Moldavia	–	0.8	1.2		
Baltic	1.0	2.9	5.2		
Belorussia	0.7	1.9	2.2		
Caucasus	2.6	3.6	4.9		
Central Asia	1.5	5.4	6.2		
Kazakhstan	2.2	5.6	6.8		

hand, the current policy of extending the capacity of existing industrial plants rather than building new ones should reduce the demand for building materials. On the other hand, any acceleration of the policy of developing uninhabited regions east of the Urals requires whole new economic and social infrastructures to be provided, creating a rise in demand for construction materials.

The production of cement has stabilised at about 120–130 mn tons a year, and is likely to grow very slowly to the end of the century. The future demand for cement is difficult to predict. It involves not merely the need to provide homes and social facilities for the natural increase in population (which, by itself, requires 700,000 new dwellings each year) and eliminating the pressures caused by migration from the countryside to the cities, but also the extent of regional population shifts, brought about mainly by the need to develop Siberia. If the present rate of housing construction is maintained, the entire population should be living in a post-war house by the end of the century. However by this time, the demolition of the badly-built houses dating from before 1960 will be taking place, and it seems reasonable to assume that 2 mn new dwellings will be built each year until into the next century.

Cement requirements for the construction of industrial, commercial and infrastructural buildings depends not only on the economic growth rate, but also on the extent of industrial location. The building of completely new factories in new regions requires far more cement than the enlargement of existing factories, and it also means that new roads need to be built (generally from concrete in the Soviet Union) as well as offices and public buildings.

Although there was hardly any growth in output by the cement industry during 1975 to 1980, a rise of 22.8% in Soviet gross domestic product was achieved. On this basis, it can be assumed that the sort of growth in GDP that may be anticipated up to 2000 will require an annual cement output of 128 mn tons in 1985, 131 mn tons in 1990 and 137 mn tons in 2000. The Eleventh Five Year Plan target of 140 to 142 mn tons in 1985 seems both optimistic and unnecessary given the new trends in the nature of construction work.

One of the principal results of improvements in construction technology has been the rapid growth in the production of precast concrete sections. This is essentially a post-war development, with production of one million cubic metres in 1950 having increased one-hundred fold by 1980. It is unlikely that the output of concrete sections will grow much beyond current levels before the end of the century, in view of the probable stabilisation in the rate of house-building and cement production. In fact, it may well decline in connection with the recent successful experiments in the on-site continuous pouring of cement.

Table 5.3: Production of Pre-cast Concrete Sections (mn cu m)

Year	Output
1960	30.2
1970	84.6
1975	114.2
1980	122.2

The production of bricks will continue to decline, because the principal customers for bricks are individuals and collective farms for house-building, and the share of these dwellings has declined from 36.6% of new houses in 1960-5 to 18.0% in 1975-80. Bricks are used more infrequently by state organisations for the construction of housing, public buildings and industrial enterprises. It seems fair to assume that the output of bricks will continue to decline by 2.5% a year from 41.8 bn in 1980 to 36 bn in 1985, 32 bn in 1990 and 25 bn in 2000.

The rate of growth of output of glass has been low compared with those of other construction materials. During 1950 to 1960, it was 6.7% a year, 4.6% a year during 1960 to 1970 and 3.1% over 1970 to 1975, while the period 1975 to 1980 saw a decline of 1.9% a year. The relationship between the production of glass and that of cement is declining; this is because a substantial amount of cement is used for the construction of items which do not require glass such as dams, bridges, roads, etc. In 1960, some 3.2 sq m of glass were produced at the same time as 1 ton of cement, but in 1970 and 1980 the figures were respectively 2.4 sq m and 1.95 sq m. As with other construction materials, the level of glass production can be expected to stabilise at that of the last few years, i.e 250 mn sq m a year.

Consumption of Fuel by the Construction Materials Industry

Fuel is a very important element in the production costs of the construction materials industry, amounting to 7.9% of total costs with energy accounting for a further 4.6%, and for the cement industry the respective figures were 24.9% and 13.1%.

The most notable features of fuel consumption during the last 20 years have been the dramatic rise in the share of natural gas, from 3% in 1959 to 31% in 1980, an equally dramatic fall in the share of coal from 57% to 21%, and the continuing heavy consumption of oil products, mainly residual fuel oil.

(a) Cement

Fuel is used primarily for the production of clinker in kilns, and accounts for 37-38% of its total production cost. As clinker is the principal component of cement, the share of fuel in the total production cost of cement comes to almost 25%.

In 1980, 225 kgsf were required for the kilning of each ton of clinker. This was only 81% of the fuel rate of 1960, but it must be noted here that the fall in the fuel rate has been slower than for power stations and blast furnaces.

Table 5.4: Consumption of Fuel for the Production of Clinker

	Fuel Rate (kgsf/ton)	Fuel Consumption (mn tsf)	Estimated Output of Clinker (mn tsf)
1960	277	10.1	36.4
1970	237	18.1	76.2
1975	228	22.3	97.7
1980	225	22.5	100.0
1985 Plan	216	24.5	113.6
1990 Plan	210		

Of the two national cement-producing organisations, Glavzapadtsement and Glavvostoktsement, the latter is the more fuel-efficient, and is improving its fuel rate more rapidly. In 1980, its plants needed an average 220.8 kgsf/ton (98.1% of the national average) while in 1975 its fuel rate was slightly higher than the national average at about 230 kgsf/ton. The Eleventh Five Year Plan expects Glavvostoktsement to reduce its fuel rate by 2.7% to 214.8 kgsf/ton, due mainly to the greater use of the dry method of production. This will be introduced at major plants like Karaganda.

There is a large variation in the fuel rates of cement plants, with some of the most modern and best managed plants achieving extremely low rates. In 1981, the USSR's most fuel-efficient plant, Novospassk, required only 139.3 kgsf/ton of clinker, largely thanks to its adoption of the dry method of clinker production. On the other hand, 32 ageing and obsolete furnaces using the wet method have an average fuel rate of 331 kgsf; these are to be scrapped during 1981 to 1985.

There are four main reasons why the fuel rate has fallen in recent years: the change in the type of fuel; the increasing size and improved technology of rotary furnaces; the changing method of clinker production; and the increasing size of cement plants.

Change in the Type of Fuel. Until 1960, coal was the predominant type of fuel used by cement plants, but since then it has rapidly been replaced by natural gas and, to a lesser extent, oil. More than 70% of all rotary furnaces now operate on gas. The consumption of gas for the production of clinker has risen from 6.8 bn cu m in 1965 to 9.1 bn in 1970, 11.1 bn in 1975 and about 13 bn cu m in 1980.

Table 5.5: Type of Fuel Used for the Production of Clinker (%)

	1960	1972	1975
Coal	52.8	20.2	24.0
Natural gas	38.0	56.7	60.5
Oil	7.8	22.0	14.4
Others	1.4	1.1	1.1

Gas is replacing coal for several reasons. First, less fuel is needed – it has been calculated that using gas cuts the fuel rate per ton of clinker by 5% to 7%. Secondly, it has proved a better fuel than coal, in that its quality is more consistent, enabling a regular rhythm of work to be achieved and because it has a higher heat content. Thirdly, a number of technical advantages accrue to the cement industry from the use of gas, mainly involving the use of cheaper and simpler equipment. These are said to reduce capital construction costs by 10%.

Savings accruing from the use of gas rather than coal vary between 4.5 and 36.2 roubles/tsf depending on the location of the cement plant. Fuel oil is practically as efficient as gas, with savings of only 0.5 to 4 R/tsf in favour of gas, and furnace productivity and cement quality unchanged, although labour costs rise by 3% when oil is used.

In view of the large advantages of using gas, it can be assumed that all those plants now using coal or oil will eventually transfer to it. This is especially true of those in the Kuzbass (Chernorechensk, Yashkino, Topki and Novokuznetsk), which should eventually receive gas from the Nizhnevartovsk-Tomsk-Novokuznetsk gas pipeline. Those plants which will not be in a position to receive gas for some time, or are located close to large oil refineries, are being transferred to oil. The Akmyane plant in Lithuania, for example, is situated 30 km from the Mazheikiai oil refinery, destined to become one of the largest in the Soviet Union, and it is much cheaper to use fuel oil from Mazheikiai than natural gas piped from Western Siberia.

Very few plants use fuel other than oil, gas or coal. One is the Punana Kunda in Estonia which uses oil-shale, and because of its very advanced technical characteristics the plant has achieved a most respectable fuel rate of 218 kgsf/ton.

Method of Production of Clinker. There are two basic methods of production of clinker, the 'wet' and the 'dry' methods. The choice of method depends on the humidity of the raw materials and has an important influence on the fuel rate. The production of a ton of clinker by the wet method requires about 300 kg of coal or 200 cu m of natural gas, while the dry method requires only 170 kg of coal or 110 cu m of gas. In 1980, 240 kgsf were needed for the wet method and only 180 for the dry method.

For modern furnaces, the difference in the fuel rate between the wet and dry method is much greater. Table 5.6 compares the fuel rate of a 5 X 195 metre furnace using the wet method and a 5 X 75 metre furnace with a cyclonic heat exchanger using the dry method.

The growth of output by the dry method has been painfully slow (even before the Second World War the Spassk plant had furnaces using the dry process) because of a continuing failure to reduce the high level of humidity of the raw materials. It has even been the case that some plants equipped to work by the dry method have been forced to use the wet process. The 'Giprotsement' Institute has estimated that, while a new 150 metre wet furnace needs 204 kgsf/ton of clinker, a 60 metre dry furnace requires only 161-173 kgsf/ton. The importance

Table 5.6: Fuel Rates of Cement Kilns (kgsf/ton of Clinker)

	Gas	Fuel Oil	Coal
Wet method – operating furnace	230	234	244
new furnace	221	224	244
Dry method – operating furnace	121	124	129
new furnace	107	109	129

(from a fuel consumption standpoint) of the dry method can be readily appreciated, yet production of cement by the dry process has grown from 6.9 mn tons in 1962 to 12.8 mn in 1970 and only 18.3 mn tons (14.6% of the total) in 1980. All prospective plans envisage a gradual change to full production by the dry method, but the Eleventh Five Year Plan foresees the production of only 25.6 mn tons in 1985, or 18% of total output, and a target of 22% has been set for 1990. During the period 1980 to 1990, it is planned to introduce new capacity for the production of 10 mn tons a year of cement by the dry process; this will be achieved by the reconstruction of existing dry plants at Katav-Ivanovo, Kuznetsk, Slantsevsk, Lipetsk, Bezmein and Pervomaisk, and by the conversion of wet furnaces at Karadag, Brotsevsk and Ararat.

Cement industry economists appear satisfied with the technical level of the wet method in the Soviet Union, although it is necessary to maintain efforts to lower the humidity of slurry by making greater use of liquifiers and more effective heat exchange equipment. The technical level of the dry method, on the other hand, lags slightly behind world standards, and these technological shortcomings seem to be mainly responsible for the slow development of dry kilning.

The failure to meet plan targets for the installation of dry furnaces means that some of the savings expected from the greater use of natural gas are being lost. A new wet furnace of 185 metres in length should give savings of 11.6 roubles per tsf (in Khabarovsk) to 22.3 R/tsf (in Turkmenia) when gas is used rather than coal, and savings of 1.1-1.8 R/tsf when gas is replacing fuel oil. But for a 75-metre dry furnace, the savings rise to 24.9-36.2 R/tsf and 3.4-4.0 R/tsf when coal and oil are replaced by gas.

The Increasing Size of Plants. Larger cement plants make it more economical to lay gas pipelines to those plants still using coal or oil, and enable more efficient fuel utilisation systems to be employed. Table 5.7 shows the relationship between plant size and fuel rate in 1974.

Table 5.7: Size of Plants, Volume of Output and Consumption of Fuel in 1974

Size of Plant ('000 tons per year)	Number of Plants	Share of Output (%)	Fuel Consumption (kgsf/ton)
Less than 200	8	0.8	341
201–500	5	1.6	250
501–1,000	24	16.8	248
1,001–1,500	19	22.3	210
1,501–2,000	11	18.1	227
More than 2,000	16	40.5	228
All plants	83	100	230

The larger plants have slightly higher fuel rates because they are dominated by large new furnaces which are still being run-in. The average size of a Soviet cement plant has risen from 848,000 tons/year in 1965 to 1.4 mn in 1980. The optimal size is disputed, although the director of Bryansk Cement Plant believes that 2.5 mn tons/year is a good figure, and long-term forecasts have indicated that 50% of plants will be producing more than 1.8 mn tons/year compared with 24% in 1973.

The Use of Alternatives to Clinker. Large amounts of fuel can be saved by the more widespread use of slag from iron and steel plants and other active mineral additives, and of by-products and waste from other industries. One ton of fuel can be saved for every 8.3 tons of cement produced with clinker mixed with industrial waste products.

Particularly large fuel savings accrue from the manufacture of slag-based Portland cement, although its output declined during the period 1977 to 1981 from 35.4 mn tons (28% of total cement output) to 31.2 mn tons (25%). This is said to be due to the heavy cost of transporting the slag over sometimes huge distances; in 1981, for example, the Ust-Kamenogorsk plant imported 271,500 tons of slag over a distance of 2,029 km from its supplier in the Urals. Table 5.8 shows the sort of fuel savings that can be achieved by producing slag-based Portland cement (mark 400) compared with that using other mineral additives.

Although waste industrial products are of inferior quality, their widespread availability allows transport costs to be reduced, making their use economical. A favourite waste is ash from coal-burning power stations and the provision of dry ash to cement plants has been organised by the Burshtyn, Zmievsk, Ladizhinsk and Kurakhovsk power

Table 5.8: Fuel Rates by Type of Cement, 1980

Plant	Fuel Rate (kgsf/ton of cement)		Electricity Needs (kWh/ton)	
	Conventional Portland	Slag-based	Conventional Portland	Slag-based
Staro-Oskol	201.6	140.0	70.4	57.8
'Mikhailovtsement'	179.0	145.0	105.2	92.0
'Glinozem'	187.1	94.2	88.2	66.9
Zhigulevsk	187.1	120.3	79.5	56.3
Zdolbunovsk	193.1	116.7	57.8	55.8
Kemenets-Podolskii	190.0	145.0	91.5	84.9
Chimkent	174.5	120.6	77.1	70.2
Balakleya	188.6	114.6	78.1	63.3

stations in the Ukraine, and stations at Vorkuta, Krasnoyarsk, Slantsy (ash from oil-shale) Ryazan and Frunze. This has been used together with, or as a substitute for, slag at the Kamenets-Podolskii, Olshansk, Vorkuta, Krasnoyarsk, Gornozavodsk, Slantsy, Amvrosievsk, Balakleya and Kant plants, and the 'Mikhailovtsement' Association.

During 1981 to 1985, ash from the Syzran combined heat-and-power plant is to be made available to the Zhigulevsk combine and ash from the Gusino-Ozersk power station will be delivered to the Timlyuisk plant. Substitutes like ash should become progressively more important throughout the 1980s as it is estimated that additional potential reserves of slag are limited to only 4.9 mn tons a year, all of it from iron and steel plants except for 1.1 mn tons a year from the Novodzhambul phosphor plant in Central Asia. The cement industry takes 80% of all available slag, and it can thus expect to obtain a further 4 mn tons a year when this is organised. It should permit a further 8 to 8.5 mn tons of cement to be produced, depending on the mix of pure clinker and slag, bringing the total output of slag-based Portland cement to 40 mn tons a year by 1985. It should enable savings of 0.4–0.45 mn tons of fuel and 84–85 mn kWh of electricity to be made annually.

The Strategy for Fuel Rate Reduction. During 1981 and 1982, plans for lowering the average fuel rate of cement plants were not fulfilled. The basic reasons for this were low rates of furnace usage at some plants, with the worst culprits being the Staro-Oskolsk (Central Chernozem region) and Checheno-Ingush (North Caucasus) cement plants, and an unduly high slurry humidity level. In fact the average humidity index actually rose by 0.2% for the Glavzapadtsement organisation (which administers cement plants in the western part of the RSFSR) in 1981 instead of falling as planned. At the Bryansk plant, furnace utilisation suffered from the employment of poor quality chains which tended to break within two weeks of being hung.

However, steps have been taken which should lead to a reduction in the fuel rate in 1983 – these include an acceleration in the speed at which furnaces revolve at the Krichev (Belorussia), Balakleya (Ukraine) and Krasnoyarsk plants, and the nationwide introduction of improved types of oil burners at those plants using fuel oil.

But according to Yu.V. Kazanskii, the director of the NIItsement Institute, the most fruitful path to cutting fuel rates involves the lowering of the slurry humidity factor and the institute has elaborated a programme for reducing humidity at wet method plants by:

(a) Employing new, more effective, models of devices to thin out (and hence dry out) slurry before it enters the furnace. They will be installed at 43 plants during the 1981 to 1985 plan period.

(b) Preparations for the transfer of wet plants to a semi-dry regime by carrying out the press-filtration of slurry in 40 furnaces at 12 plants.

(c) The wider use of hydro-locks in slurry pumps – this is particularly necessary at the Belgorod plant.

The application of these measures is regarded as a matter of some urgency, because humidity control at many plants has been very poor. In some cases, water has even accumulated in the cold chambers of the furnaces after passing through the pipes with the slurry, and much heat (and hence fuel) is wasted on its evaporation.

Another necessary development is the installation of more heat exchangers, especially those designed to capture heat from furnace housings, on 23 furnaces at eleven plants; this will save 30,000 tsf a year. In the overall heat balance of a cement plant, heat losses from the hot part of a furnace have been reduced to a less significant level, accounting for 15% of all heat losses, although substantial fuel savings can still be made, as demonstrated by the experience of the Chimkent, Kant, Semipalatinsk, Savinsk and Topki plants.

Future Consumption of Fuel. Each ton of cement requires an average 0.77 tons of clinker, and assuming that this relationship is maintained, then future output of clinker can be anticipated at 98.6 mn tons in

1985, 101 mn in 1990 and 105.5 mn tons in 2000.

If it is assumed that the current pace of re-equipment of the cement industry is maintained, then by 1990 all wet furnaces of less than 118 metres in length will have been scrapped. New wet furnaces installed during the early 1970s have fuel rate norms of 222 kgsf/ton, although some of the best plants such as 'Bolshevik' (209 kgsf/ton) have achieved much better results. An average rate of 210 kgsf/ton in 2000 can be assumed because technological progress during 1980–2000 will have some impact on the norms for the new 170 and 185-metre furnaces which will account for most of the new capacity installed during the period. If it is assumed that the fuel rate falls at a regular rate over 1980–2000, then total fuel consumption can be estimated as shown in Table 5.9. By 1990, natural gas should account for all the fuel consumed by Soviet clinker kilns.

The production of cement from clinker and other materials also requires a small amount of fuel, varying between 20 and 30 kgsf/ton of cement in 1970. Taking 25 kgsf/ton as an average, and assuming no change in this rate, then the production of cement will require 3.2 mn tons in 1985, 3.3 in 1990 and 3.4 mn tons in 2000. This brings the total fuel consumption by the industry to 24.9 mn tsf in 1985, 24.7 mn in 1990 and 23.8 mn tsf in 2000.

Table 5.9: Forecast Fuel Consumption for the Production of Clinker

	1985*	1990*	2000
Production of clinker (mn tons)	98.6	101	105.5
Dry method	17.7	22.2	45.0
Wet method	80.9	78.8	60.5
Fuel rate (kgsf/ton)	220	212	193
Dry method	177	174	170
Wet method	230	223	210
Consumption of fuel (mn tsf)	21.7	21.4	20.4
Dry method	3.1	3.9	7.7
Wet method	18.6	17.5	12.7

Note: * Data for 1985 and 1990 are derived from my forecasts rather than from official plan targets, which by 1982 were looking increasingly unattainable.

(b) Precast Concrete

Plants making precast concrete sections need fuel primarily for producing steam which is used for technological, as opposed to energy, purposes. These include the warming-up of sections, acceleration of the hardening process and the preheating of materials in winter. Thermal energy is also used for the heating, hot water supply and ventilation of the factories and other non-production processes.

The most important fuel is natural gas. Some 1.4 bn cu m were used for what are described as 'construction sections' in 1965, with consumption rising to 2.1 bn in 1970, 2.8 bn in 1975 and about 2.9 bn cu m in 1980.

In 1970, the fuel rate per cubic metre of concrete amounted to 45 kgsf, varying between 30 and 60. If this rate is maintained, then it can be calculated that the sector will require 5.5 mn tsf a year between 1980 and 2000. This will consist largely of fuel oil and natural gas, with coal being used in the concrete plants of Eastern Siberia and the Far East.

(c) Glass

An important feature of the glass industry is that it can only use gaseous fuels. In the past, glass factories have had to construct special equipment for the transformation of oil and coal into gas which then has to be processed by regenerators so as to bring its heat rate up to a sufficiently high level.

During the course of production of gas from solid and liquid fuels, large amounts of thermal energy are lost. It is therefore not surprising that the transfer of glass plants to natural gas has brought immense advantages. The fuel rate has been considerably reduced. In 1975, it was estimated that only 600 kgsf of natural gas were needed per ton of glass while the necessary volume of oil was 625 kgsf, and coal 854 kgsf where a 250-sq m furnace was employed. What is notable about these figures is the dramatic improvement since 1965 in the fuel rate where coal is used; in that year 655 kgsf of oil and 1,320 kgsf of coal were needed, but it is clear that gas still has a big competitive edge over other fuels. Table 5.10 shows the effects of conversion to natural gas on the fuel rates of some factories.

Table 5.10: Fuel Rates by Glass Plants Before and After Conversion to Natural Gas (kgsf/ton)

Factory	Fuel before Conversion	Before	After
Lisichansk	coal	816	462
'Avtosteklo'	coal	741	502
'Proletarii'	coal	625	601
'Oktyabrskii Revolyutsiya'	coal	738	503
Gomel	peat	1,028	548
Konstantinovsk	coal	405	330

The average fuel saving on conversion to natural gas is about 35-40%, ranging from 2-6.1% when gas replaces oil to 44-63% where gas produced from coal is replaced, and these savings are valued at 23-24 roubles/tsf for oil replacement and 47.7-60.8 R/tsf where coal gas is replaced. Glass production costs are reduced by 5%, or 18 roubles per thousand cubic metres of gas.

In 1965, when 1.8 bn cu m of gas were used, amounting to 69.7% of total fuel consumption by the sector, the fuel rate was about 16 kgsf per square metre of glass. By 1975, gas consumption had risen to 3 bn cu m, and it was used for the production of 60% of all glass and 70% of sheet glass at a rate of 14 kgsf per sq m. This rate is likely to have fallen further given the technological improvements in the glass industry since 1975. In the Ukraine, the fuel rate for the production of sheet glass fell from 559.1 kgsf/ton to 545.5 during the three years 1975 to 1978.

Conversion to gas is continuing, because it not only leads to lower fuel costs, but also to better glass (it has a more consistent texture) and to a higher furnace productivity. The average gas-fired furnace can produce 14-19% more glass when gas is used in preference to other fuels.

(d) Bricks

The conversion of ring furnaces to natural gas from coal reduces the length of the kilning cycle by 20-25%, and lowers the fuel rate by 10-20%. The furnace productivity is raised by 30% and labour productivity by 7-12%. The consumption of natural gas for the production of bricks rose from 1.0 bn cu m in 1965 to 1.4 bn in 1970, 1.9 bn in 1975 and 2.0 bn in 1980.

The fuel rate for the production of bricks in the Ukraine declined from 236 kgsf per 1,000 bricks in 1971 to 225.3 in 1975 and 224.2 in 1978. If the same rate applied throughout the USSR as a whole, then the production of 44.68 bn bricks will have required 10.02 mn tsf in 1978 compared with 10.64 mn tsf for the production of 47.21 bn in 1975.

The manufacture of other construction materials, such as ceramic items, linoleum, etc., required 2.7 bn cu m of gas in 1965, 3.5 bn in 1970, 4.8 bn in 1975 and 5.2 bn in 1980.

Summary

In 1972, fuel to the value of 1,391 mn roubles was used by the construction materials industry, including 334 mn for cement, 170 mn for precast concrete, 271 mn for wall materials including bricks and 617 mn roubles for other materials. Oil accounted for 45.6% of the total cost of fuel, coal 27.2%, gas 26.0% and peat and shale 1.2%. The glass and porcelain industry used a further 118.2 mn roubles worth of fuel with oil (51.7% of the total) and gas (43.5%) being the most important fuels and coal (4.1%) and peat and shale (0.8%) being of minor significance.

The construction materials sector used 95 mn G-cals of thermal energy in 1975 compared with 68 mn in 1970 and 46 mn in 1965. This was mainly produced by large industrial boilers, which have been considered in Chapter 3. Only 2% of the available waste heat at construction materials plants was utilised in 1975, in spite of the large potential. Some plants, however, are making an effort in this respect. The Anzhero-Sudzhensk Glass Plant uses 0.5 tons of fuel oil per ton of glass, and in 1980 it installed a heat exchanger to capture the heat from gas expelled at a temperature of $600°C$ by its No. 1 furnace. The heat is used for preheating air blown into the furnace. Consequently, 3,500 tons of fuel oil were saved in 1981, and the fuel rate per ton of glass was reduced by 100 kg compared with 1976.

Given the assumptions concerning future growth rates of the construction industry, it can be estimated that its fuel consumption will grow very slowly from 96 mn tsf in 1980 to 98 mn in 1990 and 100 mn tsf in 2000.

Table 5.11: Construction Materials Industry* — Estimated Future Fuel Consumption (mn tsf)

	1980	1985	1990	2000
Gas	30	35	41	58
Oil	45	45	40	30
Coal	20	17	17	12
Others	1	1	1	—
Total	96	98	99	100

Note: * including glass and porcelain.

6 THE CHEMICAL INDUSTRY

In complete contrast to the iron and steel and electricity industries, the chemical industry is highly heterogeneous with more than 4,500 distinct products being manufactured in the USSR. It also differs from other industries in that fuels are consumed primarily as raw materials.

Compared with other industrialised countries the USSR has a small chemical industry in spite of rapid development in recent years. In 1965, the chemical and petrochemical industries accounted for only 4.7% of total industrial output, although by 1980 this share had risen to 7.0%. There are two main reasons for this late development. First, there has been a tendency to rely on traditional materials such as steel and wood rather than develop new alternatives such as plastics. Secondly, some sectors of the chemical and petrochemical industry involve highly complex and sophisticated technological processes, and it is only recently that their development in the Soviet Union has begun to take place.

The sectors requiring the largest inputs of oil and gas are: ammonia, chemical fibres, synthetic resins and plastics, varnish and paints, synthetic dyes, detergents and soaps (which are organised under the Ministry of the Chemical Industry), and synthetic rubber, basic organic synthesis products and carbon black (under the Ministry of Petrochemicals). These sectors will be considered individually.

(1) Basic Organic Synthesis Products

(a) Ethylene

Ethylene has traditionally been the most important base material in the USSR, both by volume of production and sophistication of production processes, and will remain so for the foreseeable future. Nevertheless, output has remained at less than 15% of that of the USA.

The Tenth Five Year Plan called for an increase of 70% over 1975 in the production of ethylene to 2.32 mn tons, but was badly under-fulfilled. However, it continued to grow at a rate of 5.4% a year thanks to the commissioning of a large new plant at Nizhnekamsk (Volga region) in 1976. Output of ethylene is likely to rise to 2.0 mn tons in 1985 as production builds up at the Budennovsk (North Caucasus) facility which became operational in 1981.

Table 6.1: Production of Ethylene ('000 tons)

	1970	1975	1980
USSR	799	1,366	1,773
USA	8,204	8,971	13,239
USSR as share of USA (%)	9.7	15.2	13.4

At first, ethyl alcohol (obtained mainly from grain and potatoes) was a major source of ethylene, with 11% of the total output of ethyl alcohol being used for this purpose in 1950. The separation of coke-oven gas and the hydrogenation of acetylene were also important sources, but by the mid-1960s the use of these methods had practically ceased.

Ethylene is now obtained from the dehydrogenation of ethane and (jointly with propylene) from the cracking of low-octane naphtha fractions derived from the straight-run distillation of oil, the pyrolysis of ethane and propane in casinghead gas and the cracking of refinery gases, principally those obtained from visbreakers and catalytic crackers. Recently, gas condensate has become an increasingly important material for pyrolysis.

Casinghead gas has proved the best raw material for the production of ethylene, with one ton of ethylene requiring two tons of casinghead gas, or 2.6 tons of refinery gas or 2.78 tons of naphtha or gas-oil. However, alternative materials to casinghead gas must be considered for the production of olefins because of the recent emergence of a number of trends – the change in the centre of gravity of oil extraction from the Urals-Volga and North Caucasus regions (which produce oil with high gas factors) to Western Siberia, the rapid growth of the organic synthesis sector (which has created a demand for feedstocks far in excess of the potential output of casinghead gas), and the vast distances between existing petrochemical plants and new sources of casinghead gas (i.e. Western Siberia). The transmission of casinghead gas by pipeline over very long distances is uneconomical, and the transportation of its liquid components in railway cisterns is prohibitively expensive.

The degree of utilisation of casinghead gas has risen from 61% in 1970 to 70% in 1980, and it will grow further as more facilities at the Tomsk and Tobolsk petrochemical complexes, which will operate off the gas, are completed.

Refinery gases are obviously a cheap feedstock for the synthesis of olefins in regions with large refineries, although the size of the petrochemical plant is limited by the size and depth of refining of its refinery

Map 6.1: Chemical Plants, European USSR

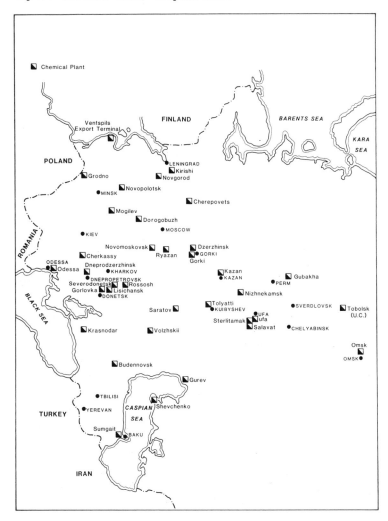

supplier. An important advantage of using naphtha is that the production of initial olefins and their derivatives can be achieved on the basis of the optimal capacity of the chemical industry, and does not depend on the capacity and structure of any particular oil refinery. The increasing size of Soviet refineries and the greater incidence of secondary processing suggest that the importance of refinery gas as a chemical feedstock can be expected to rise in the future.

The basic gas-forming processes of oil refining which yield the largest output of fractions containing olefins are secondary processes such as catalytic cracking, catalytic reforming, coking and pyrolysis. However, the depth of refining in most Soviet plants is not great, and the most valuable components of oil-refinery gas, such as propane and butane, are mostly used for bottling or for raising the octane rating of gasoline. As recently as 1975, ethane was not utilised at most refineries, although it accounts for between 9% and 20% of refinery gas. The utilisation of refinery gas has consistently failed to meet plan targets, and its output has grown slowly from 9.21 bn cu m (converted to the equivalent calorific value of natural gas) in 1970 to 15.80 bn in 1980.

The use of natural gas as a petrochemical feedstock is also a comparatively recent phenomenon. In 1974, virtually no ethane and only 40-50% of the potential volume of propane was being utilised. During the next 20 years, however, natural gas will account for an increasing share of the starting material for the production of ethylene and propylene, because its production will grow more rapidly than that of casinghead or refinery gas. In 1981, 11,900 bn cu m, or more than 36% of the USSR's proved plus probable reserves, had an ethane content of 3% or more; this is sufficient to justify its refining in gas refineries. Gas with a high ethane content is found in the Urals-Volga and Donets-Dnepr regions, in the Jurassic and Cretaceous strata of Western Siberia, Eastern Turkmenia and Western Uzbekistan and the Paleozoic in Eastern Siberia and the Far East. The biggest gas deposits with a high ethane content are Orenburg (Urals region), Vuktyl (North West region), Zapadno-Krestishchensk (Eastern Ukraine), Urengoi, Zapolyarnoe and Yamburg (Western Siberia) and Shurtan (Uzbekistan). In 1982, the completion of an ethane pipeline from Orenburg to Kazan permitted the commissioning of an ethane separation plant at the Orenburg chemical complex. The ethane is intended for the Kazan ethylene plant.

Gas condensate will also gain in importance, particularly after the Urengoi gas field begins producing it in 1983. The Neocomian deposits of Western Siberia (including payzones at Urengoi, Zapolyarnoe and

Table 6.2: Output of Ethylene by Source of Starting Material ('000 tons)

	1960	1970	1975	1980
Casinghead gases and ethane	61	24	137	177
LPG	82	324	369	89
Naphtha, gas oil and gas condensate	38	451	860	1,507
Total	181	799	1,366	1,773

Yamburg) contain 4,000 bn cu m of gas which is not only rich in ethane, with a content of 4 to 6.5%, but also yields large amounts of condensate. Between 60 and 460 grams per cubic metre of gas have been obtained, and this is enough to justify the drilling of special wells, the installation of well-head processing equipment and the laying of a condensate pipeline.

The future of naphtha cracking as a source of ethylene is unclear in view of the abundance of natural gas. The effectiveness of the method depends on the extent to which use can be made of the propane and butane fractions and other components obtained during the pyrolysis process simultaneously with ethylene. It is estimated that the consumption of naphtha per ton of ethylene will vary between 3.25 tons in a 300,000 tons/year plant and 3.87 tons in a 60,000 tons/year plant. Although ethylene tends to require more feedstock than most other petrochemical products, it needs comparatively little fuel for energy purposes.

The location of ethylene-producing plants has traditionally coincided with the sources of feedstocks, such as oil refineries, gas-fractionating plants, etc. Where ethylene is produced by the pyrolysis of casinghead gas, additional factors have been the recovery rate of gas and its ethane content. The highest gas factor has been obtained at the small West Ukraine and Saratov oilfields, but the gas has been of poor quality and inadequate for the petrochemical industry. The best gas comes from oil deposits of the Caucasus, East Ukraine, the Tatar and Bashkir republics, Kuibyshev and Western Siberia. Between 50 and 80 cu m of gas are usually obtained per ton of oil, and it contains great quantities of ethane, propane, butane and pentane. The ethane content varies from 19.5% at Romashkino (Tatar republic) through 14% at Tuimazy (Bashkir republic) to 8.7% at Shaim (Western Siberia). By comparison, the ethane content of natural gas is much lower, varying from 6% in the Volga region to 3.5% in Central Asia and only 0.4% in the North Caucasus. Yet the returns on the manufacture of ethylene from natural gas-based ethane are so high that the cost of the ethane separation equipment, amounting to 1,000 million roubles for the provision of enough ethane to make one million tons of ethylene, can be recouped in less than two years. And the cost of equipment can be reduced considerably if low-temperature separation equipment is employed. If gas from the Valanzhinskii strata at Urengoi is separated at a temperature of minus 40°C, then 20–25% of the ethane potential can be captured, and this is enough to justify the building of an ethane pipeline to the planned ethylene facilities at Tobolsk and Tomsk.

The main ethylene plants are:

Kazan	450,000 tons/year
Budennovsk	250,000
Nizhnekamsk	300,000
Lisichansk	300,000
Angarsk	300,000
Gorki	300,000

There are also two small and technologically obsolete plants of capacity 60,000 tons/year each at Kazan and Sterlitamak. The total installed capacity of Soviet ethylene plants at the end of 1981 was 2.02 mn tons.

The main Kazan plant was built by Toyo of Japan using a Lummus process, and the facility at the Prikumsk petrochemical plant in Budennovsk was built by Linde of West Germany using their own process. Linde have also won a contract to build another plant of capacity 250,000 tons/year at Kalush in the Western Ukraine, and it is rumoured that they will build another such plant at Budennovsk.

The 300,000 tons/year plants were built by the Russians with their own process, and have been given the designation EP-300. The Gorki plant is linked by a 56-km pipeline with Dzerzhinsk (Gorki oblast) where the ethylene is processed into ethylene oxide (200,000 tons/year) and ethylene glycol (133,300 tons/year). The Angarsk plant is connected by a 190-km pipeline with Zima where ethylene is transformed into ethylene dichloride, and thence into vinyl chloride and finally into 250,000 tons/year of PVC. The Lisichansk plant despatches ethylene to Severodonetsk where 240,000 tons/year of polyethylene is produced and at the Nizhnekamsk petrochemical plant the ethylene is used by a 200,000 tons/year ethylene oxide facility. Kazan and Budennovsk each have a 200,000 tons/year polyethylene plant.

A system of ethylene pipelines connects the petrochemical plants at

Kazan, Nizhnekamsk, Ufa, Sterlitamak and Salavat. The Kazan-Nizhne-kamsk link was finished in 1982, completing the 640-km system.

During the current five-year-plan period, the construction will begin of at least three new plants, each with the capacity to produce 450,000 tons of ethylene a year. They will be located at Tomsk and Tobolsk (both in Western Siberia) and at Zima in Eastern Siberia.

(b) Propylene

Propylene is produced jointly with ethylene by a number of processes. As the share of these processes in the total output of ethylene has grown, the volume of propylene jointly produced has grown at a rate faster than that of ethylene. However, ethylene still remains the most important monomer and will continue to do so. During 1975 to 1980, the production of propylene grew by 42% compared with a plan target of 60%.

Table 6.3: Production of Propylene ('000 tons)

	1970	1975	1980
USSR	302	580	824
USA	3,012	3,446	6,486
USSR as a share of USA (%)	10.0	16.8	12.7

As with ethylene, the production of propylene requires great quantities of raw materials. The most important method has been the cracking of refinery gas, but this has been superseded by the cracking of naphtha which is now accounting for all the increase in output of propylene. The predominance of naphtha cracking has resulted from the tendency to obtain ethylene by the dehydrogenation of ethane from natural gas, although it also creates problems in that it reduces the volume of resources available for catalytic reforming and the production of high-octane gasoline and aromatics.

The other important source of propylene has been the oxidation of propane at gas-fractionating plants using casinghead gas, but the only major facility planned to utilise this process in the future is that under construction at Tomsk petrochemical plant. The propane is separated from pentane and butane, and the propane content of casinghead gas varies from 12% at Tuimazy to 18% at Romashkino. About 70% of the propane potential of casinghead gas is utilised at the moment. The oxidation of propane is the cheapest method of obtaining propylene, but it is more economical to use this propane as an industrial bottled gas. It is possible to obtain propylene from ethyl alcohol or acetylene, but these processes were phased out before 1970.

The most important propylene plant, in addition to the four ethylene-propylene facilities at Nizhnekamsk, Lisichansk, Angarsk and Gorki is at Budennovsk. It was built by Linde with an annual capacity of 125,000 tons a year, and started up in 1981.

(c) Acetylene

The production of acetylene has grown very slowly compared with that of ethylene and propylene, which are cheaper to produce. The USSR currently produces about 300,000 tons a year using a wide range of processes and starting materials. This level of output will not rise, and may even fall in the future.

In 1970, about 50% of all acetylene was derived from calcium carbide, but this share has fallen dramatically in favour of the electro-cracking of methane from natural gas and the oxidative pyrolysis of gas. Oxidative pyrolysis of natural gas began at Lisichansk in the early 1960s and by 1965 was accounting for 30% of acetylene output. It is the cheapest method in all regions of the USSR except Western Siberia, which has cheap electricity and local resources of lime and coke and where the calcium carbide method costs only 85% of the oxidative pyrolysis method compared with 150% for the USSR as a whole.

The thermo-oxidative pyrolysis method has not been used widely yet, although with each ton of acetylene a volume of synthesis-gas sufficient for the production of four tons of ammonia is jointly obtained. Consequently, production of acetylene by this method takes place mainly at nitrogenous fertiliser plants. New methanol shops may be built using natural gas and synthesis-gas obtained as a by-product of acetylene production.

For the electro-cracking of methane, 12 tons of feedstocks and energy are needed for each ton of acetylene. The main advantage of the process is that different feedstocks can be used. The importance of electro-cracking will grow, mainly because of the abundance of methane. It is the main constituent of natural gas, with its share ranging from 93% in the Volga region to 98.4% in the North Caucasus, and also of casinghead gas where its share varies from 28.6% at Shaim in Western Siberia to 40% at Romashkino in the Volga region.

Some 3.3 tons of natural gas per ton of acetylene are needed for electro-cracking compared with 4.5 tons for oxidative pyrolysis. The stagnation in acetylene production means that a declining share of total gas consumption is being used in this way; in 1975 only 5.4% of all gas destined for the chemical industry went to acetylene plants compared with 6.9% in 1970 and 10.3% in 1965.

The decline of the calcium carbide method has had repercussions on the production of calcium carbide, which grew slowly from 815,000 tons in 1970 to 851,000 in 1975 but then fell rapidly to 791,000 tons in 1979.

(d) Butadiene

Butadiene is a diolefin used basically for the production of synthetic rubber. The Soviets have not published output data, but a reasonable guess suggests that they produced about 450,000 tons in 1980. The growth rate is likely to be minimal until after 1985 because of the failure to set firm plans for the construction of new car factories, the most important end product from butadiene being vehicle tyres.

As recently as 1960, decomposition of ethyl alcohol derived from grain and potatoes was the only source of butadiene, and by 1970 was still accounting for half the total output. The catalytic dehydrogenation of n-butane, introduced in 1970, has since assumed a greater importance. In 1975, it accounted for 53% of all butadiene output, with ethyl alcohol yielding 38% and the pyrolysis of light oil fractions the remaining 9%, and by 1980 the share of ethyl alcohol had declined further.

The change in the source of butadiene is particularly important, as it is a major consumer of petrochemical feedstocks and fuel, requiring three tons of material and up to 7.5 tons of fuel per ton of butadiene. The catalytic dehydrogenation of n-butane and naphtha-cracking will grow in importance at the expense of other methods such as the pyrolysis of light oil fractions and the use of the butane component of refinery gas. At the moment, the isolation of practically all the butane potential at refineries is accomplished, and there is little scope for any increase in the availability of butane. Naphtha-cracking is the most rapidly growing source, allowing very cheap butadiene to be manufactured from butylene originating in multiple-product crackers.

The biggest butadiene plants at the present time are two plants of 100,000 tons capacity a year each, located at Kazan and Nizhnekamsk. They were built by Mitsubishi, using a Nippon Zeon process, and Mitsubishi have won the contract to build two more butadiene shops at the Tobolsk Petrochemical Plant. They will produce a total 100,000 tons a year using the dehydrogenation of n-butane process.

(e) Ethyl Alcohol

As ethyl alcohol has, in the past, been an important source of ethylene, propylene, acetylene and butadiene, this seems an appropriate point at which to consider it. It is one of the oldest and best established sectors of the chemical industry, due to the large number of starting materials, including agricultural products such as grain and potatoes which have been extensively used for this purpose in the USSR, as well as the ease with which it can be produced. Moreover, ethyl alcohol was an important material for the production of butadiene and hence synthetic rubber; the Soviet Union was one of the first major producers of synthetic rubber and consequently has a long-standing ethyl alcohol industry.

The most significant features of recent years have been the slow growth rate of production and the conversion of the sector from agricultural materials to a hydrocarbon base producing synthetic ethyl alcohol. During the 1970s, output grew at an average 2.2% a year, solely as a result of higher productivity obtained at existing plants, and not until 1985-90 is any major increase in the scale of output anticipated, when new uses of ethyl alcohol will arise.

Table 6.4: Production of Ethyl Alcohol (mn hectolitres)

	1960	1970	1975	1977
USSR	17.0	28.0	31.7	32.6
USA		26.2	22.0	18.9
USSR as a share of USA (%)		107	144	172

There are three sources of ethyl alcohol: agricultural products, the synthesis of ethylene and the hydrolysis of wood. The share of agricultural products in total output has fallen from 62% in 1960 to 56% in 1970 and 30% today while that of synthesis has risen from 24% to 32% to about 60%. Wood hydrolysis is declining in importance.

There have been two main results of the switch from agricultural to hydrocarbon materials for producing ethyl alcohol. One has been a considerable reduction in production costs, and the other has been the development of processes by which rubber is obtained directly from petrochemicals, thereby by-passing the stages of production and processing of synthetic alcohol. This is achieved by the direct synthesis of butadiene and isoprene from n-butane, isopentane, isobutylene and formaldehyde. By 1970, the use of agricultural products for the manufacture of synthetic rubber had ceased entirely.

Production of ethyl alcohol by the hydrogenation of ethylene takes place at Ufa, Groznyi, Kuibyshev, Saratov, Orsk and Sumgait.

(f) Methanol

Production of methanol has grown at a steady, if not spectacular, pace since 1970 after quadrupling during the 1960s.

Table 6.5: Production of Methanol ('000 tons)

	1960	1970	1975	1978	1979	1980
USSR	231	1,004	1,447	1,809	1,774	1,900
USA		2,237	2,348	2,885	3,362	
USSR as a share of USA (%)		44.9	61.6	62.7	52.8	

The largest plants producing methanol are located at Severodonetsk in the Ukraine and Novomoskovsk in the Centre region. Two very large plants with capacities of 750,000 tons/year each are under construction at Gubakha in Perm oblast (Urals region) and at the Tomsk petrochemical Plant. They will both be operating by 1983 and should have reached capacity by 1985, bringing the annual output of methanol to 3.4 mn tons. A significant share of this will be exported. Soviet methanol exports rose from 156,647 tons in 1975 (10.8% of output) to 258,561 tons in 1980 (13.6%), and an export terminal with an eventual capacity of 435,000 tons a year is under construction at Ventspils. ICI of the UK and Klockner Chemie of West Germany have contracts with the USSR to buy methanol, although the volume involved is to be negotiated annually.

Originally, methanol was produced primarily from the products of coal processing. This proved expensive, and the transfer to natural gas lowered production costs by 25-45% depending on the plant.

Natural gas is now the basic source of methanol, with 97% of the product derived from gas. The consumption of gas per ton of methanol is smaller than for almost any other petrochemical product, and as gas is now available in most parts of the country, methanol plants are generally built near the principal customers for the product. This is why there has been such a great deal of controversy over the new plant being built at Tomsk; it will cost more to transport the methanol from Tomsk to its consumers than it would to despatch the necessary volume of gas by pipeline.

The methanol sector's share of the total volume of natural gas consumed by the chemical industry has declined from 12.1% in 1965 to 7.4% in 1970, 7.3% in 1975 and 7.0% in 1980 while the actual volume involved has risen from 0.74 bn cu m in 1970 to 2.5 bn in 1980.

(g) Aromatics – Benzene

Of the three aromatics, benzene is the most important with output growing at an average annual rate of 4.7% during the 1970s.

Table 6.6: Production of Benzene ('000 tons)

	1960	1970	1975	1978	1979	1980
USSR	506	1,036	1,427	1,655	1,606	1,644
USA		3,753	3,459	5,037	5,729	
USSR as a share of USA (%)		27.6	41.3	32.9	28.0	

In 1960, virtually all benzene was derived from a coal base, but a mere ten years later only 63.2% was coal-based, with 30.5% coming from oil and 6.3% from the hydrodealkylation of toluene.

However coal will remain a significant source of benzene. Aromatic hydrocarbons (benzene, toluene and xylene) are formed in the chambers of coke furnaces during the coking of hard coal. Crude benzene currently accounts for about 1% of the total output of coking ovens, and its composition normally depends on the quality of the coking blend and the temperature of coking. But the main concern of coking plants is to provide high-quality coke for the metallurgical industry, and this imposes constraints on both the quantity and quality of benzene.

Of the oil-based processes, catalytic reforming (mainly platforming) is expected to be the most likely source of benzene, as it provides the largest output per ton of oil. Benzene is the first aromatic hydrocarbon to be obtained from the catalytic reforming of gasoline; it is found in fractions of 62-85° with toluene being obtained between 85 and 110° and xylene between 110 and 140°. Some Soviet experts have predicted that, in the future, fractions of 62-85° will be almost completely refined into benzene. Other experts, however, believe that naptha-cracking will become the most important source.

(h) Aromatics – Toluene

The Russians do not issue data on toluene production, but a reasonable estimate for 1980 was 800,000 tons. While 51.3% of toluene was derived from coal in 1963, this share had fallen to only 23.5% in 1970 with 74.5% coming from an oil base (principally by naphtha-cracking, or catalytic reforming of gasoline) and 2% as a by-product of the styrene production process.

(i) Aromatics – Xylene

The production of xylene has grown more rapidly than that of the other aromatic hydrocarbons, at a rate of 7.9% a year during 1970 to 1980.

Table 6.7: Production of Xylene ('000 tons)

	1960	1970	1975	1978	1979	1980
USSR	42	214	327	433	435	459
USA		2,709	2,649	4,190	5,346	
USSR as a share of USA (%)		7.9	12.3	10.3	8.1	

Xylene is similar to other aromatic petrochemical products in that the share of it derived from coal fell rapidly during the 1960s, while that stemming from oil products is rising, and accounted for 93.6% of all xylene in 1970. The best xylenes are those obtained by the catalytic reforming of heavy gasolines and light kerosenes containing large quantities of alkylbenzene and very little olefin hydrocarbon. Aromatised gasolines obtained by the catalytic pyrolysis of heavy gasolines also constitute a valuable raw material.

New aromatic plants to have come on stream in recent years include:

		tons/yr	Year	Built by:	Process:
Benzene:	Budennovsk	100,000	1981	Linde	Houdry
	Kazan	160,000	1977	Toyo	Mitsubishi
	Krasnodar	150,000	1977	Chiyoda	Mitsubishi
	Nizhnekamsk	160,000		Toyo	Mitsubishi
	Ufa	120,000	1981	Eurotecnica	Houdry
p-xylene:	Kirishi	60,000	1977	Kawasaki	Arco
	Novopolotsk	?		John Brown	ICI

New plants under construction include:

		tons/yr	Built by:	Process:
Benzene:	Novopolotsk	125,000	Asahi	Houdry
	Omsk	125,000	Technip	UOP
	Ryazan	125,000	Asahi	Houdry
	Ufa	125,000	Technip	UOP
o-xylene:	Omsk	165,000	Eurotecnica	UOP
	Ufa	165,000	Eurotecnica	UOP
p-xylene:	Omsk	165,000	Eurotecnica	UOP
	Ufa	165,000	Eurotecnica	UOP

(j) Phenol and Acetone

The creation of a large-scale organic synthesis industry in the Soviet Union is said to have begun in 1949 when the joint production of phenol and acetone by the cumene method from isopropylbenzene began. Output grew rapidly until 1970, since when it has grown comparatively slowly.

Table 6.8: Output of Phenol and Acetone ('000 tons)

	1960	1970	1975	1978	1979	1980
Phenol	108	347	413	469	487	496
Acetone	54	232	279	317	332	340

Phenol and acetone are produced at the 'Orgsintez' plant at Kazan, the Groznyi Chemical Plant, the 'Orgsteklo' plant of Dzerzhinsk (Gorki oblast), the 'Nitron' plant of Saratov and others.

In the USSR, approximately 90% of phenol and 83% of acetone is produced by the cumene method, and this predominance will continue in the future. Phenol is also obtained by the catalytic reforming of gasoline.

(2) Plastics

The output of plastics in the USSR, while growing rapidly, is still only a fraction of that of the USA. The pressing need for the Russians to raise their production of plastics is illustrated by the fact that one ton of plastics can be substituted for five to six tons of ferrous or non-ferrous metals, reducing costs and labour requirements and lowering the burden on transport facilities. It has been estimated that the use of one ton of plastics in heavy engineering and the manufacture of machine tools, tractors and vehicles can yield savings of up to 2,800 roubles and reduce labour requirements by up to 1,700 man-hours.

Five types of plastics predominate in the USSR — carbamides, aminoplasts, phenolplasts, PVC and polyethylene.

The rapid growth in the production of plastics has stemmed largely from the development of the petrochemical industry. During the 1950s, the material base consisted largely of phenol, formalin, methanol, benzene and camphor, i.e. products from the coking sector which, as recently as 1958, accounted for 70% of material inputs compared with 18-20% from plants and minerals and only 10-12% from oil and

Table 6.9: Output of Plastics by Type ('000 tons)

	1965	1970	1975	1980
Total	803	1,673	2,838	3,636
Polyethylene	57	267	420	623
Polypropylene	0.1	10.2	10.9	31.9
PVC and copolymers of vinyl chloride	80.8	160	334	398
Polystyrene and copolymers of styrene	28.9	82.2	144	247
Cellulose ethers	36.0	47.9	53.4	53.7
Carbamide resins	165	346	619	752
Phenolformaldehyde resins	133	196	261	298
Mochevins and melamines	24	31.5	39.9	38.2
Ion-exchange resins	5.5	7.6	12.4	14.0
Others	272.7	524.6	943.4	1,180.2

gas. By the end of 1965 the share of oil and gas had risen to 30–35%, and it currently stands at about 90%.

Of particular importance are specialised plants based on the products of oil refineries and on natural gas. Plants using oil products specialise in polyolefins, polystyrene and copolymers of styrene, phenolformaldehyde resins, plasticisers and also initial monomers and intermediate products. Plants based on natural gas are engaged in the processing of acetylene, methanol and their derivatives. However, the extent to which the petrochemical industry's potential is realised depends on the degree to which the process of refining isolates individual hydrocarbons which, in turn depends on the technological level of the refining industry. This still lags behind that of other industrially developed countries.

An analysis of the material requirements of individual stages of production cycles has shown that it is the initial stages, the synthesis of individual monomers, which are most material-intensive, requiring 2.2–5.0 tons per ton of monomer. Although this has no influence on the location of oil- and gas-refining facilities because of the relatively small amounts of material required and the transportability of plastics, it is of considerable importance to the plastics industry, in view of the fact that the cost of materials accounts for 77–79% of total expenditure by plastics plants.

Natural gas is becoming an increasingly important material for plastics, especially carbamide resins, aminoplasts, polyformaldehyde, etc. It is calculated that 100,000 tons of plastics can be obtained from one billion cubic metres of gas and that the unit capital investment costs of plant using gas can be reduced by up to 2.5 times compared with those plants using agricultural raw materials.

From one ton of casinghead gas, some 400 kg of plastics can be

Table 6.10: Consumption of Raw Materials in Tons per Ton of Plastics and of Energy in tsf per Ton of Plastics

Product	A	B	C	D	Energy
		Raw Material			
Polyethylene	2.5	2.4	4.0	–	2.5–3.5
Polystyrene	2.0	2.0	2.3	–	3.0–3.5
Polyformaldehyde	–	–	–	3.0	12
Epoxy resin	4.3	4.2	4.5	–	5–6

Notes:
A. Casinghead gas.
B. Oil refinery gas.
C. Low-octane fractions of straight-run distillation.
D. Natural gas.

obtained. One ton of carbamide resins requires 1.2 tons of natural gas and a ton of aminoplasts requires 1.1 tons of natural gas. Energy requirements, in terms of tons of standard fuel per ton of plastics amount to 3.0–3.5 for phenolformaldehyde resins, 1.7–2.0 for phenoplasts, 6.5–7.0 for polycarbonates and 2.0–2.5 for polypropylene.

Polymerised plastics (i.e polyethylene, polypropylene, PVC and polystyrene) have high degrees of material and fuel intensity, and should therefore be produced near oil refineries or gas pipelines. Consequently, it has been suggested that 70–75% of these plastics should be produced in the RSFSR, and for some fuel-intensive synthetic resins, the RSFSR should account for 80–85%. At the moment, production is concentrated in the Volga region, but Siberia should eventually account for 35–50% of total Soviet output, although polymerised plastics should come last in order of preference after synthetic rubber, chemical fibres and synthetic fibres. In 1974, the Volga region accounted for 60% of polyethylene and 38% of PVC resins and copolymers production.

Detailed technical and economic calculations are made during the process of planning the location of specialised plastics plants. A raw materials base is being created for the large-scale multi-product manufacture of energy-intensive polymers in Siberia. Highly specialised plants of optimal capacity for the processing of polymer products are being constructed in mainly medium and small towns of the Centre, Southern and North West regions, with highly developed sectors of engineering and metalworking, light and food industries and construction. The most material-intensive plastics have mainly been produced in the Volga region, which has a large number of refineries. The production of plastics in the Caucasus and North Caucasus is being limited to the likely level of consumption by these regions, and Central Asia and Kazakhstan will be used for production only of the least water-intensive and most energy-intensive products.

By 1970, the share of the five leading regions (Centre, Volga, Western Siberia, Urals and Donets-Dnepr) had fallen to 52% of total plastics production compared with 80% in 1960, but they maintained their leading position due to a number of reasons.

(1) The transfer of the nitrogen-fixing plants in the Centre and Donets-Dnepr (i.e. Novomoskovsk and Severodonetsk) to natural gas, and the construction of new plants in those regions created a basis for the rapid development of the production of methanol, carbamide resins, caprolactam, and for the construction of large acetylene shops based on the pyrolysis of natural gas.

(2) In the Volga and North Caucasus regions, with large resources of oil and casinghead gas, and consequently where it was most expedient to develop the plastics industry, it was considered more important to satisfy the country's pressing needs for synthetic rubber and fibres, and basic substances such as benzene, xylene, phenol, ethylene oxides, etc. In 1974, the Volga region accounted for 60% of all polyethylene and 38% of all PVC resins and copolymers produced in the USSR.

(3) The major shift to West Siberia will take place during 1980 to 1985, with the construction of the Tomsk and Tobolsk plants. By 1975, it was planned that West Siberia should occupy fourth place after the Volga, Centre and Donets-Dnepr, but ahead of the Urals. These five leading regions would produce 45.6% of total output, indicating a further spatial diversification. By 1985, the Eastern regions will be producing a third of all plastics, mainly from Tomsk, Tobolsk, Omsk, Usolye-Zima, Chardzhou and Mary. Tomsk alone is planned to produce 600,000 tons of plastics in 1985, or 25% of the planned increase in national output over 1981 to 1985. So far, however, only the 100,000 tons a year polypropylene facility is operational, producing several different types of material. These include granules of polypropylene suffused with asbestos for the Vyatka Washing Machine Plant of Kirov, which requires a product highly resistant to heat and alkaline liquids. Three other shops are under construction at Tomsk. They will manufacture formalin, carbamide resin (for making furniture) and polyformaldehyde (for engineering and domestic appliances).

The most important plastics plants are:

		tons/yr	Year	Built by:	Process:
Polyethylene:	Novopolotsk	120,000			
	Budennovsk	200,000	1981	John Brown	UCC
	Kazan	120,000	1975	Salzgitter	Imhico
	Kazan	200,000	1982	John Brown	UCC
	Severodonetsk	120,000	1977	Salzgitter	Imhico
	Severodonetsk	120,000	1980	Salzgitter	Imhico
	Sumgait	60,000	?	?	?
	Ufa	60,000	?	?	?
Polypropylene:	Gurev	30,000		Tecnimont	Montedison
	Tomsk	100,000		Tecnimont	Montedison
Polystyrene:	Omsk	100,000		Litwin	Cosden
	Shevchenko	100,000		Litwin	Emejota
	Shevchenko	100,000		Litwin	Rhone Progil
	Dneprodzerzhinsk	100,000			?	?

The Shevchenko facility works in conjunction with a 300,000 tons/year styrene plant at Shevchenko, which was also built by Litwin. Some of the styrene is exported to France under a compensation agreement.

PVC: Ussolye-Zima   250,000   Klockner INA   KHD-
Pritchard engineering and a Huls process, and supplied for a 270,000 tons/year vinyl chloride plant using ethylene from Angarsk. Another vinyl chloride facility of similar size is being built at Uhde, and is scheduled for 1985.

(3) Chemical Fibres

The development of the chemical fibres industry has gradually eroded the share of natural fibres in the total output of fibres from 85.4% in 1960 to 69% in 1970 and further to 55% in 1980. This proportion is still far higher than in the USA, and it means that the USSR is devoting an unnecessarily large volume of resources to sheep-rearing and cotton-growing. One ton of chemical fibres can save 2.5 tons of cotton or wool.

The rate of growth of production of chemical fibres has been disappointingly low, with the Five Year Plan targets for 1975 and 1980 being fulfilled to the extent of only 73.5% and 80.5% respectively.

When analysed by type, it can be seen from Table 6.11 that the production of synthetic fibres is growing far faster than that of artificial fibres — by 13.0% a year during the 1970s compared with 2.9% a year. Artificial fibres are basically rayon and acetate filaments; synthetic fibres include nylon, terylene, orlon, savan and perlon. In 1980

Table 6.11: Production of Chemical Fibres ('000 tons)

	1960	1970	1975	1978	1979	1980
Artificial fibres	196	456	590	634	571	606
Synthetic fibres	15	167	365	497	529	570
Total	211	623	955	1,131	1,100	1,176
Synthetic fibres as a share of all chemical fibres	7.1	26.8	38.2	43.9	48.1	48.5

synthetic fibres accounted for 48.5% of total output; this compared with over 90% in the USA.

In 1975, the RSFSR accounted for 60% of the output of chemical fibres. They should be produced in regions with cheap raw materials, and therefore the share of the RSFSR should rise to 80-85%, including 30-35% in Siberia. Synthetic and artificial fibres should take second and third priority after synthetic rubber.

The cost of raw materials amounts to 70-80% of the production cost of chemical fibres. Each ton of viscous fibres requires five tons of materials.

In 1959, only 7% of raw materials were petrochemicals. By 1970 this share had risen to 55%, and by 1980 to 80%. This dramatic change is due to the increasing availability of natural and casinghead gas. About 20,000 tons of synthetic fibres can be produced from 1 bn cu m of natural gas and enough synthetic resins can be obtained from one ton of casinghead gas to produce 3,000 sq m of synthetic fabric. According to one expert, practically all synthetic fibres will eventually be produced on the basis of benzene, xylene and other hydrocarbons derived from petroleum in the future.

Materials for the Manufacture of Chemical Fibres

(a) Caprolactam. Caprolactam is an important input for the synthetic fibre sector. Production has grown from 15,350 tons in 1960 to 148,400 in 1970, 295,000 in 1975 and 340,000 tons in 1980. The 1980 plan target of 534,000 tons was considerably underfulfilled, mainly because the 80,000 tons/year plant at Chirchik in Central Asia, supplied by Snia Viscosa, was not completed until December 1980, and another plant (50,000 tons/year) at Grodno in Belorussia also started up late. Grodno now has two plants of total capacity 100,000 tons a year.

(b) Acetic Acid. The biggest plant, building up to 150,000 tons a year since it came on stream in 1980, is located at Severodonetsk in the Ukraine.

(c) Ethylene Glycol. While data for total output of ethylene glycol are not available, it is known that the largest plant is located at Dzerzhinsk in Gorki oblast. It became operational in 1981 with a rated capacity of 133,300 tons a year, and works on ethylene piped from the ethylene plant at Novo-Gorki. A small facility of capacity 7,500 tons a year is under construction by Salzgitter at Nizhnekamsk.

(d) Ethylene Oxide. The biggest producers of ethylene oxide are at Dzerzhinsk and Nizhnekamsk, with both plants producing 200,000 tons a year. The Dzerzhinsk plant accounts for 33% of the material required for the production of lavsan, an important intermediate material for the manufacture of chemical fibres, while the Nizhnekamsk plant produces largely for the paint industry. Both these plants were commissioned in 1981–2.

(e) Acrylonitrile. The USSR's largest plant began operating in 1979 at Saratov with a capacity of 150,000 tons a year, and is now being doubled up. A significant share of its output is being exported under a compensation agreement, but most of it supplies the synthetic fibre plants of the Volga region.

(f) DMT. This is produced entirely at Mogilev in Belorussia in a plant of 240,000 tons capacity a year. DMT is used for the production of lavsan.

(4) Fertilisers

Fertilisers are a comparatively recent industry in the USSR, and the fact that only 13.9 mn tons of inorganic fertilisers were produced in 1960 illustrates the extent to which the agricultural sector had been neglected prior to that date. Since 1960, the production of fertilisers has grown at an average rate of 10.6% a year, and the share of nitrogenous fertiliser has risen from 35% to 48%. The Tenth Five Year Plan target of 138 mn tons in 1980 was greatly underfulfilled, and the Eleventh plan has set a target of 150 mn tons for 1985; on the basis of the output record so far, it looks as if this plan will also be underfulfilled.

Table 6.12: Output of Fertilisers (mn tons)

	1960	1970	1975	1978	1979	1980
Total output	13.9	55.4	90.2	98.0	94.5	103.9
Total output at 100% nutrient content	3.3	13.1	22.0	23.7	22.1	24.8
Nitrogenous fertiliser – total	4.9	26.4	41.6	45.4	44.6	49.9
Nitrogenous fertiliser at 100% nutrient content	1.0	5.4	8.5	9.3	9.2	10.2
Nitrogenous fertiliser as a % of total fertiliser	35.1	47.7	46.1	46.3	47.2	48.0

Table 6.13: Output of Fertiliser by Region (mn tons)

	1960	1970	1975	1980
RSFSR	7.2	27.3	42.4	50.0
North West	0.6	3.7	5.8	
Centre	2.1	8.6	9.3	
Central Chernozem	− }	1.9	2.8	
Volga Vyatka	− }			
Volga	0.5	2.7	4.3	
North Caucasus	−	1.8	3.7	
Urals	3.4	5.9	14.0	
Western and Eastern Siberia and Far East	0.6	2.7	2.9	
Ukraine	3.9	11.5	18.3	19.7
Belorussia	−	6.1	11.0	13.8
Caucasus	0.5	1.3	2.0	1.9
Baltic Republics	0.8	2.5	3.7	4.6
Central Asia	{ 1.6	4.7	7.0	7.3
Kazakhstan		2.0	5.8	6.5

The production of fertiliser is highly dispersed throughout the USSR. The largest producers of nitrogenous fertilisers are the plants at Nevinnomiisk (North Caucasus), Voskresensk, Dorogobuzh, Shchekino and Novomoskovsk (Centre), Grodno (Belorussia), Cherepovets and Novgorod (North West), Kuibyshev and Bereznikovsk (Urals), Kemerovo (West Siberia), Angarsk (East Siberia), Rovno, Cherkassy, Severodonetsk, Gorlovka, Dneprodzerzhinsk and Lisichansk (Ukraine), Fergana, Chirchik, Vakhsh and Kirovokan (Central Asia), Estonia shale-chemical plant and Ionava (Baltic).

It has recently been suggested that the production of nitrogenous fertiliser has grown too quickly in relation to the other types. There is an optimal mix of fertilisers, in which the ratio of nitrogenous to phosphate fertilisers should be 10 to 9; at the moment it is 10 to 6.5, and it is possible that resources earmarked for nitrogen-fixing under the

Eleventh Five Year Plan may be diverted to the production of phosphate fertilisers.

Materials for the Manufacture of Nitrogenous Fertilisers

(a) Ammonia. The production of ammonia has grown at an average annual rate of 8.2% since 1970 to 16.73 mn tons in 1980, although the Tenth Five Year Plan target of 22.8 mn tons for 1980 was considerably underfulfilled, largely as a result of the failure to commission the huge Tolyatti complex on time. Output will probably rise to 27 mn tons in 1985 with a significant share of the increase going for export.

Nearly 93% of ammonia is produced from natural and casinghead gas, with a further 5% from coking gas. Coke once accounted for an important share of raw materials, but gas has proved much cheaper. The transfer from coke to natural gas at Novomoskovsk, for example, reduced unit costs by 45%.

The production of a ton of ammonia requires an average 1,350 cu m of gas, consisting of 675 for feedstock and 675 for the generation of energy. Some advanced plants achieve much better rates, with the 'Azot' plant of Severodonetsk (Ukraine) needing only 950-1,100 cu m per ton of ammonia, methanol, nitric acid and acetic acid. In 1975, the rate was 1,400-1,500 cu m/ton, and this impressive reduction has been achieved largely through the capture of waste heat, thereby reducing the volume of gas needed for firing the boilers.

The use of coking gas is still economical in some regions. The combination of a nitrogenous fertiliser plant with a metallurgical and coking plant can reduce the unit cost of fertiliser by 5% and, for a plant with a capacity of 100,000 tons of ammonia a year, a saving of 15 mn roubles a year can be effected. The best example is the Novolipetsk nitrogenous fertiliser plant in the Central Chernozem region, and the new Altai coking plant at Zarinsk in Western Siberia will supply a nitrogenous fertiliser plant to be built adjacent to it.

In 1975, 52.1% of all natural gas destined for the chemical industry was used for the production of ammonia. This compares with 42.2% in 1970.

Soviet ammonia capacity is planned to grow by nearly 8 mn tons over the period 1981 to 1985. The newly created Ministry of Fertiliser Production has drawn up plans for 13 new ammonia plants, each with a capacity of 450,000 tons a year, in addition to the four plants currently under construction at Angarsk, Odessa, Gorlovka and Perm. In all, 17 new plants built with foreign assistance will begin operating between 1981 and 1985, in addition to smaller plants of 200,000 tons

Table 6.14: Production of Ammonia by Source ('000 tons)

	1960	1970	1975	1980
Natural and casinghead gas	226	5,522	9,550	15,400
Coking gas	444	1,085	1,404	900
Coke and coal	443	793	684	250
Others	271	238	360	170
Total	1,384	7,638	11,998	16,720

a year at Rustavi and Kemerovo using Soviet equipment, and this compares with 20 which came on stream during 1976 and 1980.

These were located at Cherkassy (2), Dneprodzerzhinsk, Gorlovka (2) and Odessa (2) all in the Ukraine, Cherepovets and Novgorod (3) in the North West, Dorogobuzh and Novomoskovsk (2) in the Central region, Grodno in Belorussia, Rossosh in the Central Chernozem, and Tolyatti (4, making 6 at the complex with an annual output of 2.7 mn tons) in the Volga region. They were mostly built by Toyo using a Kellogg licence, except those at Tolyatti which were built by Chemico with a Benfield licence and the Gorlovka plants, built by Creusot Loire with a Kellogg process.

The Tolyatti complex is said to be the world's largest, and is likely to be extended during the 1981 to 1985 period. It is fed with natural gas from the Urengoi-Chelyabinsk-Petrovsk pipeline, and more gas will be available from the new series of pipelines following the Urengoi-Nizhnyaya Tura-Petrovsk corridor. The growth of ammonia production at Tolyatti will be assisted by the construction of a second string of the Tolyatti-Gorlovka-Odessa ammonia pipeline, the first string of which was completed in 1980. Running for 2,450 km with 400 shut-off valves, it carries 2.5 mn tons a year from the Tolyatti 'Azot' plant. Up to 0.3 mn tons a year will be distributed to farms along its route from 30 distribution points, and 2.2 mn tons will be exported annually from the Yuzhnyi terminal near Odessa.

The Novgorod plant also exports ammonia from the Baltic port of Ventspils, with Denmark and the Netherlands taking 60,000 tons a month. The Ventspils terminal has a capacity of one million tons a year, and most of the USSR's exports of ammonia, which came to 1.07 mn tons in 1979, and urea (136,000 tons) are despatched through this port. The Yuzhnyi terminal at Odessa is acquiring a loading facility for the export of 1.5 mn tons of urea a year.

During the last 20 years, the consumption of ammonia per ton of fertiliser has fallen from around 1,000 to 855 cu m. The volume of gas required by the sector has risen from 0.2 to 13.2 bn cu m a year during the period 1960 to 1980. It should rise to about 21.8 bn cu m in 1985 and as much as 33.6 bn in 1990.

(b) Urea. Soviet urea is produced in equipment manufactured and installed by Chemoprojekt of Czechoslovakia using a Stamicarbon process. These plants have a capacity of 350,000 tons a year, and three were installed during the 1976 to 1980 plan period at Cherkassy and Dneprodzerzhinsk (2). Six more are under construction at Angarsk, Berezniki, Fergana, Grodno, Salavat and Severodonetsk. The Russians also build urea plants of capacity 450,000 tons a year each with equipment imported from Tecnimont. Two of these are operating at Berezniki and Gorlovka, and one more is under construction at Kemerovo; some reports say it has become operational. Snamprogetti have built a 450,000 tons/year plant at Novomoskovsk and another three at Tolyatti, and Toyo have built a facility of similar size at Perm.

(5) Synthetic Rubber

The USSR does not publish data on the output of synthetic rubber, but it can be estimated that it produced about 1.6 mn tons in 1980.

The location of the synthetic rubber industry is largely influenced by that of the major oil refineries, and consequently the RSFSR tends to produce more rubber than it uses. Rubber is highly-fuel-intensive, and it has been proposed that 80-85% of production should be located in the RSFSR. Eventually, 35-50% of total output should take place in Siberia, but the share of Western Siberia is currently very small, and is growing only slowly.

This situation should be rectified when the synthetic rubber shops of the Tomsk and Tobolsk combines come on stream. The continued expansion of output from the Volga plants has been criticised, but the Volga region remains the largest producer, currently accounting for more than half the national output. This is likely to continue for the next few years with the further development of the Nizhnekamsk petrochemical plant which produces monomers for the synthetic rubber industry.

The largest synthetic rubber plants are situated in the Volga (Volzhskii, Kuibyshev and Nizhnekamsk), the Centre (Yefremov in Tula oblast and Yaroslavl), the Central Chernozem (Kursk), the Urals (Chaikovsk and Sterlitamak), Western Siberia (Omsk), the North Caucasus

Table 6.15: Structure of Monomer Requirements for Synthetic Rubber (%)

	1960	1975	1980*
Butadiene	80.5	52.1	42.0
Isoprene	–	29.1	37.1
Isobutylene	0.5	2.0	3.6
Chloroprene	9.0	4.5	5.8
Others	10.0	12.3	11.5

Note: * Tenth Five Year Plan target.

(Gudermes), the Caucasus (Sumgait) and Kazakhstan (Karaganda). The Nizhnekamsk synthetic rubber plant will be one of the largest of its type in the world when completed, and the Volzhskii plant is already one of the world's largest producers of isoprene rubber.

Synthetic rubber is obtained from the following monomers – butadiene, isoprene, isobutylene and chloroprene, which in turn are obtained largely from oil and gas.

Ethylene, originally used for the production of intermediate styrene, is now being used together with propylene in the production of special purpose EPDM rubber. Propylene is also used for the production of nitrile rubber. The cost of the final product depends largely on the type of raw material and the method of processing. The share of different starting materials changed dramatically during the 1960s, with that of ethyl alcohol declining from 94.5% to 15.6% in favour of pentane (the share of which rose from nil to 29.7%), n-butane (nil to 23.3%) and iso-butane (nil to 11.2%). Since 1970, the shares of butane, iso-butane, pentane and fractions of C_4 gases have increased, and by 1980 the production of monomers for synthetic rubber from ethyl alcohol had practically ceased.

Over 80% of Soviet rubber is now of the stereo-regular polyisoprene and polybutadiene (SKI and SKD) and copolymer butadiene-styrene and butadiene-methylstyrene (SKS and SKMS) types.

It is significant that in 1975, stereo-regular rubbers accounted for 42.7% of all synthetic rubber in the Soviet Union compared with only 17% in the USA and 22.5% in Japan. Current Soviet policy is for an accelerated growth in the production of stereo-regular rubber, especially of the ethylene-propylene type, the ending of sodium-butadiene manufacture, the gradual reduction in imports of natural rubber (although the need to expand trade with Vietnam and Kampuchea will sustain imports at a certain level for some years), a stabilisation in the

Table 6.16: Output of Synthetic Rubber by Type ('000 tons)

	1960	1970	1975
Sodium butadiene (SKB)	160	71	58
Copolymer butadiene-styrene (SKS) and butadiene-methylstyrene (SKMS)	117	471	516
Stereo-regular polyisoprene (SKI) and polybutadiene (SKD)	–	292	576
Chloroprene	25	76	62
Butadiene-nitrile (SKN)	4	25	40
Others	10	34	98
Total	316	989	1,350

production of butadiene-styrene rubber, and the expansion of butadiene nitrile and chloroprene rubbers.

Synthetic rubber was first produced in 1932 at Yaroslavl from ethyl alcohol. As early as 1950, 67% of all rubber used in the tyre industry was synthetic, and imports of natural rubber have now fallen to 214,654 tons in 1980 compared with 316,500 tons in 1970.

The cost of raw materials amounts to 77-78% of the production cost of synthetic rubber, and between two and four tons of materials per ton of rubber are required. Thus the importance of using efficient new materials like casinghead gas (400 kg of synthetic rubber can be obtained from one ton of casinghead gas) can be readily seen. In 1959, this share had grown to 85-90%, to 96% in 1970, and has remained at 100% since 1975.

(6) Carbon Black

Carbon black is an important input to the tyre industry. Production grew from 300,000 tons in 1960 to 691,000 tons in 1970 and about one million tons in 1980.

The industry tends to be located near its principal customers, i.e. the major tyre plants. The largest plants are situated at Omsk and Barnaul (Western Siberia), using material from the Omsk oil refinery, and at Stavropol, which uses local natural gas. The recent reconstruction of Stavropol's reactors has allowed the level of output to be maintained while annual gas consumption has been reduced from 0.32 to 0.10 bn cu m. In 1981, the Omsk plant commissioned a new 24,000 tons/year shop, bringing its total capacity to 120,000 tons/year.

For many years, the basic raw material was anthracene oil from the coking sector, and green oil produced in plants engaged in the pyrolysis of gas oil. Recently, the use of oil products has grown considerably, as has that of natural gas. In 1965, 2.6 bn cu m of natural gas (amounting to 2% of total consumption) was used for this purpose, and consumption rose to 3.3 bn cu m in 1970 and 4 bn in 1980.

Oil products are now tending to replace natural gas, especially as production is being stepped up at plants not served by gas, such as Omsk and Barnaul.

At the present time, new methods of production are being used; the thermic cracking of heavy catalytic gas-oils and oil extracts, and the catalytic cracking of gas-oils. Over the period 1965 to 1970, the volume of output of carbon black rose to such an extent due to the use of new materials and methods, that the USSR became an important exporter. In 1980, 103,835 tons were exported, mainly to Bulgaria, East Germany, Hungary and Czechoslovakia.

(7) Other Products

Other chemical products use comparatively little fuel, either as a feed-stock or as a fuel. They include pesticides, of which 470,000 tons were produced in 1980, paints (2.9 mn tons) and soap and detergents (2.579 mn tons, of which 1.012 mn tons were produced from synthetic materials). (Casinghead gas is an important raw material for paints and is replacing vegetable and animal fats.)

Table 6.17: Output of Selected Chemical Products ('000 tons)

	1960	1970	1975	1980
Pesticides	62.6	299	448	470
Paints and varnishes	1,212	2,377	3,016	2,900
Soaps and detergents	1,473	1,907	2,336	2,579
(including synthetic)	23	471	769	1,012

The production of soap and detergents take up most of the vegetable and animal fats consumed by the chemical industry. In 1970, 540,000 tons of natural oil was used by the chemical industry, compared with 650,000 tons in 1965.

The raw materials for synthetic detergents and surfactants are gas, liquid and solid hydrocarbons (i.e., propylene, benzene and paraffins), sulphuric acid and caustic soda. These are transformed into synthetic fatty acids and alpha-olefins. Between two and four tons of material per ton of synthetic fatty acids are required. The increased share of petrochemical raw materials in the production of detergents permitted the use of natural oils to be reduced considerably. The first plant for the production of synthetic fatty acids came on stream at Shebekino (Central Chernozem region) in 1953.

The first synthetic detergent plants were Shebekino (1958) and Volgograd and Angarsk in 1962. The output of synthetic detergents grew by an average 20.8% a year during 1960 to 1980, and received a substantial boost in 1982 with the commissioning of a 200,000 tons/ year detergent plant at Tura. This will be served by the USSR's first facility for manufacturing higher fatty acids, which started up at the Ufa '22nd Congress' oil refinery at the end of 1982.

(8) Consumption of Fuel

In 1972, the value of fuel consumed by the chemical industry amounted to 829 mn roubles; this included 421.8 mn roubles of oil and oil products, 352.2 mn roubles of natural gas and 47.8 mn roubles of coal and coal products. The sectors requiring most fuel (in value terms) were basic chemicals (267.1 mn R), organic synthetic products (234.8 mn R) and synthetic rubber and asbestos (173.1 mn R). Smaller amounts of fuel were used by mineral chemicals (31.6 mn R), plastics (29.5 mn R), synthetic fibres (25 mn R) and paints and lacquers (24.1 mn R).

About 205 mn G-cals of thermal energy were utilised by the chemical and petrochemical industry in 1975 compared with 150 mn in 1970 and 101 mn in 1965. This was largely produced by industrial boilers, although a significant volume resulted from the capture of waste heat from various production processes; this amounted to 32 mn G-cals in 1975 (more than by any other sector), 16 mn in 1970 and 9 mn in 1965.

Oil was the most important fuel for all chemical sectors except basic chemicals, where natural gas had become predominant in 1972 due to its widespread use for the production of ammonia and urea. Gas was also an important input to the synthetic rubber and organic synthetic products sectors, while coal had become practically insignificant except for the synthetic fibres sector.

Coal

The importance of coal has declined sharply during the last 20 years. Originally, products such as benzene, xylene, phenol, etc. were derived largely from coal, but it has since been superseded by gas and oil products. Most coal products destined for the chemical industry are obtained during the coking process, and their output is continuing to increase slowly as more new coking batteries are built to serve the needs of the iron and steel industry. During 1976 and 1980, 18 new coke batteries were built, and although most of these were designed to replace obsolete plant, the output of some chemical products, like sulphur-free benzene for the caprolactam sector, grew particularly rapidly.

Coking gas is still used, mainly in several Ukrainian plants and at Novomoskovsk (Central region), Kemerovo (Western Siberia) and Rustavi (Georgia), for the production of ammonia and nitrogenous fertiliser. Exactly half of the total expenditure on coal and coal products by the chemical industry in 1972 went to the basic chemicals sector which includes these products. Coking gas proves cheaper than natural gas for the production of ammonia and methanol in regions with full-cycle metallurgical plants.

Table 6.18: Production and Use of Coking Gas (bn cu m of natural gas equivalent)

	1970	1978	1979	1980
Production of coking gas	14.9	17.3	16.9	17.1
Used by the chemical industry	1.2	1.4	1.2	1.1

Oil Products

At the present time, oil refineries are the chief suppliers of hydrocarbon raw materials for Soviet chemical and petrochemical plants, although petrochemical feedstocks account for little more than 2% of the total output of oil. In the future, it is hoped that this share can reach 6-8% as in the USA and Western Europe.

The volume and range of materials obtained at each refinery depend on the capacity and structure of the refinery, including the depth of refining. The role of refineries as suppliers of materials will grow both in regions such as the Volga with a developed petrochemical industry but a declining level of oil production, and in the regions like Western Siberia with virtually unlimited possibilities for the production of oil-intensive synthetic products.

The volume of petrochemical material from a refinery varies between 4% and 18% of the crude throughput, depending partly on the depth of refining and partly on the location of the refinery. A refinery of capacity 6 mn tons/year with a limited extent of secondary refining can produce 75,000 tons of refinates and 125,000 tons of low-octane gasoline with 150,000 tons of gases a year, i.e. 300,000–380,000 tons of hydrocarbon raw materials, sufficient for the production of 100,000 tons of ethylene and 50,000 tons of propylene. A 12-million-ton refinery with extensive secondary refining capacity can provide up to 2 mn tons of materials. The output of feedstock from refineries in the European part of the Soviet Union should be minimised because of the growing demand for gasoline and diesel for transportation purposes, and it should be concentrated at the Siberian refineries such as Omsk and Angarsk. At the moment, most naphtha comes from the Volga refineries, particularly those like Nizhnekamsk and Novo-Kuibyshev, which are linked to large petrochemical complexes.

In 1972, 421.8 mn roubles of oil products (including refinery gas) were consumed by the chemical sector, including 138.9 mn R for organic synthetic products, 112.7 mn R for synthetic rubber and asbestos, 71.6 mn R for basic chemicals and 98.6 mn R for other sectors.

Depending on the structure of the refinery, between 40 and 200 kg of refinery gas are obtained per ton of crude, and this constitutes one of the largest sources of raw material for the petrochemical industry. The available resources increase not only with the growth in the throughput of refined oil, but also with the growth in the volume of secondary processing. The output of gas from different refinery processes (as a percentage of the weight of total output by the process) is: catalytic cracking 19.6–35.9%, catalytic reforming 9.0%, thermal cracking 6.4%, hydrocracking 9.1%, thermo-contact cracking 7.6% and coking 14.4%. The share of all these processes, except thermal cracking in the overall volume of refining is continually growing.

Although oil refinery gas provides a stable raw material for the petrochemical industry, and the processing of gas into petrochemical products is achieved easily and cheaply, its use is limited by the fact that it is also a prime source of additives for high-octane gasoline.

Insufficient use of oil refinery gas is beind made, although investment in gas-fractionating plants could be quickly recouped. The volume of LPG consumed as a raw material by the petrochemical industry has

Table 6.19: Output of Refinery Gas by Type as a Share of Crude Throughput (%)

	Thermal Cracking	Catalytic 43–102	Catalytic Cracking 43–103	Reforming	Thermo-contact Cracking	Coking
Methane-ethane-ethylene mixture	2.9	2.8	15.3	0.2	4.1	8.6
Propane	1.4	2.6	3.0	4.0	0.5	1.1
Propylene	0.6	3.3	7.2	–	1.4	1.6
Iso-butane	0.3	6.3	1.4	2.1	0.4	0.4
n-butane	0.6	1.9	0.7	2.7	0.6	0.9
Iso-butylene and n-butylenes	0.6	2.7	8.3	–	0.6	1.8
Total	6.4	19.6	35.9	9.0	7.6	14.4

grown from 0.38 mn tons in 1960 to 1.9 mn in 1965, 2.57 mn in 1970 and 3.65 mn tons in 1975.

Paraffin is used for the production of synthetic fatty acids, detergents, synthetic alcohol and additives for animal feedstuffs. It has traditionally been obtained from the North Caucasus region, and was first produced at Groznyi in 1927. In 1954, a plant producing paraffin from Volga oil was commissioned at Novo-Kuibyshev petrochemical plant, and the Volga region still produces more paraffin than any other in the Soviet Union. When the carbamide deparaffinisation process was introduced, the output of liquid paraffins grew quickly, and during the 1970s, new 'Parex' units, each producing 120,000 tons a year, were imported from East Germany and installed at several refineries including Mozyr and Novopolotsk in Belorussia, Kirishi in the North West and Volgograd and Saratov in the Volga region. While much of their output is destined for the animal feedstuffs sector, a significant proportion is used by petrochemical plants.

Gas condensate is likely to acquire greater importance as a petrochemical feedstock in future years, especially when its production at Urengoi begins to build up. While one ton of condensate is considered equivalent to 1.5-2 tons of motor fuel, it has a value equal to 5 tons of oil products destined for the petrochemical sector.

Gas

As late as the mid-1970s, it was believed that oil products (mainly naphtha and gas-oil) would continue to provide the bulk of the petrochemical industry's feedstock requirements almost indefinitely as well as cover demand by transport for gasoline and diesel. However, the slow growth in output of crude oil has lead to a reappraisal of the value of automotive products, and it is now policy for petrochemicals to switch, wherever possible, to natural gas.

Natural gas is the basic feedstock for obtaining ammonia, methanol, acetylene and carbon black, and is becoming increasingly important as a source of many other products. In 1980, 36.3 bn cu m were used, or 8.4% of total gas consumption in the Soviet Union. During the 1970s, output by the chemical industry rose at an average annual rate of 8.1% while its consumption of gas increased by 13.4% a year, and it can be estimated that the usage of oil products rose by 4-5% a year during the decade.

The importance of natural gas relative to that of other feedstocks is growing, at an accelerating pace. During the first half of the decade, gas consumption rose by 104% while output by the chemical industry

Table 6.20: Consumption of Natural Gas by the Chemical Industry

Year	Consumption of Gas (bn cu m)	Share of National Gas Consumption (%)	Total Output by the Chemical Industry (1970 = 100)
1960	1.9	4.2	
1970	10.3	5.4	100
1975	21.0	7.3	165
1978	28.8	7.8	200
1979	32.7	8.1	207
1980	36.3	8.4	218

increased by 65%, giving a gas-input/chemical-output rate of 1.6, and during the second half the respective figures were 72.8% and 32%, giving a rate of 2.28.

The value of natural gas consumed by the chemical industry has risen from a mere 17 mn roubles in 1959 to 352.2 mn in 1972, consisting of 168.6 mn R for basic chemicals, 95.6 mn for organic synthetic products, 55.5 mn for synthetic rubber and asbestos and 32.5 mn R for all other chemical sectors.

In 1980, it is estimated that natural gas accounted for 43% of fuel consumption by the chemical industry, oil 54% and coal 4%. This represents very little change over 1972, with the share of oil growing slightly, entirely at the expense of coal.

Table 6.21: Share of Different Fuels in Fuel Input to the Chemical Industry, 1972

	Gas	Oil	Coal
Basic chemicals	63	27	9
Organic synthetic products	41	59	–
Synthetic rubber and asbestos	33	65	2
Mineral chemicals	22	77	1
Plastics	21	74	4
Synthetic fibres	17	48	31
Paints and lacquers	19	65	16
Others	24	59	16
All chemicals	43	51	6

Casinghead gas is becoming an increasingly important input to the chemical industry, particularly since large new gas refineries have come on stream in Western Siberia, including Nizhnevartovsk (capacity 8 bn cu m a year), Belo-ozersk (4 bn) and Surgut (4 bn). They have enabled

Table 6.22: Composition of Gas from Selected Deposits in 1980 (%)

	Methane	Ethane	Propane	Butane	Pentane	Nitrogen
Natural Gas						
Urengoi (Western Siberia)	99.4	0.3	–	–	–	–
Medvezhe (Western Siberia)	98.1	0.2	0.0	0.0	0.0	1.3
Shebelinka (Ukraine)	93.6	4.0	0.6	0.7	0.4	0.6
Orenburg (Urals)	82.1	3.7	1.5	1.4	2.2	7.5
Vuktyl (North West)	75.7	9.1	3.1	–	7.5	3.7
Russkii Khutor (North Caucasus)	69.1	11.3	3.3	1.7	8.6	3.3
Ust-Vilyuisk (Far East)	92.5	2.8	1.8	0.9	0.4	1.4
Achak (Turkmen, Central Asia)	93.4	3.6	0.9	0.3	0.3	1.0
Gazli (Uzbek, Central Asia)	94.2	2.6	0.1	0.1	0.1	2.1
Casinghead Gas						
Tuimazy (Bashkir, Volga)	41.9	20.0	17.3	7.9		9.4
Romashkino (Tatar, Volga)	37.0	20.0	18.5	8.2		11.5
Buguruslan (Kuibyshev, Volga)	72.5	9.8	7.5	8.3		–
Staro-Groznyi (North Caucasus)	30.8	7.5	21.5	10.0		–

the rate of utilisation of potential resources of casinghead gas to be raised from 65% in 1970 to 70% in 1980 and it is planned to raise this share to 80% in 1985.

In gas refineries, the gas is dried, cleaned of impurities and separated into dry gas (basically methane) and unstable benzine, being a mixture of ethane, propane, butanes, pentane and heavier hydrocarbons. Dry gas is used as a fuel, and unstable benzine is either separated into its components at the gas refinery, or is sent to oil refineries or petrochemical plants. Liquids from the new Siberian gas refineries are to be utilised by the Tomsk and Tobolsk petrochemical plants, and a special pipeline has been laid from Ust Balyk to Tobolsk, but at the moment, all liquids are railed to petrochemical plants in the Volga region from Nizhnevartovsk or Tobolsk. The dry gas is piped at a rate of 16 bn cu m a year to the Kuzbass. Table 6.22 shows the contents of different components in natural gas and casinghead gas from various deposits.

(9) Future Consumption of Fuel by the Chemical Industry

A major problem in forecasting the future demand for fuel by the chemical industry is that of forecasting the output of the most important chemical products. The plan targets for plastics, for example, have traditionally been greatly underfulfilled; during 1976 to 1980, output should have risen by 2.9 mn tons, but an increase of only 0.8 mn tons was achieved.

The reason is that all new plastic production is to come from a small number of very large multi-product plants. In almost all cases, the construction of these plants takes very much longer than planned and, when commissioned, their build-up to rated capacity is painfully slow. This is not just a consequence of difficulties in assimilating new technology. The modern plastics plant synthesises a great many intermediate products, and the failure to supply any of these in sufficient quantities can have an adverse effect on the performance of the entire plant.

The situation concerning chemical fibres is little better, and the 1980 targets for ammonia and fertilisers were considerably underfulfilled. However, once the technological and organisational problems have been overcome, there is no reason why the output of chemical products should not grow extremely rapidly, because there is a huge potential demand for them given the amount of resources spent on more expensive alternatives such as steel, timber and natural fibres.

Table 6.23 shows how the chemical industry could develop over

Table 6.23: Forecast Output of Products by the Chemical Industry (mn tons)

	1980	1985 Plan	1985 Likely	1990	2000
Plastics	3.64	6.1	5.3	7.8	17
Chemical fibres	1.176	1.6	1.5	1.9	3
Fertilisers	103.9	150	129	161	180

1980 to 2000, with the likely rates of growth of between 1981 and 1985 assumed to apply until 2000. The output of fertiliser is likely to stabilise at about 180 mn tons a year. Although the Eleventh Five Year Plan anticipates that the production of plastics will grow at an average annual rate of 11.0% to 6.1 mn tons in 1985, chemical fibres by 6.4% a year to 1.6 mn tons and fertilisers by 7.6% a year to 150 mn tons, it is likely that the actual growth rates will amount to 8%, 5% and 4.5% a year respectively.

As fuel is used primarily as a feedstock, it is unlikely that the fuel rate will fall significantly for chemicals as a whole. But there will be major changes in the nature of fuel used, with the shares of natural gas and gas condensate falling at the expense of casinghead gas, naphtha and gas-oil, although the absolute volume of gas products used by the petrochemical industry should continue to grow. It should be remembered that gas condensate is classified under oil rather than gas in official Soviet statistics, and this convention is followed in Table 6.24.

Table 6.24: Estimated Consumption of Fuel by the Chemical Industry (mn tsf)

	1980	1985	1990	2000
Natural gas	43	50	60	80
Oil-based feedstocks (inc. gas condensate	54	82	115	170
Coal-based feedstocks	4	4	5	5
Total	101	136	180	255

Growth rates for fuel consumption of 6.1% a year are anticipated for 1981 to 1985, and 5.8% during 1986 to 1990 before falling to 3.5% a year over 1990 to 2000 in connection with the levelling out of nitrogenous fertiliser production.

So far, the discussion has centred on the requirements of fuel resources as feedstocks. In addition, small amounts of fuel (mostly natural gas), are used to fire industrial boilers and combined heat-and-power plants belonging to the chemical plants. Consumption of natural gas for this purpose has grown particularly quickly, partly thanks to the conversion of boilers burning fuel oil and coal, and in 1980 amounted to 9.7 bn cu m compared with 5 bn in 1975 and 2.3 bn in 1970. The fuel requirements of these boilers and CHPPs have been considered in Chapter 3.

The chemical industry is also an important consumer of electricity, from the national grid as well as its own CHPPs. In 1980, 107.7 bn kWh were used (8.3% of national power output) compared with 64.2 bn in 1970 (8.7%) and 19.1 bn kWh in 1960 (6.5%). However, the consumption of electricity per unit of chemical output is declining quite rapidly; in 1976–80 the gross output by the chemical industry rose by 32% while the consumption of electricity rose by only 18%.

7 THE OIL REFINING INDUSTRY

The USSR does not issue statistics on oil refining, but it can be estimated that their 45 operating refineries processed 501 mn tons of oil in 1982 and had a total capacity of 567 mn tons at year end.

During the five years 1976 to 1980, the output of oil products grew by 3.7% a year compared with a growth in crude oil production of 4.2% a year. The capacity of secondary refining plant rose by 50%, permitting a further 36 mn tons of fuel oil to be processed annually, and allowing a further 17.5 mn tons of light and middle products from the same volume of crude oil. The Eleventh Five Year Plan for 1981 to 1985 calls for an increase of 2.0% a year in product output, and given the planned 1.0% a year increase in the output of crude oil, it would appear that the Russians expect to reduce their exports of crude in favour of higher product exports.

The location of the oil refining sector is still heavily concentrated in the traditional refining regions of the Volga, Azerbaidzhan and the North Caucasus. Western Siberia, which produces half the country's oil, has only one refinery, at Omsk. This heavy concentration of refining capacity in a limited number of regions puts a heavy strain on the railway system for the transport of oil products. To supply Tashkent, for example, oil products must be hauled 2,000 km from Pavlodar or Krasnovodsk.

With the railway system under increasing strain, there has been a slight change in Soviet refinery location policy during the 1970s. While the former policy of increasing total capacity by expanding existing plant is being continued, more and more emphasis is being placed on the construction of new refineries. Five came on stream during the Tenth Five Year Plan period; these were Lisichansk (Ukraine) in 1976 and doubled up to 12 mn tons in 1979, Mozyr (Belorussia) in 1976, Pavlodar (Kazakhstan) in 1978, Nizhnekamsk (Volga region) in 1979 and Mazheikiai (Lithuania) in 1980. All are equipped with the standard 6 mn tons capacity atmospheric and vacuum primary distillation plant. Another refinery at Achinsk (Eastern Siberia) was due to start up in 1981 but did not yield its first stream of products under serial production conditions until December 1982. Plans for other refineries at Chimkent (Kazakhstan) and Chardzhou (Central Asia) have been greatly delayed. The assembly of equipment began in March 1980 at

Map 7.1: Oil Refineries, European USSR

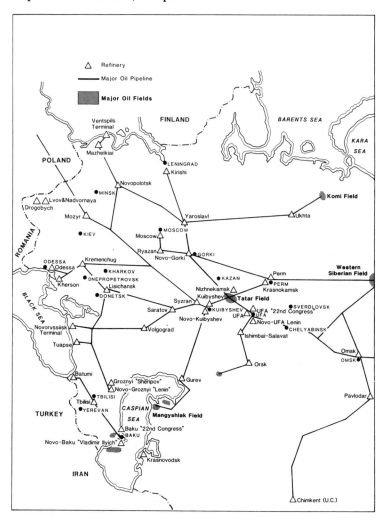

Table 7.1: Oil Refineries in Operation, end 1982 (mn tons)

Refinery	Region	Estimated Capacity
Kirishi	Leningrad	18
Ukhta	Komi	6
Mazheikiai	Lithuania	6
Novopolotsk	Belorussia	20
Mozyr	Belorussia	12
Moscow	Central	12
Ryazan	Central	15
Yaroslavl	Central	24
Groznyi 'Sheripov' and Novo-Grozyni 'Lenin'	North Caucasus	24
Tuapse	North Caucasus	6
Baku '22nd Congress'	Azerbaidzhan	26
Novo-Baku 'Vladimir Ilyich'	Azerbaidzhan	18
Batumi	Georgia	6
Tbilisi	Georgia	3
Novo-Gorki	Volga Vyatka	24
Kremenchug	Ukraine	15
Kherson	Ukraine	9
Lisichansk	Ukraine	18
Odessa	Ukraine	6
Drogobych	Ukraine	3
Lvov and Nadvornaya	Ukraine	6
Perm	Urals	24
Krasnokamsk	Urals	6
Orsk	Urals	12
Ufa, Ufa '22nd Congress', Novo-Ufa 'Lenin'	Volga	46
Saratov	Volga	15
Volgograd	Volga	12
Novo-Kuibyshev	Volga	30
Kuibyshev	Volga	6
Syzran	Volga	6
Ishimbai-Salavat	Volga	12
Nizhnekamsk	Volga	12
Omsk	Western Siberia	30
Angarsk	Eastern Siberia	30
Achinsk	Eastern Siberia	6
Komsomolsk	Far East	3
Khabarovsk	Far East	9
Gurev	Kazakhstan	3
Pavlodar	Kazakhstan	12
Krasnovodsk	Central Asia	12
Fergana	Central Asia	4
Total		567

Table 7.2: Refining Capacity by Economic Region, end 1982

Region	Refinery Capacity (mn tons)	Population, 1/1/82 ('000)	Capacity per Person (tons)
Volga	139	19,561	7.11
Eastern Siberia	36	8,451	4.26
Caucasus	53	14,572	3.64
Belorussia	32	9,744	3.28
Volga Vyatka	24	8,344	2.88
Urals	42	15,754	2.66
Western Siberia	30	13,431	2.23
South	15	7,274	2.06
North Caucasus	30	15,868	1.89
North West	24	13,611	1.76
Centre	51	29,299	1.74
Far East	12	7,170	1.67
Donets Dnepr	33	21,270	1.55
Kazakhstan	15	15,253	0.98
Baltic	6	8,344	0.72
Central Asia	16	27,404	0.58
South West	9	21,763	0.41
Central Chernozem	–	7,706	–
Moldavia	–	4,025	–
USSR	567	268,844	2.11

Chardzhou with East German experts participating, and the refinery is scheduled for start-up in 1984. It is actually located at the new town of Neftezavodsk, 90 km from Chardzhou. The Chimkent refinery should be commissioned in 1983 according to current plans, and this is likely to take place now that the 1,600-km pipeline from Pavlodar to Chimkent has been completed. A branch of the same pipeline will also serve Chardzhou, and another branch is to be built to Fergana enabling its small refinery to be supplied on a regular basis with Siberian crude.

There have been reports in the past that refineries are to be built at Arkhangelsk, Nakhodka, Vinnitsa and Zaporozhe, but no construction work appears to have been carried out yet.

When the distribution of refinery capacity is considered by economic region, it can be seen that, while only two regions (Moldavia and Central Chernozem) do not have refineries, some important regions like the Baltic, the three Ukrainian regions (Donets-Dnepr, South West and South), Kazakhstan and Central Asia are underprovided in terms of their populations. The Volga region, on the other hand, has an extremely large refining sector in comparison with its population. Table 7.2 uses regional populations as a very rough indication of demand for oil products; in fact, underdeveloped regions like Central Asia should have a much lower *per caput* demand for oil products than (for example) the Central region.

The 45 refineries are:

Kirishi (Leningrad Oblast)

Situated 114 km from Leningrad, Kirishi started up in 1966, and receives oil by pipeline from Yaroslavl. During the Tenth plan period, a para-xylene plant (the first of its kind in the USSR), an octafiner and a hydrogen plant were completed by Kawasaki in 1976, a gas liquifaction and bottling plant was added in 1977, and in 1980 a new first-phase plant of capacity 6 mn tons a year and a parex plant for producing 120,000 tons of liquid paraffin a year were installed. In 1981, a catformer of 1.05 mn tons a year was added. The capacity of the refinery is now 18 mn tons a year.

Ukhta (Komi Republic)

This is a small refinery which dates from 1939 and processes local oil and gas condensate into eight different products. It has a capacity of 6 mn tons a year, and most oil from the Komi oilfield is sent to Yaroslavl. A large parex plant is under construction; its liquid paraffin will supply a new synthetic detergent plant under construction at Ukhta.

Mazheikiai (Lithuania)

Construction began in 1970, and after lengthy delays the refinery finally began working in May 1980 when fuel oil was delivered to the nearby Akmyants cement works. The first stage, producing petrol, diesel, kerosene, lubricants and LPG, was completed in August 1980. The second stage is now under construction and will begin producing shortly. The refinery currently satisfies Lithuania's petrol and diesel requirements and exports fuel oil and LPG. It has a throughput of 6 mn tons a year, and when this is built up to the rated 24 mn tons a year, it will become the Soviet Union's largest source of products for export.

Novopolotsk (Belorussia)

Novopolotsk started up in 1963 on oil arriving through a branch of the Druzhba pipeline. Its size has increased considerably during the last five years in preparation for the completion of the Surgut-Polotsk pipeline which reached Novopolotsk in early 1981. The capacity of the Druzhba pipeline has also been increased, and the refinery can now handle 20 mn tons of oil a year. It is technologically advanced with a large volume of secondary refining capacity and produces chemical feedstocks for the rapidly growing Belorussian petrochemical industry, as well as 240,000 tons a year of liquid paraffin from two parex plants.

Mozyr (Belorussia)

The Mozyr refinery began operating in 1975 and was supplied by a pipeline bringing oil from the nearby Rechitsa field. Local oil output has been declining, however, and the refinery is now supplied mostly from the Druzhba pipeline. In 1976, the construction of the second stage began, and its main units came on stream in 1979, bringing the refinery's capacity to 12 mn tons. Mozyr produces large volumes of petrochemicals, has a 500,000 tons a year bitumen plant and produces raw materials for animal foodstuffs from its parex plant.

Moscow

This is an old refinery, built in 1934. Its capacity was doubled in 1976 in preparation for oil coming from the Komi republic through the Ukhta-Yaroslavl-Moscow pipeline. It has recently begun to receive Tyumen oil from the Surgut-Polotsk pipeline, and its current capacity is 12 mn tons a year. The Russians are upgrading the plant, and a large volume of secondary processing equipment will be installed during the 1980s. A vacuum distillation plant and a 1 mn tons a year catcracker are now being built.

Ryazan (Central Region)

This medium-sized refinery of 15 mn tons/year capacity consists basically of primary processing plant. It uses Volga oil and is now being supplied from Tyumen through a branch line from Surgut-Polotsk pipeline. A new shop for the production of lubricants was commissioned in 1980.

Yaroslavl (Central Region)

The Yaroslavl refinery works on oil from the Volga region, the Komi republic and Tyumen oblast. Oil has recently started arriving through the Surgut-Polotsk pipeline. The refinery produces petrochemical feedstocks for Yaroslavl's synthetic rubber plant, and has a primary refining capacity of 24 mn tons a year. It has 13 facilities including large catcrackers and catformers producing light and medium products for most of the Central region.

Groznyi 'Sheripov' (North Caucasus)

One of the oldest refineries in the USSR, dating from the last century, Grozyni 'Sheripov' was reconstructed in 1974, and its annual output was increased by 250%. A large volume of secondary refining capacity was installed, so as to enable increasing quantities of light products to be obtained from a declining volume of crude.

Novo-Grozyni 'Lenin' (North Caucasus)

Novo-Grozyni 'Lenin' has also been undergoing an extensive reconstruction, and in 1979 a new first-phase facility was added, bringing the total capacity of the Grozyni plants to 24 mn tons.

Tuapse (Krasnodar, North Caucasus)

A small plant of 6 mn tons capacity a year.

Baku '22nd Congress' (Azerbaidzhan)

The refinery now has a capacity of 26 mn tons a year with the start-up of a new first-phase unit with electric desalter in July 1981. A cat-former of 1.05 mn tons a year, a vacuum distillation unit for producing lubes (which have been in short supply in the Caucasus region) and a coking chamber for the production of petroleum coke were also commissioned in 1981.

Novo-Baku 'Vladimir Ilyich' (Azerbaidzhan)

The 1972 Giproazneft plant for the reconstruction of the Baku refining industry called for the capacity of this refinery to be doubled to make up for the disappearance of two small and obsolete refineries. This was accomplished in 1977, with the new first-phase unit working on Mangy-shlak oil delivered by tanker. This has created problems, because it is necessary to receive and refine the local high-quality oil and Mangy-shlak sulphurous oil separately. A large new catformer of capacity 1 mn tons a year was installed by Litwin at a cost of $50 mn in 1981, and the plant's catcrackers have been modernised and re-equipped. A new first-phase plant was completed in 1979, bringing the refinery's capacity to 18 mn tons a year, and in 1982 a 300-ton coking chamber built by the Volgogradneftemash Association was installed.

Batumi (Georgia)

This small refinery dating from 1930 handles oil brought by rail from Baku and by pipeline from the new Samgori oilfield in Georgia. It has a capacity of 6 mn tons a year.

Tbilisi (Georgia)

Tbilisi is a small, old and obsolete refinery of 3 mn tons capacity a year.

Novo-Gorki (Volga Vyatka Region)

The Novo-Gorki refinery, situated at Kstovo, came on stream in 1958. Its capacity was raised to 24 mn tons in time to receive oil from Tyumen through the Surgut-Polotsk pipeline, which reached Gorki at the beginning of 1980.

Kremenchug (Ukraine)

After coming on stream in 1966, Kremenchug was supplied with oil by rail until 1974, when the Michurinsk-Kremenchug pipeline was completed. In 1978, another pipeline was laid from Lisichansk; this is part of the system distributing oil throughout the Ukraine, and it enabled the capacity of the refinery to be increased to 15 mn tons. It has a large secondary refining capacity, and a major share of its products are distributed to Cherkassy and Kiev by a product pipeline. A lube additive plant was commissioned in 1981.

Kherson (Ukraine)

Dating from 1960, Kherson refinery is supplied by a pipeline from Kremenchug bringing Tyumen oil and another from Poltava bringing local Ukrainian oil. It has a capacity of 9 mn tons a year.

Lisichansk (Ukraine)

Lisichansk is one of the USSR's newest refineries. It began operating in September 1976 on crude received through a pipeline from Krasnodar. In 1977 a major pipeline of 1,220 mn diameter and 1,089 km long from Kuibyshev started bringing Tyumen oil. The second primary unit was completed in October 1979, and in 1980, the first part of the second stage was commissioned bringing the refinery's capacity to 18 mn tons a year. In 1980, a new catformer of 1 mn tons a year was introduced, and 1981 saw the start-up of a 2 mn tons a year hydrofiner with a high degree of automation and said to be operated by only six workers. It is estimated that diesel from the hydrofiner will enable the working life of lorry engines to be prolonged by 15-20%. A distinctive feature of the refinery is its ethylene production unit, which began operating in 1978. Eventually it will produce 300,000 tons a year and will be connected by a 36 km pipeline to the chemical plant at Severodonetsk, where the ethylene is turned into polyethylene.

Odessa (Ukraine)

Odessa has a small refinery, now working on Tyumen oil delivered by the final stage of a 4,500 km system originating in Western Siberia. It has a capacity of 6 mn tons a year.

Drogobych (Ukraine)

This is a small primary refining plant kept alive by oil railed from the new Kaliningrad field. It has a capacity of 3 mn tons a year.

Lvov and Nadvornaya (Ukraine)

These two small refineries with a joint capacity of 6 mn tons a year work on local oil from the declining Western Ukrainian field.

Perm (Urals Region)

The Perm refinery began producing in 1957 and has since been expanded on several occasions, making it one of the USSR's largest refineries with a capacity of 24 mn tons. It is notable for the production of petrochemicals with a new plant for producing ethylbenzene and styrene from low-grade oil starting up in 1975, and an ammonia and carbamide complex with an annual capacity of 1 mn tons of fertilisers coming on stream in 1980.

Krasnokamsk (Perm Oblast, Urals Region)

This small refinery, located near Perm, uses local oil and has a capacity of 6 mn tons a year.

Orsk (Urals Region)

Orsk refinery, built before the last war, processes Bashkir and Tyumen oil which arrives through a pipeline from Salavat. It has a capacity of 12 mn tons a year.

Ufa (Bashkir Republic)

Ufa refinery was built in 1936 and has been reconstructed and expanded several times. It uses local oil and is part of a complex including the Ufa '22nd Congress' and Novo-Ufa 'Lenin' refineries and a number of petrochemical plants. The total capacity of the complex is 46 mn tons a year, and its product output rose by 22% over 1976 to 1980.

Ufa '22nd Congress'

Unlike the other two refineries in the complex, which use local Bashkir oil, Ufa '22nd Congress' has been working on Tyumen oil since 1970.

With the Urals-Volga oilfields declining, and with the Urengoi-Chelyabinsk gas pipeline serving many needs formerly covered by fuel oil, the emphasis in recent years has been on installing secondary capacity, like a 1 mn tons a year catformer built in 1981 by Litwin and Technip of France. At the end of 1982, a plant was installed for the production of higher fatty acids from ethylene and aromatics derived from benzene. However, it is said that the refinery has not been working well for a number of years, and urgent measures must be taken during the Eleventh plan period.

Novo-Ufa 'Lenin'

A new catalytic cracker was installed in 1973, and a catformer intended to produce a large proportion of the USSR's high-octane petrol for Ladas was built in 1976. The bitumen plant is the chief supplier for a large part of the Volga region. The thermal cracking plants are currently undergoing construction and coking plants are being built. By 1985, the refinery will be a major producer of liquid paraffin from several parex plants.

Saratov (Volga Region)

This refinery has a capacity of about 15 mn tons. It has a large Czech-built catformer which was installed in 1973 and produces high-octane petrol for Volga cars.

Volgograd (Volga Region)

Volgograd refinery processes local oil from the Lower Volga region and Mangyshlak oil delivered by tanker. It is technologically advanced with a large volume of secondary refining capacity, and produces over 50 different products. A carbamide deparaffinisation plant was introduced in 1980, and this portends increased supplies of oil from the Mangyshlak and Buzachi peninsulas. Its current capacity is 12 mn tons a year. A parex plant produces 120,000 tons a year of liquid paraffin for the Svetloyarsk Plant of Vitamin Concentrates.

Novo-Kuibyshev (Volga Region)

After coming on stream in 1949, this refinery has become one of the world's largest with a capacity of 30 mn tons. It refines oil from local fields and from Tyumen and Mangyshlak. It has traditionally been a research centre for the oil refining industry, and a new type of fully automated parex plant which can be operated by only 12 people is being tested there. It will produce paraffin for the synthetic detergent and animal feed industries. A 1 mn tons a year catformer was installed in 1981.

Kuibyshev (Volga Region)

Kuibyshev is an old primary processing refinery with a capacity of 6 mn tons. It sends some of its residual fuel oil to Novo-Kuibyshev for further refining.

Syzran (Volga Region)

This is a small refinery of 6 mn tons capacity. A new parex plant which produces 24 tons of paraffin per 100 tons of raw material compared with the usual 14 tons has recently been commissioned.

Ishimbai-Salavat (Volga Region)

The Ishimbai refinery, built in 1934, has been incorporated into a complex with the Salavat petrochemical plant. It processes oil from local Bashkir fields, gas condensate and casinghead gas. It has a platformer producing 93-octane petrol, a Czech-made hydrofiner for processing diesel and equipment for producing dearomatized kerosene which is used for the manufacture of detergents at Sumgait, near Baku. The refinery has a capacity of 12 mn tons.

Nizhnekamsk Petrochemical Combine (Volga Region)

This is one of the newest refineries in the USSR, and the first in the Tatar republic. It is served by a new pipeline from Almetyevsk through Naberezhnye Chelny, which brings Tyumen oil arriving through the Samotlor-Kuibyshev pipeline. The primary refining facility began operating in April 1979, and three or four different petrochemical processing facilities are installed each year. The refinery now has a capacity of 12 mn tons.

Omsk (Western Siberia)

The Omsk combine dates from the early 1950s, and it has been extended many times since then. At first it worked on Volga oil through the Tuimazy-Omsk pipeline, but it is now fully converted to the refining of Tyumen oil. In 1974, the first plant in the USSR for making vehicle transmission oil was installed, and secondary capacity was further increased with the introduction of a hydrocracker in 1978. The refinery was extended further in 1979 and 1980 when a 1 mn tons a year catformer was installed by Litwin at a cost of $36 mn, and a petroleum coke plant is now being built. Omsk refinery now has a capacity of 30 mn tons a year.

Angarsk (Eastern Siberia)

This refinery is part of the Angarsk Petro-Chemical Combine and has a capacity of 30 mn tons. It uses Tyumen oil delivered through the pipeline from Samatlor to Anzerho-Sudzhensk where it joins the Trans-Siberian Pipeline. It supplies most of the Eastern Siberian region with oil products and the rapidly growing local petrochemical industry with feedstocks. During 1981 its desulphuriser and catcracker were modernised, and the pipeline for carrying ethylene from its 300,000 tons a year EP-300 ethylene facility to Zima was completed.

Achinsk (Eastern Siberia)

After several months of tests during the summer of 1981, the USSR's newest refinery began producing in December 1982. It works on Tyumen crude delivered through a second string of the Omsk-Krasnoyarsk-Irkutsk pipeline which ends at Angarsk.

Komsomolsk (Far East)

The small Komsomolsk refinery was built in 1935 with a capacity of 1 mn tons a year. It refines Sakhalin oil arriving through the Okha-Komsomolsk pipeline, and in 1979 its capacity was trebled in time for the completion of a second string of the pipeline. The refinery is not yet working at capacity; this will happen when the Mongi-Pogibi pipeline on Sakhalin is completed. Its capacity is currently 3 mn tons.

Khabarovsk (Far East)

Built in 1950, the Khabarovsk refinery of 9 mn tons capacity refines Tyumen oil sent by pipeline to Irkutsk and then railed to Khabarovsk. It now produces 16 types of product, completely satisfies the Primorskii Krai's requirements for petrol and diesel and produces fuel oil for export.

Gurev (Kazakhstan)

This small refinery was built in 1947 and enlarged in 1971. It processes local oil from the Emba field and heavy oil from Mangyshlak. Its capacity is now officially said to be 3 mn tons. A coking plant producing coke for the non-ferrous metallurgy industry started up in 1980.

Pavlodar (Kazakhstan)

Pavlodar refinery was completed in 1978, three years behind schedule.

It is fed by the Omsk-Pavlodar pipeline which delivers Tyumen oil. A second primary refining stage and a bitumen producing complex of 0.5 mn tons capacity a year started up in 1980, and in 1981 a gas bottling plant began to collect and process gas which was previously flared. The refinery now covers bottled gas demand from most of Kazakhstan. A 1 mn tons a year catcracker and a vacuum distillation unit are currently under construction, and the refinery has a capacity of 12 mn tons a year.

Krasnovodsk (Central Asia)

Krasnovodsk refinery is famous for its coking plant, the first of its type in the USSR. It was manufactured by Creusot-Loire of France and delivered in 1974. The plant started producing high-quality electrode coke for the steel and aluminium industries in 1977. Another such plant has since been installed and plans have been drawn up for a thermo-cracking installation designed to produce needle coke. The refinery works on local oil, and has been operating at much less than its rated capacity of 12 mn tons a year in recent years because of the decline in Turkmen oil production.

Fergana (Central Asia)

Built in 1959, this small refinery was extended in 1972. It is supplied by local oil from Uzbek and Tadzhik fields. Its capacity is about 4 mn tons a year, but it is considerably underutilised and has a poor record of efficiency.

According to the Eleventh Five Year Plan, the period 1983 to 1985 should see the completion of the first stages of the Chardzhou and Chimkent refineries, and new capacity should be added at Lisichansk and Pavlodar. All these new units should be of 6 mn tons a year each. The Mazheikiai refinery will be extended by 6 mn tons (some reports say its capacity will be quadrupled, implying the installation of 18 mn tons of capacity − these look rather optimistic, although it should be achieved before 1990), and Khabarovsk by 3 mn tons. It can be estimated that primary refining capacity should rise to 600 mn tons a year by the end of 1985. The Grozyni and Baku complexes are undergoing reconstruction work to enable them to process more oil from Siberia and the Buzachi field of Kazakhstan.

The most efficient plants in 1981 were Moscow, Ishimbai, Pavlodar, Gurev, Novopolotsk, Kherson, Yaroslavl and Tuapse. They have an aggregate first phase capacity of 98 mn tons a year. Four refineries failed badly to meet their targets. These were Fergana, Orsk, Grozyni 'Sheripov' and Krasnovodsk, with a total installed capacity of 34 mn tons.

Refining Technology

Improvements in refining technology have proceeded in two directions: a larger size of refinery and refining units, and a greater depth of processing with a concomitant improvement in the quality of products.

Immediately after the last war, the capacity of refining plants was very small. First-phase plants of 600,000 tons a year, thermal crackers of 450,000 tons and catcrackers of 250,000 tons a year were standard refining equipment. By 1982, domestically produced first-phase units of 6 mn tons had been standard for 17 years, and some of 8 mn tons had been installed. Catcrackers and catformers of 1 mn tons a year and hydrofiners of 2 mn tons were operating at several of the larger refineries. During the period 1976 to 1980, the volume of catformer capacity accounted for by units of 0.9 mn tons a year and more rose from 27% to 42%, while the volume share of hydrofiners of 1.5 mn tons a year and more grew from 20% to 30%. The standard size of new vacuum distillation units is 5 mn tons a year, and modern Soviet lube plants have capacities of 0.38 mn tons a year.

As long ago as 1974, first-phase plants of 12 mn tons, catcrackers of 1.5 mn tons and catformers of 1.2 mn tons had been designed, but the Russians appear to be sufficiently happy with their standard equipment, and particularly large or advanced units have been imported. These include catformers of 1 mn tons capacity which have been built at several refineries by Litwin.

During the six years 1975 to 1980, 871.8 mn roubles of oil-refining equipment was imported. This included 394 mn roubles from East Germany (mostly small crackers and Parex liquid paraffin plants produced by Chemieanlagen Grimma of Leipzig), 207.1 mn roubles from Japan, 80.9 mn roubles from Czechoslovakia, 79.9 mn roubles from France and 40.8 mn roubles from Romania.

The most pressing problem facing the refining industry at the moment is the need to upgrade its products. Fuel oil alone accounts for 42.5% of oil products by volume, and it is used for purposes which could be met more rationally by natural gas. The arrival of the two natural gas pipelines in the Urals region, for example, has enabled a large number of industrial and municipal boilers which previously burned high-sulphur fuel oil from the Ufa complex to switch to natural gas. This has improved the environment in Urals' cities and lowered costs, but has also left the refineries with a surplus of fuel oil on their hands. This problem, the so-called 'mazut problem', can only be solved by the installation of secondary refining equipment.

It has been argued that the Ufa refineries are not doing enough to overcome this problem. The programme of construction and reconstruction for the 1981 to 1985 period anticipates a decline in the share of fuel oil (mazut) in the product mix from 41.5% to 37%, but this is regarded by the Bashkirneftekhimzavod Association as insufficient. By making a greater use of vacuum distillation facilities, it is said that 'hundreds of millions of roubles' worth of light and medium products could be obtained without any increase in the throughput of crude. In the long-term, it is believed that the Ufa complex can increase the depth of refining to 85%, and a plan is being drawn up, involving the installation of visbreakers, catcrackers, hydrofiners, coking plants and lube plants.

In other regions, refineries face the problem of how to meet a growing demand for light products from a declining supply of crude. This is the case at Baku, where a considerable amount of money has been spent on rationalising the city's refineries by installing more secondary equipment such as the catformer and catcracker at Novo-Baku 'Vladimir Ilyich' refinery. However, the Baku refineries are not meeting their plan targets because of a shortage of high quality crude. This problem can only be rectified when the Grozyni-Baku oil pipeline is completed and Siberian crude begins to arrive.

Current Soviet policy is to raise the share of light and medium products from 50% to 60–65%, but at the present time existing secondary units at some refineries are underutilised. Particularly high rates of output of light products, and a corresponding fall in the share of fuel oil, took place in 1982, and this was achieved largely through the commissioning of catformers at Kuibyshev and Kirishi. The output of liquid paraffin intended for the production of animal feed additives and synthetic detergents is now increasing rapidly. The parex method of paraffin production has been installed at six refineries: Ukhta, Kirishi, Syzran, Novo-Kuibyshev, Mozyr and Novopolotsk. The Ufa complex is to get three plants during the next few years.

As the depth of refining has grown, the quality of oil products has improved. It was planned to raise the share of high-octane petrol in total petrol output from 50% to 74% during the 1971 to 1975 plan period, but it reached 84.8% in 1975. By the end of 1979, 93.8% of petrol production was high-octane. At this point, the definition of 'high-octane' was revised, and the Eleventh Five Year Plan has called for the share of 'high-octane benzine' to be raised from 64% in 1980 to 87% in 1985 and 96% in 1990. The improvement of diesel fuel has been a particularly important achievement. Soviet economists have estimated that diesel with a 1% sulphur content wears an engine out after 57,400 km, while diesel with a 0.2% content will keep it running for 88,700 km. The share of low sulphur diesel fuel (i.e. with a sulphur content of less than 0.5%) has been raised to 95.8%, including 47.2% with a sulphur content of less than 0.2%. The Eleventh Five Year Plan expects all diesel to be low sulphur in 1985. The installation of carbamide deparaffinisation plants at a number of refineries has enabled diesel with very low freezing points for the northern regions to be produced. A further aim of the Eleventh plan is a big increase in the production of lube additives, the use of which is expected to effect annual savings of 350 mn roubles for the economy.

The introduction of modern, more efficient equipment, has lead to a significant reduction in the losses of oil and oil products during the refining process. In 1980 a total of 5.7 mn tons were lost during processing, or 1.25% of throughput, and this compares with 1.51% in 1975. It is planned to reduce losses to 1.1% in 1985.

Some refineries, such as Kirishi, Yaroslavl, Mozyr, Novopolotsk and Ryazan have already reduced the loss rate to less than 0.7% a year. These are all comparatively modern plants, and the replacement of obsolete equipment at other refineries should enable the rather high national loss rate to be reduced. In particular need of attention are the Fergana and Krasnovodsk plants of Central Asia, where losses amount to 3-4% of throughput.

Oil refineries are important users of their own products and it is hoped that during 1981 to 1985, such losses can be reduced by better secondary energy usage. In 1980, they produced 11 mn G-cals of heat and steam, and the planned installation of 150 boiler utilisers should permit this to rise to 22 mn G-cals in 1985. Together with the planned reconstruction of heat exchangers at 12 first-phase plants and the modernisation of a number of furnaces, it should be possible for the refinery sector to save almost one million tons of fuel over 1981 to 1985. The planners believe that a further 0.5 mn tons can be saved by the use of refinery gases which are still flared at some refineries.

Forecast Output by Oil Refineries

While official data on the size of refinery throughput and the output of products are not available, my estimates show that in 1980 the Russians produced 72 mn tons of gasoline, 120 mn tons of diesel and medium heating oil, 205 mn tons of residual fuel oil, 30 mn tons of bitumen, 8 mn tons of LPG, 16 mn tons of aviation fuel and 19 mn tons of other products from a total throughput of 481 mn tons. Total losses, including the flaring of useless gases, might have amounted to about 11 mn tons.

The United Nations has produced estimates which are close to my own for gasoline, diesel and bitumen, but are widely different from my figures for residual fuel oil. In fact the Russians have stated that fuel oil amounts to 42.5% of their throughput, giving 205 mn tons in 1980, and the UN presumably believes that this includes bitumen and lubes.

Table 7.3: UN Estimates of Soviet Oil Product Output (mn tons)

	1970	1975	1978	1979
Motor gasoline	46.9	65.5	69.7	71.5
Kerosene	24.0	30.6	33.0	35.0
Distillate fuel oil	68.3	98.2	107.0	112.0
Residual fuel oil	93.9	131.0	140.2	145.0
Lubricating oil	6.0	8.7	9.6	10.5
Bitumen	16.4	23.6	27.0	30.0
LPG	4.5	6.3	7.0	7.5

The Eleventh Five Year Plan foresees the output of products rising by 2% a year, which suggests a 1985 target of 519 mn tons if my estimate for 1980 of 470 mn tons is correct. The share of residual fuel oil in total output is planned to fall to 38.5%, giving a 1985 target of 200 mn tons, slightly less than the volume produced in 1980, and the output of diesel is expected to rise much more rapidly than that of gasoline plus naphtha. The forecast for the output of products suggested by Table 7.4 looks reasonable in the light of the probable failure to install secondary refining capacity as quickly as planned.

These forecasts are necessarily highly tentative. They are based on a forecast of the likely demand for different products and an assumption that the plans for the construction of new refineries and expansion of existing plant, will be carried out. These involve raising the share of light and middle products from the present 43% to 77% by the end of the century, mainly by linking first-phase units, catcrackers and

Table 7.4: Forecast Throughput and Product Output of Soviet Oil Refineries (mn tons)

	1985	1990	2000
Throughput	530	570	630
Output of gasoline	80	95	130
diesel	145	165	230
residual fuel oil	210	200	150
bitumen	35	40	50
LPG	9	10	12
others	40	50	50
Total	519	560	622

visbreakers in one integrated plant, and using highly-efficient new catalysts now being produced at Novokuibyshev, Ufa, Omsk and Baku. Some of these will be employed in a new process, developed by Soviet scientists, for breaking down gudrons, and industrial tests were to begin in 1983.

Gas Refineries

The production of casinghead gas was planned to grow from 28.6 bn cu m in 1975 to 43–45 bn in 1980, but in fact rose to only 37.5 bn cu m. The introduction of 12 bn cu m of gas refinery capacity during 1976 to 1980 has enabled the rate of utilisation of casinghead gas to be raised from 57.8% in 1975 to 70% in 1980 when the remaining 30% was either flared or pumped back for the gaslift extraction of oil.

The Tenth Five Year Plan called for a utilisation rate of 80–85% to be achieved in 1980, and this required six new gas refineries to be built in Western Siberia — Nizhnevartovsk Nos. 2, 3 and 4, Yuzhno-Balyk, Belo-ozersk and Surgut. It would also be necessary to raise the rate of gas utilisation in the Orenburg, Emba and Central Asian oil-fields. With the failure to fulfil the targets of the Tenth Five Year Plan, the 85% utilisation target has been put back to 1985 according to the Eleventh Five Year Plan, and the increase from 70% in 1980 should allow the output of LPG to rise by 5 mn tons.

Apart from a 0.5 bn cu m extension to the Kazakh refinery in 1977, and the completion of the 2 bn cu m facility at Usa (Komi republic) in 1980, all new gas refinery capacity has been installed in Western Siberia.

Construction of the Nizhnevartovsk gas refinery began in 1970, and

Table 7.5: Capacity of Gas Refineries in Western Siberia (bn cu m, beginning of year)

	1975	1980	1981	1982
Nizhnevartovsk	2	8	8	8
Pravdinsk	0.5	0.5	0.5	0.5
Yuzhno-Balyk	–	0.5	0.5	0.5
Belo-ozersk	–	–	4	4
Surgut	–	–	–	4
Total	2.5	9	13	17

by 1975 the first of the planned four units of 2 bn cu m/year each was operating, in addition to the small plant at Pravdinsk. By the end of 1978 the last unit had been installed, although it did not begin operating until mid-1979. The output of casinghead gas from Western Siberia exceeds refinery capacity because it includes gas from the Fedorovsk gas cap.

In 1980, Nizhnevartovsk reached its projected capacity, enabling 70% of all gas from Samotlor to be utilised, and the Belo-ozersk plant of capacity 4 bn cu m/year was completed in 1980. Samotlor gas is now fully utilised, and the Belo-ozersk refinery will be brought to full capacity by processing gas from the Varyegan group of deposits. Belo-ozersk is connected with Nizhnevartovsk by a 70 km concrete highway. It was built by the Megiongazstroi trust and was completed in 2½ years, a year behind schedule due to shortages of materials and equipment.

In 1980, the first phase of 2 bn cu m a year was completed at the Surgut refinery, which has been built to utilise the casinghead gas from Fedorovsk and other local oil deposits, and the second stage started up at the end of 1981.

However, Tyumen gas refineries have not been working to capacity, due to a shortage of gas. This is because of the failure to fulfil the plan to build 847 mn roubles worth of collection pipelines over 1976 to 1980. Only 666 mn roubles worth was built, and consequently only 20% of available casinghead gas has been collected by the Surgutneftegaz Association. The Varyegansk and Kholmogorsk deposits have also been flaring an unduly large share of gas. On the other hand, there are difficulties with distributing the products of the gas refineries – the pipeline carrying dry gas from the Nizhnevartovsk refinery to the Kuzbass is not yet working to capacity because work on compressor stations is lagging behind schedule, and a shortage of tank cars at Tobolsk means that unstable benzine piped through the Yuzhnyi

Balyk-Tobolsk pipeline cannot be used. It is simply pumped into gas pipelines and wasted.

In 1982, 30% of Tyumen casinghead gas was flared. The Ministry of Oil and Gosplan have drawn up a programme for the construction of collection pipelines and gas refineries in Tyumen oblast up to 1990, and by 1985 losses must fall to 15%. During the Eleventh plan period, new refineries will be built at Lokosovo (to serve the new Middle Ob deposits between Nizhnevartovsk and Surgut), Tarko-Sale (for the large new deposits to be developed between Kholmogorsk and Urengoi) and Krasnoleninsk for deposits on the lower reaches of the Ob.

Technical improvements to Soviet gas refineries have centred on improving the low temperature absorption and condensation processes. Absorption has high capital costs and requires comparatively large amounts of energy, and the VNIPIgazpererabotka institute has been elaborating different ways of raising its efficiency. The low-temperature condensation process is simpler, requiring temperatures of $-35°C$ to $-45°C$ and pressures of 35 to 40 kg per sq cm. The Russians have raised the pressure to 59 kg/sq cm and lowered the temperature to $-82°$ for their Nizhnevartovsk, Belo-ozersk and Surgut plants, so as to achieve a propane recovery rate of more than 90%, but VNIPIgazpererabotka has subsequently devised ways of obtaining the same result with pressures of 35 to 37 kg/sq cm.

The USSR's second biggest gas refinery, at Minibaevo in the Tatar republic, uses a low-temperature condensation and rectification process using a double-cascade cooling cycle employing propane and ethane. With a temperature of $-60°C$, the facility is more efficient than other processes. The importance of absorption plants is declining in the USSR; they are used mainly for the processing of lean gases containing 3–5% heavy fractions.

The principal aim of current research is to double the standard size of refining units from the current 1 bn cu m a year, largely by raising the size of compressors and cooling equipment.

8 TRANSPORT

As the national economy develops, as the volume of gross production grows and as the location of industry is extended into the more remote corners of the USSR, the transportation system expands accordingly. This expansion has been accentuated by three distinct trends of recent years: first, the greater specialisation of production plants, which means that within a given sector there is a need for more transportation between different plants of the various components which make up the finished product; secondly, the greater concentration of output in a small number of leading plants; and thirdly, the economic development of remote regions of Siberia and Central Asia.

On the other hand, the Soviet economy is becoming more technologically advanced; this means that the share of output of very bulky items − steel, ores, construction materials, timber, etc. in total industrial output is declining, and it will appear from Table 8.1 that this trend more than counteracts the other three.

Table 8.1: Relationship between Freight Turnover and Gross Industrial Production

	1965	1970	1975	1978	1979	1980	1985 Plan
Freight turnover (bn ton-km)	2,764	3,829	5,201	5,949	5,986	6,165	7,090
Growth rate (1965 = 100)	100	138	188	215	217	223	256
Industrial production (165 = 100)	100	150	215	249	258	267	336

During 1976 to 1980, freight turnover rose by 18.5% while industrial production grew by 24%. During the previous five-year period the corresponding growth rates were 35.8% and 43.3%, so it can be seen that the rate of decline of the Soviet economy's transport-intensity is accelerating.

With the growth in real incomes, higher living standards, shorter working hours and longer holidays, it is natural that the Soviet citizen should want to travel more. In 1965, each citizen travelled an average 874 km by train and in 1980 he travelled 1,255 km. This does not mean that the same people are travelling further. In fact the length of the average train journey has remained remarkably constant, growing only from 88 to 93 km over 1965 to 1980. Therefore it must be deduced that a larger proportion of the population are making train journeys, and/or that people are travelling more often.

As the trends towards industrial specialisation and concentration continue, workers become more specialised in their jobs, and it might be expected that they should have to travel further to work. Moreover, as people from the countryside migrate to the towns, and large towns become larger, the distance between the large housing estates and the major factories dominating the towns grows. Thus, the average length of an urban bus journey has grown from 4 km in 1965 to 5.7 km in 1980. One of the more striking features of passenger travel has been the rapid growth of inter-city bus services, often in competition with the railways. In 1965, the total length of scheduled inter-city bus routes was 1.4 mn km, but by 1980 it had grown to 3.2 mn km, and the number of passengers carried annually by inter-city buses grew from 886 mn to 2,021 mn over the same period. A similarly dramatic growth has been registered by the trolley-bus and taxi services in the major cities, and the underground railways in Moscow, Leningrad, Kiev, Tbilisi, Baku, Kharkov, Yerevan and Tashkent.

Private car ownership is still comparatively rare, but with the stock of private cars rising by more than 900,000 units a year, car travel will grow in importance over the next decade.

All this means a steady growth in fuel requirements, consisting largely of gasoline and diesel with smaller amounts of fuel oil used by ships and riverboats, and jet fuel. Coal is no longer used now that steam traction on the railways has ceased.

In analysing the growth of the Soviet transport system, it helps to subdivide it into two distinct categories — freight and passenger transport.

Freight Transport

Most Soviet freight is carried by rail, although the share of the railways in total freight carriage has been declining steadily as the oil pipeline network has grown.

The different types of transportation tend to specialise in different types of haul. The railways carry loads destined for long journeys, with the average length of a rail journey amounting to 923 km, while that of an average road journey is only 18 km. Sea journeys are of great length, testifying to the growing size of the USSR's ocean-going fleet.

Table 8.2: Turnover of Freight (bn ton-km)

	1960	1970	1975	1978	1979	1980	1985 Plan
Freight turnover							
rail	1,504	2,495	3,236	3,429	3,349	3,440	3,950
sea	131	656	736	828	851	848	925
river	100	174	222	244	233	245	290
oil pipeline	51	282	666	1,049	1,141	1,197	1,350
road	99	221	338	396	410	432	575
Share of total (%)							
rail	80	65	62	58	56	56	56
sea	7	17	14	14	14	14	13
river	5	5	4	4	4	4	4
oil pipeline	3	7	13	18	19	19	19
road	5	6	7	7	7	7	8

Table 8.3: Volume of Freight (mn tons)

	1960	1970	1975	1978	1979	1980	1981
Total	10,793	18,379	25,619	28,340	28,461	29,254	31,123
Rail	1,885	2,896	3,621	3,776	3,688	3,728	3,762
Sea	76	162	200	229	227	228	223
River	210	358	475	546	537	568	594
Pipeline	130	340	498	589	609	630	638
Road	8,492	14,623	20,824	23,200	23,400	24,100	25,906

Pipeline transportation refers to deliveries of oil and oil products, although petrochemicals like ammonia and ethylene are now being carried in significant quantities by pipeline. Gas pipelines are not included in the analysis.

When the volume, as opposed to turnover of freight is considered, the picture is very different to that presented in Table 8.2 because of the difference in the average length of haul. When Tables 9.2 and 9.3 are considered together, the average length of haul of freight by different methods can be ascertained.

Table 8.4: Average Length of Haul of Freight (kms)

	1960	1970	1975	1978	1979	1980
All transport	175	208	202	210	210	211
rail	798	861	894	908	908	923
sea	1,724	4,049	3,680	3,616	3,749	3,719
river	474	486	466	447	434	431
pipeline	392	829	1,337	1,781	1,874	1,900
road	12	15	16	17	18	18

Railways

In complete contrast with other industrially developed countries, the Soviet rail network is steadily growing in size, at a rate of 693 km a year between 1965 and 1980. This is primarily due to major projects such as the BAM railway in Eastern Siberia and the Far East, and the Western Siberian line from Tyumen to Surgut, Nizhnevartovsk and Novyi Urengoi.

In spite of the continual expansion of the railway network, its degree of utilisation is growing, and reports of severe congestion in certain areas appear from time to time in the Soviet press. In 1965, the Soviet railways transported 18,381 tons of freight for each kilometre of track, and by 1980 this figure had grown to 26,292 tons. This is in spite of the fact that the expansion of the oil pipeline system helped to relieve congestion by carrying loads which would otherwise have gone by rail.

Other factors relieving congestion have centred round the change from steam to diesel and electric traction. Steam trains have virtually disappeared now, and in 1980 30.8% of the total length of track was electrified. Electrified lines include those most heavily used; thus in 1980 only 31% of the track was electrified, but almost 55% of all freight was carried by electric trains. Although the degree of electrification is far higher than in many other industrialised countries, it will continue to grow in spite of the tense situation as regards the supply of electricity in the European regions of the USSR. With the rapid growth of electricity supply from atomic stations, it is believed that the advantages of electrification will outweigh the greater costs. Electric trains can pull significantly heavier loads and travel faster, with the average daily run of an electric train amounting to 435 km in 1980 compared with 415 by a diesel train. In 1980, each newly built diesel engine had an average capacity of 2,784 hp while the average capacity of electric train was 7.914 hp.

The incidence of railway congestion is often mentioned in the context of the need to diversify geographically the Soviet economy, particularly in respect of the processing of bulky raw materials. It is significant that 51% of total railway freight turnover consists of the transportation of only four products – coal, oil, construction materials (mainly stone, sand and cement) and timber.

Of the products with an average length of haul of more than 1,000 km, oil and oil products are the most important. With the centre of gravity of the oil industry moving to Siberia, the average distance over which crude oil has to be transported has grown considerably, and the

Table 8.5: The Soviet Railway Network

	1960	1970	1975	1978	1979	1980	1981
Total length ('000 km)	125.8	135.2	138.3	140.4	141.1	141.8	142.8
electrified	13.8	33.9	38.9	41.1	42.4	43.7	44.8
steam and diesel	112.0	101.3	99.4	99.3	98.7	98.1	98.0
Freight turnover carried by:							
electric (%)	21.8	48.7	51.7	53.6	53.6	54.9	
diesel (%)	21.4	47.8	47.9	46.3	46.4	45.1	
steam (%)	56.8	3.5	0.4	0.1	–	–	
Utilisation – volume of freight per km of track per year ('000 tons)	15.0	21.4	26.2	27.0	26.1	26.3	

Russians have been pursuing a policy of transferring as much oil as possible to pipelines. By 1981, 95% of all crude was carried by pipeline, and the emphasis now is on building product pipelines, particularly in regions where the railways are particularly congested such as the Central region. But while the volume of oil and its products carried by pipeline is rising rapidly, to the extent that the share of pipeline in freight transportation has grown from 5.4% in 1965 to 19% in 1980, the amount of oil carried by rail is still rising, from 389 mn tons in 1975 to 422.7 mn tons in 1980. Consequently, it accounted for 10.5% of freight volume carried by the railways in 1970, 10.7% in 1975 and 11.3% in 1980.

Sea Transport

The great majority of freight turnover by sea transport consists of foreign trade. Consequently the average length of haul is very great, at 3,719 km in 1980 (after reaching 4,070 in 1971) and the turnover, which accounted for 13.8% of total turnover in 1980, is out of all proportion to the volume of transportation which accounted for only 0.8% of the total (Tables 8.2 and 8.3).

Domestic sea-transport takes place mainly on the Black Sea, Caspian Sea, White Sea and Sea of Okhotsk.

The impetus to long-distance foreign trade began in the late 1950s with the development of Soviet trade with the Third World, and particularly in 1960 with the opening of routes to Cuba. Since then, the merchant fleet has grown rapidly at an annual rate of 10.1% a year to 23.4 million gross registered tons in 1980.

The turnover of seaborne freight has been growing far slower than the size of the fleet since 1967. If the level of utilisation of freight-

Table 8.6: Merchant Shipping Fleets ('000 gross registered tons)

Year	USSR	USA
1960	3,429	24,837
1970	14,832	18,463
1975	19,236	14,587
1980	23,444	18,464

carrying capacity achieved in 1967 had been maintained, then in 1980 a fleet of 17.0 mn tons would be required. This suggests a surplus capacity of 6.4 mn tons of shipping in 1980 (cargo liners rather than tankers) and portends either a slow-down in the rate of ship-building, or a more vigorous effort to attract foreign cargoes.

River Transport

The haulage of freight by the inland waterway system has grown more slowly than that by other types of transport. Only 1.9% of all freight was carried by river in 1980, and 4.0% of the total turnover of freight was transported in this way.

The comparatively slow growth of river transport can be ascribed to the stagnation of the inland waterway network, particularly over the period 1976 to 1980 when it actually declined by 4,400 km to 142,000 km.

Table 8.6: Soviet Inland Waterways

	1960	1970	1975	1978	1979	1980
Length of waterways ('000 kms)	137.9	144.5	145.4	142.6	142.3	142.0
inc. artificial	13.3	18.6	19.6	20.5	20.5	20.5
Usage rate (tons per km)	1,523	2,478	3,270	3,830	3,775	4,001

Since 1975, the usage rate for waterways has been growing at an average annual rate of 4.1%. Coal, oil and oil products, timber and grain are the principal products carried.

Road Transport

In 1980, over 24 bn tons of freight, or 82.4% of all freight, was carried by road, but because the average journey was only 17.9 km, the turn-over of freight carried by road transport was only 7.0% of the total.

Although official statistics on the number of lorries operating in the

Table 8.8: Soviet Road Transport

	1965	1970	1975	1980
Length of road network ('000 km)	1,070	1,106	1,022	1,022
inc. hard surface ('000 km)	360	489	618	732
cement or asphalt ('000 km)	131	205	290	373
Usage rate of hard surface roads ('000 tons per km)	29.7	29.9	33.8	32.9

USSR are not published, it can be estimated that the size of the lorry fleet amounted to 7.4 mn at the end of 1981 compared with 3.8 mn in 1970. Thus the number of lorries has been growing at an average annual rate of 6.3%, and the number of lorries per kilometre of hard surface road has risen from 7.8 in 1970 to 9.8 in 1981. The lorries are also getting bigger; the average lorry produced in 1970 had a load capacity of 4.3 tons while by 1980 it had risen to 5.0 tons. The commissioning of the first stage of the Kama Lorry Plant at Naberezhnye Chelny helped to raise the average load capacity from 4.5 tons in 1978 to 5.0 tons in 1980. The quality of engines is improving, and better lorries and roads have permitted an improvement in the rate of fuel usage of 40% over the last 20 years.

Passenger Transport

In spite of the increasing extent of private car ownership, the use of public transport is still continuing to grow. In 1980, the average Soviet citizen made 257 journeys by public transport compared with 239 in 1975. These consisted of 157 by bus (143 in 1975), five by public taxi (7), 34 by trolleybus (31), 31 by tram (32), 14 by train (13), 15 by metro (12) and one by ship or riverboat (1).

Private car ownership has been growing rapidly in recent years. Since 1950, the USSR has produced over 16 mn cars, of which 25% have been exported. With the construction of the Volzhskii Car Plant at Tolyatti, annual output has grown from 344,000 in 1970 to 1,327,000 in 1980. It can be estimated that there were 9.5 mn cars in the USSR at the end of 1981 compared with 1.8 mn in 1970.

The future development of passenger transport must ·be closely related to the increase in the stock of passenger cars. This has not yet affected the growth in the utilisation of public transport. The annual number of journeys made by the average Soviet citizen grew by 4.0%

Table 8.9: Public Transport − Number of Journeys (bn)

	1960	1970	1975	1978	1979	1980	1981
Total number of							
passengers (bn)	25.8	48.0	61.1	66.0	67.2	68.5	69.5
Bus	11.3	27.3	36.5	40.4	41.3	42.2	43.0
Tram	7.8	8.0	8.2	8.4	8.3	8.3	8.2
Trolley bus	3.1	6.1	8.0	8.8	8.9	.9.0	9.0
Railway	2.0	2.9	3.5	3.6	3.6	3.6	3.6
Metro	1.1	2.3	3.0	3.5	3.7	3.8	4.0
Taxi	0.4	1.1	1.7	1.1	1.2	1.4	1.5
Riverboat and ship	0.1	0.2	0.2	0.2	0.2	0.2	0.2
Average number of							
journeys per person	122	198	239	252	254	257	259

a year over 1970 to 1980 compared with 5.3% a year over 1965 to 1970. But with the stock of private cars likely to rise to over 13 mn by 1985, it is inevitable that this will affect public transport, although to what extent is most difficult to predict.

The Russians decided many years ago that metros were the quickest, cleanest and cheapest method of urban transportation. More recently, another attribute has acquired greater significance − they can save the country a substantial volume of diesel and petrol by attracting passengers away from buses and private cars with comparatively low rates of fuel efficiency.

Accordingly, the programme to build metros in all major cities has been stepped up. By the end of 1980, the USSR had built metros in seven cities with a total population of over 20 mn − Moscow, Leningrad, Kiev, Kharkov, Baku, Tbilisi and Tashkent. Between them, they had 342 km of track, an increase of 68 km over 1975, and they carried 3.8 bn passengers. With a usage rate of 11 mn passengers per kilometre of track a year, they are the most intensively used metros in the world.

During the period 1981 to 1985, another 112 km of track, including 30 km in Moscow, 14.5 in Leningrad, 4.5 in Kiev, more than 4 in Tbilisi, 7 in Baku, 7.5 in Kharkov, 5.5 in Tashkent and nearly 12 km in Yerevan are to be built, and the Minsk, Gorki and Novosibirsk metros are to begin operating. In March 1981, the Yerevan metro began working with the first stage of 7.5 km and three stations now in use, and by 1985 it should be 12 km long with five stations. In the first few days of 1983, the tunnelling work on the Minsk metro was completed, and the start of regular services was promised for autumn 1984.

Construction of a further nine metros will begin or continue at Dnepropetrovsk, Kuibyshev, Sverdlovsk, Alma Ata, Riga, Omsk,

Table 8.10: The Soviet Metro System

	1970	1975	1980	1981
Length of track (km) – USSR	214	274	342	356
Moscow	179	217	246	184.0
Leningrad				66.1
Kiev	14	28	43	28.3
Kharkov	–			17.3
Tashkent	–	–	15	15.5
Baku	11	16	19	18.6
Tbilisi	10	13	19	18.8
Yerevan	–	–	–	7.5
No. of passengers carried (mn) – USSR	2,294	2,972	3,823	3,974
Moscow	1,628	1,966	2,318	2,377
Leningrad	418	554	717	738
Kiev	127	204	255	298
Kharkov	–	32	175	175
Tashkent	–	–	74	89
Baku	47	105	141	137
Tbilisi	74	111	143	143
Yerevan	–	–	–	17

Rostov, Perm and Chelyabinsk. By 1985, metros in 20 cities with an estimated total population of 37.5 mn will either be operating, or under construction. It can be estimated that by 1985 they will be carrying 4.8 bn passengers, and by 1990 6.1 bn. The same number of people travelling by private car would require an estimated 1.3 to 1.4 mn tons of petrol.

However, many large Soviet cities will still be without metros in 1990, including Volgograd, Donetsk, Kazan, Odessa and Ufa, all of which will have populations exceeding one million in that year. Here, the emphasis will be on trolley-buses which are slower and more unsightly than metros, but which also enable large savings in oil consumption to be made. The tram services are also to be extended, not by increasing the number of trams, but by increasing speed and unit capacity, with high-speed trams now operating in Kiev. Volgograd will have an underground tram system.

It is possible that, in spite of an estimated increase of 26 mn in the urban population of the USSR over the next ten years, the growth in demand for oil products for urban passenger transport can be kept to less than 1.5% a year. This depends, however, on the successful fulfilment of ambitious plans for the construction of nuclear power stations to provide the power for the new urban transport networks.

With the metro being by far the fastest form of urban transport, extended car ownership should have little effect on it. Moreover, it is

Table 8.11: Development of the Soviet Tram and Trolleybus Systems

	1970	1975	1980	1981	1985 Plan
Extent of the network (km)					
– total	16,412	19,978	23,136	23,791	26,700
trolley buses	8,151	11,209	14,004	14,522	16,700
trams	8,261	8,769	9,132	9,269	10,000
No. of passengers (mn)					
– total	14,084	16,198	17,290	17,192	
trolley buses	6,122	7,963	9,035	8,995	
trams	7,962	8,235	8,255	8,197	
No. of vehicles – total	37,818	41,055	44,427	45,457	
trolley buses	15,767	20,289	23,868	24,593	
trams	22,051	20,766	20,559	20,864	

the most environmentally inoffensive form of transport, and as considerable capital investments have to be recouped, it is likely that efforts will be made to attract as many passengers as possible. Trams are already declining in popularity due to their slow speed, and most of the effect of mass car ownership will be felt by buses, trolley buses and taxis. In 1980, 200 towns had trams and 158 had trolley buses. They used 6 bn kWh of electricity, but it is estimated that the wastage of power through inefficient equipment amounted to 25-30%.

It can be assumed that car production will grow from its present level of 1.3 mn a year to 1.5 mn due to the minor expansion of the Gorki and Zaporozhe plants. The doubling up of the Tolyatti car plant may be announced shortly, as Soviet planners are preparing for the population of Tolyatti to grow from 530,000 to one million by 2000. Not only has pressure for car ownership been building up among the Soviet population, but the Lada cars built at Tolyatti have become an important Western currency earner. The new Tolyatti plant should begin producing about 1988 and total car production should rise to over 2 mn a year by 1990.

Fuel Consumption by the Transport Sector

The share of the transport sector in the total consumption of fuel and energy has fallen from 19% to 10% in the period 1960 to 1980. Between 1959 and 1966, the volume of fuel consumed by the transport industry (excluding agricultural vehicles and private cars) did not increase, and its share of the total costs incurred by the transport sector fell from 15.6% to 9.3%. This was due to the conversion of the railways from steam to diesel traction, and hence from expensive coal to cheap oil. During the period 1966 to 1972, the conversion to oil continued, and the oil price rise of 1967 resulted in a big increase in fuel costs to 2,900 mn roubles. Since 1972, the use of coal has almost disappeared, with the value of oil consumption rising fairly slowly due to the process of conversion from diesel to electric traction now taking place. The value of electricity used by the transport sector (for urban passenger transport as well as electrified railways) has grown from 150 mn roubles in 1959 to 458 mn in 1966 and 820 mn in 1972.

It has been stated by Soviet officials that the transport sector uses 45-48% of the total output of light oil products in the USSR. This would have amounted to 86-92 mn tons of gasoline and diesel in 1980.

Fuel Consumption – Railways

As Table 8.12 shows, the change from steam to electric and diesel traction has resulted in a dramatic fall in the total consumption of fuel between 1960 and 1975.

Table 8.12: Consumption of Fuel and Energy by Rail Transport (mn tsf)

	1960	1965	1970	1975
Coal	42.8	15.5	4.5	–
Fuel oil	10.6	8.4	4.5	2.1
Diesel fuel	3.0	8.2	11.6	15.3
Fuel for the production of electricity*	3.8	7.4	10.1	12.8
Total	60.2	39.5	30.7	30.2

Note: * including the fuel equivalent of hydro and atomic power.

The unit consumption of fuel has fallen from 35.9 tsf per mn ton-km of total transportation (defined as ton-km of freight transport plus passenger-km of passenger transport, with one passenger-km regarded as being equal to one ton-km of freight according to Soviet analyses) in 1960 to 11.12 in 1970 and 8.51 in 1975.

It can be seen that, while the consumption of fuel by the railways (including that needed for power generation for electric trains) fell by almost 50% during 1960 to 1975, freight and passenger transportation turnover rose by 112%. Of particular importance was the disappearance of steam traction while the extent of electric traction grew faster than that by diesel trains.

Table 8.13: Estimated Total Transportation by Type of Traction (bn ton-km)

	1960	1965	1970	1975	1980
Total transportation	1,675	2,152	2,760	3,549	3,772
Freight	1,504	1,950	2,495	3,236	3,440
Passenger	171	202	265	313	332
By type of traction					
steam	951	334	97	14	–
diesel	358	968	1,319	1,700	1,701
electric	365	850	1,344	1,835	2,071

It is particularly important to reduce the volume of diesel fuel used by the railways. This is to be accomplished in two ways: first, by the programme of electrification, which is to continue at an average annual rate of 1,200 km a year for the foreseeable future; and secondly by technical improvements to engines and by increasing the speed and size of trains. Trains 1½ km long, for example, are now being used to ship coal from the Kuzbass to Moscow. The Voroshilovgrad Locomotive Plant, which makes 96% of Soviet diesel trains, has begun the serial output of 8,000 hp engines, and the construction of a 9,000 hp proto-type is now taking place.

In 1965, diesel trains required 8.47 tsf of diesel to move one million ton-km of total transport (i.e freight plus passengers). By 1970, this figure had risen to 8.79 tsf, by 1975 to 9.0 and by 1981 to 9.65. This last figure consisted of 9 tsf of diesel per one million ton-km of freight and 14 tsf per million passenger-km.

This increase in diesel usage rates has taken place in spite of techni-cal improvements to engines with the installation of fuel-saving devices, and is a result of the conversion of many of the main trunk routes to electric traction. On these routes, the trains tend to be very long, carrying large loads over immense distances. As electric trains take more and more of this traffic, the diesel trains are left with the shorter and lighter local journeys, on which freight and passengers cannot be moved so efficiently. Diesel engines have also taken over the fuel-intensive shunting functions previously carried out by steam engines.

Electric trains required 8.71 tsf of power per million ton-km of total transport in 1965, and by 1970 this figure had dropped to 7.51 tsf, with a further fall to 6.98 tsf in 1975. This rapid decline in energy consumption may, in fact, stem in part from the greater use of nuclear and hydro electricity to drive electric trains, particularly as the major East–West lines from Siberia have been electrified using cheap hydro power. Soviet economists use the standard United Nations conversion rate of 123 gsf/kWh to convert nuclear and hydro power to tons of standard fuel, whereas a more realistic rate for the USSR would be 328 gsf/kWh, this being the actual volume of fuel that would be needed to generate 1 kWh at a conventional thermal station if nuclear and hydro power were not available.

According to official data, the amount of power needed to accomplish a turnover of 10,000 ton-km has declined from 149 kWh in 1960 to 137.8 in 1965, 127.8 in 1970 and 124.6 kWh in 1975.

Fuel Consumption – Road Transport

The Russians have not published official data for the production of different types of oil products, or the volumes of their consumption by different types of transport. It can be estimated, however, that the production of diesel in 1980 amounted to 120 mn tons, of which 20 mn were exported, leaving 100 mn tons for domestic consumption.

The road transport fleet probably used about 20 mn tons of diesel, with the railways requiring 10.5 mn tons, and the rest was used by buses (3.2 mn tons), river and sea transport enterprises, and also by the farms for their tractors (now using diesel rather than kerosene), combine harvesters and trucks. Large volumes were used to power stationary motors of different types by virtually all sectors of industry, and the military was also a significant user of diesel.

Of the 72 mn tons of gasoline produced, and 58 mn domestically consumed in the USSR in 1980, it is thought that lorries used 19 mn tons and buses 2.0 mn tons. The 8.5 mn cars on Soviet roads may have used about 16 mn tons of gasoline. This is much more than the same number of cars would use in Western Europe, because the Russian cars include a disproportionately large number of taxis (both official and unofficial) which travel huge distances each year. Moreover, the scarcity of cars in the USSR tends to lead to a greater usage rate of a car once it has been purchased, in spite of the cheapness of subsidised public transport. Most of the remaining 21 mn tons of gasoline was used by agricultural vehicles (an estimated 19 mn tons) and the military.

Diesel is tending to replace gasoline as the major road transport fuel because diesel drive permits fuel savings of up to 25% over gasoline. The production of lorries and buses with diesel engines is planned to increase by 69% during 1981 to 1985, and it has been estimated that the conversion of the entire lorry and bus fleet would yield fuel savings of 30 mn tons of oil products over a five-year period. If the plan for conversion to diesel drive during 1981 to 1985 is fulfilled, and diesel lorries carry 46% of all freight transported by road compared with 36% in 1980, then fuel savings of about 5 mn tons will be made during 1981 to 1985.

As well as conversion to diesel, other methods leading to a reduction in petrol consumption are being tested. They include the use of a petrol-MTBE (methyl tertiary butyl ether) mixture; four lorries using this fuel gave petrol savings of 8% over 40,000 km when compared with four lorries using pure petrol. A mixture of petrol and methanol gives larger savings, in the order of 14–15%, but is more expensive. These tests have been carried out by the Glavmosavtotrans organisation of Moscow, which has one of the country's largest lorry fleets, and which used 1.7 mn tons of motor fuel worth 300 mn roubles in 1981. By 1985, the organisation hopes to have 100 lorries using petrol plus MTBE, 500 using petrol plus hydrogen (which is said to raise the octane rating) and 1,000 using petrol plus methanol.

It is believed that the USSR had about 7.1 mn lorries in 1980, of which 1.6 mn were operated by the agricultural sector. The 5.5 mn lorries engaged in the transport of freight used some 39 mn tons of oil products at a rate of 7.1 tons per lorry per year. The fuel rate amounted to 149 tsf per million ton-km, which is average by European standards in spite of the low fuel efficiency of Soviet lorry engines. This is because the comparative importance of the general-purpose lorry fleet means that the significance of empty return runs is lower in the USSR than in Western countries where most lorries are operated by individual specialised firms.

The poor state of service facilities for lorries means that many of them have unnecessarily high rates of fuel consumption, and even the most efficient lorry fleets can have more than a third of their lorries consuming fuel above the rated norm. This is because drivers have no incentive to save fuel, no means of accurately checking rates of fuel consumption and have generally not been trained to drive efficiently.

The Moscow Automobile Institute, together with Avtokombinat No. 1 of Glavmosavtotrans, has carried out research showing that a driver can easily reveal and remove deficiencies in engine performance without special tools, thereby reducing fuel consumption by up to 20%. But the standard training undertaken by drivers does not include instruction in how to save fuel. It is recommended by the Institute that meters for the measurement of fuel consumption ('raskhodomery') should be installed in lorries, but in spite of an 'original, competitive design' having been created by the Ministry of Automobile Transport, serial production of these instruments has not yet started. A small number of transport enterprises have started using portable testers, and their more widespread use could lead to substantial fuel savings.

Diesel engines need better fuel systems; the regulators which provide stability at maximum and minimum crankshaft revolutions are old-fashioned and inefficient, yet are still being fitted to a new generation of diesel engines, thereby eliminating the fuel-saving potential of these engines. It is reported that these technical problems are now being dealt with.

Buses used an average 21 tsf per million passenger-km, which is good by Western standards because Soviet buses tend to fill a larger proportion of their seat capacity than those in the West. New buses now being built in Lvov have advanced diesel engines and will replace ageing petrol-driven buses, cutting fuel consumption by half.

Fuel Consumption – Other Types of Transport

Riverboats and ocean-going ships used comparatively small volumes of fuel in 1980, possibly 4 mn tons of diesel and fuel oil. Fuel usage by ships has improved by 1.8 times during the last 20 years, and 2.4 times for riverboats. Riverboats, using about 2.6 mn tons in 1980, achieved a usage rate of 11 tsf per million ton-km, and diesel-powered boats now carry 82.6% of all river-borne freight because their fuel rates are 44% better than those burning fuel oil in steam boilers.

It is thought that Soviet planes used about 15.7 mn tons of aviation gasoline and jet fuel in 1980. This compares with 53.8 mn tons in the USA, 4.7 mn in the UK and 2.6 mn tons in West Germany. The fuel usage rate of planes was 100–110 tsf per million passenger-km in 1980; this is extremely poor by world standards in spite of the high utilisation rate of seat capacity because the fuel-efficiency of Soviet aero engines is very low. A new generation of engines needs only 34 tsf, and this is the sort of rate enjoyed in the West.

Electricity Consumption by the Transport Sector

In 1980, 102.7 bn kWh of electricity were used by the transport sector, consisting of 48.7 bn by electric railways, 20.6 bn by oil pipelines, 11.3 bn by gas pipelines, 8.1 bn by urban public transport (including 1.7 bn by metros), and 14 bn kWh for other functions, which include loading and unloading work by road, river and sea transport enterprises.

Table 8.14: Electricity Consumption by the Transport Sector (bn kWh)

	1960	1970	1975	1980	1985 Plan
Electric railways	10.4	32.0	43.1	48.7	57.0
Pipelines					
Oil and oil products	0.8	8.6	8.9	20.6	23.3
Gas			4.6	11.3	20.7
Urban public transport	2.6	5.1	6.7	8.1	10.0
Others	3.8	8.7	10.9	14.0	17.0
Total	17.6	54.4	74.2	102.7	128.0

The Future Consumption of Fuel by the Transport Sector

According to the Eleventh Five Year Plan, freight turnover on the railways will increase by 14-15% to 3,950 bn ton-km in 1985. This is a surprisingly small increase in spite of the planned rise in industrial production, and can be explained by the policy of transferring the transport of oil and oil products to pipelines, and by the increasing localisation of coal consumption as the natural gas pipeline network is extended. The Russians plan to slow down the increase in the volume of coal being hauled long distances from the Kuzbass to Leningrad and the western republics, and convert consumers in those regions to gas. Nevertheless, in spite of these measures the annual volume of hard coal carried by rail is expected to grow by 62 mn tons a year from 732 mn tons in 1980 to 794 mn tons in 1985, and the tonnage of oil loads will rise by 35 mn tons from 423 mn tons.

It can be expected that the average length of haul might fall slightly to 910 km in 1985, with the railways hauling a total tonnage of perhaps 4,350 mn tons, or 16% more than in 1980. The share of electrified track will rise to 34.2% of the total by 1985, with 6,000 km of track to be electrified over 1981 to 1985 while the total length of the Soviet rail network grows by 3,600 km. The share of freight carried by electric trains is likely to rise to 65% according to a speech by Minister of Communications Pavlovskii at the 26th Party Congress, thereby helping to achieve a saving of 7 mn tons of diesel fuel to be effected by freight and passenger rail transport over 1981 to 1985. Eventually, it is hoped that electric trains will carry up to 72% of all rail-borne freight. The accomplishment of technical measures such as running bigger and more powerful trains should provide savings of 3 bn kWh of electricity and 1½ mn tons of diesel a year; according to Gosplan's Institute of

Complex Transport Problems, technical improvements to transport can reduce the rate of fuel usage by 10% for the railways and 22% for lorries. During 1976 to 1980, technical improvements to the power supply systems, and the regeneration of electricity for return to the network by electric trains yielded savings of 6.6 bn kWh, and the plan target for 1981 to 1985 is 8.9 bn kWh. At the moment, power losses amount to 11-13%, but the use of more efficient equipment can reduce these to only 3-4%.

According to the Eleventh Five Year Plan, it is hoped to increase the average speed of freight trains by 2.7 km per hour, and this should raise the rate of power consumption by electric trains by 2.7%. There is to be a considerable increase in the number of passenger carriages electrically heated (by 4,000 carriages) and provided with air conditioners (by 3,000), and together with other measures designed to improve passenger comfort, this should lead to an additional increase of 0.3 bn kWh in power consumption, raising the norm by 0.2%.

It seems unlikely that the Eleventh Five Year Plan targets will be fulfilled, and a freight turnover of 3,800 bn ton-km in 1985 seems more likely, rising to 4,200 bn in 1990 and 4,800 bn in 2000. If, as seems more likely, the plan for track electrification is fulfilled, the total transportation (i.e freight and passenger) turnover by diesel trains should continue the trend of 1978 to 1980, when it fell from 1,740 to 1,701 bn ton-km, and decline to 1,600 bn in 1985, 1,500 bn in 1990 and 1,200 bn in 2000. This should permit the consumption of diesel to be reduced from 15.3 mn tsf in 1980 (10.5 mn tons of diesel) to 14.4 mn tsf (9.9 mn tons) in 1985, 13.2 mn tsf (9.0 mn tons) in 1990 and 10.3 mn tsf (7.0 mn tons) in 2000.

During the period 1981 to 1985, a 33% increase is planned for the freight turnover of the road transport industry, from 432 bn ton-km to 575 bn. This implies an increase in tonnage carried from 24.1 bn tons to 28.8 bn, assuming an increase in the average journey from 18 km to about 20 km.

Road transport, with a fuel usage rate 19 times that of the railways, accounts for about a half of all fuel consumed in the transport sector. The trend towards diesel rather than petrol-driven lorries is to be accelerated, and this will lead to a considerable growth in diesel consumption. It can be estimated that it will grow to 92 mn tons in 1985 by all sectors of transport including agricultural vehicles and the military, and perhaps 135 mn tons by the economy as a whole. This forecast takes account of planned savings by the transport sector (i.e. excluding agriculture) of 13 mn tons of light oil products during

1981 to 1985 compared with 10.2 mn tons over 1976 to 1980.

Diesel consumption by the transport sector in 1990 is likely to be in the order of 110 mn tons, and 125 mn tons by the end of the century. The reason for the abrupt slow-down in the anticipated growth of diesel consumption is the new policy for the rapid development of lorries driving on LNG.

For several years now, the Russians have been testing various types of vehicles to run on liquified gas instead of petrol or diesel. The technology has largely been developed by the Moscow Institute of Motor Vehicle Construction, and the testing has been carried out on seven models of lorries, two of buses and one taxi in Moscow, Kiev, Kharkov and Tbilisi.

Gas has a number of advantages over oil products. It is cheaper and is much less pollutive, with the emission of carbon dioxide reduced by up to 75%. On the other hand, it is bulky, with the average car unable to carry more than the equivalent of four gallons of petrol. Research is under way in Moscow to solve this problem. A car is being tested, carrying gas cooled to $-161°C$ to reduce its volume and it is hoped that eventually plastic tanks rather than steel or aluminium ones can be used to reduce weight. At Moscow's Likhachev lorry plant, a ZIL lorry using gas under a pressure of 200 ats has been designed.

A decision has been taken to begin the mass production of gas-driven vehicles during 1982, when 5,000 modified ZIL-130 lorries were to be built by the Likhachev plant, and production is to grow to 10,000 in 1983, 35,000 in 1984 and 50,000 in 1985. The Gorki Lorry Plant has begun production of its own gas-powered vehicle, the GAZ-3227. Long-term plans expect a total of one million gas-driven lorries to be running on Soviet roads in 1990, which suggests that annual output will be running at 300,000 in that year. In Donetsk, designs have been drawn up for special filling stations, which take gas directly from pipelines, process and liquify it.

There are several other reasons why diesel consumption by the Soviet lorry fleet will grow more slowly after 1985. First, the share of large lorries, which enjoy a fuel rate several times lower than the average for the sector, will increase during 1981 to 1985, with the large-scale production of MAZ lorries of 28–30 tons load capacity and new lorries from KrAZ (16 tons capacity) and KamAZ (18 tons). Secondly, the greater use of radial tyres, which are planned to account for 50% of tyre output in 1985, will lower fuel consumption rates by 3–5%. And thirdly, efforts to reduce the incidence of empty runs will be intensified over 1981 to 1985, drawing on the experience of the general-purpose lorry fleets of Glavmosavtotrans in Moscow, and some Belorussian fleets.

By 1985, 13 mn cars should be using 24 mn tons of petrol a year, and 66 mn tons will be consumed by the Soviet economy as a whole. Although this will represent only 12.5% of refinery throughput compared with 50% in the USA, the Russians have been making strenuous efforts to reduce the consumption of petrol by price increases (the price of petrol was raised in 1982 to between 30 and 40 kopecks per litre, depending on the grade) and by developing substitutes.

The most likely substitute is LNG, and the conversion of passenger cars is to be speeded up. In Tbilisi, the entire taxi fleet of 'several hundreds' is said to be operating on gas, and the City Soviet has decided that all petrol-driven public transport must be converted. Tashkent now has 130 taxis of type GAZ-24-07 working on propane-based LPG. Each gas canister contains 84 litres and lasts for 450–500 km. The long-term plan for Moscow foresees the conversion of 100,000 cars by 1990. In other cities, plans for the conversion of private cars are hindered by the lack of a filling station network, but it is likely that they will be adopted by Leningrad and Kiev in the near future. By the end of 1981, about 20,000 vehicles of all types were running on gas in the USSR, including 10,000 in Moscow and the same number elsewhere.

Other experiments have involved the use of a petrol-hydrogen mixture. Micro-buses tested in Moscow have needed only 30% of their normal petrol requirements, and three taxis on test in Kharkov made petrol savings of 40%.

Table 8.15: Forecast Fuel Consumption by the Transport Sector*

	1980	1985	1990	2000
Diesel (mn tons)	37	50	70	82
Petrol (mn tons)	37	47.5	62.5	85
Jet fuel (mn tons)	15.7	19	24	33
Fuel oil (mn tons)	0.8	0.5	–	–
Total oil products	90.5	117	156.5	200
Natural gas (bn cu m)	0.5	1	5	15

Note: * Excluding agriculture.

As well as researching into fuel substitutes, the Russians have also been designing cars with very low fuel rates. The 'Kommunar' Association of Zaporozhe, for example, has designed a car which will do 47.9 miles to the gallon. However, this will have little impact on petrol consumption, as Soviet car production is dominated by the Zhiguli (better known in the West as the Lada) cars with rates of 26-28 miles to the gallon. Taking all these factors into consideration, it can be estimated that fuel consumption by public and private transport will grow as shown in Table 8.15.

Gas Pipeline Transport

Gas pipelines are significant users of gas, as well as electricity, burning it in compressor stations. In 1980, 30.45 bn cu m of gas were used in this way, and during the period 1970 to 1980, consumption rose by an average 20% a year. The share of the total national output of natural gas burned by compressor stations rose from 2.56% in 1970 to 7.0% in 1980, and this is due to the growing importance of intercontinental pipelines from Western Siberia to the European USSR with the consequential increase in the average distance over which a cubic metre of gas is pumped. During the three years 1977-80, the increase in the volume of gas used by compressor stations has amounted to 11.97% of the increase in gas production during the same period. As the entire increase in Soviet gas output up to the end of the century is planned to come from Western Siberia, it can be confidently assumed that 12% of the increase will be spent simply on transporting the gas to its customers.

Little over 2% of total gas output (9.44 bn cu m in 1980) is lost during transport and distribution. The share has declined from 2.29% in 1970 to 2.17% in 1980, although it reached a low of 1.96% in 1978. The main cause of losses is from cracks in pipelines, and it might be expected that the incidence of these should decline as the technology of pipe manufacture and pipeline construction improves; on the other hand an increasingly large share of the pipeline network consists of 1,420 mm diameter pipe (which, with an annual throughput of 33 bn cu m is obviously liable to far greater losses from accidents than pipelines of smaller capacity) laid through the swamps of Western Siberia where the incidence of accidents is greater. This is because the pipe, which has to be laid during the winter when the ground is frozen, can rise to the surface during the summer when the swamp melts, and split along its weld. The pipe should be weighted down with concrete blocks, but this is not always done, and when an accident occurs, the absence of roads can lead to delays in operating the cut-off valve to stop the flow.

It is fair to assume that of every additional 8 cu m of gas produced

Table 2.16: Consumption and Losses of Gas during Transport and Distribution (bn cu m)

Year	Consumption by Compressor Stations	Losses	Total	As a Share of Output (%)
1970	4.90	4.38	9.28	4.85
1978	22.82	7.30	30.12	8.09
1979	27.20	8.34	35.54	8.74
1980	30.45	9.44	39.89	9.17

by the USSR, 1 cu m will be needed to move the other seven to their destination. This means that by 1985, the gas pipeline network will be burning 62 bn cu m (including losses) and this figure should rise to perhaps 85 bn by 1990 and 100 bn in 2000.

9 AGRICULTURE

Agriculture is a major user of petrol and diesel for tractors, combine harvesters and trucks, fuel oil and coal for heating buildings, and electricity for a wide variety of uses. During the last few years, there has been a steep rise in the volume of gas used by farms for heating buildings, drying crops, etc.

Although agriculture is regarded, not without reason, as the weakest link of the Soviet economy, it is easy to overlook the fact that a massive programme of capital investment (accounting for 27% of total Soviet investment during the latter half of the 1970s) has resulted in a post-war growth of output amounting to an average 3.9% a year for grain, 6.5% for sugar beet, 2.8% for vegetables and 4.6% for cotton.

Table 9.1: Output of Major Products (annual average) (mn tons)

Period	Grain	Potatoes	Sugar Beet	Vegetables	Cotton
1946–50	64.8	80.7	13.5	11.4	2.32
1956–60	121.5	88.3	45.6	15.1	4.36
1966–70	167.6	94.8	81.1	19.5	6.10
1971–75	181.6	89.8	76.0	23.0	7.67
1976–80	205.0	82.6	88.4	26.0	8.93
1981–85 Plan	238–243	'an increase'	100–103		9.2–9.3

The rate of growth of the livestock sector has been somewhat lower, due to distress slaughtering on a number of occasions because of fodder shortages caused by the failure of the grain harvest. Since 1950, the number of cattle has risen at an average annual rate of 2.2%, sheep by 1.3% and pigs by 4.0%.

There is still a long way to go before Soviet agriculture reaches the goal of providing an adequate balanced diet for the population and providing a sufficiently high surplus in good years to cover the short-falls of bad years. This was recognised by the Eleventh Five Year Plan, which set targets for the period 1981 to 1985 as shown in Table 9.3, but by the end of 1982 it was apparent that these targets (with the exception of those for cotton and eggs) had become unattainable.

Given the steady increase in energy capacity and other investment resources provided to agriculture in recent years, the 1981 to 1985 plan targets should have been feasible. However, the multitude of problems

219

Table 9.2: The Livestock Sector

| Year | Stock of Animals, 1 Jan. (mn) | | | | Period | Output (mn tons) | | |
	Cattle	Sheep	Pigs	Poultry		Meat	Milk	Eggs (bn)
1950	58.1	93.6	22.2		1946–50	3.5	32.3	7.5
1960	74.2	144.0	53.4	514.3	1956–60	7.9	57.3	23.6
1970	95.2	135.8	56.1	590.3	1966–70	11.6	80.6	35.8
1975	109.1	151.2	72.3	792.4	1971–75	14.0	87.4	51.4
1980	115.1	143.6	73.9	980.9	1976–80	14.8	92.7	63.1
1982	115.7	142.1	73.2	1,029.3	1981–85 Plan	17.2	98	72

Table 9.3: Eleventh Five Year Plan Targets for Agriculture (mn tons/ year)

	Actual Output 1976–1980 (ave.)	Planned Output 1981–1985 (ave.)	Actual Output 1981
Grain	205.0	238–243	
Sugar beet	88.4	100–103	60.6
Vegetables	26.0		25.6
Cotton	8.93	9.2–9.3	9.6
Meat	14.8	17–17.5	15.2
Milk	92.7	97–99	88.5
Eggs (bn)	63.1	72	70.9

faced by the rural economy — an ageing and inefficient labour force, an inadequate infrastructure (bad roads, a lack of machinery-repair and produce-storage facilities) and the continuing failure to make better use of dry-farming techniques in the semi-arid zones which provide much of the USSR's grain output — coupled with different weather conditions, has meant that the increase in investment has been accompanied by declining yields on investment. The failure of the 1981 and 1982 harvests has meant that the 1981 to 1985 grain target is now unattainable, and because more than two-thirds of Soviet grain goes to the livestock sector, this also means that the meat and milk targets should be missed in spite of substantial grain imports. Although the size of the animal herds has been maintained, the animals are being fed less, resulting in a fall in the average weight of slaughtered animals.

Total energy capacity in agriculture has grown at an average annual rate of 7.7% since 1950, including 9.4% during 1950 to 1960, 7.7% during 1960 to 1970, and 6.3% a year over 1970 to 1981.

During 1975 to 1981, the total capacity of tractor engines has been growing at an average annual rate of 4.8%, combine harvester engines by 5.2%, lorries by 5.0% and electric motors and installations by 7.8%. It is likely that these growth rates will be maintained until beyond 1985.

Because of the reduction in the number of people employed in agriculture, the increase in energy capacity is even more significant when measured per worker. It is interesting to note that while the increase over 1965 to 1970 was 3.5 hp per worker, and over 1970 to 1975 some 5.6 hp per worker, an increase of 7.3 hp per worker was achieved during 1975 to 1980. This reflects both an accelerating fall in the number of agricultural workers and a more rapid increase in the provision of energy capacity.

Table 9.4: Energy Capacity in Agriculture (mn hp)

Year	Total	Tractor Engines	Combine Engines	Lorries	Electric Motors and Installations	Animal Power	Others
1950	62.3	22.3	8.0	21.3	0.9	7.3	2.5
1960	152.9	50.3	24.7	63.2	7.2	4.7	2.8
1970	322.1	121.8	46.1	103.5	40.7	3.2	6.8
1975	457.3	169.7	59.1	131.6	85.6	2.5	8.8
1978	552.9	200.7	69.2	155.0	113.6	2.3	12.1
1979	579.4	208.4	72.2	162.5	121.2	2.2	12.9
1980	603.9	215.3	76.3	168.8	127.8	2.1	13.6
1981	632.8	224.7	80.3	176.9	134.4	2.1	14.4

Table 9.5: Provision of Energy Capacity to Agriculture

	Hp per Worker	Hp per 100 Hectares of Sown Land
1950	1.7	47
1960	5.4	74
1970	11.2	148
1975	16.8	190
1978	21.4	236
1979	22.8	248
1980	24.1	259
1981	25.5	279
1985 Plan	33.7–36.1	

In 1980, the provision of energy capacity per worker varied from 50.4 hp in Estonia and 42.4 hp in Kazakhstan, where the farms are highly mechanised thanks to the flat land, to only 9.1 hp in Azerbaidzhan and 6.0 hp in Georgia. These are mountainous republics where agriculture is dominated by labour-intensive sectors like fruit, tea, tobacco and vines. Moldavia had the highest provision of energy capacity per 100 hectares of sown land at 649 hp, and Kazakhstan (160 hp) the lowest.

The Soviet definition of 'tractor' covers a number of different types of vehicle used for many purposes. Of the annual production of tractors (after taking imports and exports into account), about three-quarters are delivered to agriculture. During the period 1976 to 1980, a total of 1,806,000 tractors with a combined capacity of 144.1 mn hp (i.e. an average of 79.8 hp each) were received, and it is planned that during 1981 to 1985 the farms should receive 1,870,000 tractors.

Table 9.6: Production and Stock of Tractors ('000)

Year	Production	Delivered to Agriculture	Stock of Agricultural Tractors
1960	239	157	1,122
1970	459	309	1,977
1975	550	370	2,334
1978	576	371	2,515
1979	557	355	2,540
1980	555	348	2,562
1981		352	2,595

Table 9.7: Capacity of Soviet Tractors

Year	Total Capacity of Tractors Produced During the Year (mn hp)	Capacity per Tractor (hp)	Total Capacity of all Soviet Tractors (mn hp)	Capacity per Tractor (hp)
1965	21.0	59.2	77.6	48.1
1970	29.4	64.1	111.6	56.4
1975	41.4	75.3	152.5	65.3
1978	47.0	81.6	179	71.2
1979	46.6	83.7	186	73.2
1980	47.0	84.7	191	74.6

Not only has the number of tractors employed by Soviet agriculture steadily grown, but capacity, measured in terms of horse-power of new tractors, has also grown. In 1965, the average capacity of tractors produced in that year was 59 hp, and in 1980 the average capacity of new tractors had grown to 84.7 hp. Consequently, while the number of operating tractors in the USSR grew by 59% between 1965 and 1980, their combined capacity grew by 146%.

There is a distinct link between the utilisation of the tractor stock and the area of sown land. During 1965 to 1980, there has been a marginal increase in the area of sown land from 209.1 mn hectares to 217.3 mn, with the number of tractors per 1,000 hectares rising from 7.71 in 1965 to 11.79 in 1980. The relationship between the number of tractors and the sown area varies considerably from region to region, depending on the share of land sown with grain. In Kazakhstan, where most of the sown land is devoted to grain, comparatively few tractors are needed because they are able to cover huge distances in long runs. In 1980, Kazakhstan had 6.52 tractors per 1,000 hectares while the Central Asian region, where the principal crops are cotton and vegetables, and where tractor operations must be carried out slowly and laboriously, had over 40 tractors per 1,000 hectares.

The average length of life of a Soviet tractor amounts to 7.6 years, and if the plan for the delivery of 1,870,000 tractors to agriculture over 1981 to 1985 is fulfilled, then the stock of tractors in 1985 should be 2.8 million, or 9.3% more than in 1980. This suggests that the number of tractors required by agriculture is tending to level out, and in the future emphasis will be placed on increasing the size and capacity of individual tractors. On the other hand, it is possible that the Russians may soon begin the large-scale production of small tractors designed specifically for private plots. This would eventually raise the tractor

Table 9.8: Combine Harvesters ('000)

	Output	Stock
1960	59.0	497
1970	99.2	623
1975	97.5	680
1980	117	722
1981		741

stock to near US levels (4.3 mn in 1980) with a consequent decline in average engine capacity.

It is apparent that the stock of combine harvesters is also starting to level out, in spite of plans such as that for 1976 to 1980 which called for the delivery of 538,000 harvesters. This plan was fulfilled; 553,000 combines were produced, of which 539,000 were delivered to agriculture and the rest were exported. At the end of 1980, the number of combines in the USSR rose to 722,000, an increase of 6.2% over 1975. During the period 1981 to 1985, it is planned that 600,000 harvesters will be delivered, and if this target is met, then the stock should reach 750,000, rising to perhaps 760,000 by 1990.

About one-third of all lorries produced in the USSR are delivered to the agricultural sector. In 1980, 268,000 lorries (including specialised vehicles like milk tankers) were received, of which 240,000 replaced scrapped lorries and 28,000 extended the stock of lorries at the disposal of agricultural enterprises to 1,596,000.

During 1976 to 1980 the total acquisition of lorries by agricultural enterprises amounted to 1,342,000 vehicles, and the plan for 1981 to 1985 calls for the delivery of 1,450,000. It can be estimated that the stock of lorries will amount to 1,750,000 in 1985, and 1,850,000 in 1990. The annual increase in the stock of lorries should fall because of the increasing size and capacity of new lorries. Between 1970 and 1980 the average capacity of a lorry rose from 3.18 to 3.65 tons, and in 1980 their total freight capacity increased by 252,000 tons or 4.5% while the number of lorries grew by 28,000 or 1.8%.

Rural roads in the USSR are generally unmade, which means that they can become quagmires in summer and equally impassable in winter when the ruts freeze. Bad roads are blamed for mechanical breakdowns which put the average rural lorry out of commission for 40 days a year, and although rural roads are being given a hard surface (mainly compacted gravel) at a rate of 23,000 km a year, it should be the end of the century before the road construction programme is complete.

Table 9.9: Lorries ('000)

Year	Delivery	Stock	Total Freight Capacity of Lorry Stock (mn tons)	Unit Capacity of Lorry Stock (tons)
1970	156.6	1,136	3.33	2.93
1975	269.4	1,396	4.45	3.18
1978	269.9	1,528	5.26	3.44
1979	266.5	1,568	5.58	3.56
1980	268.0	1,596	5.83	3.65
1981	268.0			

In the meantime, it is hoped that the increasing use of auto-trailers will reduce transport costs. Each trailer, pulled by a lorry, lowers transport costs by up to 1.5 kopecks a ton for trailers with a capacity of 8 to 10 tons, and saves 6 tons of motor fuel a year.

Pneumatic pipelines are planned for the major grain-producing regions, and a system of 650 km in length is to be built in Kazakhstan in the near future. Containers filled with grain will be blown along the pipeline, reducing transport costs fivefold. When it is remembered that transportation accounts for 40% of total agricultural costs, the vast potential of pneumatic transport can be appreciated.

A notable feature of Soviet agriculture in recent years has been the rapid growth in the capacity of electric motors, which are used to accomplish the mechanisation of a wide variety of tasks. As recently as 1960, they were virtually unknown on Soviet farms, but by 1981 were accounting for 21.2% of total energy capacity.

The electrification of agriculture is continuing to grow very rapidly, at an average annual rate of 8.5% over the period 1975 to 1980. In 1980, 111 bn kWh of power were consumed, an increase of 8.5% over 1979, but the five-year plan target for agricultural power consumption in 1985 has been set at 160 bn kWh, implying that electrification growth rates will fall to 7.9% a year. The amount of electricity used by each agricultural worker for production purposes has grown from 1,709 kWh in 1975 to 2,733 in 1980 and is planned to rise to about 4,200 in 1985.

Most of the increase in power supplies is destined for stationary electric motors, the number of which rose from 8.84 mn in 1975 to 12.20 mn in 1979 and 12.79 mn in 1980. Electricity demand for thermal processes (i.e. heating cowsheds, drying grain, etc.) is growing less quickly, but the needs of land irrigation, and drainage systems

Table 9.10: Consumption of Electricity by Farms (bn kWh)

	1975	1980	% Increase	1982	1985 Plan
Total consumption	73.8	111.0	50.4	126	160
for houses, admin. buildings	19.9	27.3	37.2	30	36
for production purposes of which:	53.9	83.7	55.3	96	124
electric motors	26.2	43.0	64.1		
heating	16.0	20.5	28.1		
lighting	5.0	8.0	60.0		
land improvement and by sector:	5.7	10.0	75.4		18
livestock	30.8	44.9	45.8		67
crops	16.1	26.6	65.2		37
processing	7.0	12.2	74.3		20

will double over the five years 1981 to 1985.

Sales of electricity to farms are heavily subsidised, with the total power bill for 1980 amounting to 837 mn roubles, or 1% of total farm revenues of 81,016 mn roubles. More than 700 mn roubles a year are spent on rural electrification with most of this going on erecting new transmission networks. The rural network now extends for more than 5 mn km and is growing at a rate of 168,000 km a year. It has 17,000 transformer substations of 35 and 110 kV, and more than 750,000 transformer points. The total capacity of agricultural transformers now exceeds 150 mn kVa.

It can be estimated that electricity consumption by farms will grow to 200 bn kWh in 1990 and 280 bn at the end of the century. Although many of the basic processes, such as milking cows and delivering water to animals, are almost fully mechanised, the demand for electricity will continue to grow as the policy of building large animal complexes is carried out. At the present time, pig-fattening complexes for 108,000 animals a year have been built, each containing 1,200 electric motors and 2,500 infra-red heaters in 40 automatic systems, receiving electricity from twelve transformers of 630 kVa each. A larger complex for 216,000 animals is being built, as well as battery farms each designed to house 4 mn poultry.

There is plenty of scope for the increased electrification of the fodder preparation and distribution processes, which can account for up to 60% of total labour expenditure on some livestock farms. In typical farms, fodder preparation is carried out by a series of electric machines with the aggregate capacity of the motors of the three basic machines (for washing roots and tubers, for cutting roots and potatoes and for fodder mixing) not exceeding 6 kW. However, these should be replaced by a universal fodder crusher driven by 10 kW motor, which cuts labour requirements by 75-90% and costs by 50-90%. The most efficient systems for the transport and preparation of 2,100 tons of fodder a year would typically involve ten electric motors of total capacity 48 kW and would reduce labour needs by 40% and production costs by 20%.

Electricity is finding increasing use in the siloing of fodder because it speeds up the process and produces better quality silage. A current is passed through electrodes buried in the fodder and a thermostat cuts it out when a temperature of 35°C is reached. The heating process takes 30-60 hours and an average 25 kWh are needed for the processing of one ton. Thus each cow, eating 15 tons of silage, will require a power expenditure of 375 kWh.

The USSR has 320,000 milking machines, each capable of milking about 120 cows. However 10% of the 43 mn milk-producing cows are still milked by hand.

Electricity is widely used for the sorting, cleaning and drying of crops, and is finding increasing use in glasshouses for additional lighting, ventilation and water circulation systems. Huge amounts of electricity will be needed to power the irrigation systems being built in Central Asia, Kazakhstan and the North Caucasus and Volga regions of Russia, as well as the drainage networks being built in the non-Chernozem zone of northern Russia. The capacity of pumping stations on the Karshi Canal in Uzbekistan, for example, has reached 500 MW, the equivalent of a small power station. It is estimated that the use of electric motors instead of pumps with individual diesel motors gives fuel savings of 130 gsf per cu m of water. Labour costs are reduced fourfold.

During the next five years, it is hoped that the prototypes of a new generation of electric tractors can be produced. The first examples were built 50 years ago, but their cables wore out very quickly, and they proved far more expensive than conventional internal combustion tractors. It is now believed that the costs of production and operation can be reduced sufficiently to make them competitive.

Practically all electricity used by farms comes from the national grid, although there are still a large number of small local power stations, owned by farms and generating electricity on the basis of tractor-type diesel engines. In 1965, there were 109,000 of these with a total capacity of 5,295 MW, and they produced 6.03 bn kWh, or 29% of total rural power requirements. But as the rural network of electricity transmission lines has been extended to even the remotest farms, these highly inefficient stations have been scrapped and in 1980 only 35,000 remained with an aggregate capacity of 2,692 MW (77 kW per station) producing 0.67 bn kWh. They are used primarily as a reserve source of electricity during power cuts.

Fuel Consumption by Agriculture

The value of fuel consumed by agriculture rose from 1,500 mn roubles in 1966 to 2,555 mn in 1972. It consisted largely of oil products, although small amounts of coal, peat and shale were used for heating buildings and, since 1972, natural gas has assumed an increasing importance for this purpose. The agricultural sector used 13.4% of all oil products in 1972, although this share has been declining steadily from 18.8% in 1959 and 15.4% in 1966.

In 1980, the consumption of oil products amounted to 56 mn tons of light and middle products, including 37 mn tons of diesel and 19 mn tons of gasoline, and grew by 1.5% over 1979. Small amounts of fuel oil were used for heating purposes. More than half the oil products were used in the RSFSR, and a surprisingly large amount, 9.5 mn tons, was consumed in Kazakhstan. This compares with only 6.0 mn tons in the Ukraine, which manages to provide a much greater volume of output, and is a reflection of the extremely extensive nature of agriculture in Kazakhstan, where grain yields average 1.08 tons per hectare over 1976 to 1980 compared with 2.61 in the Ukraine. It is arguable whether the continuing efforts to grow grain in some of the more marginal areas of Kazakhstan can be justified in the light of the considerable expenditure of oil and other materials involved.

Table 9.11: Consumption of Oil Products by the Agricultural Sector, by Region, 1980 (mn tons)

USSR	56.0
RSFSR	32.0
Ukraine	6.0
Belorussia	1.8
Baltic	1.8
Moldavia	0.8
Caucasus	1.0
Kazakhstan	9.5
Central Asia	3.1

While fuel consumption by tractors is a function of the area of sown land (with consumption by combine harvesters being a function of the land area sown to grain), the amount of fuel used by lorries will vary roughly with the tonnage of produce grown, the average carrying capacity of the lorries, the rate of utilisation of lorries (which depends on the share of empty or half full runs) and the average length of journey by lorries between the fields and the granary, fertiliser store, seed store, repair workshop, etc. It is probably impossible to calculate the rate of efficiency of fuel use by agricultural transport and equipment given the large number of variables involved, but Soviet economists all agree that it is very low compared with that obtained by Western farms.

Losses of fuel from poorly maintained storage tanks are causing considerable concern as well as the perennial problems of pilferage. Efforts are being made to effect savings; Ukrainian farms are said to have saved 156,000 tons of diesel in 1980 compared with the consumption norm of 1975, but there is still substantial scope for further reductions in consumption.

One method likely to be widely employed is the laying of underground product pipelines to farms from a central oil product despatch point. This should practically eliminate losses from transshipment, and may help to prevent pilferage by reducing the number of people involved in the distribution of products. It is estimated that the heavy capital costs can be recouped in one year because of the large savings that can be made by reducing the size of the local road tanker fleet. Work has commenced in several parts of the USSR, such as Kazakhstan, where a lack of good roads make distribution by tanker particularly expensive, and the Stavropol krai in North Caucasus, where all the farms in the Korovsk region are to be linked by a pipeline system.

The consumption of natural gas has grown during the 1970s at an average annual rate of 22.0% from 0.67 bn cu m in 1970 to 3.37 bn in 1977 and 4.89 bn in 1980. While used mainly for the heating of buildings such as cattle sheds, it is finding increasing use for the drying of damp grain and the storage at a constant temperature of fruit, mixed feed, etc. Plants burning 30, 60 and 120 cu m/hr have been designed by the VNIIpromgaz Institute, and the first such fruit storage plant began operating in 1975 at the Dzhandosov state farm in Kazakhstan; it has five hermetically sealed chambers with a capacity of 500 tons of fruit, and its temperature is maintained at 0-4°C by a compressor refrigerator powered by a 60 cu m/hr gas plant designated the URGS2A. The gas plant runs on liquified gas delivered to a GNS2A generator from two underground reservoirs with a combined capacity of 4.2 cu m of liquified gas. A period of industrial testing demonstrated that apples, grapes and pears could be stored in perfect conditions for lengthy periods, and shortly afterwards another plant of capacity 120 cu m/hr was installed at a grain elevator at the Sukhomi flour mill in Georgia. Increasingly wide use is now being made of these plants.

Piped gas is also being used to an increasing extent, especially on farms within 50 km of trunk pipelines, or on the outskirts of towns. While it is mostly burned in boilers to provide steam and hot water, the direct burning of gas in glasshouses is beginning to take place. The best method involves the installation of small gas burners along the walls of glasshouses. This gives an efficiency rate approaching 100%, gives a good micro-climate with a raised carbon dioxide content and accelerates the growth of plants. The use of gas for infra-red heaters is also growing.

As well as fossil fuels and electricity, agriculture also uses a substantial volume of thermal energy. Much of this is obtained as waste heat from power stations or the compressor stations of gas pipelines, and yields considerable fuel savings. A glasshouse complex working on heat from the Lithuania Power Station, for example, saves one million roubles a year. However, at many other large stations, a huge potential remains unused. Kursk atomic power station (2,000 MW) emits 900,000 cu m of water at a temperature of $28-32°C$, and its use in glasshouses would save 3,000 tsf per hectare per year.

According to the Ministry of Gas, 280 hectares of glasshouses could be supplied by heat from compressor stations operating in 1980 and a further 310 hectares could be heated by stations to be built during 1981 to 1985. This would enable 1 mn tsf/year to be saved, but the use of this heat is currently said to be 'insignificant'.

Only 1% of surveyed geothermal resources are used at the present time, mainly in the North Caucasus. Use of the remaining 99% would provide the fuel equivalent of up to 40 mn tsf a year. A programme has been elaborated to build 174 hectares of glasshouses heated by geothermal energy during 1982 to 1990 in the North Caucasus, Azerbaidzhan and Central Asia. The largest geothermal station currently operating is at Mostovsk in Krasnodar oblast. Water from a depth of 3,000 m is delivered at $60°C$ to glasshouses, then is piped at $40-50°C$ to livestock complexes and for the manufacture of silage. It is then sent at $20-30°C$ to ponds to assist fish-breeding, and is finally pumped back into the ground to maintain the underground water reservoir. Geothermal energy is also used to heat houses and administrative buildings and for the washing of wool and production of concrete.

It can be estimated that the total consumption of fuel by the agricultural sector in 1980 amounted to 102 mn tsf compared with 85 mn in 1970 and during the period 1970 to 1980 it rose at an average rate of 1.8% a year. As well as 82 mn tsf of fuel for vehicles and machines, a further 20 mn tsf of coal, fuel oil and natural gas were used for heating and other purposes. As well as 4.9 bn cu m of natural gas, about 5 mn tons of fuel oil and 12 mn tons of hard coal were burned by the agricultural sector in 1980.

Future Consumption of Fuel

The relationship between fuel consumption and the output of agricultural produce is very weak. Tractors and combines have to cover the sown area irrespective of its yield and the amount of produce grown on it, and the volume of fuel used by lorries depends on the inputs to agriculture as well as its output.

Strenuous efforts can be expected to reduce the wastage of fuel resources, and it is a reasonable estimate that whatever happens to the fortunes of agriculture (the avowed aim of producing one ton of grain per inhabitant by 1990, or 280 mn tons, is technically feasible, but most unlikely unless the infrastructural problems of agriculture can be solved), fuel requirements by vehicles and machines should grow very slowly to 62 mn tons in 1990. With petrol-driven trucks being phased out in favour of diesel-powered vehicles, the consumption of diesel should rise from 37 mn tons to 50 mn while that of gasoline falls from 19 to 12 mn tons. A tentative estimate of 65 mn tons in 2000 (60 mn diesel and 5 mn gasoline) looks reasonable.

As more grain elevators are built, and more fuel is needed for crop-drying and storage, the consumption of natural gas is likely to grow rapidly, particularly as it will replace coal in the Ukraine and the western USSR, and fuel oil in the Urals and Volga regions. There should also be a substantial increase in the volume of gas used for the heating systems of livestock complexes, replacing other fuels including firewood, which is still used to a large extent by farms throughout the USSR. An estimate of fuel consumption for these purposes might be 22.5 mn tsf in 1985, 25 mn in 1990 and 28 mn in 2000. The overall fuel requirements of agriculture should grow by 1.2% a year to 115 mn tsf in 1990 and then by 0.6% a year to 122 mn tsf in 2000.

Table 9.12: Forecast Consumption of Fuel by Agriculture

	1985	1990	2000
Vehicles:			
Gasoline (mn tons)	15.5	12	5
Diesel (mn tons)	44	50	66
Other purposes:			
Natural gas (bn cu m)	8.5	12	20
Coal (mn tons)	8	8	4
Fuel oil (mn tons)	3	3	1
Total (mn tsf)	110	117	132

It seems to be taken for granted by many Western observers that the volume of fuel exported by the USSR is regarded by Soviet planners as a residue after the country has satisfied its own needs. In fact, it is likely that exports play a major role in the planning balance, in financial rather than volume terms, and any shortfall in production makes itself felt through a reduction in fuel available for domestic needs rather than a decline in exports. Exports are needed to finance imports of equipment which the USSR could only produce itself at a prohibitive cost in terms of money and time, and are therefore considered more important than the domestic production of other, less vital, items. Since 1978, exports have also assumed a further, equally vital, importance in that they are necessary to help the USSR pay for its imports of grain which have been averaging 40 mn tons a year during the recent period of poor harvests.

The Soviet Union is planning to increase its exports of gas while striving to maintain oil exports at current levels and using atomic power and inefficient, but cheap, resources of coal to produce electricity. During the next twenty years, it will have to raise sufficient hard currency to service and repay its debts (now about 17 bn dollars), finance heavy imports of grain and meat, and fulfil its role as lender of the last resort for its profligate allies in Eastern Europe. It has been asked whether the Soviets are prepared to continue playing this role, but their support for Poland during 1981 and 1982, which involved them in distress selling of oil, gold, diamonds and timber during particularly weak market conditions, appear to confirm their commitment to honour Eastern Europe's debts to the West while simultaneously taking various steps to attract countries like Poland more securely into the Soviet economic and political orbit.

Consequently, large (and increasing) exports, which inevitably means fuel during the next decade at least, figure very prominently in the various options open to Soviet planners. And while crude oil has traditionally dominated the fuel export pattern, natural gas is proving far cheaper to produce, and hence more profitable to export, even after its heavy transportation costs have been taken into account. It is likely that Soviet oil exports will fall during the rest of the 1980s, but the Russians will be hoping to increase their gas sales so as to cover the

Table 10.1: Exports of Fuel and Energy by the USSR

	1960	1970	1975	1978	1979	1980
Crude oil (mn tons)	17.8	66.8	93.1	121.1	117.7	115.8
Oil products (mn tons)	15.4	29.0	37.3	42.1	42.7	43.3
Total oil (mn tons)	33.2	95.8	130.4	163.2	160.4	159.1
Coal and coke (mn tons)	14.9	28.7	30.3	30	·28	26
Natural gas (bn cu m)	0.2	2.2	19.3	37.0	48.4	57.3
Total fuel (mn tsf)	59.8	167.6	238.9	306.3	314.5	320.6
Electricity (bn kWh)	0.0	5.2	11.3	12.2	15.2	19.1

decline in oil exports and to effect an absolute increase in total fuel exports.

The principal feature of Table 10.1 is the rapid growth in exports of oil and oil products from 33 to 159 mn tons over the period 1960 to 1980, or by 8.1% a year. Exports of gas were due to treble over the period 1976 to 1980 to 58 bn cu m, or 13.3% of production, and this target was almost achieved. Electricity is exported to Finland, Norway, Greece, Poland, Hungary and Bulgaria, and may eventually be sent to the GDR and West Germany. The value of fuel exports has grown dramatically since 1973, as can be seen in Table 10.2.

Fuel is exported to different regions of the world according to different motives. An important destination is the rest of Comecon, which took nearly half of Soviet petroleum exports in 1980, and where the principal motive is that of trade specialisation, although political considerations are also important. The USSR is the only Comecon member, apart from Romania, to produce large quantities of oil, and it exports oil to these countries in exchange for industrial products. It has a political, as well as economic, obligation to supply the rest of Comecon, and accordingly it sells oil at prices lower than the world market price. Under the 'Bucharest formula', prices amount to the average of the world market price for the previous five years, and this means that in 1980 Comecon countries paid only 60% of the world price for oil bought under annual contracts from the USSR. During the first half of 1980, Poland, for example, paid 65-69% of the world price. The aim of the Bucharest formula is to soften the impact of world price rises on the economies of Comecon countries. Oil prices rise regularly but gradually, their level for several years in advance can be roughly estimated by Comecon planners, and they are generally significantly lower than world prices.

Means other than price rises are needed to encourage the Eastern

Table 10.2: **Exports of Fuel by Value (mn roubles)**

	Crude Oil and Products	Solid Fuel	Natural Gas	Electricity	Total	Share of Fuel in Total Exports
1973	2,403	432	92	100	3,027	19.2
1974	4,352	565	213	113	5,243	25.3
1975	5,908	1,005	451	159	7,523	31.4
1976	7,676	1,021	751	168	9,616	34.3
1977	9,400	1,046	1,023	194	11,663	35.1
1978	10,052	965	1,473	228	12,718	35.6
1979	14,517	983	2,089	280	17,869	42.2
1980	18,085	1,101	3,687	400	23,273	46.8

European countries to economise on oil. These take the form of limits to the volume of oil sold under term agreements; the Eleventh Five Year Plan has stipulated that term sales will amount to 400 mn tons over 1981 to 1985. Thus, the level of term exports is not expected to grow beyond the 80 mn tons exported in 1980. But the USSR will supply additional oil at prices calculated from a formula based on Opec prices excluding those of the African producers. Such oil must be paid for in hard currency, but the Eastern European countries will still prefer Soviet to Opec oil because its supply is less subject to political upheavals, wars, etc. Soviet strategy, on the other hand, is to encourage them to look elsewhere for their oil, leaving more Soviet oil available for export to the West.

One of the main reasons for this strategy is that continuing sales of oil to Eastern Europe are simply resulting in larger Soviet trade surpluses with those countries. There seems little likelihood of the Eastern European countries being able to raise their exports sufficiently to bring their trade into balance let alone pay off the deficits which have accumulated against them in recent years. On the contrary, the deficits have been increasing from year to year, and for Soviet oil deliveries to continue at current levels amounts to a further substantial subsidy in addition to that existing under the Bucharest formula.

In addition, a trade surplus of $2.83 bn has accumulated over 1978 to 1981 with Vietnam, $2.76 bn with Mongolia and $1.0 bn with Cuba. These countries, together with North Korea, import about 14 mn tons a year of Soviet oil at prices even lower than those charged to Eastern Europe.

The USSR is forced to choose between leaving its allies to stand on their own feet, or effectively giving its oil away. It can be expected to

Table 10.3: Soviet Trade Surpluses with Eastern European Countries, 1978-1981 ($ mn)

	1978	1979	1980	1981	1978–1981
Bulgaria	218	217	336	927	1,698
Czechoslovakia	79*	278	168	369	736
East Germany	400	462	836	499	2,197
Hungary	46*	503	342	1*	798
Poland	216*	189	1,241	2,357	3,571
Romania	10*	17	142*	143	8
Total CMEA	267	1,666	2,781	4,294	9,008

Note: * Deficits.

try and find a compromise resulting in significant cuts in oil deliveries while raising supplies of natural gas and electricity under agreements involving Eastern European participation in pipeline and power station construction.

The Russians do not seem to be enjoying much success in their plans to cut oil deliveries to Eastern Europe, and as recently as July 1982 they were still reaffirming their aim to sell a total 400 mn tons of crude and products over the five years 1981-5. But if cuts in Russian deliveries are achieved, they will not necessarily lead to oil shortages in Eastern Europe, because all these countries are significantly exporters of oil to Western Europe. While Romania has traditionally exported domestically-produced oil since before the last war, other countries like East Germany, Poland, Czechoslovakia, Hungary and Bulgaria have recently begun exporting products refined from Soviet crude to the West for hard currency. These sales reached a peak of 12.5 mn tons in 1980 before falling to 10.2 mn tons in 1981, and it can be argued that any cut in Soviet crude deliveries is more likely to lead to hard currency balance of trade problems than fuel shortages. It is probable that the countries involved will cut exports, which are not as profitable as in the past due to the decline in product prices, in conjunction with more stringent oil-saving measures.

In 1980, the Soviet Union supplied other socialist countries with 91 mn tons of crude and products, 18.2% more than the 77.7 mn tons of 1975. Of this, 80 mn tons went to Eastern Europe with the rest going to Cuba, Vietnam and North Korea.

It can be estimated that in 1981, Soviet oil deliveries to Eastern Europe fell by about 2 mn tons, with East Germany, Hungary and Poland accounting for most of the decline, although there was a small

Table 10.4: Destination of Petroleum Exports by Volume and Value

	1975	1976	1977	1978	1979	1980
Volume (mn tons)	130.4	148.5	161.1	163.1	160.4	159.1
Socialist countries	77.7	84.0	88.0	90.0	90.0	91.0
Capitalist countries	52.7	64.5	73	73	70.0	68.0
OECD	39.1	50.2	58.6	60.7	58.9	57.0
Others	13.6	14.3	14.0	12.0	11.0	11.0
Value (bn roubles)	5.9	7.7	9.4	10.1	14.5	18.1
Socialist countries	2.7	3.2	4.2	5.2	6.4	8.0
Capitalist countries	3.2	4.5	5.2	4.9	8.1	10.1
OECD	2.8	3.9	4.4	4.3	7.2	9.1
Others	0.4	0.6	0.8	0.6	0.9	1.0

increase in sales to Romania and Yugoslavia. Persistent rumours suggested that reductions would be more severe in 1982; it was said, for example, that Czechoslovakia would get 2.5 mn tons less, a fall of 13.2%, and East Germany's quota was to be cut by 2 mn tons, reducing its total oil imports from 21 to 19 mn tons. Although Hungary has already survived a considerable cut in imports over the three years 1979 to 1981, it was thought that a further cut of 2 mn tons might be made, bringing Soviet supplies down to 5.5 mn tons. The Russians have promised to maintain deliveries to Poland at 1981 levels, but the healthy state of Bulgaria's economy, together with the substantial reduction in oil consumption achieved since 1975, gives scope for a cut of about 1 mn tons. In all, it was thought that Soviet exports of crude and products to Eastern Europe would be reduced by up to 8 mn tons in 1982.

In the event, it seems that the cutback has been very much less than this at about 3 mn tons, with 75 mn tons being delivered.

Prices of oil sold to Western countries have risen in line with world prices, and oil sales have grown to a level which enables the USSR to achieve a surplus on its trade with the OECD countries. Its surplus rose from $0.9 bn in 1979 to $3.2 bn in 1980, but fell back to $2.8 bn in 1981. In 1980, the Soviet Union sold 57 mn tons of crude and products, worth 9.11 bn roubles, to the OECD, and 11 mn tons worth 1.0 bn roubles to developing countries.

In spite of forecasts by some Western observers that oil sales to the West are due to suffer a precipitous decline, they continued to grow until 1979, when they fell by 4% over 1978. There were further falls of 3% in 1980 and 2.3% in 1981. Exports of crude oil to OECD countries fell from 36.3 mn tons in 1978 to 31.0 mn in 1981, but sales of

Table 10.5: Soviet Oil Sales to OECD Countries (mn tons)

	Total Volume					(including Products)		
	1977	1978	1979	1980	1981	1979	1980	1981
Finland	10.66	9.76	10.45	9.70	9.90	3.09	2.73	2.56
France	4.76	4.75	6.12	8.38	8.08	0.89	1.56	1.82
Netherlands	2.30	2.45	5.66	7.24	8.03	4.89	6.71	7.52
Italy	9.68	8.95	6.38	6.90	6.68	0.45	0.52	0.72
West Germany	8.04	8.89	9.33	6.88	5.00	3.21	3.17	3.88
Belgium	1.60	3.52	2.72	4.26	4.24	1.82	2.01	1.83
Switzerland	2.55	3.09	2.21	2.63	2.62	2.11	2.37	2.27
Sweden	3.55	4.32	4.30	2.35	1.33	2.95	1.80	0.77
Austria	1.93	1.98	1.73	1.51	1.73	0.01	0.01	0.02
Spain	0.64	0.45	0.88	1.38	1.28	0.04	0.06	0.24
Denmark	2.14	2.54	2.03	1.30	0.92	0.32	0.11	0.13
Greece	2.14	2.10	1.08	1.27	1.64	0.12	0.38	0.45
UK	4.66	4.49	2.89	1.21	1.56	0.74	0.92	0.87
Japan	0.59	0.56	0.65	0.53	0.54	0.60	0.44	0.45
Portugal	1.00	0.80	0.83	0.52	0.65	–	0.02	–
Iceland	0.43	0.38	0.36	0.36	0.29	0.36	0.36	0.29
Norway	0.83	0.83	0.82	0.20	0.51	0.13	0.03	0.18
Turkey	n.a.	n.a.	n.a	0.19	0.22	n.a.	0.19	0.22
Ireland	0.40	0.41	0.37	0.18	0.21	0.22	0.18	0.21
USA	0.69	0.44	0.06	0.03	0.27	0.06	0.03	0.27
Total OECD	58.59	60.71	58.89	57.00	55.70	22.02	23.58	24.70

Table 10.6: Soviet Oil Sales to OECD Countries (value in mn $)

	1977	1978	1979	1980
Finland	1,041	983	1,677	2,438
France	472	620	1,468	2,170
Netherlands	237	287	1,183	1,094
Italy	887	1,067	1,135	1,704
West Germany	833	1,098	2,053	1,006
Belgium	159	219	375	574
Switzerland	314	201	360	826
Sweden	340	344	696	557
Austria	190	189	269	386
Spain	53	123	126	353
Denmark	212	230	401	342
Greece	85	234	186	69
UK	480	449	477	408
Japan	76	107	146	164
Portugal	104	75	118	130
Ireland	49	na	na	89
Norway	85	68	101	48
Turkey	na	na	na	79
Ireland	37	48	80	38
USA	64	150	244	17
Total OECD	5,739	6,492	11,095	12,499

products rose from 24.2 to 24.7 mn tons. This was due to a rise in the sale of diesel from 14.8 to 15.8 mn tons and of petrol from 0.5 to 1.3 mn tons, while exports of naptha rose from 2.6 to 3.7 mn tons.

The principal Western customers are Finland, France, West Germany and Italy, with the Netherlands and Belgium becoming more important in 1979/80 as the Russians took advantage of soaring spot prices on the Rotterdam and Antwerp markets. The increasing price of oil during the last few years has meant that, although the volume of oil sales during 1978 to 1981 declined, income has been rising, from $5.7 bn in 1977 to $12.5 bn in 1980. However, for some countries the value of imports shown in Table 10.6 obviously does not match the volumes of deliveries indicated in Table 10.5, and it is apparent that the value figures are understated.

During the last few years, the Russians have found it increasingly difficult to sell crude oil to the West because of the post-1979 decline in Western demand for oil. They insist on linking the prices of their oil to world prices, more specifically to that of UK Forties 36.5° oil, and when demand is falling, the West tends to cut its imports from the Soviet Union first. Consequently, they have been pushing sales of products, where they can use the spot market to make price cuts. This enables them to maintain their market share in volume terms, because they find it easier (and more profitable) to sell products rather than crude in conditions of falling demand.

The Russians have found it difficult to provide more products for export because their refineries operate at close to capacity in supplying domestic needs, so they have consequently been selling crude to Eastern European countries, who refine it and export the products to the West. An important factor assisting this trade has been the successful efforts by Eastern European countries to reduce their crude requirements by upgrading their refineries to produce more light and middle products and less fuel oil. Consequently, 12.5 mn tons of Soviet oil, consisting of 1.4 mn tons of crude and 11.1 mn tons of products, found its way to the West in 1980 from Eastern Europe, and this compares with 8.4 mn tons in 1979 and 6.7 mn in 1978. Accordingly, the total volume of Soviet oil consumed by OECD countries rose from 67.4 mn tons in 1978 to 69.5 mn in 1980 before falling back to 65.8 mn tons in 1981.

Since the middle of 1981, the Russians have been badly affected by the slump in world crude prices. The price of their Romashkino $32.4°$ crude to north-western Europe has closely followed that of UK Forties oil, and until the spring of 1982 remained ahead of the OPEC marker price, reflecting its higher quality.

Table 10.7: Changes in Soviet Oil Prices ($/bl)

		Romashkino $32.4°$	UK Forties $36.5°$	Saudi Light $34°$
1980	May	34	33.75	26
	July	36	36.25	28
1981	March	39.25	39.25	32
	June	38.58	39.25	32
	August	36.78	35	32
	November	35.80	35	32
	December	35.49	36.50	34
1982	June	31.20		
1983	April	28.00		

Not only are Soviet planners trying to overcome the financial consequences of declining oil sales by increasing the share of products, but they are also trying to upgrade the mix of product exports. They are particularly keen on raising sales of naphtha and diesel at the expense of heavier products. Table 10.8 shows that they have been successful in this respect, with the share of naphtha and gasoline in

Table 10.8: Exports of Oil Products to OECD Countries ('000 tons)

	1979					1981				
	Naphtha	Petrol	Diesel	Fuel Oil	Total	Naphtha	Petrol	Diesel	Fuel Oil	Total
Netherlands	1,891	298	2,356	177	4,893	1,672	370	5,192	256	7,517
West Germany	403	25	2,390	183	3,213	1,359	506	1,574	353	3,876
Finland	–	–	1,537	1,527	3,095	–	–	1,045	1,487	2,556
Switzerland	–	22	1,961	131	2,114	–	59	2,165	37	2,268
Belgium	32	–	1,537	249	1,823	–	160	1,416	240	1,830
France	187	25	472	125	889	292	16	1,415	50	1,816
Sweden	–	–	812	2,066	2,950	–	–	500	272	772
Others	428	125	1,492	896	3,042	363	145	2,502	922	4,070
Total OECD	2,941	495	12,557	5,354	22,019	3,686	1,256	15,809	3,617	24,705

Table 10.9: Soviet Market Share of Oil Imports by the European OECD (%)

	Crude		Products		Total	
	1980	1981	1980	1981	1980	1981
European OECD*	6.27	6.29	30.15	27.93	9.27	9.52
Finland	54.16	68.20	91.18	93.66	61.14	73.35
Iceland	–	–	63.36	53.66	63.36	53.66
Switzerland	5.67	8.83	27.68	28.89	19.98	22.13
Austria	17.49	22.33	0.26	0.69	13.34	17.33
Netherlands	1.05	1.32	23.50	23.99	9.22	11.40
Belgium	6.73	8.33	20.08	19.66	9.80	11.09
Norway	3.68	10.89	0.99	5.99	2.60	8.48
Denmark	17.56	13.28	1.43	2.06	8.84	7.48
France	6.01	6.59	12.29	13.11	6.64	7.42
Greece	5.05	6.40	6.31	12.73	5.37	7.42
Portugal	6.04	8.55	2.02	–	5.52	7.20
Italy	6.84	6.57	3.55	4.65	6.39	6.29
Sweden	3.06	3.66	13.98	7.40	7.62	5.18
West Germany	3.70	1.38	8.47	11.12	5.00	4.30
Ireland	–	–	4.48	4.74	2.94	4.11
UK	0.63	1.87	9.92	9.56	2.15	3.39
Spain	2.70	2.19	1.32	4.87	2.59	2.43
Turkey	–	–	6.31	10.71	1.43	1.59

Note: * Soviet share of all imports from outside the European OECD. Data for individual OECD members refer to the Soviet share of imports from all sources.

total product exports rising from 15.6% in 1979 to 20.7% in 1981, while the share of residual fuel oil fell from 24.3% to 14.6%. Although there has been a small decline in the volume of crude plus product sales by the USSR to the OECD during 1978 to 1981, the Russians have managed to maintain their market share, thanks to their policy of pushing product sales.

North America accounts for nearly half of the OECD's total oil imports, and as very little Soviet oil finds its way on to the American market, it is more useful to examine changes in the Soviet share of the Western European market. In 1977, 9.00% of European imports (by volume) came from the USSR, and by 1980 this share had risen to 9.27%. It subsequently rose to 9.52% in 1981.

The All-Union Association 'Soyuznefteksport' is responsible for exporting Soviet oil. In Western Europe, a number of joint oil companies have been set up in collaboration with Western firms, including Suomen Petrooli and Teboil (both in Finland), Nafta in Britain, Nafta (B) in Belgium, Nafta (It) in Italy, DFN in Denmark and Sovoil in Switzerland. At the end of 1978, Soyuznefteksport was reorganised on a cost-accounting basis into four specialised divisions, each of which is expected to make a profit. These are Euronafta, which co-ordinates the Association's efforts to sell crude oil and products to Western Europe, Internafta, which deals with Eastern Europe, Vostoknafta (Africa and the Near and Middle East) and Dalnafta (Far East and America).

The Association controls seven transport organisations with offices at the ports of Novorossiisk, Odessa, Tuapse and Batumi on the Black Sea, Ventspils and Klaipeda on the Baltic and Nakhodka on the Pacific seaboard. In addition to these ports, oil terminals are also located at Reni (an inland port on the Danube) and Vladivostok in the Far East. Soviet tankers carry about 70% of oil exports by Soyuznefteksport, with the rest despatched along the Druzhba Pipeline to Eastern Europe.

Exports of gas are rising rapidly, and the Russians have been pushing their gas sales with a view to increasing their hydrocarbon exports now that oil exports are beginning to fall.

Soviet gas exports flow across Czechoslovakia in the so-called Transit Pipeline which carried 37 bn cu m in 1980 to Western and Eastern Europe. In 1981, its third string was completed, raising its capacity to 53 bn cu m a year. Exports to Western Europe then travel through a pipeline system originating at Baumgarten on the Austrian-Czech border. Built by Ruhrgas, OMV of Austria and Gaz de France, it was originally intended for the Consortium Project, under which Iran would sell casinghead gas to the USSR, with the Russians selling a similar amount to Western Europe.

The construction of a fourth string of the Transit Pipeline began in 1982. It will be part of the Yamal Pipeline from Urengoi to Western Europe, and will eventually carry 40 bn cu m of gas a year. Up to 16 bn of this, destined for Italy, Austria and Yugoslavia, will leave the Transit system in a branch line through Hungary, passing into Austria at Szentgotthard. Under the terms of the contracts concluded so far with West Germany (for 11.2 bn cu m a year, including 0.7 for West Berlin), Italy (8.5 bn), France (8 bn), Austria (1.5 bn) and Switzerland (0.34 bn), the Russians can expect to receive $7.2 bn a year at 1981 prices when the pipeline is operating at full capacity. Over the 25-year period of the contracts, they should receive a revenue of $180 bn at 1981 prices, which may prove sufficient to pay off Comecon's debts to the West.

Sales of gas to Eastern Europe are at concessionary prices, averaging $88.4 per 1,000 cu m in 1980, compared with the average of $111.4 charged to Western Europe. These are calaculated under the terms of

Table 10.10: Exports of Natural Gas

	Volume (bn cu m)				Value (mn $)			
	1977	1978	1979	1980	1977	1978	1979	1980
Socialist	19.4	20.7	28.5	31.7	818	1,014	1,717	2,803
Czechoslovakia	6.2	6.7	8.6	8.7	259	332	513	683
East Germany	4.7	4.8	5.6	6.5	200	235	335	545
Poland	3.5	3.5	5.1	5.3	146	170	302	470
Bulgaria	3.7	3.9	4.0	4.5	155	189	239	352
Hungary	1.3	1.4	3.3	3.8	58	67	194	347
Yugoslavia	–	0.4	0.9	1.9	–	20	75	264
Romania	–	0.0	1.0	1.0	–	1	59	142
Capitalist	12.0	16.3	19.9	25.6	593	1,133	1,480	2,832
West Germany	4.0	6.9	8.7	11.8	197	465	585	1,115
Italy	3.6	3.7	5.3	7.1	178	245	392	784
Austria	3.0	2.7	2.8	3.0	150	212	259	331
France	0.3	2.1	2.1	2.8	13	146	174	456
Finland	1.1	0.9	0.9	0.9	54	65	70	146
Total gas exports	31.4	37.0	48.4	57.3	1,411	2,147	3,198	5,635

contracts signed by Eastern European countries and the USSR within the framework of a CMEA programme for the joint development of Soviet gasfields. One example of such a contract is that which involved all Eastern European countries in the building of the Soyuz gas pipeline from Orenburg to Uzhgorod, with Poland, Czechoslovakia, East Germany, Hungary and Bulgaria undertaking to build a sector each in return for 2.8 bn cu m of gas a year at concessionary prices, while Romania supplied equipment in return for 1.5 bn cu m a year. Czechoslovakia also undertook to build a pipeline equipment repair plant at Kamyshin, which was completed in mid-1982, and also receives gas in lieu of transit payments for Soviet gas passing across its territory en route for Western Europe.

These contracts have generally proved lucrative to Eastern Europe. Poland, for example, recouped the cost of building its sector of the Soyuz gas pipeline within 2.5 years thanks to the low price of Soviet gas. All Eastern European countries will be participating in building the Yamal pipeline to Western Europe, with the East Germans building 454 km and seven compressor stations in the Western Ukraine and Tambov oblast, Yugoslavia erecting buildings for compressor stations, Bulgaria erecting housing for construction workers, and other countries providing equipment and manpower. In return, they will receive commensurate volumes of gas from the pipeline, and from a second string to be built along the Yamal corridor which will serve Eastern Europe.

Exports of coal and coke are believed to have declined from 30.3 mn

Table 10.11: Exports of Coal and Coke ('000 tons)

	Hard Coal			Coke		
	1970	1980	1981	1970	1980	1981
Austria	806	782	79	107	–	–
Belgium	274	216	94	–	–	–
Denmark	544	n.a.	n.a.	116	–	n.a.
Finland	449	589	806	598	776	715
France	1,526	781	307	–	–	–
West Germany	32	199	n.a.	–	–	n.a.
Greece	55	25	26	–	–	–
Italy	2,039	1,013	n.a.	–	–	–
Netherlands	33	–	n.a.	–	–	–
Sweden	555	475	157	126	–	–
Others	4,044	n.a.	n.a.	291	n.a.	n.a.
Total West	10,357	n.a.	n.a.	1,238	n.a.	n.a.
Bulgaria	5,065	6,732	7,051	136	–	–
Czechoslovakia	2,706	3,173	n.a.	40	–	n.a.
East Germany	3,319	n.a.	n.a.	1,498	n.a.	n.a.
Hungary	378	649	662	559	665	503
Poland	1,125	743	772	–	–	–
Romania	410	n.a.	n.a.	841	n.a.	n.a.
Yugoslavia	1,139	1,880	n.a.	1	–	–
Total East	14,142	n.a.	n.a.	3,075	n.a.	n.a.
Total	24,499	n.a.	n.a.	4,313	n.a.	n.a.

tons in 1975 to 26 mn in 1980, largely as a result of the decline in the domestic output of coal. Bulgaria is the principal customer for Soviet coal; it produces very little hard coal itself, and the Soviet Union supplies almost all its requirements. Czechoslovakia buys over 3 mn tons a year because its output of hard coal was stabilised at 27-28 mn tons a year, and East Germany imports about 2.5 mn tons a year. All other Eastern European countries import significant amounts of Soviet coal. The main Western customers are Japan, Italy, France and Austria.

Future Fuel Exports

Oil

If the current five-year plan targets are fulfilled, then the USSR should be in a position to export 140 mn tons of oil in 1985 compared with 159 mn tons in 1980. Although the Soviets do not publish their plan targets for foreign trade, it can be surmised that the planners have expected domestic consumption to rise to about 490 mn tons in 1985 with oil production planned to grow to 630 mn tons, and assuming constant stock levels, this implies a planned 140 mn tons of exports.

Towards the end of 1980, the Russians announced that they would maintain exports of crude and products to Eastern Europe during the five-year plan period of 1981 to 1985 at 1980's level of 80 mn tons, selling a total of 400 mn tons over the period. This pledge was re-iterated as recently as September 1982. It can be safely assumed that the level of supplies to the other socialist countries will be maintained, and this implies that oil exports to the West are planned to fall from 68 mn tons in 1980 to 49 mn tons in 1985.

However, the failure of agriculture to meet its plan targets for 1981 and 1982, with grain production falling considerably short of the average 238–243 mn tons a year planned for 1981 to 1985, has meant that foreign trade plans have had to be revised. It was hoped that grain production could rise to a level sufficient to obviate further heavy imports from the West, but in fact imports rose to a record 40 mn tons in the 1981/2 import season. It has therefore been necessary to keep oil exports to the West at as high a level as possible, particularly as spot crude and product prices have been falling. This explains the projected 8 mn tons/year cut in supplies to Eastern Europe in 1982, and with the commissioning of new stages at the Lisichansk and Mazheikiai re-fineries, the Russians can now produce a sufficient volume of products for export to the West, whereas they previously had to deliver crude to Eastern Europe for refining and re-export to the West.

Another important trend apparent during the first two years of the Eleventh Five Year Plan period has been the failure of industry to meet its planned growth targets. During 1981 to 1985, industry was planned to expand by 26% at an average annual rate of 4.7%. The annual target for 1981 was 4.1%, but a growth of only 3.4% was obtained, and the annual target for 1982 was consequently raised to 4.7%. However, 1982 saw the lowest rate of growth of industrial output since the war at only 2.8%, and towards the end of the year it had become apparent that the Five Year Plan target was unattainable. Accordingly, a growth of 3.2% was planned for 1983.

There are many reasons for the collapse of the Eleventh Five Year Plan, including labour shortages in the newer industries, poor plant capacity utilisation and the failure to commission sufficient electricity generating capacity (the plan target of 69,000 MW over 1981 to 1985 looks likely to be hopelessly underfulfilled), but a fortuitous consequence of this has been a lower-than-expected demand for all oil products, resulting in a Western-style oil glut during 1981 and 1982.

Moreover, the major policy change of 1980 to concentrate investment resources on the production and transportation of gas is being followed through. The production of gas greatly overfulfilled its 1981 plan target, and the 1982 target was also overfulfilled. The pipeline construction programme is being successfully carried out with the pipelines from Western Siberia to the Ukraine and the central regions of Russia being built at rates unprecedented in world practice. The conversion of oil- and coal-burning facilities to gas is also being accomplished at rapid rates. Some oil-burning power stations such as the 3,000 MW Syrdarinsk in Uzbekistan have already been fully converted to gas, and several others, like the 2,800 MW Ryazan station in the Central region, are to be converted in 1983/4. Other stations are being adapted so as to burn gas in summer, and existing dual-fired stations burning fuel oil for seven months and gas for five are having the gas-burning period extended by two months. A 300 MW set can save 100,000 tons of fuel oil a year in this way.

The current five year plan has called for the scrapping of an unprecedented volume of thermal power station capacity with new sets burning coal (at Zuevka, Ekibastuz, Perm and several Siberian stations) and gas (Azerbaidzhan, Surgut, Pechora and most heat-and-power plants) replacing obsolete sets burning oil. While the process of converting power stations to gas is simple and quick, with building the gas pipeline being the most expensive and time-consuming task, the replacement or conversion of a very large number of much smaller oil-burning facilities will prove more difficult and time-consuming. Nevertheless, it is hoped to make substantial savings at power stations alone, with their annual consumption of fuel oil planned to decline by nearly 40 mn tons between 1980 and 1985.

Needless to say, the successful accomplishment of the atomic power programme is absolutely essential to any attempt to forecast the future demand for fuel oil. If atomic stations are not built on schedule, then obsolete oil-burning sets will be kept running, and oil consumption will not fall as much as planned.

A further factor affecting the potential for oil exports is the extent to which new secondary oil-refining equipment can be installed. If the rather demanding plans of the current plan period are achieved, then it should be possible for the annual production of gasoline and diesel to grow by 5.5% a year from 188 mn tons to 245 mn tons a year over 1981 to 1985. However, there are indications that construction work at many refineries is behind schedule, and that the plans to meet a rapidly growing demand for light and middle products from a slowly growing throughput of crude are not being met. Domestic demand for crude oil is rising more rapidly than anticipated, and this is confronting planners with a hard choice between meeting domestic demand, or trying to maintain exports at the highest levels. If atomic power stations and secondary refining plant could be built on time, then the planners could avoid having to make this choice, and this was one of their principal considerations when the guidelines for the Eleventh plan were being drawn up.

They seem to be trying to solve the problem by adopting the least-cost solution of a temporary cut in oil exports to Eastern Europe. This should, in fact, be advantageous to the USSR in that the prices they obtain for product sales to Western Europe are much higher than the prices they have been charging Eastern Europe for crude oil. The Eastern European countries will suffer a decline in foreign exchange earnings, although this decline can be minimised if they can make further improvements in their oil usage rates. All these countries consume far too much oil for their size, structure of industry and stage of economic development, and the substantial cut in oil imports by Hungary (while achieving small increases in its volume of industrial production) demonstrates the potential for oil saving which every country in Eastern Europe enjoys. It is likely that the cuts in Soviet supplies will be restored when and if the Russians catch up on their badly lagging construction programme for nuclear power stations and secondary refining plant.

The cuts could be restored even earlier if the Russians cannot sell their oil to the West. In 1979, OECD countries bought 1,346 mn tons of crude and products from outside the region. In 1980, imports fell to 1,185 mn tons, or by 12%, and in 1981 there was a further fall of 12% to 1,043 mn tons. The USSR is surviving the slump in Western demand comparatively well, with their market share rising from 4.37% of total OECD crude plus product imports in 1979 to 4.81% in 1980 and 4.97% in 1981. In 1982, there was a substantial increase in the volume of Soviet oil exports to the OECD as the Russians sought to match the decline in price by an increase in volume, thereby maintaining their revenue from oil sales. As there is no sign (at time of writing) of the Western recession ending, the Russians must now be asking themselves how long the recession will last, and what further price cuts they will need to make to maintain their exports in a declining market.

Taking all these considerations into account, it can be tentatively estimated that oil exports will fall to 120-130 mn tons in 1985 and further to 80-100 mn tons in 1990. Exports to the West will fall slightly to 45-55 mn tons in 1985, and should fall sharply thereafter to 0-30 mn tons in 1990.

Gas

The size of Soviet gas exports to the West depends on the date of completion of the Yamal gas pipeline and the amount of gas contracted by Western gas utilities. At the moment, it seems likely that sales to the West will reach 35 bn cu m in 1985 with a further 40 bn cu m going to Eastern Europe. During the following five years, gas exports could nearly double to 140 bn cu m a year, with 70 bn cu m sold to Western Europe and a similar amount to Eastern Europe. The revenue from rapidly expanding gas sales should more than make up for declining oil sales.

Coal

Coal and coke exports should rise slightly by 1985 over 1980 in spite of the difficulties experienced by the Soviet Union as a result of the recent decline in domestic production. The Russians have long-term commitments to countries like Bulgaria and East Germany with little hard coal of their own, and they are unlikely to break these obligations. It is possible, however, that Poland may be asked to supply more coal to other Eastern European countries as a means of paying off its debt to them. Soviet exports to Japan, which have been declining in recent years, should begin to pick up in 1983 when the first coking coal seams at Neryungri are opened up, and the Russians begin to carry out their contract to supply an eventual 4 mn tons a year of coking coal to Japan; the contract calls for the delivery of 80 mn tons of coal over 20 years. Total coal exports are likely to rise to 28 mn tons in 1985 and 30 mn in 1990.

Total fuel exports are likely to decline from 320.6 mn tsf in 1980 to 300 mn in 1985 but the rapid growth in gas exports after 1985 should enable exports to rise again to 320 mn tsf in 1990. During the 1990s, oil exports could be maintained at 80-85 mn tons a year (although those to the West should largely disappear) while exports of gas may grow to 150 bn cu m a year. The Russians will not raise fuel exports above the level necessary to bring in the required amount of foreign currency and finance the required volume of imports. It is thought that they will be happy to peg fuel exports at 300-320 mn tsf a year for the rest of the century.

11 OTHER FUEL-CONSUMING SECTORS

Of the fuel-using sectors not considered elsewhere in this book, only non-ferrous metallurgy and engineering burn appreciable amounts of fuel directly.

Non-ferrous Metallurgy

More than 10% of the total costs of the non-ferrous metallurgy sector are spent on fuel and energy, with some sectors such as aluminium spending up to 24% of their outlays in this way. Electricity accounts for 55% of fuel and energy costs, low temperature thermal energy (i.e. steam and hot water) 22% and primary fuel 23%.

Table 11.1: Consumption of Gas and Electricity by the Non-ferrous Metal Industry

	1970	1980
Natural gas (bn cu m)	2.29	6.96
Electricity (bn kWh)	67.3	105.5

Natural gas is the most important primary fuel, being used for so-called 'technological purposes' as well as for the generation of power; more than 30% of all gas used by non-ferrous metallurgy is spent on smelting, conversion, the intensification of work in anode and wirebar furnaces and for preheating metal prior to rolling. Natural gas proves as effective in non-ferrous metal smelters as in blast furnaces, and its use in preference to alternative fuels is said to save the country 100 mn roubles a year. The Norilsk combine alone is said to save 30 mn roubles a year and cut labour needs by 6,000 workers when using Messoyakh gas rather than hard coal.

The copper industry uses about 30% of total gas consumption by the sector, or about 2.1 bn cu m in 1980. For heating reverbatory furnaces for the smelting of copper and nickel, gas competes with coal dust and oil and can be used in conjunction with oxygen. At present, ten furnaces have been converted to gas, with a consequent improvement in furnace productivity of 11–50% depending on the specific conditions of the plant. Between 140 and 240 kgsf are required for the smelting of each ton of copper, and several technical advantages result from using gas (for example the useful floor area of the furnace can be increased by 10–11%) leading to a reduction in the conversion cost of 2 to 20 roubles per ton of copper. Table 11.2 compares the characteristics of a 225 sq m furnace burning coal dust, fuel oil and natural gas.

Table 11.2: Characteristics of Copper Smelting using Different Fuels

	Coal Dust	Fuel Oil	Natural Gas
Furnace productivity (coal dust = 1)	1.00	1.15	1.27
Fuel rate (kgsf/ton)	180	171	155
Oxygen requirements (cu m/ton)	53	46.8	28.4

At anode furnaces, conversion to natural gas reduces the length of the smelting period and reduces waste, but has very little impact on the fuel rate. The productivity of a 63 sq m anode furnace is raised by 4% but the fuel rate remains at 108.3 kgsf per ton of anode copper. The best results are obtained from the conversion of wirebar furnaces to gas – the fuel rate is reduced by 31% to 167 kgsf/ton compared with 218.4 kgsf at oil-fired furnaces. At modern furnaces burning gas with an efficiency rating of 39.7%, the fuel rate falls to only 113.5 kgsf/ton.

In the past, the use of electric furnaces for copper smelting has not been very economical, but this may change with the introduction of autogenous smelting in units working on a continuous operating basis. These are said to cut electricity consumption by half.

The USSR does not issue data on its non-ferrous metal industry, prsumably for security reasons. Estimates suggest that about 130 mn tons of ore yielding 1.2 mn tons of copper a year are being mined at the present time.

The aluminium sector burned just over 1 bn cu m of natural gas in 1980. The largest consumers are the caking kilns and alumina calcination furnaces. After conversion of a caking kiln to natural gas, its productivity rises by 29–46% compared with oil-fired furnaces, and by 5% compared with those burning coal dust, and its fuel rate falls to 167 kgsf/ton compared with 171 when fuel oil or coal dust are used. An alumina calcination furnace requires 169 kgsf of gas per ton compared with 174 for an oil-fired furnace.

The production of aluminium is heavily dependent on large amounts of electricity which explains why most of the largest plants are located in Eastern Siberia, close to major hydro plants such as Bratsk and Krasnoyarsk. Fortuitously, Eastern Siberia and the Far East are believed to contain over 80% of Soviet bauxite reserves. In 1980, an average of 17,590 kWh of power was needed for the production of a ton of aluminium, but it is planned that the introduction of new electrolysis equipment should reduce this figure to 17,000 by 1985. In 1981, the Novokuznetsk Aluminium Plant reduced its unit power consumption by 629 kWh/ton.

The USSR is estimated to produce 2.3 mn tons of primary aluminium a year from about 10 mn tons of bauxite, of which perhaps 3.5 mn are imported. New smelters processing imported bauxite into alumina have been commissioned at Nikolaev in the Ukraine, and will work on power from the nearby South Ukraine atomic power station. They have a capacity of 1 mn tons of bauxite a year.

The main fuels required by the lead industry are coke (of which about 230,000 tons a year are used) and natural gas. Gas is used primarily as a technological fuel, replacing coke in the smelters. It is blown into the furnaces enriched with oxygen in a hot blast for the deoxidisation of lead ore, leading to an increase of up to 78% in the productivity of the smelt and permitting a reduction of 8.9% in the consumption of coke. However, average losses of lead in the discarded slag rise from 1.5% to 2.25%.

The coke savings are considerable when a hot blast of gas and oxygen (requiring 236.6 kg of coke and 73.1 kgsf of gas per ton of lead) is compared with a cold blast of oxygen, when 343.8 kg of coke were required. There is also a useful reduction in the expenditure of electricity, from 136.4 to 89.4 kWh per ton.

Although the USSR has proved plus probable lead reserves of 18 mn tons, mostly in Kazakhstan, the annual output of about 760,000 tons does not cover consumption, which has been growing fairly rapidly to over 800,000 tons a year, and lead has to be imported. New sources are to be opened up in the region of the BAM railway.

Natural gas is the principal fuel for the production of zinc. It is used for the drying of concentrates, the drying and formation of zinc cakes and for the production of zinc powder, etc. When gas is used to replace fuel oil in furnaces for the formation and drying of cakes, furnace productivity is raised by 65%, the expenditure of the reduction agent, coke fines, is cut by 20 kgsf/ton of zinc, and fuel consumption falls by 20–25.6% for the drying of cakes and by 6.9% for formation. For an average zinc plant as a whole, the conversion from fuel oil to a gas/oil mixture reduces fuel costs by 3%, from 98.5 kgsf of oil per ton of zinc to 95 kgsf of gas and 0.57 kgsf of oil.

Non-ferrous metal plants require large volumes of thermal energy, and many have been making strenuous efforts to save energy by making better use of their vast amounts of waste heat. The reconstruction of the roasting furnaces at Chelyabinsk Zinc Plant has allowed sufficient waste heat to be captured to supply half the entire plant's thermal energy needs, thereby saving more than 20,000 tsf a year. The USSR's largest zinc plant at Ust Kamenogorsk in Kazakhstan has drawn up a five-year plan for the use of secondary energy resources. The plan foresees the conversion of all smelters and kilns to vapour quenching, the establishment of heat exchangers in boilers, and the capture of waste heat given off by rotary furnaces. At the moment, seven devices installed to make use of secondary energy permit savings of 36,000 tsf a year by providing half the plant's thermal energy needs. The modernisation of kilns will enable them each to produce 35 tons/hour of steam, and by the end of 1985, it is planned that the plant should be saving a further 86,000 tsf a year compared with 1980.

With reserves of 23 mn tons, the USSR produces just over 1 mn tons of zinc a year. Consumption is about the same, with small volumes of imports matched by similar exports.

Very little data of any sort is available on the other sectors of the non-ferrous metal industry, and still less on their fuel consumption rates. The vital importance of this industry to Soviet economic development and the substantial reserves of practically all types of metal known to exist in Eastern Siberia and the Far East, principally in the zone of the BAM railway and near the route of the planned Berkakit-Tommot-Yakutsk railway, will ensure that output of non-ferrous metals will continue to grow as a first-priority measure. The importance of natural gas will grow at the expense of fuel oil as the gasfields of the Vilyui basin are opened up during the current and future plan periods. But fossil fuel will continue to play a minor role compared with that of electricity, consumption of which will rise as new electric smelters are commissioned in close proximity to new hydro stations in Eastern Siberia.

Table 11.3: Forecast Consumption of Gas and Electricity by the Non-ferrous Metal Sector

	1980	1985	1990	2000
Natural gas (bn cu m)	6.96	8.0	9.4	12.0
Electricity (bn kWh)	105.5	121	135	165

Engineering and Metalworking

The engineering and metalworking sector uses a small amount of fuel, amounting to 47.7 mn tsf in 1980. It is one of the least fuel and power intensive sectors of Soviet industry, with fuel accounting for only 1.1% and power 1.9% of its total costs in 1980. While output by the sector rose by 11.6% a year between 1970 and 1975, its consumption of fuel rose by 3.4% a year, and of electricity by 6.7% a year. During 1975 to 1980, the respective growth rates were 8.2%, 3.5% and 4.4%. The sharp fall in fuel and power consumption per unit of output is attributable to the improvement in metal-working techniques and to changes in the mix of engineering products, with light engineering (requiring comparatively little fuel and power) gaining at the expense of heavy engineering.

Table 11.4: Consumption of Fuel and Power by the Engineering and Metal-working Sector (mn tsf)

	1970	1975	1980
Total fuel	33.9	40.1	47.7
Natural gas	22.4	27.7	34.3
Others	11.5	12.4	13.4
Electricity (bn kWh)	65.6	90.7	112.5

Natural gas is the most important fuel and it has slowly been replacing fuel oil and coal. Just under 29 bn cu m were burned by the sector in 1980, or 6.7% of total gas consumption (including exports). In 1975, 23.4 bn cu m were used (8.1%) and in 1970 18.9 bn cu m (9.6%). It is used basically for heating metal prior to forging and thermal processing.

Gas-fired furnaces were used for 64% of metal-heating for forging, fuel oil for 26% and electric furnaces for 10% in 1975. Since then, it is likely that electric and gas furnaces will have improved their share with that of oil-fired furnaces declining. The type of fuel has an important influence on the efficiency of metal heating, with losses of metal amounting to 3-3.5% for oil furnaces, 2-2.5% in gas furnaces and 0.5% in electric furnaces. It also affects the uniformity of heating, working conditions (which are better with gas and electric furnaces) and the possibilities for automation.

The consumption of fuel per ton of processed metal varies between 50 and 939 cu m of gas, and averages 276 kgsf a ton for serial production by a group of modern mechanised furnaces with productivities of 10 to 15 tons/hour, and where heating takes place in two stages — in ring furnaces followed by semi-holding furnaces or fore-hearths. The fuel rate is much the same for gas or fuel oil, but oil-fired furnaces cost 25% more to build because they need to be bigger with larger ventilation systems, and 10% more to operate. Overall savings amount to between 1 and 4.2 roubles/tsf depending on the type and capacity of the furnace. When gas-fired furnaces are used in preference to electric furnaces, savings are much greater at 10.4 to 46.4 roubles per tsf. In the Ukraine, savings from using natural gas rather than fuel oil for thermal processing amount to 1.11 roubles/ton, and instead of coal they rise to 7.63 R/t. When metal is being heated prior to forging, savings are estimated at 2.28 and 10.83 R/t respectively.

Thermal processing is employed to improve the structure of the metal after it has been subjected to forging or mechanical processing. While electric furnaces are widespread in the USSR, gas furnaces tend to have a larger throughput. Table 11.5 shows the fuel rates of gas and electric furnaces of different types with different productivities.

Table 11.5: Rates of Fuel and Power Utilisation for Thermal Processing

Process	Furnace Type	Productivity (tons/hour)	Gas Furnace (kgsf/ton)	Electric Furnace (kWh/ton)
Normalisation	Pusher-type	1.3	97.0	325
	Box-type	0.3	92.6	350
Nitrocementation	Box-type	0.095	136.5	610
Cementation + hardening + tempering	Box-type	0.2	498.2	1,410
Hardening + tempering	Conveyor	0.8	109.0	582

While the metalworking sector uses gas and fuel oil as well as electricity, the engineering industry depends mainly on electricity and thermal energy, usually obtained from general purpose combined heat-and-power plants or, in the case of very large factories, from in-house CHPPs.

The engineering and metal-working sector is the largest industrial user of thermal energy, with 210 mn G-cals utilised in 1975 compared with 180 mn in 1970 and 122 mn in 1965. However, practically no waste heat is captured (only 2.3 mn G-cals in 1975) although there is considerable scope for large savings to be made. A major problem is the shortage of measuring instruments able to determine the true levels of thermal energy consumption. Consequently, it is difficult to establish well-founded norms of fuel and energy expenditure. Of 46 ministries participating in the sector, only the ministries of electronics, machine tools and agricultural machinery can provide the necessary data on departmental thermal energy consumption. More than 40% of all engineering enterprises are unable to measure the amount of steam and hot water which they take from general-purpose distribution networks, and a third of all enterprises owned by the ministries of oil and chemical engineering, automobile production and energy engineering have not yet started using heat exchangers in their boilers and furnaces.

However, some large enterprises are making the effort: Uralkhimmash of Sverdlovsk for example, has a forge-press shop where powerful hammers use 20 tons/hour of steam which was formerly wasted at a temperature of 130°C. Now, a boilerhouse has been built where thermal energy from exhausted steam is used to heat water for the factory, saving 16,000 cu m of gas a day. A number of recuperators have been built in the forge-press shop where heating furnaces heat up the metal in preparation for forging, so as to capture heat from furnace gases.

The ratio of electricity usage to engineering output has been declining rapidly during the 1970s, when output rose by 168% compared with a growth in power consumption by engineering and metal-working of only 71%. This is because the heavy engineering sectors like the manufacture of metallurgical plant (which increased by 54%), mining machinery (64%) and railway equipment (64%) grew comparatively slowly while those sectors using little power like instrument manufacture grew very quickly.

The Eleventh Five Year Plan expects electricity consumption to rise to 129 bn kWh in 1985, or 16.2% of industrial power consumption. This assumes that the plans for output of engineering products will be met, which was looking increasingly unlikely by the end of 1982. It is more likely that no more than 124 bn kWh of power will be required in 1985, growing to 145 bn in 1990 and 185 bn by the end of the century.

It is likely that the growth in demand for natural gas will slow down when the serial production of gas-fired furnaces for the metal-working industry is organised. At present, all furnaces are manufactured to individual specifications; this means that the application of fuel-saving components cannot be standardised with the result that many furnaces have unnecessarily high fuel rates. The Ministry of the Electrical Engineering Industry was instructed several years ago to organise the serial output of furnaces, but has failed to do so, and some of its furnaces for heating metal for forging and stamping have fuel rates more than three times those of analogous foreign furnaces. They have inefficient gas-burning equipment, and lack heat exchangers, automatic heat regulators and control devices. More than half of the enterprises belonging to the chemical engineering and heavy engineering ministries operate gas-burning equipment without adjustment valves, more than 33% of all engineering enterprises do not regulate their consumption of natural gas with the result that industry burns much more gas than it needs.

It can be assumed that during the next twenty years or so, many of these deficiencies will be overcome, and gas consumption will accordingly grow very slowly to 39 bn cu m in 1985, 44 bn in 1990 and 55 bn in 2000.

12 THE FUTURE SUPPLY OF FUEL

My estimates suggest that demand for the three most important types of fuel, oil, gas and coal, will rise from 1.863 mn tsf in 1980 to 2,900 mn in 2000. Demand is defined in its mildest sense, i.e. including exports, which are regarded by Soviet planners as being just as crucial to the Soviet economy as the adequate provision of fuel for the home market.

Table 12.1: Forecast Demand for the Main Types of Fuel (mn tsf)

	1980	1985	1990	2000
Oil	863	900	940	1000
Gas	516	735	950	1200
Coal	484	510	550	700
Total	1,863	2,145	2,440	2,900

The forecast for 1985 of 2,145 mn tsf compares with the official plan target of 2,178 mn tsf, and implies an average annual growth rate for fuel production of nearly 2.9%. During the following five-year plan period, it is thought that the growth rate will fall slightly to 2.6% a year, with a slowly growing output of oil accompanied by the continuing rapid growth of the gas industry, and production of coal beginning to accelerate as the development of the Ekibastuz and Kansk-Achinsk basins begins to pay off. During the 1990s, all these trends will continue, at a slower pace than before, with growth rates falling to an average 1.75% a year.

Table 12.2: Forecast Demand for the Main Types of Fuel

	1980	1985	1990	2000
Oil (mn tons)	603.2	630	660	700
Gas (bn cu m)	435.2	620	800	1,000
Coal (mn tons)	716.4	750	815	1,000

The estimates of Table 12.2 should be regarded as absolute minimums. They have been calculated on the assumption that the Soviet economy will grow much more slowly than at any time since the war (with industrial output growing by an average 2.5-3.0% a year), that the Soviets will be only moderately successful in their attempts to cut

Map 12.1: Hydrocarbon Basins of Western and Eastern Siberia

① West Siberian Basin ④ Anabar Anteclize
② Evenki Sineclize ⑤ Vilyui Sineclize
③ Lena-Anabar Trough ⑥ Aldan Anteclize

▨ DEPOSITS OF OIL & GAS

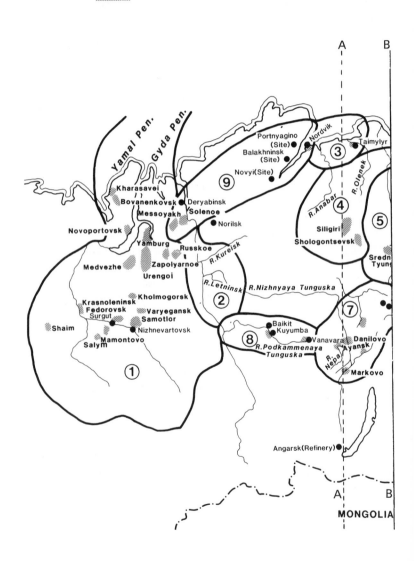

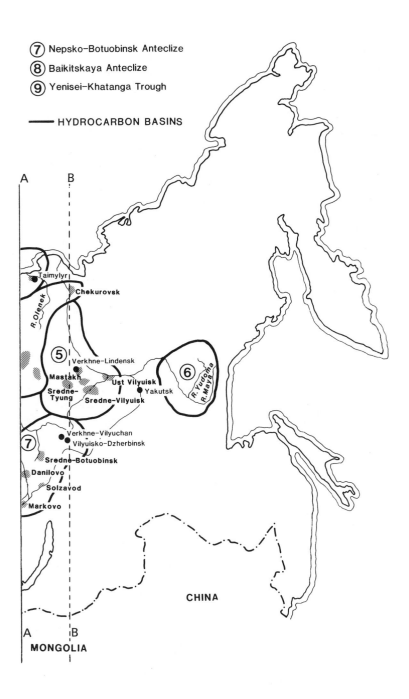

(7) Nepsko-Botuobinsk Anteclize
(8) Baikitskaya Anteclize
(9) Yenisei-Khatanga Trough

—— HYDROCARBON BASINS

the unit rate of fuel consumption, and that their exports will only be adequate to fulfil their obligations to Eastern European countries and to allow sufficient hard currency earnings to pay off debts and import essentials. If fuel production could be raised above the levels of Table 12.2, then this would provide possibilities for larger exports (and hence imports) rather than faster domestically-generated economic growth. The potential for faster growth is constrained by many factors which cannot be removed simply by the production of more fuel. It is the labour shortage and the rigidity in employment which inhibits the movement of labour from one factory or industry to another (this being necessary for the more rapid growth of labour productivity), which are the biggest single problems faced by Soviet industry rather than the supposed fuel shortages as perceived by some observers in the West.

Is the Soviet Union able to produce the quantity of fuel which the demand forecasts of Table 12.2 suggest it will need in the years ahead? It will be necessary to slow the decline in output by the older fuel-producing regions, and to open up new fields in increasingly remote and undeveloped parts of the country, where vast amounts of investment resources and manpower must be employed. The history of those regions which currently provide most of the USSR's fuel has been covered adequately in other books, and it is the purpose of this chapter to look at the regions which must yield increasing volumes of fuel in the future – Western Siberia and the Kara Sea, the Timano-Pechora region and the Barents Sea, and Eastern Siberia and the Far East (oil and gas), Central Asia (gas), and the Kuzbass, Ekibastuz and Kansk-Achinsk fields (coal).

Western Siberian Oil and Gas Fields

The Western Siberian basin is the world's largest oil- and gas-bearing province, covering 3.35 mn sq km and containing a larger volume of oil and gas than any other such basin including the Persian Gulf. About 55% of the region is potentially oil and gas bearing, and a further 17% is marginally promising. At the beginning of 1982, proved plus probable (Soviet definition) reserves of gas amounted to 30,000 bn cu m, and estimated proved plus probable oil reserves were about 8,500 mn tons; in all, the region had about 32,700 mn tons of oil equivalent of hydrocarbons, with perhaps a further 100,000 mn tons of oil equivalent of potential reserves.

These reserves are almost entirely located in Tyumen oblast, with small amounts of oil in Tomsk and Novosibirsk oblasts, and oil and gas in that part of Krasnoyarsk krai which lies within the Western Siberian basin. Most of Tyumen oblast's oil is found in the Khanty-Mansiisk autonomous region, an administrative subdivision of the oblast, while practically all the gas is found in another such subdivision, the Yamalo-Nenetskii region.

Structure

The basin is bounded by the Urals to the west and the Eastern Siberian platform to the east, and extends northwards into the Kara Sea, where its offshore area covers 330,000 sq km. The basin is filled with Mesozoic and Cainozoic sediments which, in the north and beneath the Kara Sea, overlie Triassic strata. The depth of the basement varies from 2,000-2,100 m on the western periphery, to 3,500 m in the centre and up to 11,000 m in the north. So far, the deepest exploratory well has been pushed to a little over 5,000 m in the Nadym area.

Five major series have been defined, apart from the Triassic and Paleozoic which has yielded oil at considerable depths in Tomsk oblast: These are:

(1) The Zavodoukovsk Series (Lower and Middle Jurassic) with a thickness of 200-700 m at depths of 1,200-6,000 m.

(2) The Poludinsk Series (Upper Jurassic and Lower Cretaceous) is 50-500 m thick at a depth of 1,100-3,100 m. This contains some of the most productive oil-producing horizons including the Kolumzinsk and Tarskii, which contain several of the largest producing reservoirs of the Surgut and Nizhnevartovsk arches.

(3) The Sargatinsk Series (Lower Cretaceous), 10-700 m thick at depths of 1,000-2,500 m. Within this series, the Nizhnevartovsk, Cherkashinsk and Nizhnealymsk horizons are particularly important, containing the shallowest reservoirs of the Middle Ob oilfields.

(4) The Pokursk Series (Lower and Middle Cretaceous) is most important for its Uvatsk horizon which accounts for most of the massive gas reserves in the northern part of the basin. It is 300-1,000 m thick at depths of 400-1,200 m.

(5) The Derbyshinsk Series (Upper Cretaceous) contains few oil and gas deposits, but its Kuznetsov horizon effectively caps the northern gas deposits.

The basin has been divided into three tectonic regions. An Outer Tectonic Belt, running round the periphery of the basin, contains open structures with elevations of up to 300 m dating to the Jurassic, and oil and gas have generally been found in stratigraphic traps. The Central Tectonic Region, in which the major oilfields are found, has major isometric closed structures up to 500 m high, with local uplifts of up to 500 sq km. The Northern Tectonic Region contains the gasfields and has linear closed structures with elevations of up to 1,500 m and local uplifts of up to 2,000 sq km.

Exploration

Although it is said that geophysical work has been carried out since 1948, little more than half of the basin has been covered by detailed seismic survey by 1980. Work is still continuing, even in those areas which have already been surveyed, and where the use of modern equipment is revealing new structures.

The Ministry of Geology's principal local organisation in the region is Glavtyumengeologiya, consisting of five production associations administering 28 exploration expeditions. The most important of these, in terms of new oil and gas discoveries, belong to the Yamalneftegaz-geologiya Association, based in the Yamal-Nenetskii Autonomous Region. They include the Karsk expedition, which is currently engaged in proving up the super-giant Bovanenkovsk gas deposit on the Yamal Peninsula, and the Tazovsk expedition, which discovered Urengoi in 1966 and is now concentrating on exploring the Russkoe heavy oil deposit and drawing up detailed maps of Urengoi and Yubileinoe gas deposits. The Urengoi expedition was specially established for appraisal drilling at Urengoi, but has also been discovering other gas and oil deposits in the Urengoi area, while the Nadym expedition has been drilling to depths of 5,000 metres in the search for new payzones at Medvezhe. The most recent expedition is the Tambeisk, created in 1980 to work the northern shore of the Yamal Peninsula.

The explorationists are assisted by a special geophysical organisation, the Yamalneftegazgeofizika Trest. During the 12 years of its existence, its 20 crews have surveyed 600,000 sq km and prepared 111 structures for exploratory drilling, which lead to the discovery of 47 oil and gas fields, including Urengoi, Yamburg and Bovanenkovsk.

The three most important organisations operating in the oil-producing region are Megionneftegazgeologiya, which is based in Megion and is responsible for exploration of the Nizhnevartovsk field (which includes the Samotlor deposit), the Obneftegazgeologiya Association of

Surgut, which discovered Fedorovsk, Kholmogorsk and Muravlenkovsk and is now working on four new areas, and the Pravdinsk Association, which is now concentrating on the proving up of the Krasnoleninsk field west of Surgut.

The Ministry of Geology has set up other organisations to explore Tomsk and Novosibirsk oblasts, but they accomplish only a fraction of the work carried out by Glavtyumengeologiya.

By 1975, 1,200 local uplifts had been found in the Western Siberian basin. Of these, 800 had been prepared for deep drilling, and 500 had been drilled, revealing oil and gas deposits. About 200 structures were abandoned as dry, although it is thought that some of these (principally in the Middle Ob and the Nadym-Pur regions) have flank pinch-outs which may prove productive.

The 220 deposits contained 487 pools (174 gas and 313 oil), and at 65 of the deposits, 158 shows were found (143 oil and 15 gas). A further 95 shows (91 oil, four gas) were encountered in 51 other localities. Most of the oil deposits were discovered in Neocomian strata and the gasfields in Senomanian strata.

Table 12.3: Distribution of Oil and Gas Pools by Age, 1975

	Triassic and Jurassic	Lower Cretaceous and Senomanian	Upper Cretaceous	Tertiary	Total
Basin area (mn km^2)	2.6	2.9	3.0	3.4	3.4
Promising area (mn km^2)	1.8	1.6	0.2	–	1.8
Rock volume (mn km^3)	1.42	3.36	0.74	0.79	6.3
Gas pools	59	84	31	–	174
Oil pools	121	189	3	–	313
Total	180	273	34	–	487

For organisational purposes, the basin has been divided into 31 zones. Exploration work has so far concentrated on 12 zones, and oil and gas fields have been found in 11 of these, as shown in Table 12.4.

The Priuralsk zone covers 105,000 sq km in the western part of the region and lies within the basin of the Northern Sosva river. It contains the Shaim oilfield including the Shaim, Mortyminsk, Teterevsk, Kammenoe, Leminsk, Yakhlinsk and other deposits, and has a large number of promising (although small) structures.

Table 12.4: Distribution of Oil and Gas Pools by Exploration Zone, 1975

	Gas	Oil	Total
Priuralsk	28	34	62
Frolovsk	6	11	17
Kaimysovsk	6	25	31
Vasyugansk	19	33	52
Paiduginsk	6	3	9
Middle Ob	3	180	183
Nadym Pur	39	25	64
Pur Tazov	9	1	10
Gyda Peninsular	7	0	7
South Yamal	30	0	30
Ust Yeniseisk	21	1	22
Total	174	315	487

The Frolovsk zone lies on the right bank of the Ob to the north-west of Surgut. It is important for the Jurassic and Aptian complexes of the Krasnoleninskii arch. The Yem-Yegovsk and Palyanovsk deposits are the most important.

The Kaimysovsk zone lies in the Omsk and Tomsk oblasts in the Om-Tara and Ob-Irtysh interfluves. Several small deposits, such as Usanovsk, Urnensk, Chupalsk, Multanovsk and Khokhryakovsk have been found in the Upper Jurassic, but their oil reserves are small. The oil is 29.3-30.0°, 0.4-0.8% sulphur, 2.2-3.2% paraffin, with a light fraction content of 14–15% and 33.6-36.4% at 200° and 300° respectively.

The Vasyugansk zone is located in the central part of the Ob-Irtysh interfluve, and consists of the Aleksandrovsk, Pudino and Srednevasyugan regions. It has an area of 93,000 sq km, and extends as far north as the Kolik Yegansk deposit on the Vakh river in Tyumen oblast. The oil is very high quality with 34.6-37.4° API, 0.3-0.4% sulphur and 31.2-33.0% and 46.5-57.5% light fractions at 200° and 300°.

The Middle Ob zone has an area of 136,000 sq km, and by 1975 about 150 local uplifts had been found. The major deposits are Samotlor, Fedorovsk, Megion, Ust Balyk, Zapadno-Surgut, Sosninsk, Medvedevsk, Vatinsk, Salym, Savuisk, Alekhinsk, Kogolymsk, Povkhovsk, Tyumen, Urevsk and many more. Oil from the Surgut field is heavy and sulphurous with an API of 27.3-30.4° and a sulphur content of 1.2-1.8%. The light fraction up to 200° amounts to 14.0-17.5% and 29.1-36.8% up to 300°. Oil from the Nizhnevartovsk field is of much better quality with an API of 32.1-39.0° and a very low sulphur content of little more than 0.1%, occasionally rising to 0.8%.

The Nadym-Pur zone contains the USSR's two largest gas deposits, Urengoi and Yamburg as well as several other giant deposits.

The Pur-Tazovsk zone includes three gas and condensate deposits (Zapolyarnoe, Tazovsk and Suzunsk), one gas (Yuzhno-Russkoe) and one oil/gas (Russkoe).

The South Yamal zone covers all the Yamal Peninsula, and includes some important multi-layer deposits of gas and condensate, such as Novoportovsk, Arkticheskoe, Nurminsk, Sredne-Yamal, Bovanenkovsk and Kharasavei. Of these, Kharasavei is said to be the biggest, with potential gas reserves of several trillion cubic metres.

Since 1975, there has been a considerable increase in the volumes of exploratory drilling by the Ministry of Geology, and appraisal drilling by the Ministries of Oil and Gas at operating fields. By 1975, only 6.5 mn m of exploratory drilling had been carried out since 1948. In 1975, 728,000 m were drilled, including 556,000 by Glavtyumengeologiya, and as the reserves-to-production ratio was growing very slowly, it was apparent that the rate of exploration must increase. However, the infrastructural shortcomings took their toll and the volume of drilling actually fell, with Glavtyumengeologiya drilling only 533,000 m in 1977. Things improved in 1978, when drilling increased by 56% to 831,000 m; 30 new structures were examined and the plan for new oil reserves was fulfilled. After a fall to 763,000 m in 1979, the drilling metreage rose by 36% in 1980 to 1,037,000 m, with 30 new structures explored and nine new deposits (including 23 pools of oil and gas) discovered.

By 1980, the number of discovered oil and gas deposits had reached 273 with more than 600 pools. During the period 1976 to 1980, a large amount of exploratory work was carried out on the Yamal and Gyda Peninsulas in the far north, in the Tazovsk area (i.e. in the vicinity of the Russkoe oil deposit), in the Tarko-Sale area, in the region of the Kogolymsk and Kholmogorsk deposits between Surgut and Tarko Sale, along the Agan river in the vicinity of the Varyegansk group of deposits, and to the west of Surgut on the Krasnoleninskii arch.

During the Eleventh Five Year Plan period, Glavtyumengeologiya plans to drill 10 mn m of exploration wells, or more than the total drilled in Western Siberia between 1948 and 1980. This will consist of 3 mn m in the Yamal-Nenetskii gas field area and 7 mn m in the Khanti-Mansiiskii oilfield area. The Yamalneftegazgeologiya Association plans to raise its drilling rate from 400,000 m in 1982 to 1 mn m in 1985, and given the large volume of gas reserves already discovered in the area covered by the Association, it may seem more logical to direct some of the Yamal crews to the more southerly oilfields. However, it is believed that large oilfields will be discovered in the Yamal-Nenetskii region in the 1980s.

Oil pools, some of which are known to be substantial, have been discovered beneath the gasfields. Wells drilled to 2,850-3,100 m at Urengoi yielded oil more than ten years ago, and oil rings have been found at Medvezhe, Yamburg and Zapolyarnyi. For more than one-third of the gasfield region, oil is believed to account for 50-70% of total hydrocarbon reserves of the predominant Mesozoic strata. A flow of high quality oil has been obtained from several wells at Yen Yakhinsk in the Urengoi area, and in the eastern part of the Yamal-Nenetskii region, the Krasnoselkupsk Oil Exploration Expedition has been set up to examine some promising new finds in the Verkhne Chaselsk region on the Chaselka river, 500 km NNE of Nizhnevartovsk. The new town of Tikhii, which is being built near the old settlement of Urengoi and which is expected to have an eventual population of more than 150,000 has been described as a future base city of gas and oil workers, implying that sizeable oil deposits have already been found in the area.

But major oil finds in the north of Tyumen oblast are more likely to come from the Gyda Peninsula and the northern part of the Yamal Peninsula. It is no accident that the Ministry of Geology has called its local organisation the Karsk Oil Exploration Expedition, indicating that its primary interest is the search for oil rather than gas. While the Nurmin mega-arch, containing most of the Yamal Peninsula gas finds, has also yielded oil capped by the Se Yakha suite at 2,200 m, it is in the Sredne-Yamal arch where the biggest discoveries are likely to be made. It has even been hinted that large oil deposits have already been found, and that the Russians wanted the Yamal gas pipeline project to involve opening up the Yamal Peninsula because this would facilitate the development of the new oilfield.

On the other side of the Gulf of Ob, the Gyda Peninsula should be the object of intensive exploration work in the 1980s.

In 1981, 1,150,000 m of exploratory wells were drilled (10.9% more than in 1980), 36 new areas were explored, and ten new deposits were found, including nine of oil and one of gas condensate. In 1982, there was another healthy rise in the drilling rate with 1,400,000 m of hole drilled; however, this means that the rate must average 2,480,000 m a year over 1983 to 1985 for the five-year plan target to be fulfilled. The Ministry of Geology has expressed its misgivings about this happening, saying that a further 100,000 workers are needed unless labour productivity can be improved by up to 35%. This does not seem likely given the increasingly difficult terrain being explored.

Production

The Western Siberian basin is the most important source of oil and gas in the USSR. In 1981, it yielded 335 mn tons of oil, or 55.0% of the total national output of 609 mn tons. The production of gas amounted to 192 bn cu m, or 41.3% of the nationwide production of 465 bn cu m; this consisted of 176 bn of natural gas and 16 bn cu m of casinghead gas from the oilfields. During the next ten years at least, Western Siberia will account for all the anticipated increase in oil and gas production by the USSR.

Table 12.5: Production of Oil and Gas

	Oil (mn tons)		Gas (bn cu m)	
	USSR	Western Siberia	USSR	Western Siberia
1975 Actual	491	148	289	36
1980 Actual	603	312	435	156
1981 Actual	609	335	465	192
1982 Plan	614	354	492	230
1982 Actual	612	350	501	232
1983 Plan	619	375	529	270
1985 Plan	630	399	630	357
1985 Forecast	630	399	620	347
1990 Forecast	660	480	800	550
2000 Forecast	700	500	1,000	800

While the guidelines of the Eleventh Five Year Plan suggested a target of 375-395 mn tons for Western Siberia in 1985, the final target approved by the Communist Party Central Committee and Council of Ministers was raised to 399 mn tons. The Russians have not broken down the target by field, but it is thought that Tomsk oblast is expected to produce 14 mn tons and Tyumen oblast 385 mn, compared with 10.5 mn and 323.5 mn tons respectively in 1980.

The production of oil in Western Siberia is administered by the Glavtyumenneftegaz Association in Tyumen oblast and the Tomskneft Association in Tomsk oblast. Glavtyumenneftegaz consists of five associations, each administering one of the five distinct groups of fields currently being worked. These are Nizhnevartovskneftegaz, centred on Nizhnevartovsk, Surgutneftegaz, centred on Surgut, Yuganskneftegaz based in Nefteyugansk, Noyabrskneftegaz located in the new town of

Table 12.6: Production of Oil in Western Siberia (mn tons)

	1980	1981	1985 Plan
Tyumen oblast	302.2	323.5	385
Nizhnevartovskneftegaz	201.5	207.4	212
Surgutneftegaz	49	55.2	75
Yuganskneftegaz	45.5	50.7	50
Noyabrskneftegaz	*[1]	4.2	36[2]
Shaimneft	6	6	12
Tomsk oblast	10.5	10.5	14
Total	312.7	334.0	399

Notes: 1. Included under Surgutneftegaz. 2. Some reports say the target is 25 mn tons.

Noyabrskii on the Surgut-Urengoi railway, and Shaimneft, which operates from Urai.

During the Eleventh Five Year Plan period, output by Nizhnevartovskneftegaz will grow very slowly because its largest deposit, Samotlor, has reached its peak level of production of 155 mn tons a year. While some Western pundits believe that Samotlor has been overworked and is now set to experience a precipitous decline, the Russians have claimed that, having taken 13 years to produce its first billion tons, Samotlor will yield its second billion in only six years. This suggests that they expect it to produce at current levels, if not more, until 1988 at least. Declines by some of the older deposits will be more than compensated by increased output by the Varyegansk group of deposits, 100 km north of Nizhnevartovsk on the Agan river.

Production by Surgutneftegaz should continue to grow as more of the small deposits extending north-westwards from Surgut are developed, although the association's largest deposit, Fedorovsk, has now stabilised at nearly 30 mn tons a year. Output by Yuganskneftegaz has stabilised at about 50 mn tons a year in spite of the continuing developmet of the giant Mamontovo deposit. The Salym deposit which, in terms of ultimate reserves, is believed to be even bigger than Samotlor, will not be producing significant volumes of oil until after 1985. This is because the application of new production techniques is necessary to speed up the migration of the oil, which is found in impermeable bituminous shales of the Bazhenov suite.

Noyabrskneftegaz was created in July 1981 out of the Kholmogorneft directorate of Surgutneftegaz to administer the Kholmogorsk and Karamovsk deposits. Since then, the association has also brought the Muravlenkovsk and Sutorminsk deposits on stream; the latter is expected to be one of the largest of the new deposits to begin operating in Western Siberia during the 1980s, and it will be worked from gigantic artificial islands from which up to 80, as opposed to the conventional 24, inclined wells will be drilled. Noyabrskneftegaz has been set the task of producing 82 mn tons over the 1981 to 1985 period.

Shaimneft works a number of small deposits of oil found in strati-graphic traps some distance from the main groups of Middle Ob oil-fields. While small, they are numerous, and the completion of a pipeline running all the way from Urai to the Trans-Siberian Pipeline at Yurgamysh will enable more deposits to be worked in the future. Previously, the pipeline ran only to Tyumen, where the oil had to the transhipped for transport on the heavily congested Trans-Siberian Railway.

Long-term Prospects

Looking ahead to 1990, the head of the Tyumen oblast committee of the Communist Party, Bogomyakov, and the head of the Tyumen oblast's exploration organisation Glavtyumengeologiya, Farman Sal-manov, have both claimed that the oblast can provide 500 mn tons of oil if the necessary capital investment in exploration and development is provided. In fact, the same sort of increase during 1986 to 1990 as that planned for 1981 to 1985 is more likely, leading to a possible output of 480 mn tons in 1990.

This will necessitate the opening-up of new fields. Some of these were earmarked for development by what is believed to have been an early variant of the Eleventh Five Year Plan considered by Gosplan, under which oil production in Western Siberia would have risen to 460 mn tons in 1985 at the expense of the more rapid growth of the gas industry. In the end, the variant was rejected in favour of one which envisages a moderate growth of the oil sector in favour of a very rapid development of the gasfields. Consequently, the working of the new deposits has been put back to the Twelfth plan period, 1986 to 1990, and beyond.

The new deposits are located in four main areas.

(1) The Krasnoleninskii arch contains several medium-sized and a number of smallish deposits located on the River Ob, 250 km west of Surgut. The field began producing in 1981 when oil began to flow from the first well of the Yem Yegovsk deposit, and a pipeline has been laid connecting it with the Shaim field. Its proximity to the River Ob means that the field can be developed comparatively quickly and cheaply, in spite of the large number of wells that must be sunk to tap the small

deposits. It may be giving 30 mn tons a year by 1990.

(2) The Surgutneftegaz Assocation was expecting, at one time, to be set a target of 100 mn tons in 1985 compared with 49 mn in 1980, with several small to medium deposits 100 to 200 km north-west of Surgut being developed. With the task of providing an infrastructure apparently too daunting, it was decided to cut the target back to 75 mn tons, and the original target was postponed to 1990. Meanwhile, the settlement of Lyantor, 120 km north-west of Surgut on the Pim river is being developed (it had a population exceeding 3,000 in mid-1982) not only to work the Lyantorsk deposit, but to provide a base for further expansion to the north-west.

(3) A new group of deposits in the vicinity of Tarko Sale, located at kilometre 455 on the Surgut-Urengoi railway, is scheduled for development during the 1985 to 1990 period. The principal deposits will be Vostochno-Tarkosalinsk and Severo-Kharampursk, and their high gas factor means that it will be uneconomical to develop the field until the Tarko-Sale gas refinery has been built. So far, it has not been started, which is probably why the development of the oilfield has been delayed. Its proximity to the railway will assist the oilmen, and it will subsequently serve as a base for the development of large deposits of oil discovered in the Krasnoselkupsk area, 225 km north-east of Tarko-Sale.

(4) The production of oil from the gasfield region should start during 1986 to 1990, probably from the Severonadymsk deposit. This appears to be an oilfield in its own right, rather than an oil ring at a gas deposit. There is also said to be sufficient oil in a ring at the Gubkin gas deposit to justify commercial exploitation.

Gas condensate reserves of sufficient size to justify the cost of their exploitation have been discovered at the Urengoi, Yamalsk, Bovanenkovsk, Zapolyarnyi and other deposits. At the moment, research work is being carried out into ways of raising the recovery rate from the 40–60% typical at present to nearer 80%.

Most of the condensate will be piped to the Tobolsk and Tomsk petrochemical plants, and some will be processed in the Urengoi condensate refinery into gasoline and diesel for local needs. This should permit considerable savings in the cost of transporting oil products into the gasfields. Most gasoline and diesel is shipped down the rivers Irtysh and Ob from the Omsk refinery, and then up the Nadym river to Nadym, from whence it is railed to Novyi Urengoi. Supply is both expensive and unreliable and the construction of even a small-scale condensate refinery at Novyi Urengoi should yield savings in transport costs of 1 mn roubles a year. Experiments have been carried out by Chelyabinsk Polytechnic and the BakuVNIIgaz Institute at Urengoi and Medvezhe in Western Siberia, and Mastakh, Sredne Vilyui and Markovo in Eastern Siberia.

The viability of condensate production at Urengoi, where it is found in the deepest horizons, should be assisted by the presence in the condensate reservoirs of enough ethane and propane-butane to justify the building of a large gas refinery. Its products, ethane and liquified gas, could be piped to Siberian chemical plants.

It was originally believed that the large-scale production of condensate could begin at Urengoi before 1985, but design work for the pipeline from Urengoi to Surgut was only started in early 1982, and the installation of the first gasfield equipment to handle condensate began in summer 1982. It is hoped that 0.34 mn tons can be produced in 1983 for processing by a small local refinery, but the transport of condensate out of the region will not begin until 1986 at the earliest. Condensate is included in data on the output of oil in the USSR.

From 1990 onwards, the centre of gravity of the Tyumen oil industry could move to the north as the Middle Ob deposits decline, and large oilfields believed to exist in the Kara Sea and on the Yamal and Gyda Peninsulas are opened up. No announcements of very large finds have yet been made, but the growing activity of the Karsk expedition, looking for oil on the Yamal Peninsula, has resulted in the discovery of significant amounts of oil in Jurassic structures at Novoportovsk and Bovanenkovsk. The search for oil is still continuing at Bovanenkovsk.

By 1990, it is hoped that the two 'problem' fields of Salym and Russkoe will be producing appreciable amounts of oil. Salym was discovered in 1963 in the Bazhenovskii shale formations which stretch 1,000 km from north to south, and several hundred from east to west.

The Bazhenovskii suite consists of Upper Jurassic bituminous argillaceous strata varying from 5 to 40 m thick. Flows of light, high quality oil have been obtained from about 30 distinct areas, and some of these are of commercial importance with daily yields of up to 370 cu m a day. Some of these areas lie adjacent to currently worked oil deposits, and others are in close proximity to trunk oil pipelines. Unfortunately, there are no precedents anywhere in the world for the exploration of such a suite, or for the estimation of its oil reserves, or even for delineating the boundaries of its oil deposits.

Most studies of the Bazhenovskii suite have concluded that the accumulation properties of oil reservoirs depend primarily on the extent to which the rock is fissured, although this view is challenged by some geologists who point out that fissuring has not taken place in more than a third of the studied areas, and that vertical fissuring is particularly uncommon. They argue that it is the presence and location of thin plates, layers and sheets, and the nature of the spaces between them, which determine the rate and extent of oil migration. These inter-plate spaces are essentially a new type of trap, and consequently require a different approach towards elaborating ways of exploiting them.

The total in-place reserves of the Bazhenovskii suite have been esti-mated at as much as 620 bn tons, although the recovery rate is unlikely to exceed 20%, and only then with the drilling of an immense number of wells over a period of a great many years. While some 15 deposits have been found in these shales, Salym is the most significant. Lying 100 km west of Surgut, to the south of River Ob, it has seven payzones, although only one of these, at a depth of 2,800 to 2,850 m, is of practical significance.

The deposit has anomalously high pressure of 421 ats, compared with normal pressures for 2,800 m of 289 ats. But the pressure falls quickly when wells begin producing, and well-yields decline due to the poor oil migration characteristics of the deposit. Trial production began in 1974, and in 1976, 1.4 mn tons was produced from 25 wells. Re-search into its geological structure is continuing, and on 4 October 1979, a controlled nuclear explosion was carried out in an attempt to fracture the rock and stimulate migration. The results of the experi-ment have not been published, but if it proved successful, then large-scale production of oil could start quite soon. However, it is more likely that these problems will not be solved satisfactorily, and the deposit will have to be worked extremely intensively with tens of thousands of wells, each giving a trickle of oil of perhaps 1 ton a day after an initial yield of 800 tons a day. This scenario will only be feasible when technical progress has provided equipment of much greater efficiency and durability than that currently employed, i.e. when a 2,800 m well can be drilled with one bit in ten days. The necessary technology is not likely to exist before 1990, and that is why these forecasts do not anticipate the large-scale development of Salym until after this date. In the meantime, one of the explicitly stated tasks of the Ministry of Geology for the Eleventh plan period is the further study of the Baz-henovskii suite and a more precise estimate of its reserves.

Russkoe deposit is situated along the Russkoe river, 680 km north-north-east of Samotlor, and is unique in Western Siberia, with geologists still puzzled as to why such a deposit exists where it does. It was discovered in 1968 and much effort has been put into exploring it, with eleven rigs engaged in exploratory drilling in 1977. The setting up of the Zapolyaryeneft directorate by the Nizhnevartovskneftegaz Association in 1978 suggested that it was going to be developed fairly soon, but the daunting problems posed by a complete lack of infrastructure have made this unrealistic. Various tertiary recovery methods will have to be employed to get a respectable recovery rate for the heavy oil, and the necessary amount of work involved means that a year-round link with the outside world must be established. A railway line running north-east from Urengoi, eventually reaching Dudinka, has been suggested, but this is unlikely to be completed before 1990.

The development of new fields in the Western Siberian basin during the 1990s may probably do little more than compensate for the decline of older fields. The forecast growth in oil output by the region from 480 mn tons in 1990 to 500 mn in 2000 must be extremely tentative.

Gas Production

Soviet strategy for the development of gasfields is more clear-cut. A comparatively small number of deposits contain vast quantities of gas, and it is likely that by the end of the century, no more than ten deposits will be yielding 800 bn cu m a year between them.

The whole increment in Soviet gas production between 1980 and 1985 will come from Urengoi, whose output is planned to grow from 50 to 250 bn cu m. At one time, it was planned that the Yamburg deposit, 250 km further north on the Gulf of Tazovsk, should come on stream before 1985, and there is evidence that the Gas Ministry was even considering opening up the Yamal Peninsula deposits by the mid-1980s. In a scathing criticism of these plans, the secretary of the Tyumen oblast committee of the Communist Party, writing as recently as 1978, accused the Ministry of Gas of dismissing the smaller deposits in more accessible regions (such as Zapolyarnoe, Gubkin, Yubileinoe and Komsomolsk) as 'small fry' that could be left for later, and of wanting to push on to Yamburg before a firm base had been created at Urengoi. In his article, Y. Altunin describes Yamburg as the Ministry of Gas's 'little flower', and says that they even want to 'perch on the end of the world' by extracting 35 bn cu m a year by 1985 from the Kharasavei deposit on the Yamal Peninsula. Eventually, the objections of local figures like Altunin prevailed, and it was decided that the whole increase in output would come from Urengoi, whose target would be raised to 250 bn cu m in 1985 compared with 190 bn under the original variant.

Yamburg will not come on stream until 1986. In 1979, it was announced that infrastructure construction work had begun, but after the change in development strategy, the advance party abandoned its base and did not return until January 1982. During the summer of 1982, the delivery by sea of prefabricated panels for housing and technical equipment for the gasfield began to build up rapidly.

Urengoi is the world's largest gasfield. Its proven plus probable reserves exceed 10,000 bn cu m and exploratory drilling is continuing with a large new payzone at a depth of more than 4,000 m discovered in early 1982. It began producing in April 1978, and under its initial development programme it was rated to peak at 100 bn cu m a year. This was subsequently revised to 180 bn in 1980, and the decision taken during the formulation of the Eleventh Five Year Plan to channel an increased share of investment resources into the gasfields at the expense of the oil industry led to a further revision to 250 bn cu m a year in 1985.

Work at Urengoi has been plagued with problems resulting in a continual underfulfilment of plan targets. This ostensibly has been due to the late installation of gas treatment plants, but the difficulties are much more deep-seated. Until May 1982, the gasfield's main city, Novyi Urengoi, was accessible only from the north. Freight was brought by sea through the Arctic Ocean and down the Gulf of Ob, transshipped to riverboats at Novyi Port, and then carried down the Nadym River to Nadym. Here, it was again transshipped to a railway line belonging to the Gas Ministry before it eventually arrived at Novyi Urengoi.

While icebreakers permit year-round navigation as far as Novyi Port, the Nadym River is ice-bound for seven months a year, leaving a transport window of only five months from mid-April to mid-September. Capacity of the Nadym River is only 2 mn tons of freight a year, and this is destined for many other customers as well as Urengoi gas workers. In fact, little more than 750,000 tons per year have reached Novyi Urengoi. However, the railway line connecting the old settlement of Urengoi with the outside world to the south has now been extended 80 km west to Novyi Urengoi, allowing the year-round delivery of an eventual 10 mn tons a year of freight.

Once equipment has reached Novyi Urengoi, it has to be stored until winter when it can be hauled to its final destination by tracked vehicles. In summer, the region is a vast swamp, which makes building all-weather roads vital to Urengoi meeting its gas production targets. Road-building is expensive, costing about one million roubles per kilometre, because the swamp has to be cut away and replaced with a sand foundation. Lack of roads is probably the greatest single cause of Urengoi's troubles. After four years of development, the field has only 30 km of hard surface road.

Transport problems do not cause, but merely compound, existing infrastructural shortcomings. More than one-third of Novyi Urengoi's 40,000 inhabitants are still in temporary housing and the provision of services for them is proceeding painfully slowly. However, the development of the region should accelerate now that a 500 kV power transmission line from Surgut power station has reached Urengoi.

Until the power line was completed, the provision of power to the gasfield settlements was undertaken by small gas turbine power stations of type PAES-1600, PAES-2500 and others. With sets of 10–20 MW each, they generated electricity costing 8 kops/kWh, or nearly ten times that now being supplied from Surgut power station. Not only did these small stations use unduly large volumes of fuel per kWh of power, they also required a large number of operating personnel. The Nadymgasprom and Nadymgastroi trests alone employed more than 500 workers simply to operate their small power stations, and a third of all workers employed by Urengoigazodobycha were energy workers.

During 1981 to 1985, the Gas Ministry will be concentrating its efforts on the development of Urengoi, and during 1986 to 1990 it will be working primarily at Yamburg, as well as drilling additional wells to maintain the peak level of output at Urengoi. Some reports suggest that Urengoi's annual production levels could even go as high as 350 bn cu m a year, but this is unlikely unless appraisal drilling to more than 4,000 m comes up with some big pools. After 1990, several smaller (but still 'giant' according to Soviet classification) deposits will be worked including Yubileinoe, Zapolyarnyi, Komsomolsk and Gubkin, and production should be building up on the Yamal Peninsula. The Yamal fields of Kharasavei and Bovanenkovsk will probably be worked in conjunction with a gas liquifaction plant which may be built towards the end of this decade.

Table 12.7: A Tentative Forecast of Gas Output by Deposit

	1980	1985	1990	2000
Total	156	347	550	800
Urengoi	50	240	300	300
Yamburg	–	–	100	300
Yamal Peninsula	–	–	50	100
Others*	106	107	100	100

Note: * Principally Medvezhe until 1990, thereafter Yubileinoe, Zapolyarnyi, Komsomolsk and Gubkin, and including 20–30 bn cu m/year of casinghead gas.

Eastern Siberia

Eastern Siberia currently yields about 4.5 bn cu m of gas a year, and no oil apart from a tiny amount of heavy oil at Nordvik on the northern coast. The Messoyakh gas deposit in the extreme north-west of the region belongs to the Western Siberian basin, and its annual output, together with that of the nearby Solenoe, amounts to 4 bn cu m. It is piped to the major non-ferrous metallurgical centre of Norilsk. The gas deposits of the Vilyui lowlands produce about 0.5 bn cu m/year, which is piped to Yakutsk.

The region is often cited by Soviet officials as the next in line for development when the Western Siberian oil and gas fields begin to decline, and the guidelines for the Eleventh Five Year Plan specifically called for the acceleration of exploration work in Eastern Siberia. The potentially oil- and gas-bearing area of the Siberian platform covers more than 3 mn sq km, or 25% of the total area of the USSR in which oil and gas may be found. Yet only 1 mn m of exploratory hole was drilled here during the 15 years 1965 to 1980, and this amounts to no more than 1.3% of all exploratory work in the USSR. And most of this drilling was for gas; only 350,000 m of wells were drilled in the search for oil, 0.7% of all oil exploration work in the USSR. This implies that 650,000 m were drilled in the search for gas, or 2.4% of the national total.

Eight main areas are being surveyed with varying degrees of intensity:

Yenisei-Khatanga trough (mainly gas).
Vilyui sineclize (mainly gas).
Evenki sineclize (oil and heavy gas condensate).
Lena-Anabar trough (oil).
Baikitskaya anteclize (oil and light condensates).
Nepsko-Botuobinsk anteclize (oil and light condensates).
Anabar anteclize (bitumens)
Aldan anteclize (bitumens)

There are many other smaller areas with potential for hydrocarbons, particularly bitumens.

The Yenisei-Khatanga basin is believed to have a substantial potential, given that the Jurassic sediments in the Balakhninsk area are 2,000 m thick, with the most productive strata (Volgian and Berriassian) having a thickness of several hundred metres. Although the geophysicists appear to be enjoying some success, the drillers have been slow to follow it up with V.Yu. Zaichenko of the Ministry of Geology complaining that a lengthy period occurred before 28 structures discovered by seismic teams were drilled. Commercial gas flows have ben obtained at the Balakhninsk site on the northern shore of Khatanga Gulf, and seismic parties are now concentrating on the Portnyagino region to the north of the Balakhninsk discovery. The existing gas deposits of Messoyakh and Solenoe, now giving 4 bn cu m a year, are being developed further, and two new deposits in the same area, Severo-Solenoe and Pelyatkinsk, are being tested. The production of gas by these deposits is currently constrained by demand from Norilsk, and consequently it is not likely to grow very much unless vague plans for large-scale liquifaction are carried out. There are reports that oil shows have been obtained in the Novyi area, although the precise location is not known.

The Nizhneyeniseisk expedition is responsible for exploring the lower reaches of the Yenisei river, and it has high hopes of finding oil at the Khabeisk and Deryabinsk sites which are now being drilled. So far, Khabeisk (which is 300 km north-west of Norilsk) has only given gas, with the first well yielding 1¾ mn cu m a day from a depth of 2,046 m.

The Lena-Anabar trough is an easterly extension of the Yenisei-Khatanga trough, and it probably extends offshore. It has heavy, viscous oil from Triassic and Permian strata, and several crews from the Khatanga Oil Exploration Expedition have been working on ascertaining the likely size of reserves. Exploration wells have been sunk in the Smolensk, Vladimir and Kostroma sites on the Anabar river. The Russians are hoping to make commercial finds here because the oil can be transported more easily out of the region than from any other Eastern Siberian field. It would be collected by tankers from the Mys Neftyannyi terminal near Nordvik.

Exploration for oil took place near Nordvik as long ago as 1938/41, and heavy oil was found in Jurassic and Triassic strata at depths of 2,000–2,500 m, with well yields of up to ten tons a day. The small oil deposits are capped by thick salt domes.

The Vilyui basin consists of the Vilyui lowlands and the Lena valley, and extends northwards to the mouth of the Lena where it adjoins the eastern end of the Lena-Anabar trough. It covers an area of 120,000 sq km. Exploration began during the mid-1930s, and so far more than 30 gas and gas condensate deposits have been discovered, with proved plus probable reserves of more than 500 bn cu m.

While it has been said that the surveying of potential condensate deposits has been completed, the region is regarded as the most promising in Eastern Siberia and the Far East for new gas finds. However the north-western corner, thought likely to contain the biggest gas fields, lies within a hydrate formation zone, and the Ministry of Gas has been making a special effort to study the characteristics of hydrate formation in the Vilyui Basin and Messoyakh deposit (Krasnoyarsk krai).

The three most important deposits are Sredne-Viluisk, Mastakh and Sobo-Khain. The biggest is Sredne-Viluisk, with several payzones between 1,000 and 3,200 m deep in sandstone from the late Permian through the Triassic to the late Jurassic. So far, only the small Ust Vilyui gas deposit (located at the confluence of the Vilyui and Lena rivers), and the Mastakh gas and condensate deposit have been developed, with a total output from start-up to 1980 of 5 bn cu m. During the Eleventh Five Year Plan period, it is planned to raise annual output to 2.5-3 bn cu m a year, with a network of pipelines being built to supply mining towns in the Yakutsk republic. However, insufficient effort is being made to utilise the large reserves of condensate, some of which is being produced jointly with gas at Mastakh. The deposit is flowing 30 cu m of condensate a day, equivalent to six tons of gasoline and eight tons of boiler fuel, because the production of condensate has not been catered for by the local Yakut planning organisations. The Yakut Gosplan has 'solved' the problem by transferring storage tanks from other areas where they are equally necessary. Mastakh will produce 7,000 tons of condensate in 1982, but its rational utilisation has still not been organised.

Exploratory work in the Vilyui region is now being concentrated on the Khapchagai region, where several new gas deposits have been found, and on proving up the reserves of the large Sredne-Tyungsk deposit. It was hoped that Sredne-Tyungsk would give commercial flows of oil, but the Vilyuisk Oil Exploration Expedition has only succeeded in finding gas. During 1982, two promising new gas discoveries were made in the region at Taas-Yuryakhsk and Verkhne-Lindensk.

Earlier plans for the piping of Yakutsk gas to populated regions of the Far East such as Khabarovsk and Vladivostok and for export to Japan have been shelved for the moment, but could be revived during the latter half of the 1980s. This will be more likely if major condensate deposits are found, and the large-scale development of Yakutsk fields should be assisted by the completion of an extension of the 'Little BAM railway' from Berkakit through Tommot to Yakutsk. Design work is now taking place, but the construction of the line is not likely to be before tracklaying on the BAM railway is completed at the end of 1984. On this assumption, it should be 1987 before the 730 km Berkakit-Yakutsk line is finished.

The Nepsko-Botuobinsk anteclize lies to the west of the Vilyui basin. A number of structures which could contain oil, light condensates and perhaps gas have been found, generally fully closed by thick Lower Cambrian salt domes. Exploration of the promising Sredne-Botuobinsk, Verkhne Vilyuchansk and Vilyuisko-Dzherbinsk areas is taking place, and a commercial flow of oil was obtained for the first time in the Yakutsk republic from a 1,900-m-deep well at Sredne-Botuobinsk in 1981, although oil rings have also been located at the Yaraktinsk and Ayansk condensate deposits. The oil has density of 820–845 gms/cm³, a boiling point of 105–150° and a pour point of −30° and is heavy with its light fractions having migrated into the more substantial condensate reservoirs. Another interesting feature is its low reservoir temperature of only 6–13°. However, exploration work has been extremely slow, and the failure to fulfil drilling plans year after year has brought sharp criticism from the Ministry of Geology.

In the Danilovo area, 200 km south of Yerbogachen on the Nizhnyaya Tunguska, appreciable reserves of gas have been discovered and the first oil was found in November 1980 when a well yielded 100 tons a day.

The prospects for gas production are limited by the tendency for hydrate formation in the more promising Cambrian reef horizons, and geologists of the Lenaneftegazgeologiya Association's Srednelensk Expedition are pinning their hopes on finding large quantities of oil at Sredne-Botuobinsk. They would need to be large before exploitation could begin as a pipeline would have to be built through difficult terrain for 1,100 km to the nearest refinery at Angarsk. The pipeline would follow the upper reaches of the Lena for much of its length, and would also be fed from the Markovo oil and condensate deposit, located 50 km north-east of the BAM settlement of Tayura. Markovo was discovered in March 1962 in the Lower Cambrian.

In 1982, Sredne-Botuobinsk flowed oil from 1,900m, but yields are unknown. The first oil deposit to be found in that part of the Nepsko-Botuobinsk anteclize lying in the Irkutsk oblast was Atovskoe, discovered in 1939 when a well yielded five tons of oil a day. The oil was good quality with a 52.6% content of light fractions and a 0.4% sulphur content, although it was rather waxy with a 4% wax content. Some time later, exploratory drilling led to further oil strikes in the Solzavodsk and Bystryansk areas.

The Baikitskaya anteclize (sometimes called the Tungusskaya

anteclize, as it follows the Podkammenaya Tunguska river from west to east) shares many features of the Nepsko-Botuobinskaya anteclize with accumulations of oil and condensate capped by Lower Cambrian salt domes. Most exploration work has been taking place at Vanavara, where potentially productive structures in Lower Paleozoic and Pre-Cambrian strata are being examined. The most important oil discovery has been made at Kuyumba, where commercial flows of oil were found at a depth of 2,340 m in Paleozoic reefs.

The Evenki sineclize, north of the Baikitskaya anteclize, is being explored by the Yeniseineftegazgeologiya Association. Flows of oil, gas and condensate have been obtained by the Turukhansk expedition in the Yenisei valley in the region between the Kureisk and Letninsk tributaries. The Turukhansk expedition is stepping up the pace of its operations, and in 1981 it drilled more than 10,000 m for the first time.

In the south-west of the Siberian platform on the Kamovskii Arch, several shows of oil have been obtained, and the Evenki expedition has found oil along the Kochechym tributary of the Nizhnyaya Tunguska. These hydrocarbons are closed by Lower Cambrian salt domes in the southern part of the sineclize and Devonian salt domes in the north.

The Anabar anteclize contains vast quantities of bitumen, with some estimates suggesting the presence of 12,000 mn tons of which 8% could be recoverable. The bitumen was formed from heavy oil which lost its gas components because of the absence of a salt cover. The biggest deposits are the Vostochno-Anabar (on the Anabar arch), the Khoik-skoe and Solo-oliiskoe (Olenek arch) and Chekurovskoe in the Kharaulakhsk salient to the east of the Lena estuary. But the largest concentrations of bitumen are thought to lie in the Shologontsevskii area and along the Siligir river.

The Aldan anteclize could contain as much bitumen as the Anabar arch, with deposits of heavy oil likely on its eastern edge in the Yudoma and Muisk valleys. The Russians believe that they could refine the bitumen into useful products at a cost less than 50% higher than current average refining costs, but the fields are unlikely to be developed before the mid-1990s because of the problems of exploitation and transporting the bitumen out of the region.

The Eastern Siberian region displays an extremely high degree of geological complexity, and this is one of the reasons for poor effectiveness of exploration work. By 1981, oil deposits large enough to warrant immediate commercial exploitation had not been discovered, while gas reserves were said to be growing too slowly. It is planned to increase exploratory drilling metreage by 50-60% in the USSR over 1981 to 1985 compared with 1976 to 1980, although the increasing well depths mean that the number of structures to be explored will rise by only 29%, and their area should be 15% greater. In Western Siberia, the volume of drilling should rise by 110%, and in Eastern Siberia, 140%.

The Timano-Pechora Oil and Gas Region

The Timano-Pechora oil and gas region is located in the Komi republic and Arkhangelsk oblast in the North West economic region. It has been described as having 'great significance' for the further development of the Soviet oil and gas industry, thanks not only to the size of its reserves but also its comparative proximity to the heavily populated areas of European Russia.

The on-shore part of the basin is believed to contain a potentially petroliferous area of 300,000 sq km, and a further 750,000 sq km of the Pechora Sea (part of the Barents Sea) may yield oil and gas. It is bounded on the west by the Timanskii Ridge, and in the east by the Urals mountains extending northwards into the Pai Khoi Ridge and Novaya Zemlya Island. Oil is concentrated in the southern part of the Izhma-Pechora basin, where the largest producing field is the Yarega heavy oil deposit, 10 km south-west of Ukhta; the Kolvinsk megavale, the southern part of the Khoreiversk basin (i.e. in the vicinity of the Vozei and Usa oilfields, which account for nearly all the Komi republic's current output of oil) and the Varandei-Adz'vinsk structural zone. Gas and condensate is found mainly in the Pechora-Kozhvinsk megavale, the Shapkino-Yur'yakhinsk and Laisk zones (including the Laya-Vozh gas deposit), the Denisovsk Basin and the Verkhne Pechora Basin, which contains the giant Vuktyl gas and condensate deposit.

The region's oil and gas is found in three complexes – the Carboniferous-Lower Permian (50.9% of all proved plus probable hydrocarbon reserves, including 37.8% of the oil and 74.6% of the gas), the Middle Devonian-Lower Frasnian (41.6%, including 51.9% of the oil and 22.2% of the gas) and the pre-Middle Devonian, mostly Silurian and Lower Devonian, accounting for 3% of hydrocarbon resources.

During the three years 1978 to 1980, 42 structures were examined. Most of these (36 in all) were explored by the Ukhta Territorial Geological Directorate (TGD) of the Ministry of Geology, while Komineft of the Ministry of Oil surveyed four structures and Komigazprom

(Ministry of Gas) two. The Arkhangelsk TGD has been exploring the Nenetskii region, where three significant oil finds at Taraveisk, Yuzhno-Taraveisk and Labogansk were made over 1974 to 1980, and a large oilfield was discovered at Varandei on the shore of the Pechora Sea in 1975. This last find served as convincing evidence that the area will prove to be a major producer of oil and possibly gas, and the mouth of the Pechora River is now the scene of intensive drilling activity.

For exploration purposes, the Timano-Pechora Basin has been divided into 28 oil- and gas-bearing regions. By 1958, most exploratory work had taken place in only two regions, the Ukhta-Izhminsk and Omra-Soivinsk, to the immediate west and south-east respectively of the city of Ukhta. These regions are now thought to have been fully explored, and any new deposits will be found only in stratigraphic traps. In the late 1950s, work moved eastwards of Ukhta, and in a north-easterly direction beyond Pechora to the Velyu-Tebuksk, Michayu-Pashkinsk, Pechoro-Kozhvinsk, Verkhne-Pechorsk and Sredne-Pechorsk regions, resulting in the discovery of a large oilfield (Zapadno-Tebuksk) in 1960 and a giant condensate field (Vuktyl) in 1965. While there are definite possibilities for finding more large deposits, the Ukhta TGD is believed to have been starved of funds by the Ministry of Geology, and the number of structures prepared for drilling is inadequate. Consequently, it is unlikely that large new finds will be made here before 1985, and the 1985 production targets set by the Eleventh Five Year Plan have called for increases which can only be described as modest given the large potential of the region.

In 1980, the Komi republic yielded 19 bn cu m of gas (15 bn of it from Vuktyl) and 18.1 mn tons of oil and condensate. The plan target for 1985 has been set at 21.7 bn cu m of gas and 23 mn tons of oil and condensate. The Vuktyl gasfield has peaked, and its output will decline from 93.3 bn cu m over 1976 to 1980 to 84.8 bn over 1981 to 1985, although development will continue and 30 more wells will be drilled during 1981 to 1983 bringing the total to 150. At the end of 1981, Vuktyl had reserves of 200 bn cu m of gas and 40 mn tons of condensate. The condensate is sent through a 200 km pipeline to the gas refinery at Sosnogorsk. The exploitation of a new gas deposit, Zapadno-Soplesskoe 80 km from Vuktyl, began in November 1981 and it should reach its rated capacity of 2 bn cu m a year by 1985.

During 1975 to 1980, the output of oil plus condensate grew from 11.1 to 18.1 mn tons, with the increase stemming from the development of two new oil deposits, Usa and Vozei; by 1980, Usa was accounting for 75% of the Komi republic's oil. But while production has grown steadily, it has failed to meet plan targets. The northernmost oilfield in the USSR, it was connected with the small refinery at Ukhta by a pipeline completed in 1975 and then extended to the larger refinery at Yaroslavl by 1978. Production shortfalls were due to delays in the construction of the 100 km Synya-Usa branch line of the Kotlas-Vorkuta railway. It was to have been ready in 1978, but did not reach its destination until December 1979. Casinghead gas from Usa oilfield is now being processed by the Usa gas refinery, completed in January 1980, and the dry gas will be used as a fuel for the Pechora power station, now under construction.

Of the 79.3 mn tons of oil and condensate produced by the Komi republic over 1976 to 1980, 67.5 mn tons came from Usa and Vozei. However, several other small deposits have begun to produce oil during the last few years including the promising Severo-Sabinoborsk. More than 1 mn m of development wells were drilled by Komineft and Komigazprom in 1981, and over 1981 to 1985, they plan to drill a total 5.5 mn m.

Evidence of Russian plans to step up exploration work in the Komi republic is the expansion of the seismic surveying organisation Pechora-geofizika. In 1975 it had 14 teams operating, in 1980 21 and by 1982 there were 25 teams including nine working on the Bolshezemelsk tundra. During the 1981/2 field season they carried out 10,000 km of seismic profiles.

The most interesting feature of exploration in the Timano-Pechora basin is the search for oil in the Barents Sea from drilling ships purchased from Finland. Three ships were ordered from the Rauma Repola yard at Poti, and so far two have been delivered – the 'Valentin Shashin', which arrived at Murmansk in late-1981, and the 'Viktor Muravlenko' (July 1982). They are currently drilling at undisclosed positions, thought to be near the mouth of the Pechora river. The ships have seven propellors controlled by a computer which measures the speed and direction of the current and wind, and switches the propellors on and off so as to maintain the position of the ship.

The long-term commitment by the Russians to exploration of the Barents Sea is illustrated by the creation of a semi-submersible fabrication plant at the Vyborg shipyard, 125 km north-west of Leningrad. The first platform was due for completion in 1983, but fabrication work actually finished a year ahead of schedule in August 1982, and more rigs are now being built. They will be able to drill to depths of 6,000 m in up to 200 m of water, and have similar specifications to the

'Shelf' series now being built at Astrakhan for exploration of the Caspian Sea.

Kazakhstan

Kazakhstan has three producing oilfields, of which the largest is Mangyshlak with an area of 70,000 sq km, and which consists of two major deposits, Uzen and Zhetybai. Production has declined from 20 mn tons in 1975 to only 13 mn in 1981 due to difficulties in tapping the field's heavy oil. In spite of the greater use of gaslift and other enhanced recovery methods, output is likely to decline further in the future as resources are channelled to newer fields which are easier to work. However, some reports state that 700,000 m of exploration wells will be drilled at Mangyshlak during 1981 to 1985 in the search for deposits of lighter oil at depths of up to 5,000 m. Some ten new structures will be explored, and geologists believe that the Mangyshlak field can eventually yield up to 130 mn tons a year.

The second largest Kazakh field is the Emba, situated on the northern shore of the Caspian Sea. Exploitation began in the 1909–12 period when the Dossor and Makat deposits were opened up. After being worked for many years, the field gave only 3.9 mn tons in 1981. During the last few years, output has been rising slightly, mainly from the new Tortai deposit, where wells drilled to 3,000 m are giving yields of 450 tons a day.

The third field is situated on the Buzachi Peninsula, north of Mangyshlak, and was established in 1977 with reserves of more than 150 mn tons. It is being rapidly developed so as to keep up Kazakh production until the heavy oil problems at Mangyshlak are solved. While the oil is mostly heavy, it lies at depths of only 250 to 800 m, and can be extracted comparatively cheaply by the drilling of a large number of wells. So far, three deposits have been opened up – Kalamkas (1979), Karazhanbas (1980) and Severobuzachinsk (1981), and their oil is piped to Shevchenko from whence it is shipped across the Caspian to the Baku refineries. Output is planned to grow to 5 mn tons in 1985 from 1.5 mn tons in 1981, and off-shore drilling will take place from a specially-built 100 km-long dam because the sea is not deep enough for exploration vessels.

Kazakhstan as a whole is planned to produce 23 mn tons in 1985 compared with 18.7 in 1980 and 19.1 mn in 1981. Some of the increase will come from a new oilfield which will be established in the

Caspian Depression in the southern part of Aktyubinsk oblast. It will centre on the Zhanazhol deposit, which the newly-created Oktyabrskneft Association brought on stream in 1982. By the end of 1981, 30 exploratory wells had yielded large quantities of light oil from two payzones lying between 3,000 and 4,500 m deep, and four other sub-salt deposits had been found in the Caspian Depression. More than 30 other areas are being examined to depths of up to 4,500 m, and over 1981 to 1985, 300,000 m of exploratory wells will be drilled. The cost of drilling to such great depths through salt layers which may be up to 800 m thick is so high that only the discovery of giant deposits providing very large well yields will justify the extensive development of the Caspian Depression oilfield.

Central Asian Gas

Central Asia is the second most important gas-producing region in the USSR, and should remain so until the next century, although its share of national output will continue to decline as production from Western Siberia grows. The largest fields are in the Turkmen republic, where output is planned to increase from 70.5 bn cu m in 1980 to 85 bn in 1985.

Most of Turkmenia's operating deposits have peaked, or are declining, and ten new ones must be developed for the 1985 target to be met. These include the Dauletabad-Donmez group of deposits, discovered in 1976, near Serakhs on the border with Iran. First reports suggested that the field might contain 100 bn cu m of gas over 400 sq km, but by 1979 25 exploratory wells had been drilled giving yields of 1 to 1.5 mn cu m a day from depths of 2,500 m, and it was believed that reserves of 1,000 bn cu m over 2,000 sq km existed in the area.

Development began in May 1980, and the construction of the first gas preparation installation began in June 1981. Gas will start flowing in 1983 with the completion of a 150 km pipeline linking the field with the Central Asia-Moscow trunk line at Mary — its construction began in June 1981 and by November 1982 it was crossing the Kara Kum Canal. The field is expected to yield 8 bn cu m in 1983, building up to 40 bn cu m/year by 1986.

Dauletabad-Donmez will account for most of the production increase by the Turkmen republic up to 1990, but important contributions will come from Mollaker, Uch Adzhi, Severnyi Balkui and Erdekli. The development of Mollaker began in January 1981, and gas began flowing to Mary power station towards the end of 1981. Uch Adzhi is located 120 km north-east of Mary on the Samarkand-Ashkhabad railway line, which should assist construction rates. The installation of equipment began in June 1981, and production should start in 1983. Severnyi Balkui will give 3 bn cu m/year with production beginning in late 1982. The Erdekli condensate deposit on the eastern shore of the Caspian Sea also began producing in 1982, delivering gas through the Okarem branch of the Central Asia-Moscow pipeline.

Drilling is continuing at Shatlyk, which currently accounts for about half of the republic's annual production. Although the deposit has peaked at about 37 bn cu m/year, many more wells must be drilled to maintain this level, and the recent discovery of a large new payzone at 5,000 m may enable the annual yield to go above 40 bn cu m.

During the 1990s, the Sovetabad deposit will be responsible for sustaining the Turkmen gas industry. It should come on stream during the Twelfth Five Year Plan period (1986-90) with reserves estimated in mid-1982 at 1,380 bn cu m.

The Uzbek republic is also an important producer of gas. The decline of the once-prolific Gazli deposit has been compensated by the development of other, smaller fields, enabling output to stabilise at about 35 bn cu m a year. It should remain at this level until 1985, by which time the Shurtan deposit should be yielding 16 bn cu m a year (plus 800,000 tons of condensate, 500,000 tons of ethane and 400,000 tons of propane and butane). By 1990, its annual output could reach 25 bn cu m; reserves have been put at 500 bn cu m, and exploration is continuing.

The other major field is the Mubarek group of deposits in the Karshi Steppe which produce highly sulphurous gas. This is cleaned in the Mubarek gas processing plant with a capacity of 15 bn cu m a year, and the Eleventh plan expects a further 10 bn cu m of capacity to be added by 1985.

Kansk-Achinsk Coalfield

It is thought that Soviet coal production will rise from 716 mn tons in 1980 to 750 mn tons in 1985 (against a plan target of 775 mn tons), 815 mn tons in 1990 and 1,000 mn tons in 2000. While plan targets for 1990 have not been published, it has been officially stated that output from open-cast pits must rise from 269 mn tons in 1980 to 315 mn in 1985 and 390-400 mn in 1990. Production from deep mines is therefore

Table 12.8: Characteristics of Coalfields in the Kansk-Achinsk Basin

	Itatsk	Berezovsk	Uryupsk	Nazarovo	Irsha Borodino	Abansk
Proved + probable reserves (bn tons)	29.4	18.2	16.9	1.9	3.6	29.6
Seam thickness (metres)	30–96	8–70	40–50	10–21	20–50	2–24
Depth of coal (metres)	10–500	12–300	7–300	2–200	10–78	40–80
Overburden ratio (cu m/ton)	0.8–4	1–4	1.3–3.	1.4–3.7	1	1–3.5
Ash content (%)	9	7	7	12	9	11
Moisture content (%)	36–40	32	35	39	33	33
Heat rate (kcal/kg)	3,300	3,830	3,670	3,110	3,740	3,780

planned to grow from 447 mn tons in 1980 to 460 mn in 1985, and if this is maintained, then it is clear that planners are hoping for a total coal production of 850-860 mn tons in 1990. However on past performance, they are not likely to hit such a target, and 815 mn tons seems more reasonable. Practically all the increase will come from three fields – Kansk-Achinsk, Ekibastuz and the Kuzbass.

The Kansk-Achinsk coalfied is so named because it stretches for 600 km along the Trans-Siberian Railway through the towns of Kansk and Achinsk. Its reserves are known to exceed 140 bn tons, and are believed to be much larger with some sources claiming the presence of 247 bn tons of which 100 bn can be mined in open-cast pits. Forecast reserves have been put tentatively at 450 bn tons. Proved reserves stood at 74 bn tons in 1981, of which 64 bn can be mined open-cast.

The workable seams have a thickness of up to 96 m and are either horizontal or very slightly sloping. The overburden consists basically of loose sand or clay-based material, not requiring drilling and blasting prior to removal by excavators, The overburden rate varies between 0.8 and 4 cu m per ton of coal. Production costs are estimated at 7 to 8 roubles a ton (including the heavy capital costs of providing an excavator assembly plant, transport networks, housing and amenities, etc.) or 30% of those of the Donbass. However, the coal is poor-quality lignite (calorific value 3,200–3,900 kcal/kg) with a low ash (6-13%) and high moisture (up to 40%) content, and cannot be transported due to a tendency to spontaneous combustion. The sulphur content is fairly low at 0.1-0.9%.

In 1981, 41 mn tons were produced, with 25 mn tons coming from the Irsha-Borodino mine 65 km south-west of Kansk, and 16 mn tons from the Nazarovo mine 30 km south of Achinsk. These mines enjoy very high labour productivity of 883 tons a month at Irsha-Borodino and 946 tons/month at Nazarovo, and very low production costs of 1.08 R/t and 1.11 R/t at the two mines. The coal is burned in local power stations, and its conversion into electricity for transmission westwards is the only way in which more of the coal can be used at the present time.

The first stage of the Kansk-Achinsk project envisages the creation of seven coal mines producing 330 mn tons a year from seams of up to 70 m thick in the Berezovo area at the western end of the basin. These are: Berezovo No. 1 (55 mn tons a year), No. 2 (50) and No. 3 (50), Uryupsk No. 1 (27), Itatsk No. 1 (60), No. 2 (50) and No. 3 (40). At the same time, the Irsha-Borodino field may be expanded to 65 mn tons a year.

The mines will feed eight, and possibly ten, adjacent power stations with an aggregate capacity of 51,200-64,000 MW, producing 320-400 bn kWh a year, and burning between 250 and 300 mn tons of lignite annually. The cost of the electricity is expected to be no more than 0.4 kopecks per kWh, or less than 40% of the national average; this means that the power can be transmitted over a huge distance and still prove competitive with power from new atomic stations. It is planned that this first stage should be completed by 1995, but this seems very optimistic in view of the problems that remain to be overcome, and it may be well into the next century before the mines are working at rated capacity. When the second and third stages are completed, Kansk-Achinsk is expected to yield 1,000 mn tons a year including 280 mn tons/year from the Berezovo and Uryupsk system of quarries, 360 mn tons/year from Itatsk and Barandatsk, 300 mn from Abansk and 70 mn tons/year from Bogotolsk, all of it from open-cast mines. The Minister of Power, Neporozhnyi, confirmed the target of 1,000 mn tons a year at the November 1982 Plenum of the Communist Party, although it is unlikely that this level of output can be achieved before 2050.

At the moment, three major projects are under construction. These are: the first stage (13.5 mn tons a year) of the Berezovo No. 1 mine which is projected to produce 55 mn tons a year when completed; the Berezovo power station of eventual capacity 6,400 MW with eight sets of 800 MW each; and the Krasnoyarsk excavator plant, the first stage of which is designed to assemble ten bucket-wheel excavators a year.

The mine is located near the city of Sharypovo, the population of which will eventually rise to 250,000 as the mine's workforce grows. According to the Eleventh Five Year Plan, the mine was to start producing in 1983, but in fact it began yielding coal towards the end of 1982, and by the end of the year, 2 mn tons had been produced.

Overburden removal is being undertaken by large walking dragline excavators with buckets of 100 cu m capacity, and bucket-wheel excavators with a capacity of 5,000 and 10,000 tons an hour in conjunction with frost-resistant conveyors and 180-ton capacity dumpcars made by the Minsk Auto Plant.

There are signs that the Russians are becoming increasingly worried about the massive pollution certain to ensue from the creation of the complex. The burning of up to 300 mn tons of lignite a year in a comparatively small area should devastate the environment, with an estimated 500,000 tons of sulphur anhydride and 100,000 tons of ash a year released into the atmosphere.

The water resources of the area, centred on the Chulym river and the Beloe lake are wholly inadequate for the provision of 160-230 cu m of water per second required by each power station, and a large number of huge reservoirs will have to be built. The first of these will be Verblyuzhegorsk, and eventually the diversion of water from the Krasnoyarsk Sea must be accomplished.

Apart from burning Kansk-Achinsk coal in power stations, other options open to the Russians include the liquifaction of coal, and its transportation westwards by pipeline.

At the moment, a small plant for the hydrogenation of coal is under construction. It is planned to start working in 1983, and will produce 2.5 tons of oil a day from ten tons of coal. The construction of a plant able to process 75 tons of coal a day should start shortly.

During the current five-year plan period, a pipeline is to be built from the Kuzbass to Novosibirsk. It will carry coal mixed with water on a 1:1 basis, and pumped as a pulp along the pipeline. If this pipeline works successfully, then a project for building a similar pipeline for 4,000 km from Kansk-Achinsk to Moscow will be carried out. It will be able to move 50 to 60 mn tons of coal a year, and the share of coal in the pulp will be higher than 50% because it will be mixed with water and methanol. Research has shown that the methanol can be easily extracted from the coal in Moscow, where it can be used in petrochemical plants or as an additive for petrol. The pipeline will therefore be carrying two fuels. It should be stressed, however, that these proposals are only tentative at the present time.

Ekibastuz Field

Like the Kansk-Achinsk project, the programme for the Ekibastuz field in Kazakhstan envisages the creation of a series of mineside power stations burning coal delivered directly by conveyor from the opencast mines. Five stations of a total capacity of 20,000 MW are envisaged; three of the stations are now being built on a flowline basis, and the first is more than half finished.

The coalfield currently has a capacity of 72 mn tons a year, with two giant mines accounting for 70 mn tons. These are the Tsentralnyi, which was completed in 1970 and is able to produce 20 mn tons a year, and Bogatyr, which reached its planned capacity of 50 mn tons a year in 1981. The field produced 66 mn tons in 1980 and about the same in 1981. The 1985 target has been set at 83 mn tons, considerably less than the 115 mn tons envisaged as recently as 1978. This revision is due to the extremely slow progress in overburden removal at the new Severnyi mine which is now being built, and which should be yielding 20 mn tons a year by 1990. By this time, output by the Vostochnyi mine should also be building up, and with the extension of the existing mines, it is possible that Ekibastuz will be producing 170 mn tons a year by 2000.

Ekibastuz is a fairly small coalfield compared with Kansk-Achinsk and the Kuzbass. Its proved plus probable reserves were put at 14 bn tons in 1980, and the coal has a low heat rate and a high ash content of 30-35%. However the field can be worked very cheaply because the overburden ratio is only 1.5 to 1.

In 1981, 15% of Ekibastuz coal was burned in-place, 25% was sent to other consumers in Kazakhstan, and 60% was sent beyond Kazakhstan, including 53% to the Urals. It is planned that by 1990, 40% of the coal will be burned in-place, and exports beyond the borders of Kazakhstan will be reduced. This will become possible despite the decline of Urals coalfields like Chelyabinsk, Kizel, Yegorshinsk, Karpinsk and South Urals, because other fields in the Urals have sufficient reserves of coal to satisfy long-term demand. The Korkinsk and Dalnebulanashsk areas can yield 2.5 mn tons a year of brown coal, the Bogoslovsk, Volchansk, Yelovsk-Taborsk and Kama deposits are said to have considerable coal reserves, and the Tyulgansk open-cast pit in Orenburg oblast, which began producing in 1982, will eventually give 3.5 mn tons a year. On the basis of preliminary surveys, it is thought that the East Ural deposit can produce 4 mn tons a year.

Kuznets Coal Basin

The Kuzbass is the USSR's second largest producer of coal after the Donbass, providing 145 mn tons in 1981. It has total reserves estimated at 725 bn tons distributed over an area of 27,000 sq km, making it the third largest coal basin in the USSR after the Tunguska and Lena basins. The reserves of steam coal amount to 519 bn tons, and coking coal to 206 bn tons. Its proved plus probable reserves of 66.4 bn tons are mainly found in thick seams at comparatively shallow depths with generally straightforward geological conditions. More than 85% of reserves lie at depths of less than 300 m, with 60% at less than 200 m and perhaps 33% can be mined by open-cast methods.

The coal is of high quality with an average heat rate of 5,920 kcal per kg. It is generally found in seams of 1.3 to 3.5 m thick, which account for 40% of total reserves, although thick seams of more than 10 m account for only 5%. The coal has a low content of ash, sulphur and phosphor, and has an average propensity for dressing. The hydrogeological conditions are fairly straightforward. About 60% of reserves lie in gently-sloping seams, 15% in inclined seams and 25% in steeply-falling seams.

These mining conditions mean that large, highly mechanised mines like Raspadskaya near Mezhdurechensk can be sunk. Raspadskaya produces 6 mn tons of coking coal a year, and is expected to eventually yield 7.5 mn tons a year. More than 90% of coal extraction is carried out with the use of continuous mining machines, and the coal is moved from the face to the surface entirely by conveyor. Each face gives more than 1,500 tons a day at an average cost of 7.5 roubles a ton, and labour productivity at 140 tons a month is three times the national average.

It is estimated that the Kuzbass could produce up to 500 mn tons a year for 1,000 years. Immediate plans are more modest, with most of the planned increase in output to 167 mn tons in 1985 coming from open-cast mines which currently account for 33% of total output. The oldest open-cast mine, the '50 Years of October', gave 4.5 mn tons of coking coal in 1981, but the reconstruction programme envisages a capacity of 12 mn tons a year by 1985, eventually rising to 20 mn tons a year. The construction has begun of the Taldanskii pit (projected capacity 30 mn tons a year) and another major pit at Tarakan is being built. By 1995 the production of coal from open-cast mines is planned to double to 100 mn tons a year, with the Kuzbass producing more than 200 mn tons from open-cast and deep mines.

The Karakan pits are to be worked by the Kemerovougol Association. They have proved plus probable reserves of 2.8 bn tons located in at least 52 workable seams lying almost horizontally one above the other. Perhaps 16 of the seams can be worked open-cast, and the highest seam, which is 15 m thick can be exploited with an overburden ratio of 3 to 1. During the first stage of the development, Karakanskii Nos. 1–2 quarries will be commissioned in 1984, and will be producing 30 mn tons a year by 1990.

In the distant future, an output of 550 mn tons a year is envisaged, consisting of 300 mn tons of steam coal and 250 mn tons of coking coal. Production from open-cast pits is expected to grow to 150–200 mn tons a year, mainly from the Karakan and Yerunakovsk mines.

13 CONCLUSION

Soviet fuel requirements in 1980 amounted to 1,997.3 mn tons of standard fuel, consisting of 1,676.7 mn tsf utilised by the domestic economy and 320.6 mn tsf of exports. The requirements were met by the production of 1,905.7 mn tsf, the generation of hydro-electric power worth 22.6 mn tsf, the acquisition of 48.8 mn tsf from other sources (basically secondary energy resources such as coking gas, blast furnace gas, etc.) and the import of 16.8 mn tsf, and stocks were drawn on for 3.4 mn tsf.

Fuel needs per rouble of gross social product, and per rouble of industrial production have been declining. The decline was very rapid between 1965 and 1970, slower between 1970 and 1975, and between 1975 and 1980, fuel requirements per rouble of GSP declined very slowly (by 2.6%) while fuel consumption per rouble of industrial production actually rose slightly. In the following analysis, fuel consumption includes exports; this procedure is justified on the grounds that exports are necessary to pay for imports of machinery and equipment which assist the growth of industrial production and the GSP.

Table 13.1: Relationship between Fuel Consumption (including Exports) and Major National Economic Variables

	1965	1970	1975	1978	1979	1980
Fuel consumption (mn tsf)	1014.5	1284.9	1651.1	1899.0	1935.9	1997.3
Gross social product (bn R)	420.2	643.5	862.6	995.7	1032.4	1072.3
Fuel consumption (tsf/1,000 R of GSP)	2.41	2.00	1.91	1.91	1.88	1.86
Industrial production (bn R)	229.4	374.3	511.2	577.7	595.1	616.3
Fuel consumption (tsf/1,000 R of industrial production)	4.42	3.43	3.23	3.29	3.25	3.24

Between 1965 and 1970, every 1,000 roubles' increase in annual GSP required an increase of 1.21 tsf in the provision of fuel. Between 1975 and 1978, the comparable figure was 1.86 tsf, but in 1978 to 1980, it fell to only 1.28 tsf. A similar trend was observed in the marginal increase in fuel consumption required to sustain the marginal increase in industrial production. This suggests that improvements in the fuel rate began to make themselves felt in 1978 to 1980 as increases in the GSP and industrial production were accompanied by very small increases in fuel needs.

Table 13.2: Relationship between the Marginal Increase in Fuel Consumption and the Marginal Increase in the Major Economic Variables

	1965–70	1970–5	1975–8	1978–80
Marginal fuel consumption (tsf/1,000 R of GSP)	1.21	1.67	1.86	1.28
Marginal fuel consumption (tsf/1,000 R of industrial production)	1.87	2.67	3.73	1.77

On the basis of the forecasts for fuel production of Chapter 12, it can be calculated that the provision of fuel and energy will grow at an average annual rate of 2.8% over 1980 to 1985, and 2.7% over 1986 to 1990 before falling to 2.0% during the last decade of the century. This is in spite of the rapid development of the atomic power sector, especially during the 1990s when atomic stations will be built on a flowline basis, enabling installed capacity to grow by 10,000 MW a year to 160,000 MW in 2000. The slow growth in energy provision should also take place in spite of the accelerated development of huge open-cast pits in the Siberian coalfields, which should permit coal production to grow more rapidly than has been the case during the 1970s. However, it should be remembered that Kansk-Achinsk and Ekibastuz coals have low heat rates, and the average annual growth in coal production in terms of standard fuel should amount to only 1.3% over 1980 to 1990, and 2.4% over 1990 to 2000.

Table 13.3: Forecast Provision of Energy, 1980–2000 (mn tsf)

	1980	1985	1990	2000
Fuel	1,906	2,190	2,500	3,000
Others*	91	100	120	200
Total	1,997	2,290	2,620	3,200

Note: * Hydro and atomic power (converted to standard fuel at 123 gsf/kWh), secondary energy, imports and stock changes.

It is thought that the production of natural gas will grow by 7.3% a year during 1980 to 1985, 5.3% over 1985 to 1990 and 2.4% a year during the 1990s. Gas should overtake oil as the most important fuel in 1990 (it passed coal in 1980) and by the end of the century it should be accounting for over 40% of total fuel production. The marked slowdown during 1990 to 2000 is attributable to the fact that, in spite of the growing extent of gas liquifaction to replace diesel and petrol for driving vehicles, gas should have reached its saturation point in that there is no further scope for conversion from other fuels to gas. Refineries should be producing no more than 150 mn tons of residual fuel oil, the bare minimum that can be expected given the likely quality of the oil and structure of the oil-refining sector (which should be determined by economic rather than technological considerations) at the end of the century. Official Soviet statements have claimed that the output of light and middle products will account for 75% of total products in 2000.

Oil production should continue to grow very slowly as output by Western Siberia peaks and new fields in Eastern Siberia and the Barents and Kara Seas are opened up. The Russians are believed to be pacing the exploitation of their oilfields so that increases in production (albeit very small ones) should be maintained into the next century. Output should rise at an average annual rate of 0.8% over 1980 to 1990, and 0.6% a year during the 1990s. More important than the low rate of production growth is the anticipated deterioration in quality, with the share of high-quality low-sulphur light oil from the Nizhnevartovsk field in Western Siberia falling as the production of heavy oil from Siberia increases. This trend may be partly offset by the growth in production of gas condensate, but it ensures that the oil refineries must continue investing heavily in secondary refining plant. Towards the end of the century, it may prove necessary to begin the large-scale exploitation of the Olenek bitumen fields in Eastern Siberia; by this time, the necessary technology could be available to enable bitumen and heavy oil to be exploited and refined sufficiently cheaply.

Table 13.4 shows how the demand for different types of fuel could grow during 1980 to 2000.

A gross social product of perhaps 1,270 bn roubles is likely for 1985, which, given the anticipated energy availability of 2,290 mn tsf, suggests an energy/GSP rate of 1.80 tsf/1,000 R. This compares with 1.86 in 1980 and 1.91 in 1975, and implies a marginal energy/GSP rate of 1.46 tsf/1,000 R. This is significantly better than the 1.65 of 1975 to 1980, and is due to improving fuel rates.

All the indications are that, far from experiencing an energy crisis characterised by acute shortages, the Soviet Union should be able to see

Table 13.4: Forecast Demand for Fuel by Sector (mn tsf)

	Total[1]	Coal	1985 Gas	Oil	Others
Household and municipal[2]	190	80	65	18	27
Power stations	585	232	169[3]	167[3]	17
Centralised boilers	212	40	122	50	–
Iron and steel	152	91	54	7	–
Construction materials	98	17	35	45	1
Chemicals and oil refining	136	4	50	82	–
Transport[4] (inc. gas pipelines)	258	–	75	183	–
Agriculture	110	6	10	94	–
Others	156	12	81	63	–
Exports	300	28	89	183	–
Total	2,197	510	750	892	45

	Total	Coal	1990 Gas	Oil	Others
Household and municipal	200	80	80	20	20
Power stations	634	264	200	150	20
Centralised boilers	243	50	133	60	–
Iron and steel	149	85	60	4	–
Construction materials	99	17	41	40	1
Chemicals and oil refining	180	5	60	115	–
Transport (inc. gas pipelines)	350	–	106	244	–
Agriculture	117	6	14	97	–
Others	186	12	102	72	–
Exports	320	30	170	120	–
Total	2,478	550	966	922	41

	Total	Coal	2000 Gas	Oil	Others
Household and municipal	220	80	90	30	20
Power stations	730	380	260	90	–
Centralised boilers	306	80	160	66	–
Iron and steel	145	77	66	2	–
Construction materials	100	12	58	30	–
Chemicals and oil refining	255	5	80	170	–
Transport (inc. gas pipeline)	452	–	138	314	–
Agriculture	132	3	24	105	–
Others	250	10	145	95	–
Exports	330	50	180	100	–
Total	2,920	697	1,201	1,002	20

Notes:
1. Includes peat, shale and state-supplied firewood, but not fuels gathered by the population.
2. Local boilers and stoves plus gas for cooking. Centralised boilers also supply the household and domestic sector.
3. The Eleventh Five Year Plan target is 190 mn tsf of gas and 151.5 mn tsf of oil. It is assumed that the ambitious conversion programme will not be fully carried out.
4. Includes other sectors with large transport costs, e.g. forestry, fishing, construction and the military.

out the end of the century comfortably placed to sustain economic growth rates of 3–3.5% a year during 1980 to 1985, about 3% during 1985 to 1990 and 2–2.5% during the 1990s. In fact, it could achieve significantly better growth rates than this, especially if the basis for *détente* with the West could be re-established, and/or a reduction in military expenditure negotiated. But this would almost certainly create difficulties with fuel supply as it is unlikely that the provision of energy could be increased by very much beyond the forecasts of Table 13.3, and in any case it is by no means certain that the Soviet leadership would wish to see the supply of energy grow much faster than the rates implied by Table 13.3. As it is, total fuel production during 1980 to 2000 is likely to amount to just under 50 bn tons of standard fuel, including over 13 bn tons of oil, nearly 15.5 trillion cubic metres of gas and 16.7 bn tons of coal, and it is unlikely that planners would want to deplete resources more rapidly than this.

It was argued in Chapter 1 that the economic growth rates forming the foundation of the above analysis are the minimum rates necessary to provide the population with a steadily rising standard of living and to enable the USSR to maintain its superpower status with the necessary military and foreign aid expenditure. While faster growth rates are possible, they will have to be accompanied by the introduction of additional new fuel-saving technology plus the provision of incentives applicable right down through the industrial chain of command to the individual machine operator, truck driver, etc., so that the full benefits of such technology can be realised.

REFERENCES

Journals

Annual Bulletin of Coal Statistics for Europe, United Nations
Annual Bulletin of Gas Statistics for Europe, United Nations
Ekonomicheskaya Gazeta
Ekonomika Promyshlennogo Proizvodstva
Elektricheskaya Stantsiya
Energy Statistics 1976/1980, OECD
Gazovoye Promyshlennost
Geologiya Nefti I Gaza
Hydrocarbon Processing
Izvestiya
Khimicheskaya Promyshlennost
Monthly Bulletin of Statistics, United Nations
Narodnoe Khozyaistvo RSFSR v 1980 g.
Narodnoe Khozyaistvo SSSR v 1980 g.
Narodnoe Khozyaistvo Ukrainskoi SSR
Neftyannoye Khozyaistvo
Planovoye Khozyaistvo
Pravda
Promyshlennaya Energetika
Prospects for Soviet Oil Production, A Supplemental Analysis, CIA, 1977
Sotsialisticheskaya Industriya
Soviet Studies
Stal
Statistics of Foreign Trade, Series C, OECD
Steel Market, United Nations
Summary of World Broadcasts, BBC
Teploenergetika
Tsement
Ugol Ukrainy
Vestnik Statistiki
Vneshnyaya Torgovlya
Voprosy Ekonomiki
Zheleznodorozhnyi Transport

Particular thanks are expressed to the Economist Intelligence Unit, London, for their permission to reproduce items from various issues of *Quarterly Energy Review, USSR and Eastern Europe.*

Books

N.I. Anikin, *Finansovo-Ekonomicheskaya Deyatelnost Transporta,* Moscow, 1974

N.P. Bannyi, *Ekonomika Chernoi Metallurgii,* Moscow, 1975

B.P. Belgolskii et al., *Ekonomika, Organizatsiya I Planirovanie Proizvodstva Na Predpriyatiyakh Chernoi Metallurgii,* Moscow, 1973

G.F. Borosovich, *Devyataya Pyatiletka Khimicheskoi Promyshlennosti,* Moscow, 1973

N.I. Bulyanov, *Neft I Gaz V Narodnom Khozyaistve SSSR,* Moscow, 1977

V.M. Bushuev, *Khimicheskaya Industriya V Svete Reshenii XXIV Sezda KPSS,* Moscow, 1973

YU. Chepchugov, *Sebestoimost Prokata I Puti Ee Snizheniya,* Moscow, 1973

M.V. Feygin, *Neftyanye Resursy, Metodikha Ikh Issledovaniya I Otsenki,* Moscow, 1974

M.K.H. Gankina, *Perevozka Gruzov,* Moscow, 1972

A. Gorshkov, *Tekhniko-Ekonomicheskie Pokazateli Teplovykh Elektrostantsii,* Moscow, 1974

V.N. Kalchenko et al., *Toplivnaya Baza Ukrainskoi SSSR,* Kiev, 1978

N. Kazanskii, *Geografiya Putei Soobshcheniya,* Moscow, 1975

F.K. Klepko, G.V. Tersh, *Ekonomika Proizvodstva Sbornogo Zhelezobetona,* Kiev, 1971

N.D. Lelyukhina, *Ekonomicheskaya Effektivnost Razmeshcheniya Chernoi Metallurgii,* Moscow, 1973

A.G. Lifshits, *Sebestoimost Stali I Puti Ee Snizheniya,* Moscow, 1974

Yu.M. Malyshev, *Ekonomika Organizatsiya I Planirovanie Neftepererabatyvayushchikh Zavodov,* Moscow, 1975

Mazover & Probst, *Razvitie I Razmeshchenie Toplivnoi Promyshlennosti,* Moscow, 1975

A.M. Nekrasov, A.A. Troitskii, *Energetika SSSR v 1981 – 1985 g.,* Moscow, 1981

Oil, Gas and Energy Databook, Petrostudies, Stavanger, 1978

V.V. Osmolovskii et al., *Ekonomika Obogashcheniya Rud Chernykh Metallov,* Moscow, 1972

A.S. Pavlenko, A.M. Nekrasov, *Energetika SSSR v 1971 – 1975 g.*, Moscow, 1972

D.I. Popov, *Povyshenie Effektivnosti Metallurgicheskogo Proizvodstva*, Moscow, 1972

S.L. Pruzner, *Ekonomika Organizatsiya I Planirovanie Energeticheskogo Proizvodstva*, Moscow, 1976

G.S. Ryps, *Ekonomicheskie Problemy Raspredeleniya Gaza*, Leningrad, 1978

V.K. Savelev, *Elektroenergeticheskaya Baza Ekonomicheskikh Raionov SSSR*, Moscow, 1974

E.S. Savinskii, *Khimizatsiya Narodnogo Khozyaistvo I Prportsii Razvitiya Khimicheskoi Promyshlennosti*, Moscow, 1972

N.E. Siderov, *Tekhnicheskii Progress Iznizhenie Energoemkosti Produktsii Chernoi Metallurgii*, Kiev, 1974

G. Smirnov, *Syrevaya Baza Neftekhimicheskoi Promyshlennosti*, Moscow, 1971

A.L. Staroselskii, L.N. Alekseenko, *Ekonomiya Materialnykh Resursov V Chernoi Metallurgii*, Moscow, 1977

A.P. Stepanov *et al.*, *Ekonomika Ugolnoi Promyshlennosti*, Kiev, 1974

B.Ye. Tarasov, *Sebestoimost Chuguna I Puti Ee Snizheniya*, Moscow, 1973

Vneshnyaya Torgovlya – Statisticheskii Sbornik 1980, Moscow, 1981

V.D. Yakobson, *Ekonomika Khimicheskoi Promyshlennosti*, Moscow, 1975

V.I. Yegorov, *Ekonomika Neftepererabatyvayushchei I Neftekhimicheskoi Promyshlennosti*, Moscow, 1974

D.G. Zhimerin, *Energetika Nastoyashchee I Buduschchee*, Moscow, 1978

Note on the References

Practically all the material for this book is taken from Soviet publications – books, journals, newspapers and unpublished dissertations. In only a few cases, for example where Soviet fuel consumption is compared with that by Western countries (page 30 etc.) or where exports of Soviet fuel are quantified by Western importing countries (page 239 etc.), are Western sources used. The principal Western sources are those published by the United Nations and the OECD, and a full list is provided on page 300. The magazine *Hydrocarbon Processing* has been used for identifying Western suppliers of petrochemical equipment as listed, for example, on page 153. The BBC's *Summary of World Broadcasts – Weekly Economic Report* has been used extensively, although mainly to confirm data obtained from Soviet sources. Private communications by individuals, Soviet and Western, have proved invaluable in some cases. The maps were drawn by Tim Hadwyn, cartographer of the School of Geography, Leeds University.

Otherwise, all sources are Soviet, and the most important of these are listed on pages 300-2. In all, some 176 books have been studied and 40 magazines have been regularly monitored since 1971. All daily issues of *Pravda, Izvestia* and *Sotsialisticheskaya Industriya* have been monitored since 1968, and a large data bank has been built up from which material for this book has been drawn. In some cases, source data is found to conflict; this is thought to be due to the use of different definitions by different Soviet authorities, and I have attempted in particular cases to standardise data from various sources using my own estimates where necessary. The forecasts to 2000 are my own, taken from my own model of the Soviet economy which is designed to quantify the minimum necessary level of economic activity rather than an anticipated level of activity.

If references had been provided for every significant item of information, then their number would have run to over 4,000. This is a consequence of the nature of the subject because there are no comprehensive Soviet books relating to the subject of fuel consumption in its entirety, and those dealing with consumption of a particular fuel seldom disaggregate the consumers by industry. It is plainly impracticable to list each reference, and readers wishing to know the source of a particular item of data are invited to write to the author at the School of Geography, Leeds University, Leeds LS2 9JT.

INDEX